RELIGIOUS ARCHITECTURE AND ROMAN EXPANSION

Religious Architecture and Roman Expansion uses architectural terracottas as a lens for examining the changing landscape of central Italy during the period of Roman military expansion and for asking how local communities reacted to this new political reality. It emphasizes the role of local networks and exchange in the creation of communal identity, as well as the power of visual expression in the formulation and promotion of local history. Through detailed analyses of temple terracottas, Sophie Crawford-Brown sheds new light on "Romanization" and colonization processes between the 3rd and 1st centuries BCE. She investigates the interactions between colonies and indigenous communities, asking why conquerors might visually emulate the conquered, and what this can mean for power relations in colonial situations. Finally, Crawford-Brown explores the role of objects in creating cultural memory and the intensity of our need for collective history – even when that "history" has been largely invented.

Sophie Crawford-Brown is an assistant professor in the Department of Art History at Rice University. A scholar of the art and archaeology of pre-imperial and early imperial Italy, she has been the recipient of fellowships from the Archaeological Institute of America, the University of Tübingen's Institut für Klassische Archäologie, and the American Academy in Rome.

RELIGIOUS ARCHITECTURE AND ROMAN EXPANSION

TEMPLES, TERRACOTTAS, AND THE SHAPING OF IDENTITY, 3RD–1ST C. BCE

SOPHIE CRAWFORD-BROWN
Rice University

CAMBRIDGE
UNIVERSITY PRESS

CAMBRIDGE
UNIVERSITY PRESS

Shaftesbury Road, Cambridge CB2 8EA, United Kingdom

One Liberty Plaza, 20th Floor, New York, NY 10006, USA

477 Williamstown Road, Port Melbourne, VIC 3207, Australia

314–321, 3rd Floor, Plot 3, Splendor Forum, Jasola District Centre, New Delhi – 110025, India

103 Penang Road, #05-06/07, Visioncrest Commercial, Singapore 238467

Cambridge University Press is part of Cambridge University Press & Assessment, a department of the University of Cambridge.

We share the University's mission to contribute to society through the pursuit of education, learning and research at the highest international levels of excellence.

www.cambridge.org
Information on this title: www.cambridge.org/9781009445115

DOI: 10.1017/9781009445122

When citing this work, please include a reference to the DOI 10.1017/9781009445122

First published 2025

Printed in the United Kingdom by CPI Group Ltd, Croydon CR0 4YY

A catalogue record for this publication is available from the British Library.

Library of Congress Cataloging-in-Publication Data
NAMES: Crawford-Brown, Sophie, 1987- author.
TITLE: Religious architecture and Roman expansion : temples, terracottas, and the shaping of identity, 3rd-1st c. BCE / Sophie Crawford-Brown, Rice University, Houston.
DESCRIPTION: Cambridge : Cambridge University Press, [2024] | Outgrowth of the author's thesis (doctoral)–University of Pennsylvania, 2019, under the title: Daedala tecta : architectural terracottas and cultural memory in Republican Italy. | Includes bibliographical references and index.
IDENTIFIERS: LCCN 2024029599 (print) | LCCN 2024029600 (ebook) | ISBN 9781009445115 (hardback) | ISBN 9781009445108 (paperback) | ISBN 9781009445122 (epub)
SUBJECTS: LCSH: Temples–Rome. | Architectural terra-cotta–Rome. | Cultural appropriation–Rome. | Architecture and society–Rome. | Rome–Colonies. | Rome–History–Republic, 265-30 B.C.
CLASSIFICATION: LCC NA323 .C73 2024 (print) | LCC NA323 (ebook) | DDC 726.0937/09014–DC23/eng/20240708
LC record available at https://lccn.loc.gov/2024029599
LC ebook record available at https://lccn.loc.gov/2024029600

ISBN 978-1-009-44511-5 Hardback

To my parents

CONTENTS

ACKNOWLEDGMENTS

So many have contributed to my thinking and to this project that I'm afraid anything I can say here will be hopelessly insufficient. I will limit myself to naming a few of those without whom this book could not have taken shape. Brian Rose first urged me to look at the architectural terracotta fragments from Minturnae in the Penn Museum. Thanks to him, this "look" became a dissertation, and was then expanded and reworked into the study presented here. I am forever grateful for his steadfast mentorship through my graduate studies and beyond, and for the guidance and friendship of Ann Kuttner and Jean MacIntosh Turfa, who have been fundamental at every stage of this work. I would also like to thank Tom Tartaron and Joseph Farrell for their support during my time at Penn, as well as Joan Connelly, Nancy de Grummond, and the late Larissa Bonfante for getting me there in the first place.

The research presented in this book could not have been accomplished without the generous support of the American Academy in Rome (AAR). I thank Kim Bowes, Lindsay Harris, and John Ochsendorf for their guidance and for their support of my conference, "Minturnae Between Lazio and Campania/Minturnae tra Lazio e Campania"; Giulia Barra for her supernatural skills in securing permissions to visit sites and museums; and the entire staff of the AAR for the countless individual and collective efforts that make it such an ideal place to research and work. Special thanks go to the AAR library staff, in particular Sebastian Hierl and Paolo Imperatori, and to my fellow fellows of 2016–2018.

My research in Italy was further supported by a John R. Coleman Traveling Fellowship of the Archaeological Institute of America, as well as by grants from the Penn Museum, the Salvatori Research Awards, and the Penn graduate group in the Art and Archaeology of the Mediterranean World. I thank the Direzione Regionale Musei Lazio (ex Polo Museale del Lazio) and the Direzione Regionale Musei della Toscana (ex Polo Museale della Toscana) for allowing me to access sites and storerooms during my time in Italy, and Giovanna Rita Bellini for allowing me to examine the material at Minturnae. At the Penn Museum, special thanks go to Marie-Claude Boileau, Ann Brownlee, Lynn Makowsky, and Alessandro Pezzati.

Archaeological research ultimately relies on people, and I am indebted to the many scholars who facilitated my work and who exchanged ideas with me as my thinking on architectural terracottas progressed over the years. Among them, I would like to particularly thank Stefan Ardeleanu, Francesco Belfiori, Seth Bernard, Dorian Borbonus, Caroline Cheung, Dan Diffendale, Marco Germani, Andrea De Giorgi, Ann Glennie, Alexander Ekserdjian, Elizabeth Fentress, John Hopkins, Rudolf Känel, Lynne Lancaster, Pier Giorgio Monti, Daira Nocera, James Packer, Dario Panariti, Jane Shepherd, Allison Smith, Valentin Veldhues, Natalie Wagner, and the late Russell T. Scott and Maria José Strazzulla. Erika Harnett, who examined the sculptures from Minturnae for her 1986 dissertation and who first noticed the archival photos of terracotta pedimental sculpture in the Penn Archives, deserves credit for her major contributions to the study of Minturnae. I am grateful for her generosity in sharing and discussing this material with me. The digital reconstructions presented here were produced in collaboration with Indiana University's Virtual World Heritage Lab and Flyover Zone Productions. I thank Bernard Frischer, Nathanael Tavares, Matthew Brennan, and Kelly McClinton for guiding me into the world of digital reconstruction. Members of the Cosa Excavations team have been an invaluable support, and I would also like to thank colleagues at the University of Tübingen for hosting me so graciously in 2016—in particular, Richard Posamentir, Thomas Schäfer, Philipp Baas, and Manuel Flecker.

Parts of this research were presented at various conferences and colloquia over the years, including at the American Academy in Rome, the Annual Meetings of the Archaeological Institute of America, the Associazione Internazionale di Archeologia Classica, Humboldt-Universität zu Berlin, the Institut für Klassische Archäeologie at the Eberhard Karls Universität Tübingen, Florida State University, the New York Workshop of Etruscan Art, the Royal Netherlands Institute in Rome, the University of Virginia, and the University of Toronto. I thank the organizers, moderators, and attendees for the chance to discuss my work and for their insightful feedback.

Seth Bernard, Ingrid Edlund-Berry, John Hopkins, Ann Kuttner, Brian Rose, and Jean MacIntosh Turfa offered invaluable comments on the manuscript at various stages, and this book has been greatly improved by their feedback. Needless to say, any shortcomings are my own.

My deep gratitude goes to my colleagues at Rice University, and I would like to particularly recognize the support of Graham Bader, Leo Costello, and Kathleen Canning. The illustration program for this book was generously supported by an award from Rice's Creative Ventures Fund and by the Art History department. Thanks go to Dallin Evans for stepping in to illustrate objects when no photo could be procured, to Bill Howze for his work in obtaining image permissions, and to Kelley Vernon for her assistance with the entire image program. Special thanks to Chelsey Denny and Irene Kwan, who day after day make everything possible.

I am grateful to Beatrice Rehl for her staunch support and kindness throughout the publication process, and to the entire production team at Cambridge University Press for their patience, input, and guidance.

My gratitude to my family surpasses my powers of expression. To my parents, who have supported and encouraged me at every step, I can only say thank you from the deepest of me. I am grateful to my brother Jack, to my loving grandparents, and to Niti, Aunt Anne, and Uncle Nick for their mystifying belief in me. To Andrea, Milo, and Tullio – you are my lights, every day and always.

ABBREVIATIONS

Cosa II

Brown, F. E., E. H. Richardson, and L. Richardson. 1960. *Cosa II: The Temples of the Arx. MAAR* 26. Rome: American Academy in Rome.

Cosa III

Brown, F. E., E. H. Richardson, and L. Richardson. 1993. *Cosa III: The Buildings of the Forum: Colony, Municipium, and Village. MAAR* 37. University Park: Pennsylvania State University Press for the American Academy in Rome.

Cosa IV

Bruno, V. J. and R. T. Scott. 1993. *Cosa IV: The Houses. MAAR* 38. University Park: Pennsylvania State University Press for the American Academy in Rome.

Cosa V

Fentress, E. ed. 2003. *Cosa V: An Intermittent Town, Excavations 1991–1997. MAAR* Suppl. 2. Ann Arbor: University of Michigan Press for the American Academy in Rome.

Pyrgi

1970. *Pyrgi. Scavi del Santuario etrusco (1959–1967)*, in *Notizie degli scavi di antichità* XXIV, II supplemento. Rome: Accademia Nazionale dei Lincei.

ONE

INTRODUCTION

1.1 ROOFS AS SYMBOLS

In 1920s Germany, a debate broke out that had been simmering for centuries – the *Dächerkrieg,* or "War of the Roofs." Ostensibly an architectural and aesthetic disagreement, this clash was in fact deeply rooted in conflicting views of national identity.[1] It involved the attempted introduction of flat roof architecture in a German landscape traditionally characterized by steeply pitched roofs. The most striking example of the *Dächerkrieg* can be seen in Berlin, where Bruno Taut, Hugo Häring, and Otto Rudolph Salvisberg constructed the Onkel Toms Hütte (Uncle Tom's Cabin) housing complex in 1926. Unmistakably modern, these buildings were symptomatic of broader rationalist trends related to political reform and the improvement of living conditions. They were, in other words, designed to evoke and promote the egalitarianism of an idealized future. Each featured a flat roof. Closely following their completion, detractors of Onkel Toms Hütte sponsored the construction of the Am Fischtal colony just across the street (Figure 1). Though built later, these houses looked older. Their steeply pitched roofs voiced a strong note of resistance, visually contrasting the modernist development with a sharp assertion of German architectural patriotism.[2]

Although often couched in language of practicality, the flat roof controversy was at its core a struggle of national identity. Flat roof supporters took them as symbols of innovation, equality, and "Mediterranean or universal culture,"

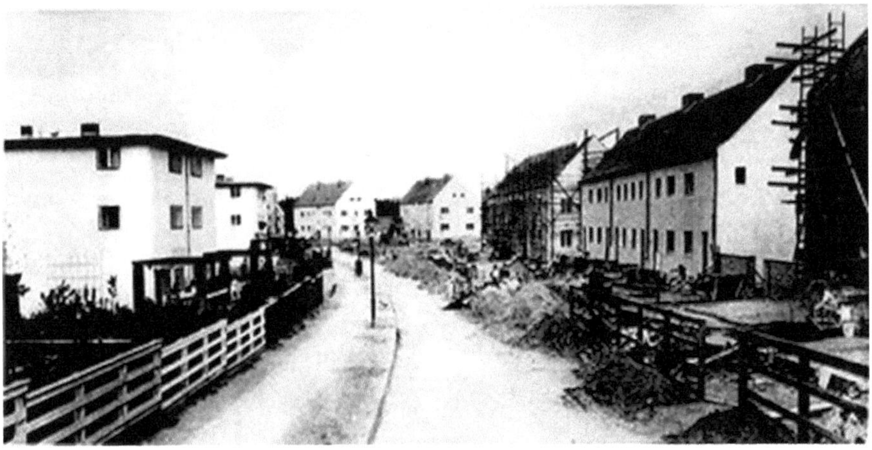

1. On the left, the Onkel Toms Hütte colony with its flat roofs. On the right, the pitched roofs of the Am Fischtal colony built across the street in response. Photo: *Berliner Tageblatt*, September 9, 1928, open access.

while growing nationalist voices decried the flat roofs as nomadic and "oriental."[3] In the nationalist view, architecture was determined by *Blut und Boden*, and in a German context this meant pitched roofs.[4]

The present study takes us more than 2,000 years before the German *Dächerkrieg* and focuses on the region of what is now central Italy. Still, the flat roof controversy offers a useful reminder of the fierce symbolic value that roofs can carry. This is often overlooked in a contemporary context – we are no longer trained to look *up*. In many ancient societies, however, the roof constituted the focal point of a building. One might think of the prominence of the roof in much of East Asian architecture. In China, the particular form of roofs as well as details of their construction constituted highly visible representations of hierarchy and status. Traditional palace halls, for instance, had hipped roofs – the type reserved for the most eminent buildings.[5] Next in importance were hip-and-gable roofs, followed by overhanging gabled roofs, flush-gable roofs, and finally pyramidal roofs.[6] Inca architecture, which we now often associate with massive stone walls, would in reality have been dominated by the thatched and wooden roofs that occupied over two-thirds of the building's height.[7] Because the Inca considered certain types of wood to be sacred, the very materials of the roof would also have conferred a special sanctity.[8]

The invention of terracotta roofing in the Mediterranean world appears to have been symbolically charged from the start. Terracotta tiles have been found at a wide range of Bronze Age sites on mainland Greece, and there is growing consensus for their architectural use on roofs beginning in the Early Helladic Period (c. 3100–2000 BCE).[9] The House of the Tiles at Lerna remains the most famous example but is certainly not unique. Terracotta tiles have been found at sites like Akovitika, Kolonna, Thebes, and Zygouries in association with structures that resemble one another architecturally, all following the basic layout of the Lerna building.[10] This has led Daniel Pullen to suggest that EH II societies were in fact each centered around a House of Tiles structure.[11] The presence of rooftiles would have distinguished these important buildings, marking each as a seat of power and the center of the community.

More recently, evidence has surfaced for the use of rooftiles on multiple buildings at certain Early Helladic sites. Ceramic tiles were uncovered across the islet of Mitrou, for instance, and Kyle Jazwa has suggested that rather than intracommunity competition, their use would have constituted "a point of pride and distinction relative to neighboring villages in East Lokris."[12] Early Helladic ceramic roofs must certainly have been eye-catching. Some tiles still preserve traces of paint and were probably placed alongside unpainted versions to lend the roof a patterned and multicolored appearance.[13] Tiles and schist slabs also seem to have been used concurrently. The patchwork-quilt quality of these roofs, with their varied colors and textures, would have heightened their prominence and contrasted sharply with neighboring buildings.

Terracotta tiles were apparently abandoned following the Mycenaean period, and the archaeological record remains strangely silent until the (re) introduction of terracotta roofs in the early 7th century BCE.[14] This time, however, they were here to stay. The early Temple of Apollo at Corinth is usually considered the first building to boast a full terracotta roof, and the literary tradition ascribes to Corinth a driving role in the invention and diffusion of this technology.[15] "Protocorinthian" architectural terracottas differ from their prehistoric counterparts in following standard sizes (they are moldmade) and in incorporating different types of elements, each destined for a specific spot on the roof.[16] The use of the mold would have a profound effect on the future of terracotta roofing across the ancient Mediterranean, as it allowed for the large-scale manufacture of numerous identical elements that could repeat along the roof's edge in a continuous pattern. Traveling artisans seem in some cases to have carried their molds with them, and we find examples of terracottas derived from the same molds at politically distinct sites from the Archaic period onwards. The retention of molds also allowed for one-off repairs of damaged elements, thus lengthening the lifespan of a roof. As we shall see, this possibility was one factor that enabled the highly conservative approach to roof decoration in central Italy during the last few centuries BCE.

Following their introduction at Corinth, terracotta roofs soon became a staple of religious architecture in Archaic Greece, where they were used almost exclusively for temples and treasuries. It appears to be from Greece that terracotta roofing spread across the Mediterranean, reaching Italy in the mid-7th century BCE and Asia Minor in the early 6th century.[17] In both areas, the use of architectural terracottas quickly expanded to include "secular" buildings as well as religious, and roofs of this type became popular vehicles for elite display.[18] At the Phrygian site of Gordion, for instance, well over 4,000 architectural terracotta fragments have been found.[19] Many are decorated with motifs derived from Greek luxury objects such as metal, ivory, and textiles, or from Near Eastern royal iconography. The imagery of the terracottas themselves thus carried messages of wealth and prestige.[20] Interestingly, striking similarities exist between some 6th century BCE roofs at Sardis and Didyma and contemporaneous examples from mainland Greece, despite the fact that most other roofs at these sites followed the local Lydian tradition.[21] Nancy Winter has suggested that these Greek-style roofs may in fact have played a role in King Kroisos' gift exchange with Delphi and Sparta.[22] Regardless, they must have been fairly conspicuous when first introduced at Sardis and Didyma, their foreign style marking them as badges of power on an international scale.

The social meaning making possibilities of terracotta roofs were by no means limited to instances of elite display. These roofs could also bear specific geographical referents, as is well demonstrated by the appearance of certain treasury buildings at sites like Delphi and Olympia. At the latter, the Treasury of Gela constitutes the "Sicilian roof *par excellence* found on Greek soil," its roof featuring a decorative program that explicitly evokes Geloan architecture.[23] Its large size – the building itself as well as the roof are the largest among Olympia's treasuries – would have further called attention to this structure, whose terracotta roof loudly proclaimed its identity. A similar situation is attested for the so-called rosette roof at Olympia. Its roof closely mirrors that of an Archaic temple at Siris, the city to whom the treasury presumably belonged.[24] These treasury buildings vividly illustrate the ways in which terracotta roofs could signify particular cities, temples, and artistic traditions. The Greek mainland-style roofs that surrounded them would have rendered their Italic forms all the more conspicuous and evocative.[25]

The meanings of such similarities, however, are not always so straightforward, and the evidence from central Italy is particularly complex in this regard. Nearly identical architectural terracottas, sometimes made from the same mold, have been uncovered at a range of central Italic sites from the 7th century BCE onwards.[26] In most cases, no obvious political connection is apparent between sites, and we even know of instances in which the same terracotta types appear at towns that were in active conflict with one another. A striking instance are the 4th century roofs from the Scasato II temple at Falerii Veteres and the Capitoline temple in Rome, some of whose terracottas mirror one another so closely as to have perhaps been made by the same artisans. Falerii and Rome, however, were at war at this time.[27] As we shall see in Chapter 3, the use of remarkably similar architectural terracottas at a range of apparently unrelated sites becomes standard between the 3rd and 1st centuries

BCE. In such cases, the temporal dimension appears to be emphasized above the geographical, with architectural terracottas intended to evoke a more generalized sense of antiquity – albeit in a locally specific context. The symbolic power of these images is by no means lessened by this shift but speaks instead to the remarkable versatility of architectural terracottas as a medium of expression. They could be, and were, worked to diverse effects over the millennia of their use across the ancient Mediterranean.

The rapid spread of terracotta roofs must have been due not only to their practical utility and aesthetic appeal but also to their potential as creators of social meaning.[28] A terracotta roof, after all, provides a grand and highly visible canvas for projecting messages to and about a community. The material is itself evocative. Architectural terracottas are molded directly from the land and are thus intimately tied to their local landscapes. Their frequent association with religious architecture and their eye-catching placement on prominent buildings contribute to an impression of authority. They are objects that tower above a viewer's head and overwhelm that viewer with a carefully curated set of images.

It is therefore hardly surprising that terracottas take on an almost mythological connotation in much of the literary record. Pliny shows a particular interest in the early history of terracotta roofing, relating the story that Butades first introduced figural decoration to terracotta roofs and that modeling in terracotta was brought to Italy by Demaratus, father of the future king Tarquinius, who fled Corinth accompanied by three coroplasts.[29] The evocatively named Vulca was said to have been summoned to Rome from Veii to build the terracotta statues for the Temple of Jupiter Optimus Maximus on the Capitoline – an anecdote that places terracotta at the center of this momentous building's construction.[30] What's more, tradition held that the terracotta chariot for the temple had miraculously grown in the furnace.[31] Because terracotta usually shrinks during firing, this event was interpreted by the Etruscan seers as an omen of great power.

Roof tiles make meaningful appearances in other literary contexts as well, suggesting not only the deep symbolic power they held in the ancient imagination but also the flexibility with which social symbols could be applied to them. In Tacitus' *Germania*, the *lack* of roof tiles is a sign of barbarity.[32] Dio reports that the wealth of senators, and thus how much they contributed toward military efforts against Antony in 43 BCE, was based on the size of their roofs – four obols for every roof tile.[33] Roof tiles are also used to great narrative effect in accounts of warfare and urban violence.[34] During the Roman invasion of Veii, for instance, the local women and slaves pelted their enemies with roof tiles.[35] After Marius had shut Saufeius, Glaucia, and Saturninus in the Curia during the violence of 100 BCE in Rome, a crowd stoned them to death with roof tiles from the senate building.[36] Perhaps most

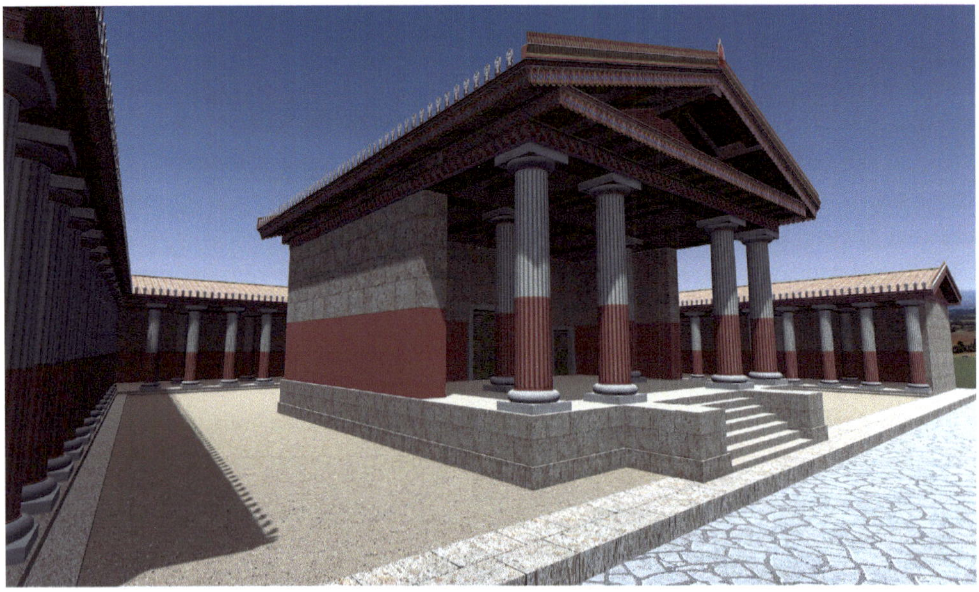

2. Digital reconstruction of the tripartite temple at Minturnae, placed for optimal visibility along the Via Appia. Missing here is the pedimental statuary that would have served to further emphasize the roof. Digital model produced by the author in collaboration with Indiana University's Virtual World Heritage Lab and Flyover Zone Productions.

memorable of all, Plutarch records how an old woman hurled a roof tile at Pyrrhus during his attack on Argos in 272 BCE.[37] He was knocked unconscious and promptly beheaded. Besides the practical utility of rooftiles in urban combat (they are readily available and deadly when dropped from a height), their association with houses, temples, and public buildings adds an unmistakably symbolic quality to their military application.

In the literary as well as the archaeological record, we have widespread evidence for terracotta roofs as emblems of authority, wealth, and place. Their role as meaning-makers and message-bearers is a fundamental aspect of their use in 3rd–1st century Italy, where temples were dominated spatially and artistically by brightly painted terracotta roofs. Temples themselves were typically situated in highly visible locations – atop hills, beside major roads (Figure 2), or overlooking a port. They were designed to be seen, and their terracotta roofs were the showstopper. What local communities were trying to convey with these roofs, and why these messages mattered, are the questions that drive the following chapters.

1.2 SCOPE AND ORGANIZATION OF STUDY

This study focuses on architectural terracottas from central Italic temples dating roughly between the 3rd and 1st centuries BCE. It is primarily concerned with non-pedimental terracottas (antefixes, revetment plaques, simas, cornices, etc.),

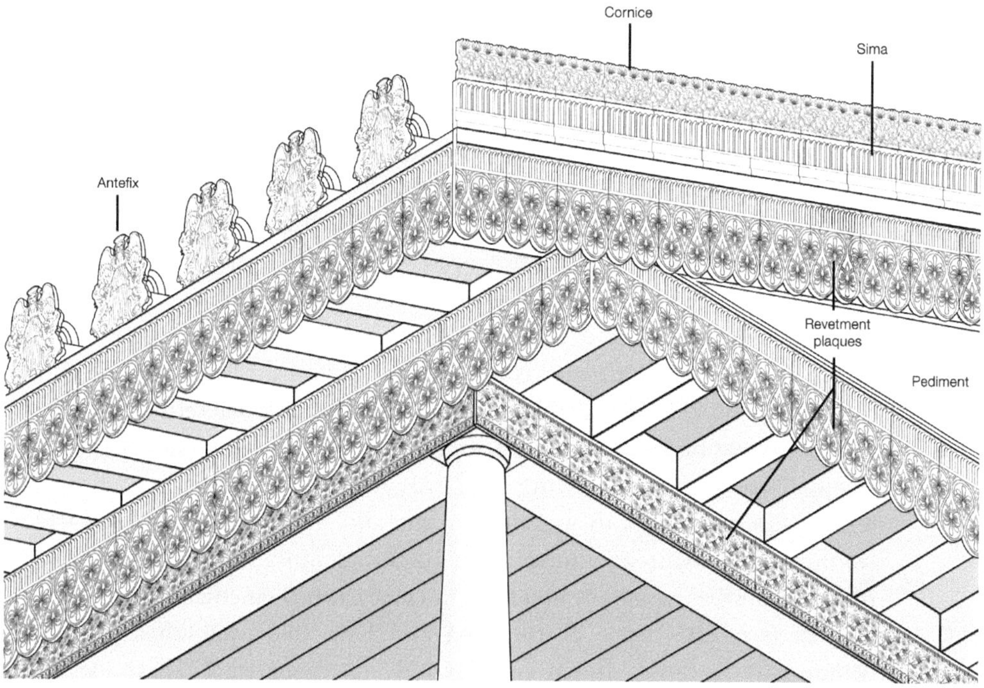

3. Drawing showing the elements of a terracotta roof referred to most frequently in the text. Illustration by Jennie Anderson.

which typically constitute the best-preserved and most numerous elements of a roof's decorative program (Figure 3). The surviving fragments of terracotta pedimental sculpture from the last few centuries BCE are often dishearteningly incomplete, rendering it impossible, in most cases, to confidently reconstruct a full scene. This has obvious implications for our ability to ascribe meaning to a given image group, and it is for this reason that the focus here will be on the more "certain" elements of the decorative program. Still, the evidence for pedimental sculpture will be discussed in relation to the non-pedimental terracottas of specific roofs as relevant. When possible, both will be used in tandem to address broader issues of local identity and the overall visual impact of temples.

Despite their obvious importance and ubiquity, pan-tiles and cover-tiles will also be largely omitted. This is because their production and form generally follow a different trajectory than other terracotta roofing elements – they vary much less, and the choice of different pan-tile types seems more connected to workshop tradition and to practical considerations such as defense against inclement weather.[38]

It would be of great value for a future study to examine tiles, pedimental sculpture, and other architectural terracottas in a holistic catalogue of central Italic roofs from the last few centuries BCE – a goal that will become more feasible as these objects receive increased scholarly attention and publication. An exhaustive catalogue is not my intention here. Instead, I aim with this study to identify certain widespread trends in architectural terracottas of the 3rd–1st centuries and to relate them to broader scholarly questions concerning colonization, identity, and material culture. These objects have rarely been meaningfully engaged in the historical discourse of this period and have much to offer our understanding of central Italy's changing political and religious landscapes during the tumultuous period of Rome's expansion.

To this end, two principal case-studies – the colonies of Cosa and Minturnae – will be used throughout as points of reference for addressing these larger themes. Both were colonies founded near the coast in the early 3rd century BCE and have yielded large numbers of architectural terracottas. These two sites have been chosen and paired, however, primarily for their differences: Cosa is north of Rome and was founded in confiscated Etruscan territory, Minturnae is to its south in the land of the Aurunci; Cosa was a colony of Latin right, Minturnae was a Roman colony; Cosa was founded ex-novo, Minturnae was built beside an ancient famous sanctuary; Cosa's architectural terracottas are well-recorded and have been published in detail, Minturnae's are little known and meagerly documented.[39] These sites thus offer two related but opposing poles for considering the use of architectural terracottas in colonies more generally.

Following this overview, the remainder of Chapter 1 offers a sort of prelude to the study. It traces the history of scholarship on Italic architectural terracottas and highlights a number of lingering problems and uncertainties, which will be taken up in the subsequent chapters.

Chapter 2 addresses one of the primary impediments to the study of 3rd–1st century Italic architectural terracottas: questions regarding their chronology and the problematic ways in which they have traditionally been bound up in assumptions regarding so-called "Romanization." Cosa plays a particularly important role here, as the typology established for its terracottas by Lawrence Richardson rests heavily on the idea that (1) many popular terracotta types were first produced in Rome and were considered "Roman" and (2) that the decoration of temples in towns like Cosa deliberately imitated that of Rome. After discussing the Cosa chronology and its problems, I survey the surviving terracottas from Rome itself in order to demonstrate that there is currently no actual evidence that these types appeared in Rome earlier than in other central Italic towns. This is essential for allowing us to shed the "Romanization" baggage and to examine the architectural terracottas from a fresh perspective – asking what *they* can tell us and not what we can read onto them.

Chapter 3 turns to the five most widespread decorative roofing elements for temples in 3rd–1st century central Italy: the revetment plaque with addorsed palmettes, revetment plaque with looped palmettes, *potnia theron* antefix, strigilated sima, and perforated cornice with triskelia and figure-eights. These elements appear on numerous temples in this period, often all together, and are in fact so common that we can refer to them collectively as constituting a "standard temple kit." As I show, each of these elements derives from earlier prototypes that are attested in Etruscan and Latial zones already in the late 6th or 5th century BCE. Their widespread adoption on later temples thus represents a conscious act of archaizing. This tendency is further illustrated by the fact that even when temple roofs were renovated during the 3rd–1st centuries BCE, they were often furnished with terracotta types nearly identical to those being replaced. Patrons and communities evidently strove to retain as far as possible the original appearance of their sacred buildings and did so through a highly conservative approach to terracotta decoration. This suggests that already by the 3rd century BCE, certain terracotta types were strongly associated with sacred architecture and with notions of ancient religious practice.

Whereas Chapter 3 focuses on architectural terracottas that were widespread on central Italic temples, Chapter 4 turns to the ways in which towns sought to emphasize a specifically local identity through their temple roofs. The case-studies of Cosa and Minturnae are discussed in detail. Cosa's temple terracottas closely mirrored those of the older Etruscan temples that still dotted the region, despite the fact that Cosa was a new colony founded as a result of Roman conquest. The strong similarities between Cosa's various temple roofs suggest that commissioners were less concerned with differentiating individual structures and more interested in creating an overarching and recognizable visual identity for the new town – one that was specifically rooted in local architectural traditions. A local-oriented and archaizing tendency is detectable at Minturnae as well, where allusions to the ancient Auruncan sanctuary of Marica were incorporated into the religious architecture of the Roman colony and where every new generation of temples appears to have consciously referenced the last through its terracotta decoration. The contrasting terracottas of the triple-cella temple and surrounding triporticus in Minturnae's *area sacra* brought together different traditions in order to create an original program whose imagery was immediately readable for diverse viewers.

Chapter 5 asks why new colonies turned so invariably and deliberately to the visual culture of their conquered enemies. This is largely connected, I argue, to the fact that colonial populations themselves were extremely heterogenous. Newly thrown together, colonists as a group had no single visual culture to import. In the absence of collective memories and traditions, communities turned to invention. Architectural terracottas proved particularly expedient in this context, as they allowed colonies to visually shape a collective identity and to broadcast it across their sacred buildings.

Finally, Chapter 6 jumps forward in time to examine the legacy of architectural terracottas during the period of the Augustan Principate. Italic architecture changed fundamentally with the large-scale exploitation of the Luna marble quarries beginning in the mid-1st century BCE. Precisely as marble began to replace terracotta on temple roofs, however, a new type of architectural terracotta was introduced. Even more than their predecessors, the so-called Campana reliefs were explicitly archaizing in their iconography, style, and material. While architectural terracottas had long been used to define and assert specific local identities, they were now employed to express an idealized Augustan vision of a pious and *unified* Italic past.

1.3 A NOTE ON TERMINOLOGY

In this study, I essentially follow the conventional terminology of the field. Still, some terms are worth specifying at the outset. I use "mid-to-late Republic" to refer generally to the period from the 3rd century BCE to the rise of Octavian in the later 1st century BCE. My use of "Republic" and "Republican" pertains primarily to Rome itself, to areas under Rome's direct control, and to earlier scholarship that conceptualizes Italic history in terms of the Roman Republic. It is important to note, however, that many of the areas under discussion here were not legally or conceptually part of the Roman Republic before the 1st century BCE. In such cases, I will privilege the use of dates rather than terms like "Republic," which risk collapsing diverse experiences into a single historical trajectory.

Words like "Roman" and "Etruscan" can also be misleading, implying more exclusionary and clear-cut cultural divisions than are actually attested by our evidence.[40] I use "Etruscan" and "Etruscans" here to refer to the places in which the Etruscan language dominated, to the people living in those places, and to the objects and structures deriving from those places. Similarly, I use Roman in relation to people living in Rome, things happening in Rome, and activities launched specifically from within Rome, whereas the term will appear in scare quotes when referencing the broader connotations it has been assigned in prior scholarship. Finally, "archaizing" is used here to refer not to the Archaic period specifically but to anything made to look older than it is.

I am aware that my use of geographic indicators will inevitably be vague. By "central Italy," I generally mean the area between the Liris River to the south and the Arno River to the north, but these are certainly not strict markers and sites on either side of those boundaries will be referenced. Similarly, while my focus is on the west side of Italy (roughly the modern regions of Tuscany and Lazio), sites from interior and eastern Italy will also come into play.

In general, I take "local" to mean the area (including the towns, roads, sanctuaries, and associated cultural activities) with which a person is closely familiar. This would of course include the town in which a person lives but also the places that person visits on a fairly regular basis. Places within a person's "local" area are likely to be accessible for a round-trip journey within one day. Of course, what constitutes "local" would have varied slightly from person to person depending on occupation and economic status. For those without a cart or horse, local trips would be done on foot, meaning that they could cover less distance in the same amount of time compared to elites or even to artisans who might transport equipment by cart. In other words, some places would have effectively been closer for certain groups of people than for others. The disparity in travel times would have increased with the construction of major roads across Italy during the last centuries BCE.[41]

I use "region" and "regional" to refer to larger geographic areas that share certain physical and cultural characteristics (for instance, the core area of Etruscan culture could be considered a "region"). I use "local region" as an intermediary between these two scales. The "local region" would thus include places that are more distant geographically than the purely "local" but still comfortably within an individual's frame of reference (for instance, a place one visits once a year or once every few years for a religious festival, market, or similar). A person traveling within their local region or their region would recognize certain shared cultural features but would be less intimately familiar with places and place-names than in their local surroundings. Familiarity is assumed to increase as one moves from the regional scale, to the local region, to the truly local.

1.4 THE STUDY OF ARCHITECTURAL TERRACOTTAS

With the themes, organization, and terminology of the current study established, it will now be important to lay some groundwork for what follows by examining the basic features of terracotta roofs – how they were made, how they have been studied, and what we still do and do not know about the processes of manufacture, sale, and use. These topics will reappear throughout the subsequent chapters in connection to the evidence and arguments presented therein.

Despite the importance placed on them in antiquity, architectural terracottas have received relatively little study compared to works in marble or bronze. This is likely due to their humble material, often fragmentary survival, and traditional relegation to the category of "mere ornament." While the "high art" represented by stone sculpture has captivated collectors and scholars from the Renaissance onwards, terracottas have been dismissed as imitative, repetitive, and even primitive. It is worth emphasizing that this attitude toward ornament represents a modern bias, as numerous art historical studies have by now eloquently demonstrated.[42] Recent work has also increasingly emphasized the strong symbolic power of vegetal ornament in Augustan art, as well as of frames and framing in Roman art more generally.[43] Given the high preponderance of vegetal motifs on architectural terracottas of the 3rd–1st centuries BCE, as well as their visual role in literally framing temple roofs, they have much to contribute to these broader scholarly dialogues.

The study of Archaic Italic terracottas has made great strides, due in large part to the work of Nancy Winter not only in cataloguing them but in emphasizing how much they can reveal about elite expressions of power as well as regional and Mediterranean-wide networks of cultural exchange.[44] Despite this, terracottas of the 5th–1st centuries BCE continue to be relatively under-published and understudied. As these chapters aim to show, such objects are anything but unimaginative. They arguably constitute the largest body of art to survive from the last centuries BCE, and are critical to our understanding of a historical period that is notoriously patchy. Because they adorned temples in every Italic town from the Archaic period through the early Empire, they offer a fundamental visual record of Italy's changing religious landscape and allow us to ask how communities *chose* to represent themselves through visual culture.

Study of architectural terracottas can also have profound implications for the reconstruction of architecture and of sites' topographical development more broadly. Besides their foundations, the buildings of pre-1st century BCE central Italy were constructed predominantly of organic materials that have since disintegrated. The terracottas that decorated their roofs are in many cases all that survive of a building and thus stand as fundamental witnesses to a lost architectural history. In the city of Rome, for instance, the evidence of architectural terracottas more than triples the known number of religious buildings dating between 450 and 350 BCE.[45] This in turn has implications for traditional narratives regarding production declines after the fall of the monarchy.[46] Similarly, architectural terracottas can provide evidence for the reconstruction of buildings. John Hopkins has persuasively argued for the massive scale of the Capitoline Temple in Rome based on the monumental size of its surviving terracottas.[47]

Despite their importance for tackling a range of historical problems, and despite a marked acceleration of interest in recent years, architectural terracottas have still not been adequately incorporated into much of scholarly discourse. A brief survey of the key studies will be useful in tracing the trajectory of scholarship on these objects. One of the very first catalogues of architectural terracottas was published in 1912 by Herbert Koch, entitled *Dachterrakotten aus Campanien mit Ausschluss von Pompei*. Six years later, Alessandro Della Seta included a survey of Etrusco-Italic temples and their decoration in his catalogue of the Villa Giulia Museum. His classification rapidly became standard and is frequently referenced even in recent works.[48]

Della Seta divided Italic terracottas into three phases:

Phase 1: mid-to-late 6th century BCE; comprising chiefly friezes depicting processions of chariots, horses, warriors, and women.[49]

Phase 2: late 6th to mid-5th century BCE; distinguished from the first phase by greater use of terracotta decoration and by the inclusion of new ornamental (geometric and vegetal) and figural elements.[50]

Phase 3: late 4th and 3rd centuries BCE, perhaps into the 2nd century; "Hellenistic" phase, characterized by a change in imagery and an emphasis on mythological scenes for pediments.[51]

It was not until 1940 that another major work on this topic appeared – Arvid Andrén's two volume *Architectural Terracottas from Etrusco-Italic Temples*.[52] Andrén retained Della Seta's tripartite division but revised the chronology and extended the third period to include terracottas from the 1st century BCE:[53]

Period 1: late 7th century–second half of the 6th century BCE; consisting primarily of "square or rectangular plaques decorated with figured motives executed in low relief enhanced by painting."[54]

Period 2: second half of the 6th century–late 5th century BCE; the "most brilliant stage of development," including a far greater variety of decorative elements and motifs.[55]

Period 3: late 5th–late 1st century BCE; distinguished primarily by the introduction of pedimental figures as well as other "characteristic ornamental designs."[56]

Andrén stated from the outset that his was a "preparatory work" and that he had sought to "collect as large a material as possible . . . in order to obtain a sure basis for general conclusions, well knowing, however, that much material still remains inaccessible or unknown, and that new discoveries may wholly or partially alter earlier views."[57] Tellingly, he prefaced this remark by drawing attention to the overwhelming lack of contextual information available for architectural terracottas. As Riemer Knoop lamented in his 1993 reappraisal of Della Seta's and Andrén's works, this is a situation that was not much improved upon in the intervening decades, and the same remains generally true today.[58] Even when terracottas are scientifically excavated and well-documented, stratigraphy rarely offers more than a terminus ante quem, and the dating of architectural terracottas has relied overwhelmingly on stylistic analysis. Indeed, it has often been the case that architectural terracottas "date strata and not vice versa."[59] As we shall see in Chapter 2, this has been particularly problematic at sites like Cosa. The fragile nature of any proposed date for individual terracotta elements has not been sufficiently recognized in site chronologies and related studies. Terracotta typologies, such as Lawrence Richardson's for Cosa, are often assumed to have more grounding in stratigraphy than is actually the case.[60] This can lead not only to the incorrect dating of terracottas from other sites but to inaccurate reconstructions of sites' topographical development.

Maria José Strazzulla highlighted this problem in an important article published in 1977 and called for a more rigorous and comparative approach to the study of terracottas across Italic sites (see Section 2.2). The first *Deliciae Fictiles* conference, held fifty years after the publication of Andrén's study, represented a major step in this direction. The subsequent meetings and corresponding publications (1993, 1997, 2006, 2011, 2019) have dramatically improved our understanding of Italic architectural terracottas by drawing together a wide range of individual case studies alongside more general essays. The series' primary contribution has been in presenting new research in a centralized format, allowing for geographic and chronological comparisons across a wide range of sites. The Archaic period is by far the best represented in these volumes.

The publication in 2009 of Nancy Winter's monumental *Symbols of Wealth and Power: Architectural Terracotta Decoration in Etruria and Central Italy, 640–510 B.C.* marked a major step forward in the study of early Italic roofs.[61] Winter begins with the earliest Italic architectural terracottas of the mid-7th century BCE, which include both "undecorated or modestly decorated" as well as "decorated" examples. The latter are best known from Poggio Civitate and Acquarossa, and Winter attributes the terracottas from these sites to workshops operating between c. 640/630 and 590/580 BCE.[62] Her study culminates c. 510 BCE with the shift from Della Seta's First to Second Phase, marked by a "change from figural to floral decoration as well as by larger scale and new forms."[63] It is a testament to Della Seta's enduring influence that his periodization is still employed, albeit cautiously, in a study produced nearly a century later.[64]

Terracottas of the so-called Second Phase have only recently received systematic treatment in Claudia Carlucci's 2021 *Terrecotte architettoniche etrusco-laziali. I sistemi decorativi della II fase iniziale.* Her chronological framework begins more or less where Winter had left off, with the late 6th century BCE construction of Temple B at Pyrgi, generally considered the first complete example of the new system.[65] The Sassi Caduti temple at Falerii Veteres (Civita Castellana) with its terracottas dating just before the mid-5th century marks the late limit of her study.

Major strides have thus been made in the study of Italic architectural terracottas over the last century, and detailed analyses of terracottas from specific sites (mostly dating to the Archaic period) have in turn allowed for more holistic analyses of broad chronological periods. Despite these advances, however, a number of questions remain unresolved – particularly for the post-5th century BCE material. The following sections survey several key topics and problems in our understanding of Italic architectural terracottas, including the uneven treatment of chronological periods, issues of chronology and typology, pedimental sculpture, manufacture and logistics, polychromy, patrons and commissioners, and workshops and workers. Many of these are discussed here briefly in order to establish context, as they will reappear in connection with the interpretations and arguments presented subsequently.

1.5 KNOWNS AND UNKNOWNS

1.5.1 *Uneven Research on Chronological Periods*

First, a reflection on the history of scholarship itself. Though abbreviated, the preceding overview reveals a habitual emphasis on Della Seta's and Andrén's phases 1 and 2. Terracottas of the Archaic period are currently far better understood than their counterparts from the last centuries BCE, which tend to receive only incidental treatment in studies primarily concerned with architecture, topographical development, cult practice, etc.

This unevenness can be traced back to the divisions first proposed by Della Seta, and still followed, albeit with important adjustments, in much of current scholarship. In Della Seta's system, Phase 1 lasts only a few decades, while Phase 2 endures a little over half a century. Phase 3 includes well over a century of material. The chronological imbalance between Phases 1–2 and 3 is even more apparent in Andrén's modified system, in which Periods 1 and 2 last roughly a century each, while Period 3 lasts four.

There are several possible explanations for this. First, Della Seta and Andrén simply knew of fewer late examples. Second, the production of decorative terracotta was at that time thought to have ended with the Republic, if not well before. Finally, and most problematically, it is extremely difficult to accurately date many terracottas produced between the 4th and 1st centuries BCE.

The last few decades have seen a flowering of scholarship on central Italic architectural terracottas from before the mid-5th century BCE. The publication of Winter's and now Carlucci's monographs have successfully supplanted Andrén's volume for these earlier periods, offering a welcome updating of his chronology and commentary in the wake of more recent discoveries. Contributions to the *Deliciae Fictiles* series and numerous site-specific publications have provided a strong framework for examining this material. The 4th–1st century terracottas, however, remain extraordinarily understudied.[66] No catalogue has replaced Andrén's in the intervening eighty plus years, and it remains the primary point of reference. In this vacuum, scholars have relied heavily on Richardson's problematic Cosa typology, published in 1960. More specialized studies such as Patrizio Pensabene and Maria Rita Sanzi Di Mino's catalogue of terracotta antefixes in the Museo Nazionale Romano, Strazzulla's monograph on terracottas from the Venetia Romana, the various excellent articles of Rudolf Känel, and site-specific publications have marked important steps forward.[67] Still, a comprehensive updated catalogue remains an urgent desideratum. Känel studied the 3rd and 2nd century material in his dissertation and is currently working toward an updated publication, which would represent an enormous contribution to the study of terracottas.[68] As discussed above, the present study takes a broader and more contextual approach to this material. Rather than offering revised typologies or catalogues, my aim here will be to identify wider trends in architectural terracottas of the 3rd–1st centuries and to relate their use to current debates regarding "Romanization," colonization, and identity-formation.

1.5.2 *Chronology and Typology*

Beyond the role that scholarly interest has played in the treatment of architectural terracottas from different chronological periods, there are a number of limitations imposed by the archaeological record itself. Significantly, architectural terracottas are almost always found in secondary or tertiary archaeological contexts. When they were removed from a temple roof in antiquity, either due to damage or to large-scale renovations, they were often buried in large undifferentiated pits within the sacred temenos.[69] This means that terracottas produced over a period of several hundred years may be found within the same deposit and that stratigraphic analysis has been of minimal help in establishing a chronology for central Italy.[70] In the absence of more objective criteria, scholars have (not unreasonably) turned to stylistic analysis in order to trace the development and diffusion of particular terracotta types. Unfortunately, this too has proved unreliable. The chronology issue will be taken up in detail in Chapter 2, in order to shed preconceptions derived from outdated "Romanization" theory and to ask what information we can reliably glean from the objects themselves.

1.5.3 *Pedimental Sculpture*

Non-pedimental architectural terracottas, which comprise the core of this study, include elements such as antefixes, simas, cornices, revetment plaques, acroteria, and roof-tiles. Despite the often-elaborate decoration of these objects, they can rarely be described as narrative.[71] This may partly explain their frequent neglect compared to pedimental terracottas, which have the appeal of being sculptural and therefore more easily equated with "high art."

There have been several attempts to reconstruct 3rd–1st century pediments and to connect them with specific myths or historical events. Scholars such as Mario Torelli and Françoise-Hélène Massa-Pairault in particular have emphasized the symbolic meaning of pedimental decoration in colonies and other Italic towns vis-à-vis Rome.[72] Most surviving pediments, however, are quite fragmentary.[73] Because their reconstruction remains a matter of some controversy, it is difficult to say even what scene is depicted, let alone its supposed political overtones.

Furthermore, pedimental terracotta sculptures have often been discussed only in relation to one another, with minimal reference to their broader context or to the building's other decorative elements.[74] One wonders if this may partly explain the unsettling fact that such sculptures are currently dated almost without exception to the 2nd century BCE.[75] More dedicated study of this material in relation to the topography and development of specific sites is needed. As noted above, pedimental sculpture will be discussed in what follows when possible, though in many cases the surviving fragments are too sparse to allow for confident arguments regarding a scene's overall message.

1.5.4 *Manufacture and Logistics*

Despite the interpretative problems noted above, the technical aspects of architectural terracotta production are relatively well understood. Roland Hampe and Adam Winter's study, published in 1965, presented key insights into modern (though essentially pre-industrial) production processes in Greece and Southern Italy.[76] Their observations seem broadly applicable to earlier periods, as demonstrated in Charlotte and Örjan Wikander's detailed analysis of manufacturing techniques at Acquarossa and Örjan Wikander's more recent study of tiles at Poggio Civitate.[77] The following overview draws heavily on these works and particularly on Winter's thorough research synthesis in *Symbols of Wealth and Power.*[78]

At least for the Archaic period, there is good evidence that clay for architectural terracottas was gathered locally.[79] After the clay was purified (e.g., by sedimentation, levigation, sifting, or grinding), temper was usually added. The amount of temper varied depending on the clay and could be drawn from minerals like quartz, feldspar, sand, stone, or from ceramic materials or grog such as ground potsherds, bricks, or tiles.[80] Access to water was also necessary and had to be added in very controlled amounts in order for the clay to reach optimal plasticity.

By and large, techniques for shaping architectural terracottas followed a common pattern. Tegulae seem generally to have been manufactured using a wooden frame, the impressions of which can sometimes be observed on the edges of a finished tile.[81] Imbrices could also be formed in frames and then draped over a semi-cylindrical object to shape them as they dried.[82]

Decorated terracottas (antefixes, simas, revetment plaques, cornices, etc.) were created using a mold (matrix). These molds, in turn, were made from an original patrix, which was usually sculpted in clay in an additive modeling process.[83] The resulting mold captured a negative impression of the patrix. It could be retouched if necessary and was then dried and fired. The use of molds allowed for mass production of nearly identical terracottas, which could be embellished or altered by the addition of stamps, incised details, or handmade elements. Separately made pieces could also be joined together – a common practice for antefixes. The decorated vertical plaque would be formed in a mold and then joined to a cover-tile while both were leather-hard. Some examples preserve clear evidence of scoring, and dilute clay could be added along the join to help the pieces adhere.[84] A layer of slip might then be added to the surface, as well as painted decoration.

After all this had been completed, the finished piece must first be dried to a leather-hard state, followed by a longer period of final drying in the shade. Depending on the season, this could take anywhere from three days to a month.[85] Workshops must therefore have required a considerable amount of space to accommodate the various roof elements as they dried.

Terracottas were then fired in a kiln in three stages: oxidation, reduction, and reoxidation.[86] As with pottery, the success of the firing depended in large part on the correct execution of all previous steps. Temperatures around 900 to 1,000 degrees Celsius were optimal for terracottas, but in reality these often seem to have been lower, and firing temperatures probably varied.[87] Access to reliable kilns would thus have been another key requirement for artisans.

The processes of drying and firing impacted the size of the finished product. Shrinkage can occur during both stages, substantially reducing the overall size of the piece. This means that the mold is slightly smaller than the patrix, and the resulting terracottas are smaller than the mold. While shrinkage can vary considerably, we might consider an average rate of 10 percent for each firing, resulting in a 20 percent size difference between generations.[88] Due to minor differences in clay and firing, even terracottas of the same generation may exhibit slight variations. The size of terracottas is further reduced when "remolding" is performed – that is, the fashioning of a new mold from an existing architectural terracotta. Size differences between otherwise nearly identical terracottas can thus provide important insights into modes of production and reuse of molds for distinct building phases.

1.5.5 Polychromy

While some architectural terracottas have retained their paint extraordinarily well (Figure 4), the monochrome appearance of most surviving fragments is a far cry from their original vibrance. When color has faded in recent times (a common occurrence), excavation reports sometimes furnish information on the object's appearance at the moment of discovery. In the last decades, the use of non-invasive scientific techniques such as pXRF has added significantly to our knowledge of ancient polychromy, and a more widespread application of these methods to architectural terracottas would be of enormous value.[89]

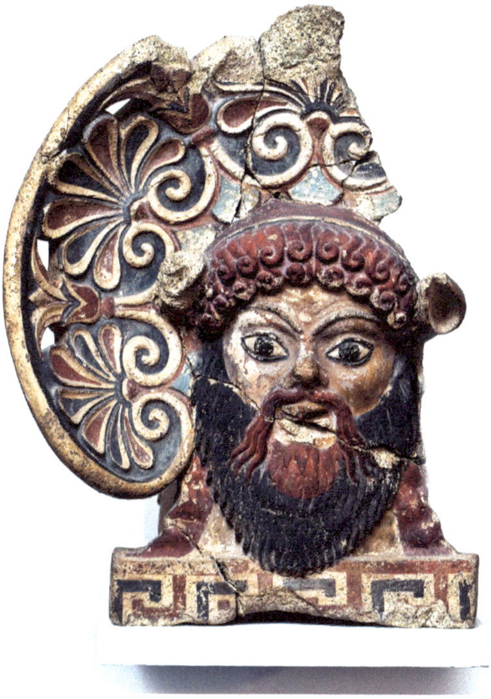

4. Antefix with head of a satyr, showing preserved paint. Said to be from Cerveteri, c. 470–460 BCE. Copenhagen: Ny Carlsberg Glyptotek, HIN 55. Courtesy of the Ny Carlsberg Glyptotek, Copenhagen.

In general, earlier architectural terracottas were dominated by a black-red-white color scheme, though the precise tone of the blacks and reds varies in the preserved examples. The color palette expanded considerably starting in the second half of the 6th century BCE to include a range of browns as well as gray-blue, green, and blue.[90] By the 4th century, most painters of architectural terracottas made use of a base coat over which they applied a vivid range of colors and shades.[91] These broad shifts in polychromy practices can thus aid in dating architectural terracottas, at least generally.

1.5.6 *Patrons and Commissioners*

Beyond questions of chronology and manufacture, which are fundamental for reconstructing the appearance of temple roofs, the present study is largely concerned with how *people* interacted with these objects. Mobility and cross-cultural interaction will be key themes of what follows, and Chapter 5 in particular will address the diversity of these objects' potential viewers. Questions surrounding patrons and artisans will also return in more detail later on, but it will be worth laying out some basic features of our evidence (or lack thereof) from the outset.

Unfortunately, we have very little information about the patrons and commissioners of temple terracottas. The Vulca anecdote is often cited as evidence that patrons seeking a particularly splendid product might summon well-known artisans from elsewhere. Even if this were the case, how much say did patrons have in the appearance of the finished product? Pliny, citing Varro, states only that Tarquinius Priscus gave Vulca the contract to make the statue of Jupiter.[92] No details regarding Tarquinius' specific requirements, nor Vulca's artistic input, are mentioned. And while the Vulca episode is undeniably appealing given the general lack of literary evidence, it comes several centuries after the events it records and is likely anachronistic. We must also be wary of the literary tendency to seek (or even invent) artistic founding figures, especially at a time when Romans sought to define their own artistic heritage in contrast to that of Greece.[93]

A few scattered references hint at patron involvement. Cato the Elder (*de agr.* 135.1) recommends buying tiles at Venafrum, suggesting that discerning consumers might be aware of which towns exceled in certain products. The *lex parieti faciundo* from Puteoli, dated to 105 BCE, offers a rare case in which the local magistrates who are commissioning a wall across from the town's Serapis temple specify the precise manner in which tiles should be nailed to the eaves.[94] Neither of these examples, however, help us with decorated architectural terracottas, and any conclusions must for the moment rely predominantly on inference. The specific ways in which commissioners and patrons wielded their influence during the construction process must in reality have varied considerably, with some patrons (like those at Puteoli) taking an active interest in architectural details and others contenting themselves with the selection of a trusted workshop to which they would then have left the majority of the decision-making. It is thus the finished roofs themselves that can perhaps offer the greatest insight into these processes. After having examined a number of architectural terracottas and full roof programs, we shall return to the question of patrons' objectives and viewers' perceptions in Section 5.2.1.

1.5.7 Workshops and Workers

As in the case of patrons, little in the archaeological record provides direct information on the workshops and artisans that actually produced architectural terracottas. As a result, interpretations range significantly, and no position has found widespread acceptance. On one side are those who consider workshops to have been stable and geographically fixed, while others have proposed a system of traveling groups of artisans.[95]

There are problems with both. If workshops were fixed, could they stay in business when a major project was not underway? Did they regularly produce other types of clay products instead?[96] Would it have been feasible to export finished architectural terracottas to other towns, given the considerable weight of these objects and the risk of breaking along the journey?[97] On the other hand, the logistical requirements for producing architectural terracottas are enormous and would not have been simple for itinerant artisans to manage. As we have seen, one needs large quantities of good-quality clay, water, sand, kilns, wood, matrices, paints, and large open areas suitable for drying the terracottas before firing, not to mention a labor force and other assorted equipment and materials.[98] There is also the possibility that artisans traveled with some, but not all, of their materials. The molds necessary to fashion a complete roof have been estimated to weigh roughly 300–400 kgs, compared to the astonishing 40 metric tons of the finished product.[99] At Satricum, the so-called Campanian roof includes a large number of terracottas apparently derived from Campanian molds and using Campanian temper.[100] It thus offers tantalizing evidence for an intermediate solution to the stable/itinerant models.

Several other sites are frequently invoked in this debate. Evidence for a stable workshop in the Archaic period, for instance, comes from the discovery of a large stoa-like structure at Poggio Civitate, which has been interpreted as a workshop for the production of architectural terracottas.[101] A mold was found on the structure's floor, as well as neatly stacked cover- and pan-tiles. The nearly seventy cover-tiles evidently had not yet been fired and were laying on the floor to dry when the building went up in flames. As people ran from the workshop, their footprints were preserved in the clay (Figure 5).[102]

Few other central Italic sites, however, preserve evidence of terracotta production. While no workshop has been found at Acquarossa, clay analysis shows that the architectural terracottas were indeed produced locally.[103] Given the need for extensive space as well as the potential fire hazard, the Wikanders have suggested that Acquarossa's terracotta production likely occurred in the vicinity of the site but not in its center.[104] Indeed, the dearth of excavated production facilities might simply reflect their usual placement away from the larger structures and centers that are the focus of most fieldwork.

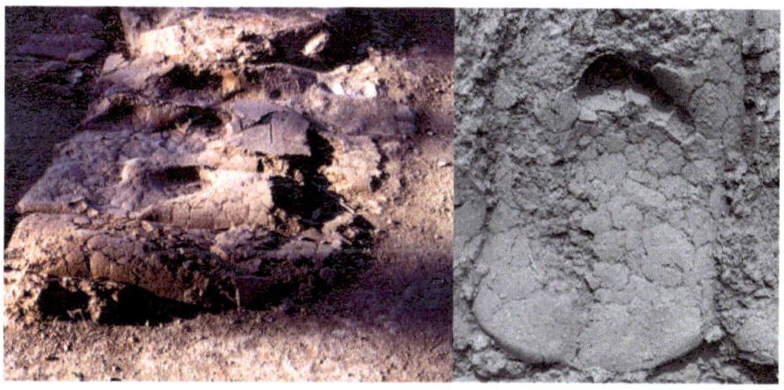

5. In-situ cover tiles from Poggio Civitate with footprints preserved. Courtesy of the Poggio Civitate Archaeological Project.

Terracottas dating between the late 6th and 1st centuries BCE have been found at the Selvasecca villa, but interpretations vary considerably regarding the site's function. A number of molds for producing architectural terracottas were found during excavations, as well as a tufo block with three cavities interpreted as molds for different types of roof tiles.[105]

Andrén viewed the Selvasecca site as a production center that supplied neighboring cities with architectural terracottas for their temples. Martin Söderlind has since challenged this notion, pointing out Selvasecca's remote location away from major cities or crossroads – factors that would impede distribution of terracottas elsewhere.[106]

Of particular interest is the fact that molds uncovered at Selvasecca are predominantly second generation, and Söderlind has suggested Tarquinia and Orvieto as the origin of their prototypes.[107] He estimates that using second generation molds would reduce the size of the terracottas by about 20 percent, making them perhaps more suitable for a private dwelling.[108] Based on Selvasecca's remote location, Neutron Activation Analysis of the clay, and the various recorded findspots of the terracottas, Söderlind proposed that the terracottas were in fact manufactured for use at the villa itself. While his arguments are convincing in many respects, it seems difficult to entirely rule out the possibility of Selvasecca as a production center. The terracottas and tiles represent an extensive chronological spread, and it is conceivable that the function of the site could have undergone significant changes during this time. As Söderlind himself notes, the evidence for large-scale manufacture at Selvasecca is particularly strong for roof-tiles of the later phases.[109] Two tiles preserve letters, interpreted as an Etruscan "L" in one case, and as a Latin "CL" in the other. Andrén and Berggren associated these with a certain Gaius Licinius.[110] If, as they suggest, he was a member of the Etruscan family Lecne, he might share ancestral ties with the suggestively named P. Licinius Tegula and Licinius Imbrex.[111]

A large roof-tile uncovered in 1975 at Pietrabbondante offers a rare glimpse into the lives, and even personalities, of its makers (Figure 6). It was found in a heap of tiles (many stamped with the Oscan letters *hl*) by Temple B – the structure to which it is thought to have belonged.[112] The tile measures 94 x 66 cm and is dated by Adriano La Regina to the early 1st century BCE.[113] Remarkably, it features a bilingual inscription in Oscan and Latin:

hn. sattiieís. detfri
seganatted. plavtad

(Detfri[114] of Herens Sattiis / signed with a footprint)

HERENNEIS. AMICA
SIGNAVIT. QUANDO
PONEBAMVS. TEGILA

(Amica of Herennius / signed when / we were placing the tile)[115]

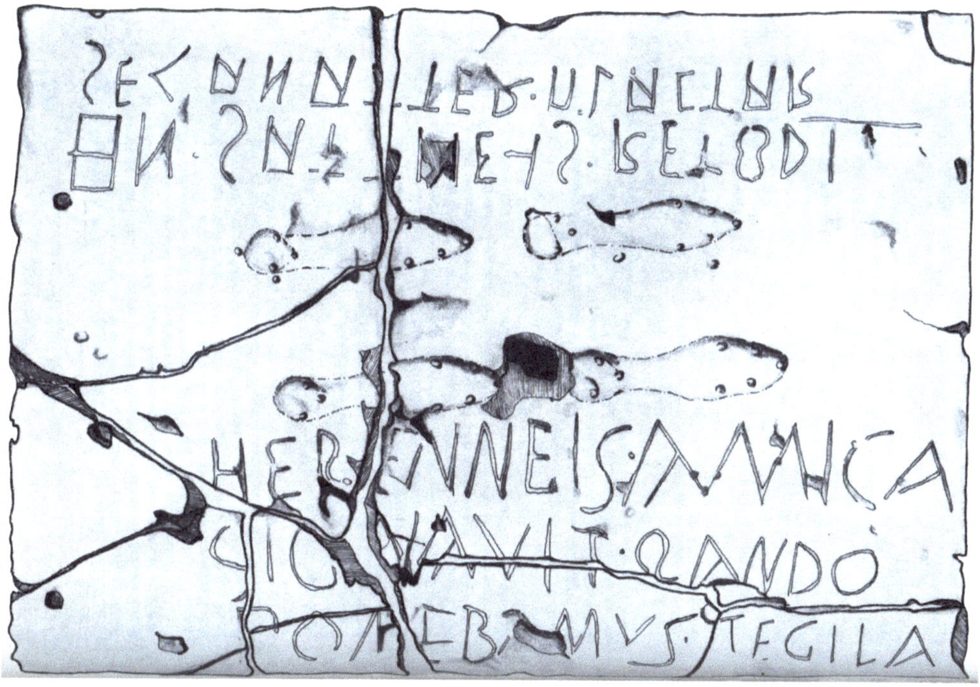

6. Roof-tile from Pietrabbondante inscribed in Oscan and Latin. Image after La Regina 1976, 285.

The women's shoeprints are visible between the two inscriptions and were added, along with the text, while the tile lay to dry and the clay was still wet. Whether the women worked regularly as tile-makers, or were called in for a large commission, is impossible to say. Nor do we know if they manufactured decorative pieces in addition to roof-tiles. Still, it is of great interest that not only are they women as well as literate slaves, they are of different backgrounds but apparently bilingual and able to communicate with ease.[116]

La Regina has suggested that their master, Herennius Sattius, owned a tile manufacturing business at Venafrum.[117] This is based primarily on the fact that the Sattii are well-attested epigraphically at Venafrum and that Cato the Elder cites the town as producing high quality tiles.[118] As has been pointed out, however, the logistical obstacles of transporting finished tiles into the mountains would have been substantial, and it seems more likely that the tile was produced at or near the site.[119]

A handful of additional inscribed architectural terracottas also appear to record artisan names. As with the Pietrabbondante tile, many of these suggest a fair degree of mobility and cross-cultural interaction. A fragmentary inscription at Fregellae reads [—]THVMA[—] in Latin letters but must be a name of Greek origin (Figure 7).[120] At Arretium, Cnei Urste is named in Etruscan, though his *praenomen* equates to the Latin Gnaeus and the *gentilicium* to the

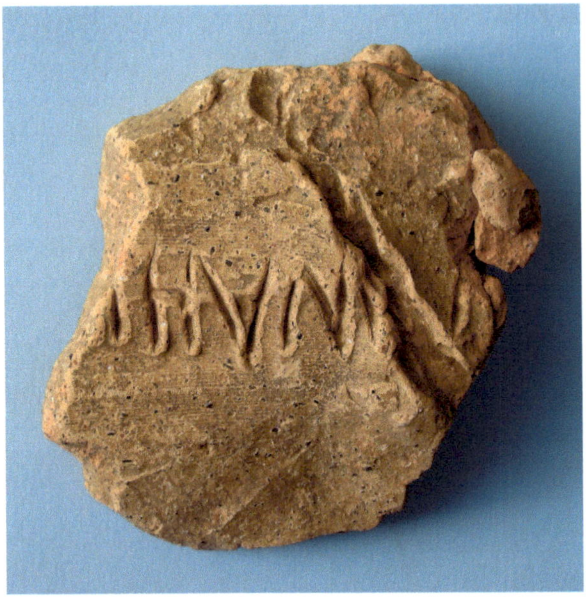

7. Terracotta fragment from Fregellae with [—]THVMA[—] inscription. Courtesy of the Ministero della Cultura – Soprintendenza Archeologia, Belle Arti e Paesaggio per le province di Frosinone e Latina. Photograph courtesy of Rudolf Känel.

Greek Orestes.[121] Indeed, Seth Bernard's analysis of the epigraphic evidence from the last three centuries BCE suggests a level of mobility amongst makers of architectural terracottas that is roughly equivalent to that of other types of building workers.[122] This strongly supports the idea that at least some coroplasts were itinerant.

Maria Bonghi Jovino has suggested that many workshops may have been "polyfunctional" and that traveling artisans could have been "hosted" by local workshops.[123] This would nicely solve the problem of transporting materials and equipment, while also accommodating for the well-attested movement of artisans and particular designs.

In actuality, the situation must have varied considerably over time and from place to place. It is unlikely that a single model existed for the production of architectural terracottas, and we must allow for the possibility that stable workshops, itinerant artisans, as well as the hosting of traveling artisans and the transportation of moveable equipment such as molds took place concurrently. There must have been some infrastructure to serve and maintain the temples of the local area. At the same time, there is now substantial evidence that artisans *were* moving around central Italy, as well as molds and/or finished products. Architectural terracottas from sites like Cosa, for instance, can be linked to examples from the immediate area (which could suggest stable workshops or artisans moving from site to site within a relatively restricted geographical zone) as well as to examples known from much more distant sites (suggesting a wider trade network and artisans, molds, or finished products traversing greater distances). Given the current state of our evidence, it seems probable that those involved in temple commissions and upkeep made use of both local and traveling artisans and that this was a core feature of architectural terracotta production from the very beginning.[124]

1.5.8 Moving Forward

While our knowledge of Italic architectural terracottas has increased in leaps and bounds over the last decades, a number of core questions remain unresolved. The categorically understudied examples dating to the last centuries BCE have not been adequately incorporated into discussions of this period, despite the fact that they constitute one of the largest bodies of material culture evidence to reach us. But this is changing, and their potential for shedding new light on long-standing scholarly debates is slowly being realized. It is a particularly exciting moment for the study of these objects. As interest in them expands, and the architectural terracottas from individual sites are published and added to the growing corpus, we will see the feasibility not only of detailed catalogues but of a wider conversation regarding their use, appearance, chronology, and role in shaping the central Italic landscape during a period of momentous change. The following pages seek to push the discourse in that direction by demonstrating just how much these objects can tell us, if only we can ask the right questions.

NOTES

1 Pommer 1983.
2 Miles 2016: 4 provocatively refers to this as "an ideological and architectural struggle for aerial supremacy."
3 The "oriental" associations of the flat roof were made particularly clear in a doctored photograph of the Weissenhof Siedlung (Stuttgart) published in 1934, where it is depicted as an "Arab village." At various points, the negative connotations of flat roofs also included associations with Socialism and Bolshevism (Pommer 1983: 160, 165).
4 An idea articulated explicitly by Paul Schultze-Naumburg (Pommer 1983: 165).
5 Ledderose 2000: 135; Steinhardt 2019: 161.
6 Steinhardt 2019: 161. Ledderose draws attention to the technical features that accompany these different roof types. Palace halls, for instance, employed a distinct type of tie beam within the roof frame (Ledderose 2000: 135).
7 Nair 2015: 104.
8 Nair 2015: 121, 137. See also p. 223 n. 50 on the view that the Spanish considered such roofs a threat precisely for their symbolic overtones.
9 Dates hereafter are BCE unless otherwise noted. For the tiles, doubts regarding their architectural use stem from the fact that like many architectural terracottas, these are found in secondary contexts or contexts of presumed reuse, and are not manufactured to follow standard sizes. As Winter points out, however, there is no reason to assume that standardization was the norm in Mycenaean times, as it was in later periods (Winter 1993a: 8–9).

The discovery context for the House of the Tiles at Lerna, where the tiles were found atop a thick layer of debris covering the floor, strongly suggests that they were originally placed on the roof (Caskey 1954: 23–27; Winter 1993a: 8). On the earliest tile roofs, see recently Marzolff 2017.

10 Pullen 1986.

11 Pullen 1986.

12 Jazwa 2018: 171.

13 Jazwa 2018: 162.

14 On the history of Greek terracotta roofs until c. 480 BCE, see Winter 1993a.

15 See the discussion in Winter 1993a: 19–21.

16 For a description of the Protocorinthian system, see Winter 1993a: 12–18.

17 On early terracotta roofs in Italy, see Winter 2009. Turfa 2022 contextualizes the advent of tile roofs in Etruria in relation to engineering advances – specifically, the use of the tie-beam truss. For the Asia Minor architectural terracotta tradition, the fundamental reference is still Åkerström 1966, although the chronology presented there has been altered by more recent finds.

18 On domestic contexts for early Italic architectural terracottas, see, e.g., Winter 2009 esp. 7–142. For a synthesis of different types of buildings employing architectural terracottas in central Italy between 640 and 510 BCE, see Winter 2009: 567–570.

19 Many were discarded in early excavations, so the actual number must be significantly higher: Glendinning 2005: 83, 85.

20 Glendinning 2002: 33–35.

21 See, in general, Åkerström 1966; architectural terracottas from the Sardis excavations are published in Ramage 1978.

22 Winter 1993b.

23 Winter 1993a: 289–290.

24 Mertens-Horn 1990: 241–243; Winter 1993a: 297–298.

25 Winter 1993a: 313.

26 The most famous being the so-called Veii-Rome-Velletri system; Winter 2009: 311–393, and see the recent summary remarks in Lulof and Smith 2017: 7–9.

27 See the discussion in Hopkins 2022: 109–110. On the similarities between the roofs, see Galluccio 2016: 280–283.

28 On the spread of tile roof technology across the Mediterranean world, see recently Winter 2022.

29 Pliny *HN* 35.151–152.

30 Pliny *HN* 35.157, citing Varro; also Pliny *HN* 28.16 and Plut. *Publ.* 13.

31 Plut. *Publ.* 13; Pliny *HN* 28.16.

32 Tac. *Ger.* 16.

33 Dio 46.31.3.

34 Barry 1996.

35 Livy 5.21.10.

36 App. *B. Civ.* 1.4.32.

37 Plut. *Pyrrh.* 34.2.

38 On the manufacture of, and differences in, Italic pan-tiles, see Shepherd 2006, 2007, 2015, 2016.

39 Cosa's architectural terracottas have been consistently presented in the Cosa volumes, the most thorough treatment being Richardson's in *Cosa II.* Valentina Livi is engaged in a long-term project to catalogue the terracottas from Minturnae, but her full results have not yet been published. See also Crawford-Brown 2019b for a discussion of the archival evidence and surviving fragments from Minturnae.

40 The problematic nature of the term "Roman" has been a topic of considerable scholarly interest over the last decades and will be addressed throughout this study. For a recent discussion of the narrowness of traditional approaches to "Etruscology," see Stoddart 2020:

1–23. Hopkins 2024 offers an extended analysis of the entangled realities of artistic production in 7th–3rd century BCE central Italy. For more general discussions of the problems with identifying clearly defined, distinct "cultures" in ancient Italy, see among others Terrenato 1998; Versluys 2013; Ricci 2019.

41 See Laurence 1999; as well as Kolb 2019 for case studies across the wider geographic area of the Roman Empire; on the roads and routes of ancient Italy generally (including by sea), see Isayev 2017 esp. 71–87; see also Hitchner 2012 on Roman roads in relation to economic growth.

42 The study of ornament is particularly well-developed in Islamic art history, see, e.g., the classic work of Oleg Grabar (1992). For comparative approaches with a broad chronological and geographic span, see Grabar 2010; Necipoğlu and Payne 2016. For Greco-Roman art, see Porter 2010; Lipps and Maschek 2014; Dietrich and Squire 2018; as well as Schultz and von den Hoff 2009 on approaches to Greek architectural sculpture. Hölscher 2009, while highlighting the paradox of "a high degree of cultural significance and, at the same time, a rather low degree of direct, communicative impact" in Greek architectural sculpture (61), sees the Roman approach as generally more concerned with viewer readability. In both contexts, he argues that architectural sculpture "distinguishes public buildings, enhancing their cultural significance by aesthetic beauty and semantic meaning" (62). Guest 2016 focuses on the Italian Renaissance but has much to offer regarding Roman predecessors. In addition to the extensive bibliographies provided in the above works, see also van Eck 2020 for a bibliographic essay on ornament in Europe.

43 E.g., Büsing 1977; Sauron 1982; L'Orange 1985; Kellum 1994; Castriota 1995; Cohon 2004; Caneva 2009, 2010; Pollini 2012; Cofer 2015; Crawford-Brown 2022; and the many contributions of Dominik Maschek (e.g., Maschek 2008a, 2008b, 2010, 2012, 2014). On frames, see recently Platt and Squire 2017a.

44 Her fundamental study is Winter 2009, but see also Winter 2002, 2022, Winter, Iliopoulos, and Ammerman 2009, and Winter 1993a, 1993b on the Greek context, among many others.

45 Hopkins 2022: 111.

46 Hopkins 2022.

47 Hopkins 2010, 2014, 2016.

48 For problems with Della Seta's system, see Knoop 1993.

49 Della Seta 1918: 128–132.

50 Della Seta 1918: 134, 138. For Phase 2 in general, 132–144.

51 Della Seta 1918: 144–157.

52 At the time, P. J. Riis was independently working on a classification of Etruscan sculpture (including a large number of terracotta antefixes), which appeared in 1941. Andrén's system, however, has proved more influential.

53 Knoop finds particular significance in Andrén's use of the "chronologically much stricter term 'Period,'" compared to Della Seta's "*fasi*"; Knoop 1993: 62.

54 Andrén 1940: CXXX ff.

55 Andrén 1940: CLI ff.

56 Andrén 1940: CCXI ff.

57 Andrén 1940: V.

58 Knoop 1993.

59 Knoop 1993: 64.

60 See the discussion in Sections 2.2–2.3.

61 An early report on her progress appeared in *Deliciae Fictiles II* (Winter 1997). Winter also published the definitive study of early Greek architectural terracottas (Winter 1993a), as well as shorter studies of the relationship between early Greek and Italic examples, e.g., Winter 2002.

62 Winter 2009: 50.

63 Winter 2009: 4.

64 Winter (2009: 4) notes that Della Seta's distinction is "not always clear-cut, and there are occasional roof elements that embrace characteristics of both phases."

65 Carlucci 2021: 14; on the Pyrgi temple, see also Colonna 2000.

66 Hopkins (2022) recently called attention to this problem for the 5th and 4th centuries in particular.

67 Pensabene and Sanzi Di Mino 1983; Strazzulla 1987; Känel 1991, 2000, 2010, 2015, 2019, to name just a few.

68 Känel 2001, published in microfiche in 2004, is unfortunately not widely available.

69 Glinister 2000.

70 Sometimes architectural terracottas are found where they had apparently fallen, but here too it is difficult to know how separated the construction and destruction events are chronologically. In rarer cases, sacred deposits containing representative roof elements and other objects can offer better insight into the phasing of the roofs, or at least offer a terminus ante quem.

71 A possible narrative function has been suggested for the unusual *Piazza della Cortina* antefixes at Praeneste (e.g., Gullini 1973: 777), for instance, though this is difficult to prove given their fragmentary state. A handful of additional non-pedimental terracottas appear to display a narrative scene, but these are the exception rather than the rule.

72 Torelli 1993, 1999; Massa-Pairault 1985a, 1992 (esp. pp. 215–245), 2000.

73 Even the most complete surviving examples, such as the Via di San Gregorio pediment, remain the subject of fierce controversy (see Chapter 2 n. 74).

74 Alexander Ekserdjian recently reexamined much of this material in his dissertation at Columbia University (Ekserdjian 2023), offering a refreshing approach that looks at Italic terracotta pedimental sculpture in relation to representations of gods in sanctuaries more generally, thus adding important context. His study, currently being worked into a monograph, constitutes one of very few analyses of this material in anglophone scholarship to date.

75 The development of the closed pediment in Italy has been variously described by scholars, but most accept the Belvedere temple in Orvieto as the earliest example (e.g., Strazzulla 1977: 41). Other exceptions to the "2nd-century rule" include the groups from Lo Scasato, Vignale, and Tivoli. The pedimental groups from Catona, Bolsena, Fucoli at Chianciano, Cosa (Temples B and D and the triple-cella temple), Luni, Talamonaccio, Vetulonia, Volterra (Temple A), and Camposcala at Vulci have all been assigned dates in the first half of the 2nd century BCE. Sculptures from Chieti, Civitalba, Nemi, and Rome (the Via di San Gregorio and Via Latina groups) are typically placed in the mid-2nd century, while a late 2nd century date is suggested for terracottas from Segni (Juno Moneta temple) and Monastero at Aquileia. Because most of these groups are quite fragmentary and lacking in relevant stratigraphic data, the proposed dates should be viewed with extreme caution. For a summary of the scholarship and relevant bibliography, see Rous 2010: 232 ff.

76 Hampe and Winter 1965.

77 Wikander 1993, esp. 104 ff.; cf. Wikander 1988: 56 ff.; Wikander 2017: 129–144.

78 In addition to her own observations, Winter draws on studies of modern tile production, pottery production, experimental data, and individual archaeological case-studies including clay analyses: Winter 2009: 505–538; cf. her discussion of Greek manufacturing processes in Winter 1993a: 304–308. See also Fenelli's summary in *Enea nel Lazio* 1981: 265–269.

79 E.g., Ammerman et al 2008; Winter, Iliopoulos, and Ammerman 2009; Winter 2009: 512, 525–526 nn. 104–108. Clay analyses at Acquarossa, Poggio Civitate, Veii, and Rome reveal an overall tendency toward using local materials, while the evidence from Satricum may suggest the transportation of at least some elements from farther afield (Knoop 1987).

80 Winter 2009: 512.

81 For the two principal types of Italic tegulae as well as features of their respective manufacture, see Shepherd 2006, 2007, 2015, 2016.

82 Hampe and Winter 1965, esp. 28, 107–108, 208, Abb. 17–18; Shepherd 2006: 169–172 and figs. 137–144, 2007: 56–58 and figs. 3–5. See also the detailed discussion (with emphasis on the evidence from Acquarossa) in Wikander 1993: 104 ff.

83 Winter 2009: 513–514, see esp. n. 38. The patrix could also be made of wood, stone, or metal. Winter notes that the clay patrix was likely used in a bone-dry state, rather than fired, in order to avoid additional shrinkage.
84 Winter 2009: 518 and fig. 8.2.
85 Hampe and Winter 1965: 183; Winter 2009: 523–524.
86 Winter 1993a: 305 and Winter 2009: 524–525.
87 Winter 2009: 524. Recent scientific studies of architectural terracottas are helping to elucidate this picture, e.g., García Giménez et al 2005; Barone et al 2017; Fugazzotto et al 2021; Russo et al. 2022.
88 Söderlind 2006: 120 and n. 20. Knoop more conservatively suggests that a terracotta resulting from remolding will have dimensions at least 5.2 percent smaller than those of the original. In most observed examples, however, the disparity appears greater. Knoop's case studies show an inter-generation shrinkage rate of 10–14 percent in one example, and 5.8–18.9 percent (with an average of 8–14 percent) in the other: Knoop 1987: 219–222, see also Figures 1–4.
89 Recent archaeometric studies of terracottas from Gela (Barone et al. 2017), Rome (Fugazzotto et al. 2021), and Alba Fucens (Russo et al. 2022), among others, have amply demonstrated the utility of applying these methods more broadly.
90 For an overview of colors and painting techniques in the Archaic period, see Winter 2009: 520–523.
91 For a discussion of shifting techniques, Rescigno and Sampaolo 2006.
92 Pliny, *HN* 35.157: "Vulcam Veis accitum, cui locaret Tarquinius Priscus Iovis effigiem in Capitolio dicandam."
93 The linguistic similarity between "Vulca" and "Vulcan/Volcanus" (a god associated with fine workmanship) might further caution us against accepting the Vulca story at face value.
94 *FIRA* III^2 153, *CIL* X, n. 1781.
95 For stable workshops, see, e.g., Andrén 1971[1974]; Riis 1981: 47–48. For traveling workshops, see Vagnetti 1966; Cristofani1981b: 195–197, Comella 1985; Bruni 1985: 126–127. For an overview of the problem, see Bonghi Jovino 1990: 48–54. Winter, Iliopoulos, and Ammerman 2009 offers a welcome examination of the spread of architectural terracotta production technology in the 6th century BCE using petrographic analysis. For evidence of traveling craftsmen in ancient Italy more generally, see Bourdin 2012: 552–559.
96 Charlotte and Örjan Wikander have rightly highlighted the urgent need to study architectural terracotta production operations. They suggest that workshops might have expanded while preparing a large-scale commission and subsequently reduced and/or diversified their output in the intervening lulls. They cite the similarities between roof-tiles and storage jars, as well as the correspondence between painted architectural terracottas and white-on-red pottery of the same period at Aquarossa (Wikander and Wikander 2006: 43–44). Recent analysis of ceramic materials from Poggio Colla would seem to support the hypothesis of local workshops producing diverse products (Meyers et al. 2019). For a later workshop that appears to have produced a range of products in addition to architectural terracottas, see Shepherd 2006.
97 It is possible that architectural terracottas were transported by ship in many cases, which would have solved many of the problems connected to overland transport. The current evidence from shipwrecks, however, is insufficient to confirm this model, particularly before the 1st century CE (*pace* Lulof 2006; see Parker 1992; Strauss 2007).
98 See Andrén's (1971[1974]: 13) thorough discussion of this problem.
99 Knoop 1987: 208 n. 536.
100 Knoop 1987.
101 Nielsen 1987: 91. Tuck 2021 offers an up to date synthesis of research at the site.
102 Nielsen 1987: 91–94 and Figures 5–7.
103 Wikander 1993: 101, 168–170.

104 Wikander and Wikander 2006: 43. There is also some evidence that Acquarossa supported several different local workshops in the late 6th and early 5th centuries BCE. Given the size of the community and the number of tiled buildings, there would have been ample work to keep local artisans in business; Winter 2009: 536.

105 Andrén and Berggren 1969; Andrén 1971[1974]; Söderlind 2006: 116.

106 Söderlind 2006: 120.

107 Söderlind 2006: 118–119. According to Söderlind, these would have reached Selvasecca "by means of commercial mould or craft circulation."

108 Söderlind 2006: 120 and n. 20; this estimate assumes an average shrinkage of 10 percent for each firing.

109 Söderlind 2006: 117, 120.

110 Andrén and Berggren 1969: 61, 71.

111 For P. Licinius Tegula, see Livy 31.12; for Licinius Imbrex, see Gell. *NA* 13.23, 16. Andrén and Berggren 1969: 71; Andrén 1971[1974]: 15.

112 La Regina 1976: 284. For the "*hl*" stamp, La Regina 1966: 2667 n. 9 and tav. VII. All "official" inscriptions dating to this period from Pietrabbondante's temple and theatre are in Oscan.

113 La Regina 1976: 287.

114 The meaning of detfri is debated: it is often translated as a name, but this is not certain (see Crawford et al. 2011: 1187–1188; Clackson 2014: 715–716).

115 Text and commentary: La Regina 1976: 286 ff.; Poccetti 1979: n. 21; and especially the more recent commentary and critiques in Crawford et al. 2011: 1186–1188. Translation modified from Wallace-Hadrill 2008: 90; and Mullen 2011: 534.

116 On the significance of the tile as a "bilingual document," see Wallace-Hadrill 2008: 91–92; Mullen 2011: 533–535.

117 La Regina 1976: 287–288.

118 Cato, *De agr.* 135.1. Cf. *CIL* X 4988, 4989, 4989a, 4992.

119 Wallace-Hadrill 2008: 92, noting that workers from Venafrum could conceivably have come to Pietrabbondante for the project; see also Crawford et al. 2011: 1187.

120 Sironen 1997; Känel 2019; Bernard 2019a: 500, tab. 1.

121 Andrén 1940: 277-8, VIII:8; Bernard 2019a: 500-1, tab. 1.

122 Bernard 2019a.

123 Bonghi Jovino 1990: 48–54, esp. 53.

124 On the early evidence, see recently Hopkins 2024, esp. 33–63. Site specific discussions of local and itinerant artisans appear throughout Lulof, Mazini, and Rescigno 2019; see, for instance, Ambrosini 2019; Bacci 2019; Bernard 2019a; Campanile and Cangiano 2019; Crawford-Brown 2019c; Meyers et al 2019; Santostefano 2019; and Scatozza Höricht 2019; among others.

TWO

CHRONOLOGICAL UNCERTAINTIES AND THE "ROMANIZATION" TANGLE

2.1 INTRODUCTION

As already noted, perhaps the greatest impediment to the study of 3rd- to 1st-century Italic architectural terracottas is the near impossibility (at least at present) of dating them precisely. Certain broad parameters are provided by the objects themselves and examination of features like polychromy, clay fabric and weight, and the thickness of finished pieces can aid in establishing a general date range. Stratigraphic data can likewise be of use, although this too is complicated by the fact that architectural terracottas are almost inevitably found outside of their original contexts. The wooden beams they once decorated and protected have long since deteriorated, and most terracottas were in any case removed from buildings during renovations in antiquity and buried in large, undifferentiated pits in the vicinity. The result is that terracottas from a range of centuries may be found together in the same archaeological context.

When precise dates have been proffered for specific examples, they are usually based almost exclusively on stylistic analysis. This quickly proves unreliable, however, as many terracotta forms consciously imitate older or local examples. Traditional designs such as the perforated cornices with triskelia and figure eights or the revetment plaques with addorsed palmettes, for example, appear on Italic temples in almost identical form for roughly five centuries (cf. Figures 23, 26, 28). As I will argue in Chapter 3, these objects are often deliberately intended to inhibit chronological differentiations – their primary goal being to look old and thus temple-appropriate.

The implications of this archaizing tendency in terracotta design have not been sufficiently appreciated. Archaizing, when done well, renders stylistic analysis virtually ineffective as a dating technique on its own. While it has occasionally been possible to combine archaeological or object-based data, literary evidence, and stylistic analysis to reach a more convincing date for single examples, we can rarely pinpoint more than a 100 or 50-year span. More precise attributions should be regarded with extreme caution.

As we shall see, even those terracotta typologies that are considered most secure rest on extraordinarily shaky evidence. The construction of these typologies is, by and large, deeply entangled in now-outdated models of "Romanization." In many cases, the model has been thrown out, but the chronology it led to has lingered behind. There remains a sticky assumption in architectural terracotta studies that Rome acted as a driving force in the production and innovation of new types.

To unpack and undermine this long-held assumption, the present chapter will analyze our archaeological evidence for the dating of architectural terracottas, taking Cosa and Rome as case studies. The former has functioned as a yardstick for dating other terracottas and thus temples in 3rd- to 1st-century Italy ever since the publication of Lawrence Richardson's tantalizingly precise typology in 1960.[1] Despite its influence, Richardson's chronology has little archaeological grounding and is in fact deeply rooted in beliefs regarding Rome's primacy. The focus will then shift to Rome itself, in order to ascertain whether any evidence can be found for new types being innovated or produced there earlier than in other towns. Here and in the following chapters, I will argue for a participatory rather than leading role for Rome in the production of architectural terracottas during the last centuries BCE and advocate the use of network theory as an explanatory framework for avoiding the confines of "Romanization" and center-periphery models.

Through an examination of the evidence from Cosa and Rome, this chapter will problematize some commonly held assumptions regarding architectural terracottas of the last three centuries BCE, thus serving as a sort of second prolegomenon to the study of this material. Having highlighted here what we don't – and for the moment can't – know, I will then seek to reassemble the evidence in the chapters that follow and ask what, in a positive sense, these objects can tell us about communities, identities, and practices of visual expression.

2.2 COSA AND THE "ROMANIZING" TERRACOTTA TYPOLOGY

The site of Cosa has played a disproportionately dominant role in discussions of "Romanization" over the last decades.[2] This is largely due to the particular way in which Frank Brown presented the results of his excavations at the site. In the words of Elizabeth Fentress, Brown was essentially "'excavating' the inaccessible Rome while excavating Cosa."[3] Brown viewed Cosa as a miniature Rome – a colony intimately tied to its mother city, which it sought consciously and consistently to imitate. His unhesitating use of terms like "Arx" and "Capitolium" hints at this view, as do his identification of several private houses around the forum as *atria publica* and his suggestion that Temple B in the forum was dedicated to Concordia. More recent scholarship has dismissed the last two theories, but the terms "arx" (albeit with a lowercase "a") and "Capitolium" have been surprisingly difficult to shake.[4]

In order to avoid the connotations that such terminology carries, even if unwittingly, I advocate the use of more neutral terms to describe Cosa's topography. The elevated southwest area, traditionally designated as the "Arx" or "arx," will here be referred to as the "summit." The earliest temple in this area, for which no concrete evidence suggesting Jupiter's worship has been found, will be referred to as "Summit Temple 1" rather than the "Temple of Jupiter" – the latter term being used only in quotations and with specific reference to previous scholarship. The appellation of "Capitolium" for the summit's large 2nd-century BCE temple is similarly rejected due to insufficient evidence and will here be called the "triple-cella temple."

Cosa's development and architectural terracottas will be discussed in more detail in Chapter 4, but it is necessary to grapple here with its role in debates over "Romanization" as a prelude to that analysis. Frank Brown's characterization of Cosa as a "typical" colony has by now been analyzed, criticized, and largely discarded.[5] What has been insufficiently appreciated, however, is the major role Brown's interpretation played in Lawrence Richardson's typology for the architectural terracottas. Richardson consistently identified the "finest" Cosan terracottas as examples of Roman production or close imitation. He writes of Temple D's decoration that "the real source of the new designs is to be sought . . . at Rome itself"[6] and that the designer of the "Capitolium's" first-phase revetments "was more than simply skillful, he was brilliant, and probably he was working in or near Rome together with the first great Roman architects."[7] For the "Capitolium's" fifth decorative phase, "the Cosans seem to have sent to Rome and bought the best terracottas available."[8] Terracottas not to Richardson's taste are instead disparaged as "conspicuously provincial."[9] The language of these statements speaks for itself, belonging comfortably to the Rome-centered model of scholarship that dominated studies of colonization for decades. The central issue with Cosa, however, is that while most scholars have now rejected "Romanization" models, many continue to rely directly or indirectly on Richardson's terracotta chronology – the explicit product of his broader interpretative approach.

Because the Richardson typology is generally assumed to have far more archaeological grounding than is actually the case, it has been widely accepted and used to date terracottas, and thus entire buildings, from sites across central Italy for the last half century. The dating of 3rd- to 1st-century terracottas is now plagued by a long tradition of circular reasoning, in which newly excavated terracottas are dated based on the Richardson chronology and then are used in turn to implicitly reinforce that chronology.

Despite its popular reception, voices of dissent have been raised. Strazzulla's 1977 article questioned the misleadingly precise dates presented in *Cosa II.*[10] A case in point is the dating of Cosa's so-called "Temple of Jupiter." According to Lawrence Richardson, "since an important temple would hardly have been put up during the troubled years of the First or Second Punic Wars, a date between 240 and 220 B.C. is to be preferred."[11] As Strazzulla points out, however, several temples *were* erected in Rome during the "troubled" period of the First Punic War; and in any case, the years between the colony's foundation in 273 BCE and the effective onset of the war are more than adequate for such a project.[12] It is worth adding that while Richardson uses historical inference to date the "Jupiter" temple, and thus the terracottas, Frank Brown, in the very same volume, explicitly dates the *temple* based on Richardson's date for the terracottas.[13] The argument is manifestly circular and rests on little more than one scholar's view of historical probability.

Even as Strazzulla was calling attention to the more broadly objectionable aspects of Richardson's approach, the Cosa typology was nevertheless rapidly gaining traction due to the undeniable allure of its precision and supposed stratigraphic grounding. Rabun Taylor revisited the chronology in 2002 and further exposed its heavy dependence on subjective stylistic criteria. Richardson's interpretation, Taylor argued, is governed by two principal assumptions: (1) "the orderly, linear nature of stylistic changes" and (2) the "notion that forms undergo recognizable evolutionary cycles progressing from an incipient, inferior phase to full maturity . . . then a 'baroque' or 'mannerist' stage, which leads to degeneracy."[14] As Taylor so well demonstrated, such linearity is fundamentally undermined by the fact that many terracottas belonging to Richardson's "classical moment" bear striking similarities to centuries-older Etruscan examples.[15] Still, Richardson's typology has remained a touchpoint. Twenty-five years after the publication of Strazzulla's article, Taylor lamented that too many terracotta studies still "take the Cosa typology as gospel."[16] The same could probably be said today.

2.3 ARCHITECTURAL TERRACOTTAS AND COSA'S STRATIGRAPHY

Strazzulla and Taylor have masterfully dissected the problems of connoisseurship in relation to the Cosa typology. The fact that it remains so influential must largely be due to Richardson's assertions of strong archaeological support. Cosa's stratigraphy, however, is anything but straightforward, and a reexamination of the archaeological evidence is crucial if we are to fairly evaluate the terracotta chronology and to understand if any support exists for the dating of these objects.

Cosa II presents a very precise account of the SW summit's ("*arx*"'s) development, for which it repeatedly claims conclusive archaeological evidence.[17] The relevant structures are an early temple (the "Temple of Jupiter") whose precise location has been a topic of debate for decades, the modestly sized Temple D dated to the first quarter of the 2nd century BCE, and the triple-cella temple ("Capitolium") dated to the second quarter of that century.[18]

It should first be noted that the summit was hardly undisturbed when excavations began in 1948. Not only had it been the site of medieval constructions, but barracks and an antiaircraft observation post had been established there by Italian soldiers during World War II.[19] Furthermore, the *Cosa II* volume was published in 1960 and thus does not represent a complete account of archaeological work on the summit. Additional excavations were undertaken in this area between 1965 and 1968 and yielded numerous architectural terracottas and other objects that may have implications for the summit's chronology and development. The results of these excavations, however, have never been fully published, and we remain fundamentally reliant on the data provided in *Cosa II*.[20]

Based on the combined criteria of archaeological context, fabric, and style, Richardson divided the excavated architectural terracottas into ten recognizable phases, with an additional list of miscellaneous and unattributed types. The principal groups were each assigned to a specific building and phase and dated as follows:

- "Temple of Jupiter," original decoration, 240–220 BCE (Figure 8)
- "Temple of Jupiter," redecoration of 170–160 BCE
- "Temple of Jupiter," subsequent repairs, post-160 BCE
- Temple D, original decoration, 170–160 BCE
- Temple D, redecoration of 100–75 BCE
- "Capitolium," original decoration, c. 150 BCE (Figure 9)
- "Capitolium," 2nd period (1st repair), c. 120 BCE
- "Capitolium," 3rd period (1st redecoration), c. 100 BCE
- "Capitolium," 4th period (2nd repair), end of the first quarter of the 1st century BCE
- "Capitolium," 5th period (2nd redecoration), mid-1st century BCE

The high number of repairs and redecorations reflect Richardson's stated belief that architectural terracottas had to be replaced every twenty to twenty-five years due to wear and breakage.[21] Taylor has already challenged this claim, pointing out that Temple B at Cosa seems to have utilized the same series of terracottas for its entire 250-year lifespan.[22] Indeed, once fired, terracottas are remarkably durable. Evidence from across central Italy now strongly suggests that terracotta roofs could remain in place for extended periods and that a two-

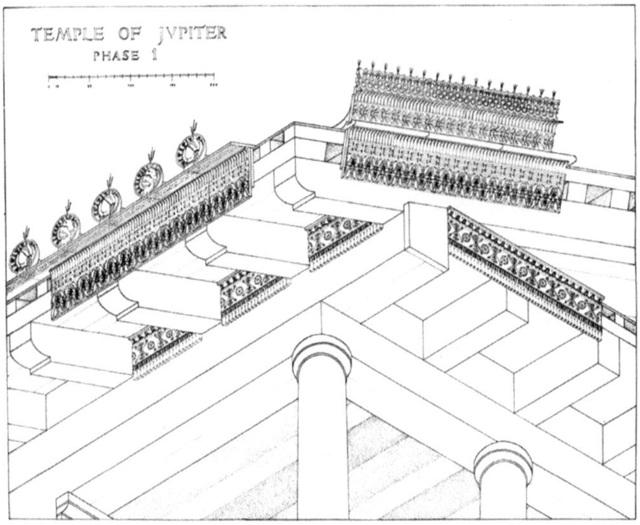

8. Original decoration of Cosa's so-called "Temple of Jupiter," as reconstructed in *Cosa II*. Courtesy of the American Academy in Rome, Cosa Archaeological Collection.

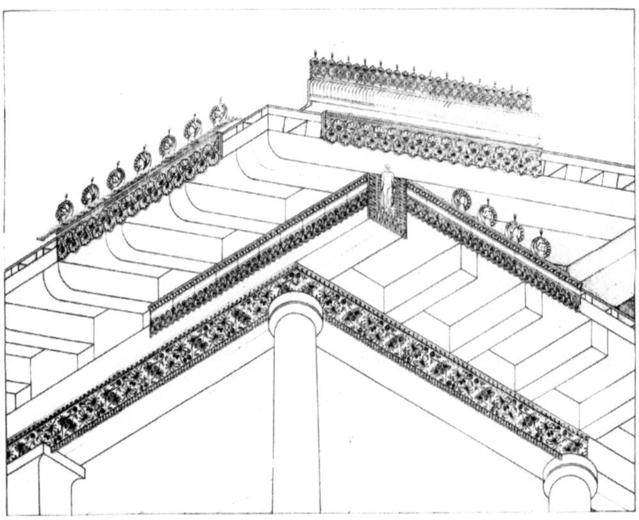

9. Original decoration of Cosa's so-called "Capitolium," as reconstructed in *Cosa II*. Courtesy of the American Academy in Rome, Cosa Archaeological Collection.

century lifespan was probably not exceptional (see Chapter 3). It is likely that individual repairs were made to buildings as needed – particularly for the more exposed and more easily replaceable elements like perforated cornices and antefixes. A full redecoration every twenty to twenty-five years is simply insufficiently attested, at Cosa as elsewhere, and Taylor advocates reducing the number of the triple-cella temple's phases from five to two and imagining only a limited repair to Temple D probably dating to the Augustan period.[23]

Russell T. Scott has convincingly argued that Temple D went up in the first quarter of the 2nd century BCE.[24] Reconstructing the phasing of its roof decoration, however, is far from straightforward. Most of the architectural terracottas assigned to Temple D in *Cosa II* were found either in the excavations of the triple-cella temple, scattered around the summit, or "in the vicinity" of the temple in areas that were not distinguished stratigraphically. For instance, not a single fragment of the shell antefixes with heads of young satyrs and maenads ("Type A"), which Richardson assigned to Temple D's original decoration, was found in a stratigraphically identified context.[25] Among the terracottas assigned to Temple D's redecoration (dated in *Cosa II* to c. 100–75 BCE), the revetment plaque with addorsed palmettes can be described only as "pre-Augustan" based on archaeological context.[26] For the perforated cornice with swastikas assigned to the same phase, no fragments were found in a stratigraphically distinguished layer.[27]

The terracottas from Temple D bear strong similarities to those of Temple B in the forum below (see Section 4.2.2.2); and in better circumstances, the latter's stratigraphy might have helped to clarify the ambiguous contexts of the summit. The area around Temple B, however, was also much disturbed by the time formal excavations began at Cosa (Figure 10). The worst affected was the zone northwest of the temple, where considerable quantities of earth and building materials had been moved during 19th-century explorations at the site.[28] More information is preserved on the southeast side of the temple, where the excavators deemed the lower levels to be stratigraphically reliable.

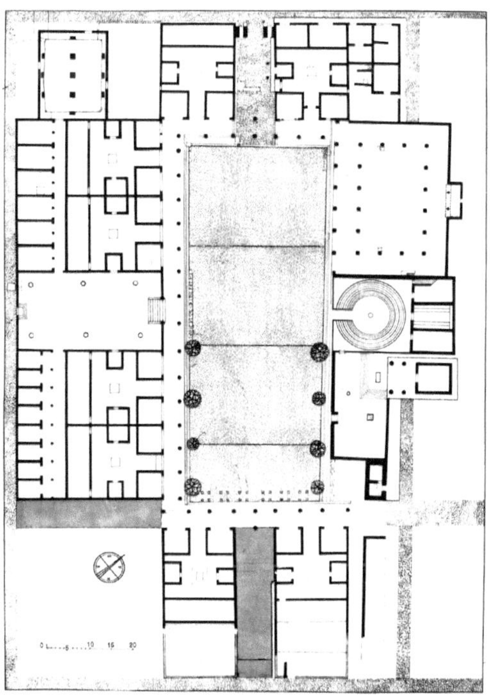

10. Plan of Cosa's forum c. 140 BCE, as reconstructed in *Cosa III*.
Courtesy of the American Academy in Rome, Cosa Archaeological Collection.

The abundance of ash deposits and objects blackened by soot links this layer to a fire that apparently destroyed the roof of Temple B sometime in the early 1st century CE.[29] However, no stratigraphy could be distinguished between this event and the foundation of the temple in the early 2nd century BCE.[30] This means that even the best-documented architectural terracottas from Temple B cannot be dated more precisely than "pre-Augustan" on stratigraphic grounds, and the majority of fragments derive from contexts that lack any stratigraphic identification whatsoever.

The lack of archaeological indicators for Temples D and B are not isolated instances, and it will be worth turning our attention in more detail to the triple-cella temple, for which Richardson claimed a particularly strong stratigraphic sequence and a "virtually infallible" system of attribution.[31] As listed above, he divided the decoration of the triple-cella temple into five main phases, dated to c. 150 BCE, 120 BCE, 100 BCE, 75 BCE, and 50 BCE. The south side of the triple-cella temple was apparently the best preserved stratigraphically, and the excavators distinguished four separate levels in this area. Level I (the "upper level") is the layer of the medieval graves, which for the architectural terracottas is of no help chronologically. Level II (variously referred to as the "lowest," "lower," or "intermediate" level) is described as the fill covering the ruin of the "Temple of Jupiter" and is dated by potsherds, lamps, amphora handles, and coins to 70–60 BCE.[32] Level III (the "conflagration level") was full of charred remains interpreted as the ruin of the "Temple of Jupiter."[33] The date of c. 75 BCE for this event is based primarily on the date of Level II, following the assumption that the fill layer was put in soon after the destruction. Finally, Level IV (the "construction level") represents material in and under the foundations of the triple-cella temple and has a terminus ante quem of c. 175–150 BCE.[34] Levels II and IV are thus the only really indicative stratigraphic markers, and as we shall see, even the dating of Level II is highly dubious.

It should at any rate already be clear that Richardson's division into increments of twenty to twenty-five years has no archaeological grounding. The chronological markers are simply too wide, and the terracotta fragments from dated contexts typically offer little more than a broad terminus ante quem. For instance, the oldest layer in which the architrave revetments, shell antefixes, and perforated cornices assigned to the original decoration of the triple-cella temple (dated by Richardson to 150 BCE) were found is Level II of the south excavations, meaning that at best they can only be dated to before 60 BCE on stratigraphic grounds.[35] This situation applies to many terracottas across the summit, including a shell antefix attributed to the original decoration of the "Temple of Jupiter" (dated 240–220 BCE) and a revetment plaque attributed to its redecoration (dated 170–160 BCE).[36] No fragment of the so-called "compluvium sima"[37] assigned to the triple-cella temple's original decoration was found in a datable context, nor any fragment of the sima with strigils assigned to its third period.[38] And these are just a few examples.

Worse still, the sparse stratigraphy that *was* identified is ignored when it does not match the proposed typology. Two fragments of the revetment plaque with looped palmettes assigned to the original decoration of the triple-cella temple were in fact found in its construction level (Level IV).[39] Richardson does not explain why a plaque used to decorate this temple was also used as building material in its foundations.

There is also considerable confusion regarding the presence of seventeen fragments of Campana reliefs in Level II. These are usually dated to the Augustan period, and Richardson assigns them to the last period of the triple-cella temple's decoration (late 1st century BCE). Level II, however, is dated in *Cosa II* to 70–60 BCE, and Richardson explains the discrepancy by suggesting that the Campana fragments had simply "strayed" there.[40] Seventeen strays is, however, a considerable number. We are left with only three possibilities: (1) the traditional dating of Campana reliefs is entirely wrong, (2) Level II dates significantly later than proposed in *Cosa II*, (3) Level II is contaminated and thus essentially useless stratigraphically.

Subsequent excavations of the houses at Cosa yielded evidence for a destructive event around 70 BCE.[41] This has often been interpreted as a piratical attack and linked to the efforts of Pompey Magnus in this period to secure the seas. Elizabeth Fentress' excavations at Cosa in the 1990s again suggested an occupation gap between c. 70 BCE and 25–20 BCE, although this is based primarily on a lack of evidence from private houses in this period.[42] Following the theory that Cosa was essentially abandoned in the mid-1st century, Taylor has suggested that Level II on the summit should be associated with the recolonization of c. 25–20 BCE.[43] However, this still does not solve the problem of the Campana reliefs. If the town was abandoned between 70 and 25 BCE, when were the Campana reliefs made? If at the moment of reoccupation c. 25 BCE, why were they used as fill material when they were still brand new? It may be the case that Level II dates even later than 25 BCE or that it actually represents multiple depositions that were not distinguished at the time of excavation.[44]

There is in fact no direct evidence that the conflagration on the summit took place around 70 BCE. This date was suggested in *Cosa II* based on the 70–60 BCE dating of Level II, which covered it.[45] It has since been retained due to its alignment with the chronology of the houses, but there is no archaeological evidence that the same event that threatened homes in the lower town also precipitated the fire on the summit.[46] The c. 75 BCE date for Level III of the south excavations must therefore be viewed with extreme caution.

We are thus left with Level IV as the most secure stratigraphic marker for the area around the triple-cella temple. A date of c. 175–150 BCE for this level is well supported by the discovery of two coins – one dating to 190 BCE found sealed in the construction layer and another dating to 175 BCE found in the mortar beneath the floor of the temple's south cella.[47] The fact that architectural terracottas were also found in this level confirms that a building on the summit was revetted with terracottas prior to the construction of the triple-cella temple in the second quarter of the 2nd century. It does not prove that this was a temple to Jupiter nor that it dates close to the foundation of the colony – though the latter is certainly likely.

The archaeological evidence for dating any architectural terracottas from Cosa's forum or summit is thus overwhelmingly lacking. While we find the occasional, though significant, terminus ante or post quem, the preserved stratigraphy across the summit is simply too broad and too ambiguous to enable the sorts of precise divisions proposed in the Richardson chronology. Despite its claims of definitive archaeological grounding, the Cosa typology is based almost entirely on stylistic judgments that are deeply entangled in Richardson's assumptions regarding "Romanization." Unfortunately, the distressingly wide chronological parameters evident at Cosa are common to many Italic sites in the last centuries BCE.

The following chapters will question the notion that towns like Cosa looked to Rome for inspiration in temple decoration, arguing for a deep reliance on local networks that relates directly to the popularity of archaizing motifs in the last three centuries BCE. Since the idea of Rome's primacy is so entrenched in terracotta studies, however, and since the goal of the present chapter is to disentangle our evidence from our expectations, it will be useful now to turn to the surviving fragments from Rome itself.

2.4 ARCHITECTURAL TERRACOTTAS FROM REPUBLICAN ROME

2.4.1 *Archaeology and Chronology*

Architectural terracottas have a rich history in Rome, with evidence for locally manufactured tiles dating back to the 7th century BCE, and a slew of Archaic temples decorated in elaborate fashion, featuring local designs as well as types common to the wider geographic region.[48] Examples continue to abound during the period of the Republic, and their development aligns closely with broader trends in central Italy. Rome's Republican terracottas are far too numerous to list here, and indeed a comprehensive study of them remains an urgent desideratum. The following discussion will highlight some of the principal bodies of evidence in cursory fashion in order to evaluate the evidence for dating Roman terracottas earlier than their central Italic counterparts, particularly for the last three centuries BCE.

Before reaching the period in question, it will be worth looking briefly to the Archaic and Early Republican material in order to establish a context both for Roman terracottas themselves and for the ways in which they have been studied. The 6th and 5th centuries are by far the best understood in current scholarship, and excavations over the last half century have revealed a substantial number of archaeologically documented examples that have allowed for new reconstructions and analyses of early Rome's terracotta roofs. Even carefully excavated terracottas, however, often leave us grasping when it comes to chronology. The iconic Temple of Jupiter Optimus Maximus Capitolinus is a case in point. Excavations in the garden of the Ospedale Teutonico between 2010 and 2014 revealed a deposit of terracottas probably buried between the end of the 3rd and mid-2nd century BCE, most of which seem attributable to this temple.[49] While an invaluable discovery, and one that allowed for previously unachievable reconstructions of the roof's early phases, the deposits themselves are anything but straightforward. The buried fragments come from multiple phases spanning several hundred years and even include terracottas that likely belonged to other temples in the area.[50] The currently accepted phasing and chronology for some examples can, however, be supported by comparisons with finds from outside of Rome.[51] The elements that have been identified for the roof's earlier phases find parallels at multiple sites in central and southern Italy, for instance in the use of perforated cornices with palmettes and looped ribbons, eaves tiles with geometric patterns, and antefixes with satyrs and maenads as well as a *potnia theron*.[52] The Capitoline terracottas differ however in their remarkable size – almost double that of their nearest relatives.[53]

Not far from the Capitoline, the Temple of Castor and Pollux in the Forum was also richly decorated with architectural terracottas soon after the close of the regal period. Excavations conducted in the 1980s revealed large deposits of terracottas, some from well-sealed layers,[54] others from fill or dump, and others from stratigraphically disturbed contexts.[55] Literary sources date the foundation of the temple to 484 BCE,[56] but a number of architectural terracottas were found beside the temple and in the fill of its podium that should, based on traditional stylistic methods, be dated to the first half of the 6th century BCE.[57] To the 5th century phase are assigned antefixes of Silenus and Juno Sospita, perforated cornices with palmettes and figure-eights, simas with a guilloche, and a range of other fragments.[58]

Investigations on the Palatine hill revealed perforated cornices and antefixes of Silenus and Juno Sospita that are remarkably similar to those from the Temple of Castor and Pollux, as well as to examples from Satricum and Falerii Veteres.[59] Other terracotta elements presumably belonging to the early 5th century phase of this uncertain structure include perforated cornices, strigilated simas, gorgon acroteria, and fragments of a cortina pendula, which can also be related to examples known from other sites in and around Rome.[60]

Of particular importance for the study of architectural terracottas in Rome are the recently published results of excavations carried out by La Sapienza

University on the Palatine's northeastern slopes and in the Colosseum valley.[61] Although these come from rigorously documented archaeological contexts, the contexts themselves are once again secondary, as the bulk of terracottas were found in large mixed deposits dating considerably later than the roofs to which they originally belonged.[62] They appear to constitute a fairly continuous sequence beginning in the late 7th century BCE and include numerous examples attested at other sites in and around Rome.[63]

Put simply, the picture that emerges of temple roofs in Archaic and early Republican Rome is one of lively activity and a tendency to employ non-unique types. A range of similar or even identical architectural terracottas are attested on multiple temples within the city and beyond its borders. As recent studies have emphasized, the strong links with terracottas from the surrounding region suggest dynamic artisan and trade networks during this period.[64] Rome must have been a major participator in these networks, but there is little in the archaeological record to indicate specific geographical points of "invention" for these various terracotta types.

As we move into the middle and late Republic, stratigraphic markers become increasingly confused, and the chronology more and more tenuous. Unfortunately, the well-documented excavations of the NE Palatine and Colosseum valley have yielded almost no architectural terracottas between the mid-Republican phase and the end of the Republic. Either no restoration took place or the later terracottas were deposited elsewhere.[65] Most of the material recovered archaeologically from other sites within Rome comes from large unstratified fill layers deposited at a much later date, which offer only a terminus ante quem. Such is the case for the repair phases of the Capitoline temple. A number of types widely popular across central Italy were uncovered, but these were found in mixed deposits and may belong to separate phases or even buildings on the Capitoline.[66] Archaeological markers are thus of limited help in terms of date and attribution.

For the later terracottas of the Temple of Castor and Pollux, a mass of fragments were uncovered that similarly frustrate attempts to identify and date phases with precision.[67] As at the Capitoline, most find parallels at other central Italic sites, and include antefixes with the head of a maenad or young Dionysus amid bunches of grapes, *potnia theron* antefixes, perforated cornices with meanders and rosettes, and revetment plaques with floral decoration.[68]

Excavations at S. Omobono have also yielded numerous terracottas dating to the post-archaic phases of the temples. Unfortunately, most are barely documented and many have been lost altogether.[69] Study of these fragments has revealed close links to examples from Lo Scasato at Falerii, and they are thus mostly dated to the late 4th/early 3rd century based on similarity rather than stratigraphy.[70] While such comparisons are useful for establishing a general chronology, they do not tell us where the type *originated.*

Up the hill, a group of terracottas uncovered on the Palatine have been attributed to the first phase (early 3rd century BCE) of the Temple of Victory.[71] Most of these, however, were found in scattered areas across the southwest Palatine, complicating the certainty of their association with particular buildings or phases. While the Temple of Victory does seem like the obvious candidate, a precise chronology for these terracottas cannot be built from the stratigraphy . They are instead, once again, dated based on stylistic similarities with terracottas from other sites. These examples find numerous parallels in Rome and in central Italy more generally and include perforated cornices, strigilated simas, revetment plaques with looped and addorsed palmettes, and *potnia theron* antefixes.[72] Several finely worked sculptural fragments have also been uncovered, which can probably be assigned to the temple's pedimental decoration and may include representations of Jupiter and Dionysus.[73]

Further evidence for terracotta pedimental statues in Rome comes from the important finds on the Via di San Gregorio and the Via Latina. The former are usually dated to the mid-2nd century BCE on stylistic grounds and represent one of the best-preserved terracotta pediments in Republican Italy (Figure 11). The reconstruction of the scene has been a topic of considerable debate, but it must have featured a standing male figure in its center, flanked by two goddesses.[74] Beyond them was a pair of male figures, with the corners

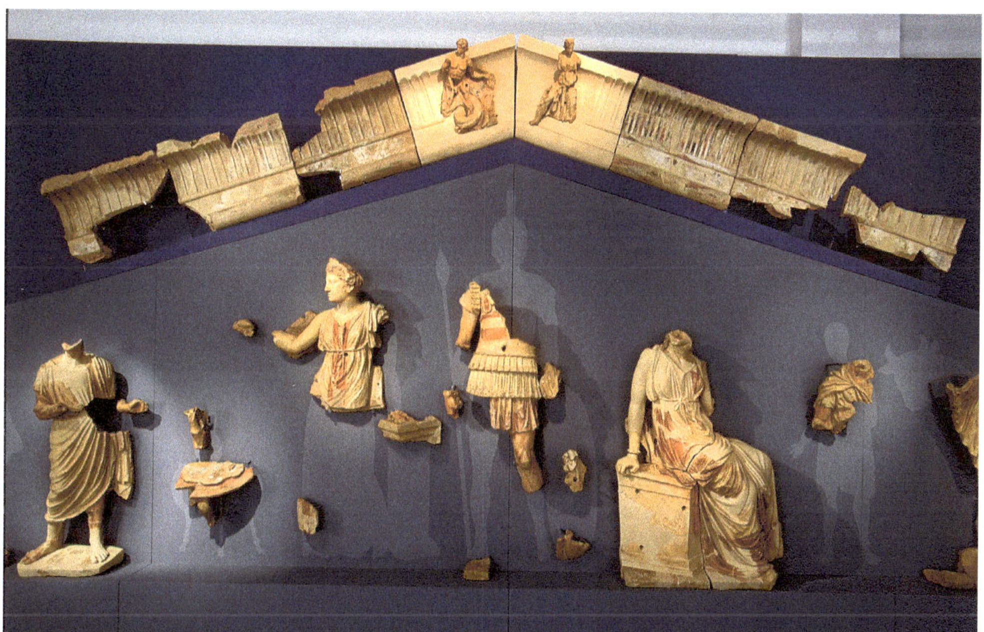

11. Central figures of the Via di San Gregorio pediment. Rome: Musei Capitolini. Archivio Fotografico dei Musei Capitolini.

occupied by *victimarii* leading animals to sacrifice. Small figures of Hercules, Hesione, and the sea monster adorned the peak of the roof. Several versions of a strigilated sima with paterae can also be associated with the temple, but little else can be said of its overall decoration.[75]

The Via Latina group is unfortunately quite fragmentary.[76] Its poor preservation impedes attempts to reconstruct a full scene, as the primary fragments consist only of a few male and female heads, a hand holding a thunderbolt, and the head of a horse. What is particularly interesting about these sculptures, however, is their decidedly archaistic style. One of the heads bears strong similarities to a terracotta statue uncovered on the Palatine hill (Figure 109), which might suggest a 1st century BCE date.[77] However, because the dating of these relies solely on stylistic criteria, and because archaizing pieces are notoriously difficult to date, the Via Latina pediment has also been placed by some in the mid-2nd century BCE.[78]

A large number of terracottas found in disturbed contexts throughout Rome are broadly dated between the 1st centuries BCE and CE but in most cases cannot be attributed to specific structures let alone phases.[79] As stone and concrete began to replace older terracotta and wood constructions, fictile revetment grew slowly obsolete. Still, it seems that in many cases certain terracotta elements were retained on structures built primarily of stone.[80] Finds from the Temple of Castor and Pollux, for example, extend all the way into the 1st century CE and include a number of fragments of Campana reliefs.[81] It is unclear whether or not these can be associated with a late decorative program in terracotta before the Augustan-period renovation of 6 CE, or whether they in some way coexisted with the imperial building.[82] A number of terracottas have also been found at the area sacra di Largo Argentina. The paucity of excavation records makes it difficult to assign these with any certainty, and their dating remains problematic.[83] Amongst the finds were numerous antefixes, including circular rosettes and antefixes with palmettes emerging from a mask, gorgon, head of a winged victory, or pair of rearing rams.[84] This is not surprising, as antefixes seem to have been one of the most enduring elements of terracotta decoration, continuing in use even after other terracotta elements had been abandoned.[85]

The examples surveyed thus far generally come from at least partially documented excavations and can therefore be associated with a particular area, if not a specific building or phase. Unfortunately, however, many fragments remain entirely unpublished or appear in catalogues produced long after their excavation. This means that information regarding provenance and excavation context is overwhelmingly lacking. Such is the case, for instance, with numerous terracottas in the collections of the Museo Nazionale Romano. Although Patrizio Pensabene and Maria Rita Sanzi Di Mino published an invaluable catalogue of the antefixes in 1983, they note at the opening that only about one-third of the objects have even a general provenance. Many come from outside of Rome and have only broad site attributions such as "Ardea" or "Palestrina." Those that do securely derive from Rome come mostly from the Tiber, where they were uncovered during large-scale construction projects in the late 19th century. It is impossible to associate them with any particular building, let alone a specific phase. The remaining terracottas in the Museo Nazionale Romano are entirely undocumented, having come to the museum from a range of large private collections. Because the collectors are known to have gathered material from the art market and from sites across Italy, the provenance of these objects remains a matter of speculation. Lacking any archaeological documentation, Pensabene and Sanzi Di Mino can offer dates based solely on stylistic criteria and on comparisons with examples from better-documented contexts *outside* of Rome.

Another important study of later terracottas from Rome (dated mostly between the 1st centuries BCE and CE) is Lucilla Anselmino's 1977 catalogue of the antefixes in the Antiquarium Comunale di Roma. Here too the material is largely unprovenanced, often derived from private collections or from casual finds in the 19th century. The better-documented antefixes occasionally preserve a vague provenance such as "Via Gallia" or "Orti Sallustiani," but these can give us only wide chronological parameters at best. Given the problems of documentation and the fact that both catalogues focus solely on antefixes, neither can help in dating other terracotta types or in reconstructing roof systems in Rome.

As we have seen, even when architectural terracottas from the mid-to-late Republic have been uncovered in more systematic excavations in Rome, it is usually impossible to assign them specific dates based on stratigraphic context. Many of the terracottas uncovered in more recent excavations (for instance, on the Palatine hill) do preserve fairly good stratigraphic information. However, the widespread practice of burying terracottas in undifferentiated deposits after their removal from the roof, coupled with the extensive rebuilding activities that have occurred throughout Rome over the millennia, render such stratigraphic contexts secondary, tertiary, or worse.[86] They can at most provide us with a broad terminus ante quem, as, for example, with the 24,600 fragments of terracottas found under the Temple of Victory.[87] And while discoveries of architectural terracottas have successfully been used to suggest the existence, location, or even the size of certain temples,[88] they can offer no clear chronological markers. In almost every case, they are dated on analogy with examples found outside of Rome.

We thus find ourselves on exceptionally shaky ground in establishing a chronology for the architectural terracottas of mid-to-late Republican Rome. And yet it is precisely in studies of this period that Rome's role as a driving force in terracotta production and dissemination has been so repeatedly and so forcefully asserted. Besides lacking in evidence, such claims even seem counterintuitive in some cases. Why, for instance, should the similarities between terracottas from Lo Scasato at Falerii Veteres and the Temple of Victory in Rome be interpreted as evidence of Rome's influence in the diffusion of artistic models in the late 4th century?[89] Falerii Veteres, after all, was repeatedly at war with Rome during the 4th and 3rd centuries (see Section 3.3.1). That Falerii Veteres' citizens should simply seek to imitate the temple decoration of their longtime enemy seems dubious at best.[90]

Even the fact that terracottas from across Italy are labeled "Hellenistic" or "Roman" should raise an eyebrow.[91] While ostensibly referring to periods of time (often quite vaguely defined), these terms nevertheless *imply* influence from, and dependence on, models originating in the Greek world or in Rome itself. Neither accounts for the role of individual Italic cities in terracotta design or development, despite the fact that countless terracottas have been found at sites across Italy from the Archaic period well into the Empire and display clear evidence of continuous local production (see Chapters 3 and 4). Again, we have no evidence that any of these types were "invented" in Rome and not in one of the many other cities in which they abound.

2.4.2 Repositioning Rome's Role

Recent work on the 6th–4th century material has already begun to undermine traditional assumptions regarding Roman influence. Patricia Lulof has interpreted the famous 6th century BCE acroteria showing Athena and Heracles, which appear at Rome as well as at Veii, Caere, Pyrgi, and Satricum, as examples of a shared visual aesthetic amongst central Italic elites.[92] In her recent monograph, Carlucci notes that the decoration of the Capitoline temple in Rome included a number of types known from other sites in the region and that its roof should not predate that of Temple B at Pyrgi.[93] She thus casts doubt on the neat attribution of decorative systems to specific centers of power in the late 6th and early 5th centuries.[94] Hopkins in particular has drawn attention to the close or even identical parallels known from sites north and south in their study of the 5th and 4th century terracottas from Rome.[95] Importantly, these include areas "that Rome purportedly controlled by the early fourth century, but also ... sites that were well-known opponents to Roman expansion."[96] As Hopkins shows, this suggests not unidirectional influence but rather high levels of connectivity and "sociocultural entanglement."[97] For the late 4th/early 3rd century, Carlucci argues for the presence of a vibrant Faliscan school of coroplasts who may have been responsible for the terracottas of Falerii Veteres' temples before the moment of Roman conquest. As already noted, many elements of these decorative programs are closely linked to examples from Rome and from areas of Roman occupation, again suggesting that similarity cannot be attributed to Roman origin or Roman influence in this period.[98]

Despite these advances, unidirectional Roman influence is often assumed in the case of colonial situations, and for the terracottas of 3rd–1st century central Italy more generally. An often-repeated claim is that during the 2nd century BCE, the bulk of architectural terracotta production shifted from earlier centers like Orvieto and Falerii Veteres to become concentrated at Rome itself.[99] This is stated as fact even by scholars who are otherwise cautious when it comes to "Romanization"[100] and is often repeated without any examples or evidence whatsoever. Only Strazzulla, who is frequently cited in this context, offers a limited discussion *after* having already stated Roman influence as a given. As evidence, Strazzulla mentions a perforated cornice found at Civitella di Chieti, which apparently shares a matrix with an example from Temple C at Largo Argentina in Rome and with another example at Luni.[101] There is, however, no archaeological reason to date the Largo Argentina example earlier than the others, nor to suggest that the matrix came from Rome rather than the other sites. Indeed, the example could just as easily be taken as evidence of traveling artisans moving about central Italy with a ready-made matrix in hand. Strazzulla goes on to cite the widespread distribution of *potnia theron* antefixes, many examples of which have been found in Rome. Because, as she writes, they are attested in Rome as well as in colonies and centers dependent on Rome, the type must have originated in the capital.[102] Once again, there is no Roman example of a *potnia theron* antefix that securely pre-dates those from other sites. *Potnia theron* is one of the most long-lived and widespread decorative motifs in Greece as well as in Italy, appearing on Italic architectural terracottas already in the Archaic period and continuing at least through the first century BCE (see Section 3.2.3).

The same applies to other terracotta types that appear on roofs in and out of Rome in the period of widespread Roman occupation. Fragments of perforated cornices with rosettes and a meander pattern uncovered during excavations of the Temple of Castor and Pollux, for instance, bear strong similarities to examples from Cosa, Luni, Ardea, Chieti, Gabii, and Alatri, as well as from the Largo Argentina in Rome.[103] The Castor and Pollux fragments, however, come from layers that the excavators deemed highly disturbed. The fragments were dated broadly to the 3rd–2nd centuries BCE based on comparanda from these other sites, which were operating in the same centuries. The situation is identical for the other architectural elements assigned to the Temple of Castor and Pollux's later phases and for the sculptural fragments as well.[104] The latter are dated based on stylistic features and comparisons with examples from sites like Arezzo and Luni to the 2nd century BCE, a period in which similar examples abounded across central Italy.[105] There is, once again, no chronological data suggesting that any of these types were used or manufactured at Rome first.

As noted above, the material from the Capitoline Temple of Jupiter – a building that is often considered the model for the spread of Roman influence par excellence – also comes from mixed deposits. Phasing attributions for the later material are based primarily on differences in fabric as well as on stylistic comparisons. Regarding the former, however, many sites have yielded examples of identical terracotta types executed in different fabrics, which have been interpreted either as instances of multiple workshops operating in tandem to speed up production or as later repairs making use of an original matrix.[106] And even when fabric can be used to confidently differentiate phases, it does not allow us to date those phases with precision. The second criterium, stylistic analysis, is also of limited help. A revetment plaque with addorsed palmettes, which has been attributed to the late 4th–early 3rd century BCE phase of the Capitoline temple's roof, offers an instructive example.[107] This is one of the most widespread types of revetment plaque, appearing across central Italy at least from the early 4th century BCE and notoriously difficult to date.[108] Galluccio's date for the Capitoline example is based on similarities with terracottas from Ardea and on the presence of a lesbian kyma in the cornice, which is thought to be an innovation of that period, replacing the strigilated cornice that is common on earlier examples.[109] The cornice with lesbian kyma, however, continues on plaques of this type well into the 2nd and 1st centuries BCE, meaning that at best we can only surmise that the Capitoline example is *not* one of the earliest iterations of a revetment plaque with addorsed palmettes.[110] Interestingly, this plaque type is apparently unrepresented in the Capitoline temple's earlier phases, which are already accounted for with other revetment types. This would seem to suggest that, contrary to models of Roman influence, the plaque with addorsed palmettes may have been added to the Capitoline temple's decoration *after* it had already become popular at other central Italic sites.

Moving beyond mold-made decoration, the evidence of terracotta pedimental sculpture similarly offers no convincing indication of Roman origin. The dating of the famous Via di San Gregorio sculptures, for instance, has varied from scholar to scholar based on proposed associations with attested temples and patrons, as well as on stylistic considerations. Stratigraphic indicators are lacking, as the fragments were uncovered in 1878 along the route of the eponymous road where they had apparently been reused as fill material in the 1st century CE.[111] The sculptures themselves share numerous iconographic and stylistic similarities with examples from across central Italy. While it seems reasonable to assume that these all date within a coherent chronological range, there is again no evidence as to *which* example was manufactured first. Style, which currently constitutes the primary dating method for most central Italic terracotta pediments, is particularly slippery for this body of material, which tends toward eclecticism and archaism.[112] Broad chronological parameters are in some cases available – for instance, that the sculptures from Fregellae ought to date before the sack of 125 BCE – but most such pediments are simply dated generically to the 2nd century BCE.

Just as stratigraphy cannot support a Roman point of origin, neither can the evidence related to manufacture. Recent analyses of workshops and artisans have increasingly revealed the fluid nature of production in the last three centuries BCE. As noted in Chapter 1, there is now strong evidence for traveling coroplasts, as well as for the existence of local production areas across the Italic peninsula.[113] The enormous weight of a full terracotta roof (roughly 40 metric tons) would have made transportation over long distances absurdly difficult and costly. Given the logistical problems, the overwhelming lack of evidence that any shared type was produced first or even primarily in Rome, the documented existence of local production sites elsewhere, and the continuity in use of architectural terracottas at many Italic sites from the Archaic period to the 1st century BCE, there is simply no data to suggest that Rome replaced earlier centers of terracotta production during the 2nd century BCE. This idea is instead a lingering reflection of outdated conceptions of "Romanization" and "Romanization" processes, which has been echoed for decades without evidence or reexamination.

Architectural terracottas have thus been used to reinforce preexisting ideas of a conscientious and unidirectional flow of Roman influence, taking a widespread central Italic phenomenon and reducing it specifically to the city of Rome. Such models assume that Rome *wanted* to be imitated and that conquered towns were eager to oblige. Not only is this idea highly problematic in itself, it is also entirely ungrounded. As we have seen over and over, there is no evidence that any of the shared architectural terracotta types originated in Rome. Nor is there reason to think that these were thought of in antiquity as intrinsically "Roman." On the contrary, later authors who were writing when Rome's power was already assured specifically characterize the city's most famous terracottas – those commissioned for the Temple of Jupiter Optimus Maximus Capitolinus – as the works of the Etruscan Vulca who was brought *to* Rome for the project.[114]

There is no doubt that Rome produced architectural terracottas from an early period and continued to generate examples of very high quality over the following centuries.[115] In all these periods, however, we simply lack the chronological precision to argue that Rome played a leading role in the innovation and distribution of specific new types. Just as for the 6th–4th century material, similarities across sites from the 3rd century onwards seem to reflect trade and artisan networks, not some broader "Romanization" of central Italy. Based on the evidence currently available, we would perhaps be most accurate in concluding that a wide range of central Italic towns, including Rome, were participating in regional trends from the Archaic period up to the early Empire. The similarities in their temple decoration likely relate to geographic proximity, healthy trade, imported ideas and styles from the wider Mediterranean world, and mobile workshops and artisans traveling from town to town.

2.5 LEAVING "ROMANIZATION" BEHIND

The insecurity of the chronology for 3rd–1st century architectural terracottas has not been sufficiently recognized, and this has implications for the broader dating of temples and building phases at sites across central Italy. Terracottas uncovered outside of Rome have often been interpreted in relation to Roman examples, which they are assumed to post-date. Given the strong and unbroken traditions in architectural terracotta production at many Italic sites, and the lack of precise evidence from Rome itself, caution is warranted.

As discussed above, the formation of these Rome-centered typologies is deeply rooted in "Romanization" theory, and approaches like Richardson's are simply symptomatic of their time. The now-infamous term "Romanization," which dates back to the writings of Francis Haverfield in the early 20th century, maintained a firm grasp on historical interpretation for much of the last century. A slew of studies, particularly since the 1990s, have sharply critiqued the term as imperialist and colonialist, objecting to Haverfield's core assumption that Roman culture was inherently superior to that of the "primitive" native populations that she conquered and that this superiority is both obvious and all-encompassing.[116] Also problematic is the term's implication of unidirectionality, as implying "a unilateral transfer of culture" from Rome to indigenous populations.[117] Early work on this topic tended to emphasize the role of local elites in transmitting Roman culture, whereas more recent studies have asked what "Roman" even means (particularly before the dawn of the Empire), and why we should assume that a given style or class of objects would have been interpreted in antiquity as intrinsically "Roman."[118] Above all, the highly variable nature and highly variable results of Rome's interactions with local populations is increasingly recognized, and current analyses tend to take a more case by case approach to this topic.[119] Cultural and individual identities are now recognized as being far more layered than "Roman" and "native." Not only are such categories reductive and usually impossible to define, they may not even be mutually exclusive.

"Romanization" has remained a nagging scholarly preoccupation for decades, and assumptions regarding Italy's homogenization over the last few centuries BCE remain entrenched in much current thinking.[120] As this chapter has shown, "Romanization" concepts underly many interpretations of 3rd–1st century architectural terracottas, which have not been reexamined in light of methodological advances in the field. There is a lingering tendency to interpret these objects in terms of "self-Romanization" – a model in which individuals and communities intentionally adopt the trappings of *romanitas* for their own gain – attributing their origin and meaning to an explicitly "Roman" context.[121]

As we shall see in what follows, the widespread use of architectural terracottas in central Italy during the last three centuries BCE instead suggests complex processes of interaction, exchange, and negotiation. It is time to shed the "Romanization" baggage that still plagues studies of Italic architectural terracottas and to ask instead what these objects can tell us about the multiplicity of experiences that resulted from Rome's contact with indigenous populations across the growing empire. I have advocated elsewhere for the use of network theory as a metaphorical model for tracking interactions in such contexts, as it allows us to work from the objects themselves without imposing any pre-set predictions.[122] Although we lack sufficient evidence to create a data-driven network model for 3rd–1st century architectural terracottas, network theory nevertheless offers an invaluable framework for *thinking* about these objects.

Put simply, network theory studies the connections ("ties") between different points ("nodes") to build a web that tracks and displays relationships. Certain nodes may be revealed as central within a particular network or cluster, and single ties between distant nodes may link otherwise isolated clusters in unexpected ways. Network theory is particularly useful as a conceptual model for tracking connections during the period of Roman expansion precisely because it reveals rather than predicts centrality within the broader system. It is also flexible and variable: Rome might be central within one network (say, the production of coinage) but function as one of many equally participatory nodes when it comes to pottery or architectural terracottas.

In this study, and especially for the case-studies presented in Chapter 4, I use network theory as an underlying explanatory framework for asking how individual cities and towns understood their respective network clusters. We cannot assume that temple terracottas were seen as inherently "Roman," or even that such an identification would have heightened their prestige and encouraged imitation. What's more, many viewers would have been entirely unfamiliar with the temples of the capital, meaning that their first mental associations would likely have been with the nearby shrines they encountered on a regular basis – those within their local areas or perhaps their local regions. This has serious implications for how we understand the intent and interpretation of architectural terracottas. It also moves us away from the traditional Rome-centered approach and allows us to work *up* by reconstructing local and regional networks from the evidence itself.

I have taken the time to lay out the problematic nature of current architectural terracotta chronologies in order to expose the "Romanization" biases imbedded within them but also to ask how we can move forward with the study of this material. A precise chronology is likely to elude us for many years to come. Even so, this rich body of material has much to tell us. The stylistic conservatism of these objects, for instance, confounds dating but speaks volumes about attitudes toward temple decoration in the last three centuries BCE. The current study will be concerned not with details of building attribution or close chronological increments but with elucidating the broader central Italic phenomena that these objects so eloquently express. In the following chapters, I will give special consideration to questions of viewer response(s), using the loose framework of network theory to consider not only the spread of objects but also the visual landscape with which viewers would have been familiar. I will ask why certain terracottas were used, what they might have meant to the people who gazed up at their sacred buildings, and how these meanings shifted and overlapped through time and space.

NOTES

1 *Cosa II*: 151–300.

2 A fundamental critique is still Fentress 2000. See also Bispham 2006.

3 Fentress 2000: 19.

4 On Brown's use of these terms, see Fentress 2000. On "Capitolia" with specific reference to the case of Cosa, Quinn and Wilson 2013.

5 See, for instance, Pelgrom and Stek 2014 for a discussion of Salmon's legacy with specific reference to Cosa – his *Roman Colonization under the Republic* included a section titled "Cosa: A Typical Latin Colony." For Gellian models of colonization in relation to Cosa, see Sewell 2014 in the same volume.

6 *Cosa II*: 198.

7 *Cosa II*: 225.

8 *Cosa II*: 269.

9 *Cosa II*: 245.

10 Strazzulla 1977. She returned to this argument in her monumental study of terracottas from the Venetia Romana in relation to specific types included in Richardson's classification. See, for instance, Strazzulla 1987: 153 n. 2, in which she also comments on the surprisingly widespread acceptance of Richardson's chronology despite its obvious failings.

11 *Cosa II*: 165.

12 Strazzulla 1977: 42–43.

13 *Cosa II*: 21.

14 Taylor 2002: 61.

15 Taylor 2002: esp. 62–65.

16 Taylor 2002: 65.

17 Of the "Capitolium," for instance, Richardson writes that the "stratification leaves no room for question about the major chronological divisions" (*Cosa II*: 206).

18 Rabun Taylor has more recently suggested that the 7.5 x 7.5 m square structure on the summit may in fact be its only early temple, Taylor 2002: 78. For the dating of Temple D and the triple-cella temple, see Scott 1992. For more on these structures, see Section 4.2.2.

19 Brown 1967; Scott 1992: 92. Excavation notebooks also refer to a WWII latrine on the site (American Academy in Rome Cosa Archives, box 131, notebook "TJ-1967" p. 26).

20 Brown 1967 gives a summary account in a few pages, and there is a two-paragraph overview in Brown 1969. Some of the finds were discussed in Scott 1992, who uses them in support of minor adjustments to the *Cosa II* chronology.

21 *Cosa II*: 169.
22 Taylor 2002: 68–69.
23 Taylor 2002.
24 Scott 1992: 95.
25 *Cosa II*: 186.
26 *Cosa II*: 202. This is due to a single fragment found in the masonry of an entrance arch dated to the Augustan period.
27 *Cosa II*: 200.
28 *Cosa III*: 154
29 *Cosa III*: 154.
30 For the date, see Scott 1992: 95–96.
31 *Cosa II*: 206.
32 *Cosa II*: 88, 188; Taylor 1957.
33 *Cosa II*: 87, 117–118.
34 The construction of the triple-cella temple is dated to c. 150 BCE in *Cosa II*, but Scott has since adjusted the chronology and would place the temple's construction between c. 175 and 150 BCE (Scott 1992: esp. p. 96 on the evidence of re-dated coins found in the construction levels).
35 *Cosa II*: 208–209, 210–211, 217–220.
36 *Cosa II*: 157–158, 175.
37 *Cosa II*: 224–225.
38 *Cosa II*: 240.
39 *Cosa II*: 213.
40 *Cosa II*: 297–298.
41 *Cosa IV* details the excavations of the town's houses. The House of the Treasure and the House of the Skeleton furnish the primary evidence for the destructive event of c. 70 BCE.
42 Referred to throughout *Cosa V*.
43 Taylor 2002: 75–76.
44 For the latter suggestion, see also Taylor 2002: 76.
45 *Cosa II*: 188 and *passim*.
46 The houses had not yet been excavated when *Cosa II* was written, and a lightning bolt is suggested as the cause of the fire (*Cosa II*: 123).
47 Scott 1992: 96–97.
48 In general, Ammerman et al. 2008; Winter 2009; Hopkins 2016; and the many architectural terracottas published in connection to specific sites around Rome (i.e., the Capitoline, Palatine, Regia, Sant'Omobono, Temple of Castor and Pollux, etc.).
49 Galluccio 2016: 237. On the excavations, see Parisi Presicce and Danti 2016.
50 Some are much smaller in scale than others, suggesting buildings of different sizes: Carlucci 2021: 440–441; Hopkins 2022: 108.
51 Galluccio 2016; Carlucci 2021.
52 For a discussion of these elements and their comparanda, see Galluccio 2016, who would however view the Capitoline temple as the earliest example of many of these types. The lack of precise chronological markers here and at other sites seems to me to preclude such a conclusion. See also Carlucci 2021, who connects the temple's decoration to developments occurring more or less simultaneously in multiple central Italic polities during this period.
53 Hopkins 2014: 115.
54 Particularly those from Trench V: Poulsen and Grønne 1988.
55 Grønne 1992; Fischer-Hansen 2008.
56 Livy 2.20.12, 2.42.5; Dion. Hal. 6.13.1–4.
57 Still another group from these excavations should date to the second half of that century. Since terracottas from an older version of a temple are often reused in the fill of its replacement, these finds would seem to suggest the presence of an earlier temple on the same site. Unless the temple's dedicatee was changed in the early 5th century, which would

be unusual, this might also indicate a cult to Castor and Pollux that pre-dated the temple of 484 BCE. These early terracottas have also been attributed to the Regia or to some other unknown structure in the area. On this problem, see Poulsen 1992: 47; Fischer-Hansen 2008: 284; Hopkins 2016: 141; and n. 42.

58 Grønne 1992.

59 Pensabene 2001: 88–90 and figs. 10–14.

60 Pensabene 2001: 89 and figs. 14–15.

61 Panella, Rescigno, and Ferrandes 2021.

62 Panella, Rescigno, and Ferrandes 2021: 272.

63 On the terracottas and their comparanda, Panella, Rescigno, and Ferrandes 2021: 163–276.

64 On common decorative systems in central Italy during the late 6th and early 5th centuries BCE, see Carlucci 2021; for the 5th and 4th centuries, Hopkins 2022, 2023.

65 Panella, Rescigno, Ferrandes 2021: 276.

66 Galluccio 2016: 278–291; Hopkins 2022: 108–109.

67 Fischer-Hansen 2008: 285.

68 Fischer-Hansen 2008: 293–299.

69 Diffendale 2018 valiantly attempts to glean as much information as possible on the Republican-era architectural terracottas from S. Omobono by combining direct study of the fragments with examination of the excavation records. Even so, most of the pieces can, at best, only be assigned to one or the other temple. Their dating inevitably relies on comparison with examples from other sites.

70 Diffendale 2018.

71 Pensabene 2001: 94–100; 2017: 205–208, 250–272.

72 On the popularity of these types in central Italy, see Chapter 3.

73 Pensabene 2001: 96–98.

74 The most thorough publication is Ferrea 2002, although her reconstruction has been heavily criticized (e.g., Strazzulla 1993, 2006a; Torelli 2004). Strazzulla argues that the two female figures should both be seated, and also rearranges the order of the animals on the left side. Her criticisms and reconstruction have been generally accepted (e.g., Coarelli 2012: 207–210), although the pediment continues to be displayed in the Capitoline Museum according to Ferrea's scheme. A more recent discussion of this pediment can be found in Kaderka 2018: 81–103.

75 Ferrea 2002: 97–107.

76 Andrén 1940: 360–363 and Pl. 109 nos. 391–392 (he refers to them as the "Via Appia Nuova" terracottas); Coarelli 1976: 26 and figs. 7–11.

77 Touchette 2015: 304.

78 E.g., Coarelli 1976: 26, who considers it earlier than the Via di San Gregorio pediment.

79 Literary sources provide minimal help in this regard, though Vitruvius does specify that terracotta decoration was still employed on araeostyle temples such as the Temple of Ceres, Pompey's Temple of Hercules, and the Capitoline temple (Vitr. 3.3.5).

80 Noted particularly in the context of terracottas from Rome in Davies 2012: 145–146.

81 On Campana reliefs in Rome, see Chapter 6.

82 On the Augustan temple and its decoration, see Nilson et al. 2009. The Campana relief fragments are listed in Fischer-Hansen 2008: 297–298, and given dates between the 1st centuries BCE and CE based on stylistic comparisons.

83 Strazzulla 1977: 46–47. Several very similar terracottas have been found in the concrete collapse of the Theatre of Pompey. Some belong to types that have been dated stylistically to between the mid-1st century BCE and the 1st century CE. However, since these new fragments were apparently used in the construction of the theatre, they must have been produced before the mid-1st century BCE. This means that the chronology is in need of serious reconsideration. I thank James Packer for showing me photos of the terracottas found in the 2011 excavations of the Theatre of Pompey.

84 Anselmino 1977 nos. 1–6, 22, 73, 90, 97, 102, 117, 138, 155–159, 182, 200, 211, 214–215; Strazzulla 1977: 46–47.

85 The same situation is attested outside of Rome, for instance, in the use of terracotta antefixes on the otherwise fully stone "Temple B" at Minturnae (Johnson 1935: 90), see Section 4.3.4.

86 On the Palatine, see Pensabene 2001: 81; 2017 *passim*. Strazzulla 2010 describes a similar situation for the Esquiline, as does Galluccio 2016: 237, 257, and *passim* for the Capitoline. On the practice of ritually burying architectural terracottas in antiquity, Glinister 2000.

87 Pensabene 2001: 87.

88 For example, their use in Pensabene 2001, Hopkins 2016, 2022, 2023.

89 Pensabene 2001: 100; 2017: 207.

90 On the decoration of the temple at Lo Scasato, see Section 3.3.1.

91 See the recent discussion of Padilla Peralta and Bernard 2022.

92 Lulof 2000. See also Winter 2009, who catalogues a number of early Roman architectural terracottas and contextualizes them within the broader sweep of central Italic production between 640 and 510 BCE.

93 Carlucci 2021: 14, 445–456. On the context of interchange of architectural terracottas between Rome and Veii, see also Carlucci 2011, and the other contributions in the same volume.

94 Carlucci 2021: 15. Although cf. her comments at 581–582, 584.

95 Hopkins 2022, in which they characterize the architectural terracottas from Rome as being "in lockstep not only with central Italy but with the western Mediterranean" (111). See also Hopkins 2016 for a discussion of early Roman architecture and architectural terracottas with explicit reference to connectivity, as well as Hopkins 2024.

96 Hopkins 2022: 109.

97 Hopkins 2022: 110 and *passim*. See also Hopkins 2023, 2024.

98 Carlucci 2004: 32; 2020: 89 and *passim*.

99 For example, Anselmino 1981: 211 states that "Roma già nel II secolo a.C. monopolizza il mercato e diventa infatti il centro propulsore di modelli e di tipi oltre che centro propagatore di prodotti." Similarly, Tortorella 1981: 219, "Si è osservato che nel II secolo a.C., decaduti ormai i grandi centri di produzione di terrecotte (come Orvieto, Civita Castellana), Roma si sostituisce a essi elaborando modelli e tipi autonomi, che si diffondono ovunque, dall'Italia centrale fino a Luni." Gualtieri, Rossini, and Moroni 2002: 148 conclude simply that "the role of Rome as propelling center of models for architectural terracottas in general, starting from 2nd cent. BC ... is unanimously acknowledged." Benjamin Rous (2010: 236) writes that "these great production centers of architectural terracottas [Orvieto and Civita Castellana] were progressively abandoned during the second century, replaced by Rome itself. The fact that Rome became a center producing new types which can be identified and mapped perhaps also makes it more feasible to accept Roman influence on subject matters. Clearly, a leading role of the capital in architectural decoration can be attested in the late republican period, which still left enough room for local variations and creativity."

100 E.g., Rous 2010, see n. 99.

101 Strazzulla 1977: 47. Two pages earlier, she gives the phrase picked up in subsequent discussions of the topic: "una volta spariti i grandi centri di produzione di terrecotte quali Orvieto e Civita Castellana, è il sostituirsi ad essi di Roma come centro propulsore di modelli e di tipi."

102 Strazzulla 1977: 47.

103 For the comparanda, see Fischer-Hansen 2008: 294–296.

104 Fischer-Hansen 2008: 285-99.

105 Fischer-Hansen 2008: 298.

106 See Chapter 3 on the evidence from Cosa.

107 Galluccio 2016: 289–291, III.3.37, tav. 23.
108 On this type, see Section 3.2.1.
109 Galluccio 2016: 291; Strazzulla 1987: 151.
110 Strazzulla 1987: 149–154 and tab. VI.
111 Ferrea 2002: 17–25.
112 See Ekserdjian 2023, who discusses the stylistic features of various pedimental groups and offers a balanced evaluation of prior attempts to date these pediments more precisely.
113 For instances of local production in this period, Celuzza 1985; Ambrosini 2019; Campanile and Cangiano 2019; and Crawford-Brown 2019c, among many others.
114 E.g., Pliny *HN* 35.157, citing Varro; also Pliny *HN* 28.16 and Plut. *Publ.*, 13.
115 For the use of local clay from the Velabrum for Roman architectural terracottas of the 7th and 6th centuries BCE, see Ammerman et al. 2008.
116 For a discussion of Haverfield, Mommsen, and the relationship between "Romanization" theories and Western imperialism more generally, see Hingley 2005, esp. 14–48. The bibliography on "Romanization" is vast. Among the many studies that address this topic, see Millett 1990; Mattingly 1997; Mouritsen 1998; Woolf 1998; Terrenato 1998a, 1998b, Bradley 2000; Keay and Terrenato 2001; Webster 2001; Hingley 2005; Van Dommelen and Terrenato 2007; Roth and Keller 2007; Wallace-Hadrill 2008; Stek 2009; Mattingly 2011; Stek and Pelgrom 2014; Stek and Burgers 2015; Aberson et al. 2016; Robinson 2021.
117 Mattingly 1997: 9.
118 E.g., the change from Millett 1990 and Woolf 1998 to Gosden 2005 and Roth 2007.
119 E.g., Terrenato 1998b; Keay and Terrenato 2001; Van Dommelen and Terrenato 2007; Roth and Keller 2007; Mattingly 2011. For a recent and pointedly specific discussion geographically, see Robinson 2021.
120 Various terms have been proffered, above all in anglophone scholarship, to replace the hated word "Romanization," but none has been widely embraced (examples include "bricolage" [Terrenato 1998a] and "creolization" [Webster 2001]). A wide range of terms deriving from postcolonial studies have been applied to ancient situations more generally (e.g., "third space," "middle ground," and "hybridity").
121 E.g., Millett 1990; Torelli 1995; Torelli 1999. For an overview of criticisms of the "self-Romanization" (in Italian, *autoromanizzazione*) model, see the discussion in Stek 2009: 11–15.
122 Crawford-Brown 2019a.

THREE

THE POWER OF THE PAST

Conscious Archaizing and the Development of the "Standard Temple Kit"

3.1 INTRODUCTION

One of the most remarkable features of post-Archaic temple terracottas is their stubborn conservatism. This stands in contrast to what came before, as a dizzying array of new types, technologies, and designs had appeared across the region during the 6th and 5th centuries. Though it must not have been obvious at the time, these early innovations would set the standard for the next five hundred years, with many forms then continuing essentially unchanged even into the 1st century BCE.

As this chapter will argue, conscious efforts seem to have been made during the 3rd–1st centuries to reference older terracottas through the use of archaizing designs even on newly built temples. This relates not only to the moment of construction, as these same designs were often retained over subsequent building phases in an attempt to preserve the temple's original appearance as much as possible. Any necessary repairs and renovations often closely followed the previous decorative plan, even when the original molds were no longer available. This traditionalist tendency further frustrates modern attempts to date architectural terracottas stylistically. Because these forms were designed to evoke an ancient and revered religious landscape, their styles intentionally confound chronological distinctions.

This interest in archaizing forms also results in a relatively high level of homogenization in roof design by the 2nd century BCE. Of course, innovation and individuality were frequently emphasized through architectural terracottas, and the manner in which discrete identities were expressed through temple decoration will be the subject of Chapter 4. Before turning to these distinctive examples, however, we must first recognize and examine the more conservative terracotta elements that became so widespread during the last few centuries BCE. As we shall see, these are deeply rooted in older central Italic designs. We have mounting evidence that terracottas could survive in place on temples for hundreds of years, with individual elements being replaced or repaired as needed.[1] This means that ancient shrines would have been visible to colonists and other inhabitants and has major implications for how we interpret the archaizing tendencies of terracottas in the period of Roman expansion.

The focus of this chapter is on a set of five terracotta types that derive from and reference earlier forms but that gained particular popularity on Italic temples between the 3rd and 1st centuries.[2] This group, which I refer to as the "standard temple kit," comprises revetment plaques with addorsed palmettes, revetment plaques with looped palmettes, *potnia theron* antefixes, strigilated simas, and perforated cornices with palmettes and figure-eights (Figure 12). By referring to these as part of a "kit" I mean that these five elements offered a basic set from which temple designers might choose. In some cases, we see the swapping out of individual elements, whereas in others the full "kit" (all five elements together) is employed.

It should be emphasized from the outset that this "standard kit" in no way implies common matrices or workshops – quite the opposite. Most of these terracottas appear to have been produced locally, and what is so striking about the repetition of designs across central Italic temples is that the decision to use them often does *not* reflect cost-saving measures such as ready-made matrices, or the availability of artisans specializing only in these types. Rather, the use of these "standard" elements seems to reflect a deliberate choice on the part of communities and commissioners.

Because these were made and used across central Italy, individual examples vary in their details. I define them as belonging to a "standard" type if their composition follows the basic format outlined below for each element. As we shall see, these core compositions are sufficiently distinctive to make local versions instantly recognizable as belonging to the larger category. It is important to stress that, at least based on the current evidence, there is no single "archetype" for each of these elements – no distinct point of origin or identifiable model that all later versions can be said to emulate. These are rather variations on a theme that, for reasons to be explored below, became particularly popular during this period of political change.

As will be emphasized here and in Chapter 4, the "standard kit" could and was frequently adapted to fit specific local contexts. Thus, while "standard" elements appeared on roofs across central Italy, the roofs themselves were

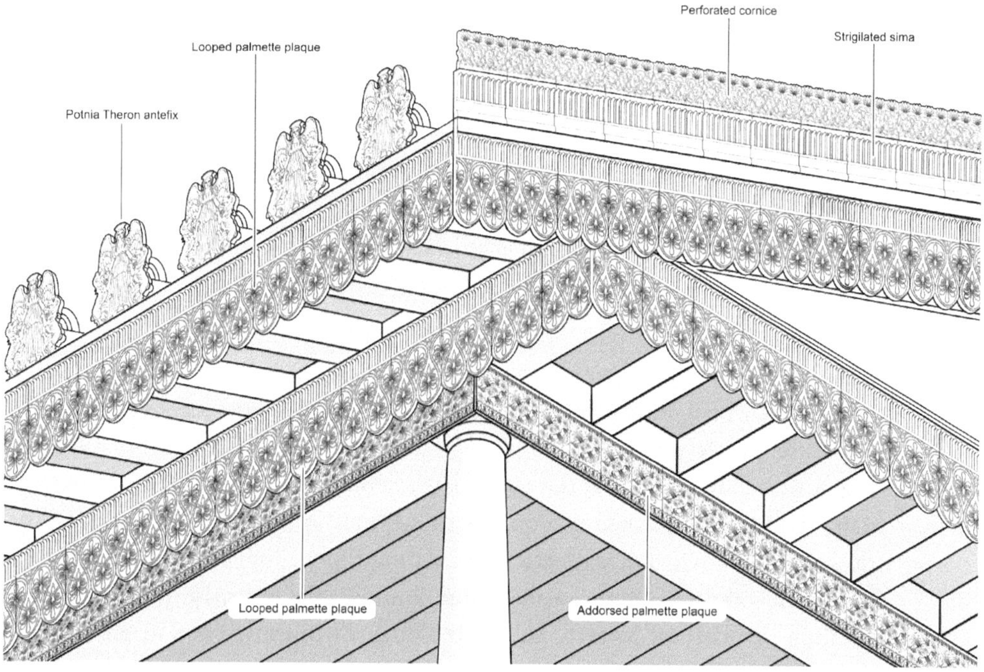

12. Reconstruction showing the elements of the "standard temple kit." Illustration by Jennie Anderson.

never identical. Individualization could be achieved through a number of means, for instance, through local variations on "standard" types, through the imagery of more variable elements such as acroteria or pedimental sculpture, or through the swapping out of a "standard" type for another version of that element (i.e., a more unusual revetment plaque in place of the standard looped palmette type). While many elements belonging to the "standard kit" featured on earlier roofs, including in combination, I do not consider them truly "standard" until the late 3rd century/early 2nd century, when their popularity across central Italic temples began to skyrocket. Before this period, the elements themselves were less common, and their use therefore followed a different logic. By the 2nd century, on the other hand, the choice to use unusual versus "standard" types must be understood against the background of the latter's immense popularity, as well as in the context of local interests and broader aesthetic tendencies in sacred architecture related to the specific historical moment.

In what follows, I will first survey the principal decorative types that constitute the "standard temple kit." Although the discussion will include a range of central Italic towns, sites with good documentation and a large corpus of terracottas, such as Cosa, will inevitably be referenced with greater frequency. A few temple roofs featuring the "standard" elements will then be examined, followed by a broader discussion of iconography and symbolism.

I will argue throughout that these popular terracotta elements are intentionally archaizing and will close by contextualizing this phenomenon in relation to the shifting political landscape of central Italy during the last centuries BCE.

3.2 ELEMENTS OF THE "STANDARD" TEMPLE KIT

3.2.1 Revetment Plaque with Addorsed Palmettes

3.2.1.1 Description

The first element of our "standard kit" is a revetment plaque that would typically have been nailed to the wooden beams of the architrave (Figure 13). Nail holes are still visible scattered across the decorated surface of many preserved examples. The plaque is typically divided into three registers: a short cavetto at the top, a large central register featuring a diagonal pair of mirrored palmettes along with s-spirals and flowers, and a row of downturned flowers or palmettes articulating the scalloped lower edge.

The decoration of the cavetto varies considerably and may include stylized petals, a Lesbian leaf pattern, an egg molding, or in some cases strigils. Below

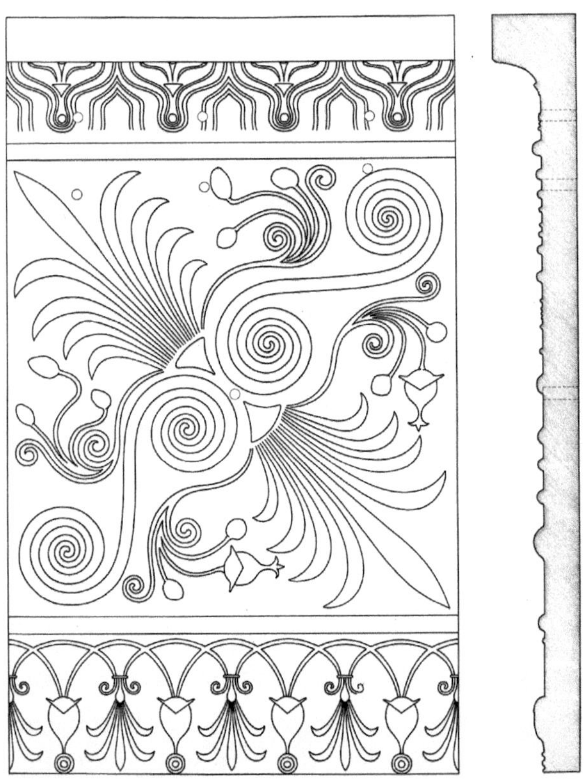

13. Addorsed palmette plaque from Cosa, Type C2:245.
Courtesy of the American Academy in Rome, Cosa Archaeological Collection.

the main register, the plaque may also be undecorated, though a horizontal band of stylized hanging flowers connected by arcing interlaced stems is common. It is the central register that dominates the composition and defines the plaque as a discrete type. The two diagonal palmettes, placed end to end so that they "point" to the lower left and upper right edges of the plaque (or to the lower right and upper left), are almost reminiscent of a thunderbolt.[3] An intricate s-spiral appears on either side, and curling vines ending in buds or flowers fill out the space between them and the palmettes.

Although color rarely survives in any complete form, excavation reports as well as some extant examples give us a clue as to the brightness and intricacy of their original polychromy. The earlier examples of this type are dominated by black, red, and white,[4] whereas a much wider range of colors is attested in the last three centuries BCE. At Minturnae, for instance, the plaques had red palmettes on a black ground, yellow s-spirals on a blue ground, with the buds yellow on magenta.[5] Interestingly, the coloring sometimes varied from plaque to plaque, even in the case of identical mold-made plaques from a single site. It is unclear whether this occurred at the original moment of production or when replacements were installed. At Minturnae, the cavettos of this revetment plaque type consist of small three-petal flowers that alternate in orientation. Examples in the Penn Museum as well as on site at Minturnae[6] show a progression from red, to yellow, to blue-green in the background (Figure 14), whereas another fragment at Minturnae[7] goes from yellow to red and then back again to yellow. A similar situation occurs at Cosa, where the ground around the palmettes may be painted either red or black and that around the s-spirals either green or light blue on fragments belonging to a single subtype.[8]

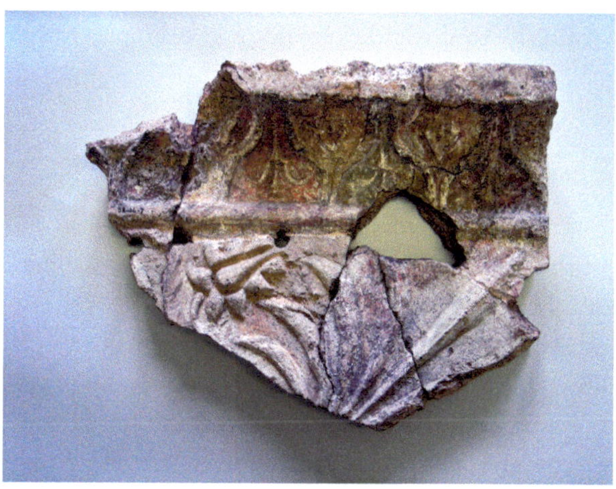

14. Fragments of an addorsed palmette plaque from Minturnae showing one of the attested color patterns for cavettos of this type. Philadelphia: Penn Museum.
Photograph by author, with permission of the Penn Museum, object no. 32-36-7.

The range is even greater between one subtype and another, with the palmettes often painted red but in some cases alternating to blue and yellow for the individual leaves.[9] Among preserved examples at Cosa, the s-spirals too may be red, yellow, or bright blue.[10]

3.2.1.2 Development

The revetment plaque with addorsed palmettes appears to be an Italic invention without obvious antecedents from the corpus of Greek architectural terracottas. It is likely, however, that elements of the design derive from earlier vase-painting and bronze decoration and were then picked up by workers in terracotta.[11] The plaque's earliest appearance on an Italic roof is a matter of some debate, with Mauro Cristofani having suggested a 5th century BCE date for a fragment from Volterra but the bulk of early examples likely dating to the early 4th century BCE.[12] It appears to have been particularly popular in Etruscan areas, appearing in almost identical form at Pyrgi, Cerveteri, Punta della Vipera, Tarquinia, Talamone, Orvieto, Arezzo, Fiesole, Populonia, and Volterra somewhere around the early 4th century.[13] As Strazzulla demonstrates, these early examples are characterized by the presence of a strigilated cavetto, a smooth lower edge, and either three berries or a flower with two berries between the palmettes and s-spirals.[14] To the Scasato I temple at Falerii Veteres she attributes the first instance of an upper border decorated with a leaf pattern rather than strigils and a row of hanging palmettes with s-spirals and bullae or medallions along the lower edge of the plaque.[15] This arrangement, which as Strazzulla notes is itself based on earlier models, becomes standard for these plaques in the 3rd–1st centuries BCE.[16] Their overall appearance is quite consistent, constituting an instantly recognizable type. Still, individual decorative details such as the polychromy or the precise form of various flowers and buds does vary considerably from site to site and even amongst examples from a single locale.

3.2.2 Revetment Plaque with Looped Palmettes

3.2.2.1 Description

The second major element of the "standard temple kit" is a revetment plaque that usually sheathed the roof's upper and raking beams (Figure 15).[17] Its short cavetto consists of a row of strigils or more rarely flowers, and the majority of the composition is occupied by the large lower register. Rows of standing and hanging palmettes encircled by looped ribbons alternate across the horizontal axis. Two full palmettes are typically delineated on the lower hanging row, while on the upper row the central palmette is complete and the two that flank it are cut in half – their full shape to be realized only by their placement beside identical plaques along the roofbeam.

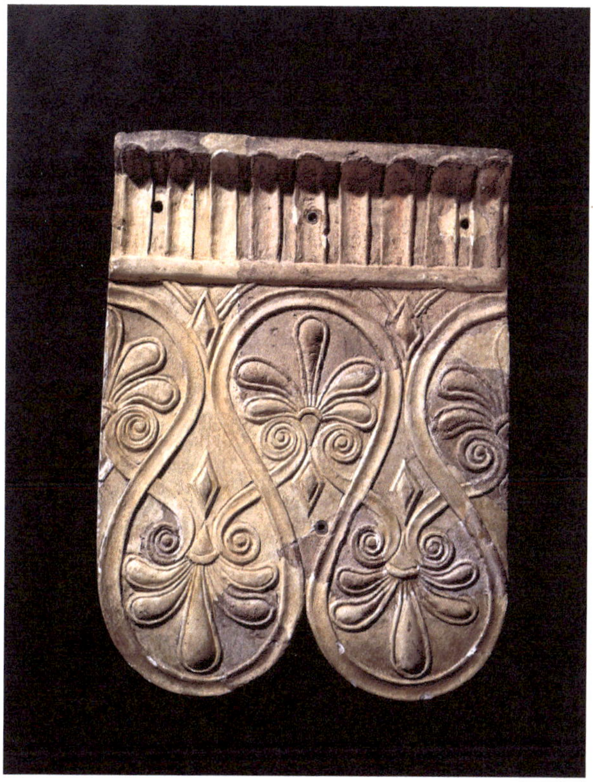

15. Looped palmette plaque from Minturnae's *area sacra*, 3rd/2nd century BCE. Philadelphia: Penn Museum.
Courtesy of the Penn Museum, object no. 32-36-5.

The palmettes themselves are highly stylized and usually consist of five or seven leaves. A pair of small s-spirals connects each standing palmette to the two that hang adjacent to it, and the space beneath each palmette is typically filled by a diamond shaped lozenge. Stylized buds sometimes appear at the top of the main register, between the looping ribbon and the horizontal band that marks the bottom of the cavetto. The lower border of the plaque is scalloped to follow the curve of the looping ribbon that encircles the hanging palmettes. This section would have projected slightly beyond the wooden roofbeam, adding additional protection and disguising the linearity of the beam. The visual effect is comparable to that achieved by the addorsed palmette plaques, which transformed the lower beams from a series of simple, straight lines to a mass of diagonal forms and swirls.

Our information regarding polychromy is patchy, with paint still sometimes preserved but better attested in reports written close to the moment of discovery. The earliest examples are again primarily black, red, and white, although the precise arrangement of these colors is not consistent.[18] Cosa offers a key body of evidence for the 3rd–1st century material, with eleven distinct subtypes of this plaque preserved. As with the addorsed palmette plaques, there appears to be considerable variation in color from one subtype to the next and even within single subtype groups. In some examples, the strigils of the cavetto alternate between red and yellow,[19] while in others they repeat in a red, black, red, yellow, red, green pattern from left to right.[20] The ground of the principal register is usually black, though in one group the excavators report that it is apparently white.[21] The palmettes themselves, the compositional focal point of the design, vary significantly in terms of color. In some the central leaf is red, surrounded by a pair of yellow, then blue, then red leaves.[22] Another group features leaves that are all yellow with the exception of the red center,[23] while still another retains the red/yellow scheme but alternates so that the central leaf is red, flanked by a yellow pair, then a red, then another yellow.[24] Red and blue repeat on the leaves of another subtype, with the central leaf sometimes red and sometimes blue.[25] Finally, one set uses red exclusively for the palmette leaves, which are delineated by white borders.[26]

3.2.2.2 Development

Like the revetment plaque with addorsed palmettes (Section 3.2.1), this plaque seems to be of central Italic origin. The earliest example may be the fragments from Pyrgi dating possibly to the 6th century BCE (Figure 16), but the type soon spread across Etruria and Latium to sites like Cerveteri, Orvieto, Falerii Veteres, Arezzo, Ardea, and Segni in the 5th and 4th centuries.[27] Strazzulla has rightly pointed out the impossibility of tracing a linear stylistic development

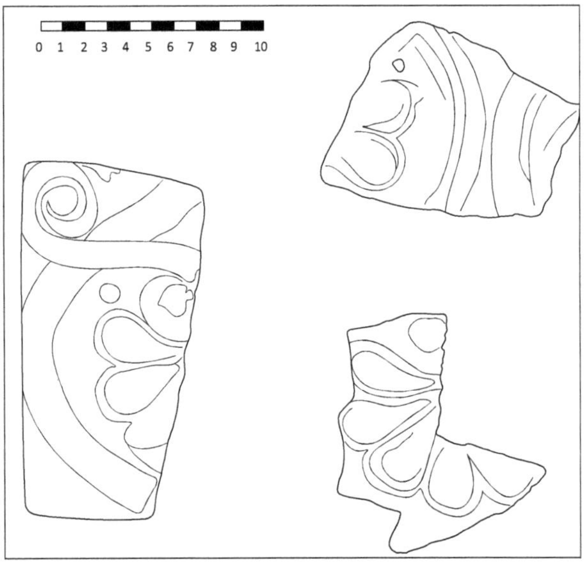

16. Fragments of a looped palmette plaque from Pyrgi, late 6th century BCE (?). Illustration by Dallin Evans, after *Pyrgi* 680 fig. 524.

amongst plaques of this type, as the basic composition remains almost entirely unchanged through the 1st century BCE.[28] Minor variations follow no apparent pattern, and identical forms suddenly reappear after a gap of a century or more.[29] By the 2nd century BCE, this plaque is present on temples across Italy. It is represented by multiple subtypes and even fabrics at most sites, indicating that when repairs were necessary it was almost exclusively replaced by near look-alikes, rather than by more novel or innovative revetments.

3.2.3 Potnia Theron Antefix

3.2.3.1 Description

Although antefixes tend to be one of the more variable elements of temple decoration in the last three centuries BCE, those featuring *potnia theron* (the "mistress of the animals") are probably the most widespread (Figure 17). Their

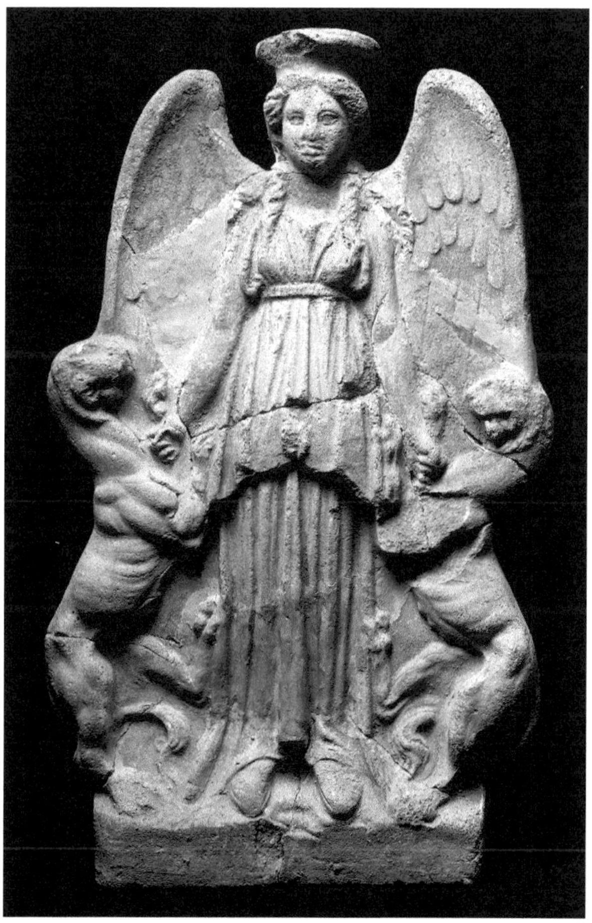

17. *Potnia theron* antefix from Temple I at Lo Scasato, Falerii Veteres, c. late 4th/early 3rd century BCE. Rome: Museo Nazionale Etrusco di Villa Giulia, inv. 3742.

iconography is fairly consistent: a standing *potnia* with prominent wings occupies the space of the antefix, which is sometimes lanceolate but more often shaped to follow her form. She is flanked by a pair of rearing felines, whose front paws she grasps. The felines usually rest one back paw on the ground and the other against the *potnia*'s leg, although in some cases she lifts them so that their heads reach the level of her chest. In a few examples, she holds out flowers or fruit to the beasts that flank her.[30] A *polos* typically crowns the goddess, its form varying from more cylindrical to more conical and its peak frequently pierced with a hole for the insertion of a meniscus. She wears a long garment, usually sleeveless, belted just under the breasts, and her hair cascades down over her shoulders.

Potnia theron antefixes are traditionally divided into two categories: the "archaistic" and "classical" types.[31] The first uses "archaizing" stylistic elements such as swallowtail folds in the drapery but is distinguished especially by the inclusion of multiple sets of wings on the goddess – one pair emerging from her shoulders, the other from her waist, and a third that may appear at her ankles. The far more diffuse "classical" type is marked by a "generally classicistic" style and a goddess with only a single pair of wings.[32] Both types appear to have been produced concurrently, and their stylistic differences do not necessarily reflect chronological distinctions.[33]

Few *potnia theron* antefixes retain their original color, though a group from Monte Rinaldo with comparatively well-preserved polychromy does offer some insight. Five subtypes of the *potnia theron* antefix have been uncovered at the site.[34] When color is preserved, it seems to have been used in a fairly consistent way within each subtype. For instance, in one set, dark red was used for the clothes, reddish-orange for the flesh, orange-ochre for the felines, blue-aquamarine for the wings, and black for the background and profile (Figure 18a and b).[35] This coloring precisely matches that of the *potnia theron* antefixes at Civitella di Chieti[36] but is certainly not the only color scheme used for this type. Some examples from Luni preserve traces of light blue on the *potnia*'s garment, while in another subtype the decoration is composed almost entirely of shades of red, with the exception of yellow for the felines.[37] An older version from Falerii (Lo Scasato I) used a light color for the *potnia*'s skin,[38] black for her hair and red for her lips, white with a red border for her garment, with her wings greenish, the lions gray, the background black, and the base painted red, white, and black.[39] As with the other elements of the "standard" kit, the coloring of *potnia theron* antefixes must have varied considerably.

Italic antefixes had a long tradition of alternating between male and female figures, whereas *potnia theron* antefixes usually seem to have stood alone. There are exceptions, however, as *despotes theron* ("master of the animals") antefixes are attested at a few sites and would likely have been paired with the *potnia*.[40] The iconography is almost identical, except that the figure is male and wears a tunic and a Phrygian cap.

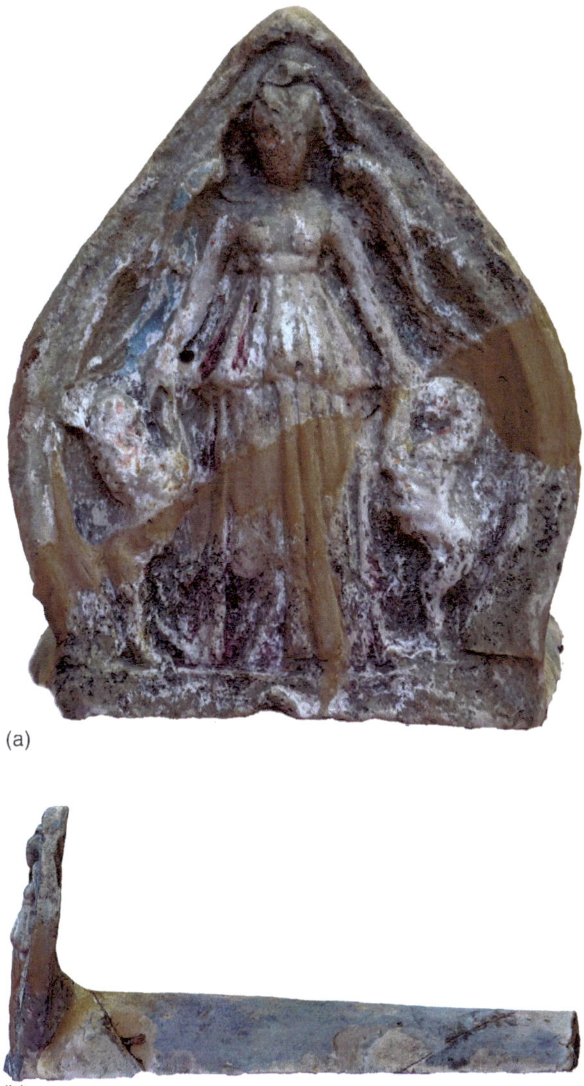

18. (A AND B) *Potnia theron* antefix from Monte Rinaldo, Type A1 in Belfiori 2020a: 219 fig. 19.
Photo courtesy of Francesco Belfiori. Research project of the Soprintendenza ABAP per le province di Ascoli Piecno, Fermo, e Macerata and the Università di Bologna, in agreement with the Comune di Monte Rinaldo.

3.2.3.2 Development

More than any other type discussed here, the *potnia theron* boasts an ancient and complex history. The Mistress of the Animals is attested already in 3rd or 4th millennium BCE Mesopotamia, and she appears on cylinder seals and other objects at sites like Nimrud in the 9th and 8th centuries BCE with many of the attributes that would later come to define her iconography.[41] In the Aegean, references to *potinija* have been found at every major site where Linear B tablets are preserved, although the term seems to denote several different Mycenaean goddesses. It is during the Orientalizing and Archaic periods in Greece that she takes on her more standard form.[42] She appears in Italy by the end of the 8th century BCE, where her iconography seems strongly related to Near Eastern influences and often suggests an association with fertility.[43] Metal reliefs depicting the *potnia theron* are attested in central Italy at sites like Satricum, Praeneste, and Caere, and the motif soon becomes popular on Etruscan bucchero vases, enduring well into the late 6th century.[44] It is perhaps an interesting coincidence that the *potnia theron* appears most commonly on handles and in the added elements of these vases, where the figure projects away from the vase's body and into space, much in the way that the later antefixes project from the building's roof (Figure 19). And in fact, the earliest instances of *potnia theron* on Italic architectural terracottas similarly appear on projecting elements. An early 6th-century acroterion from Poggio Civitate (Murlo) depicts a human figure flanked by creatures with feline heads (Figure 20), while simas with female heads from the same site have been interpreted as images of the *potnia theron* based on the felines that flanked them along the roof's edge (Figure 21).[45] Around the same time at Chiusi, cover tiles with finials also seem to show a stylized image of the goddess.[46] The related *potnia hippon* ("mistress of the horses") appears on an antefix from Pyrgi in the late 6th century, and late 6th/early 5th century antefixes from Capua (Figure 22) and Rome show her more or less in what would become her standard iconography on later architectural decoration.[47]

After this, the type appears to fall from favor for well over a century. Examples dated to the late 4th/early 3rd century BCE emerge once again at Capua, and for the first time at Falerii Veteres at the sanctuary of Lo Scasato I.[48] It rapidly spreads across Italy to become the dominant form of antefix in the 2nd century. The seeming gap in usage is suggestive and implies that the

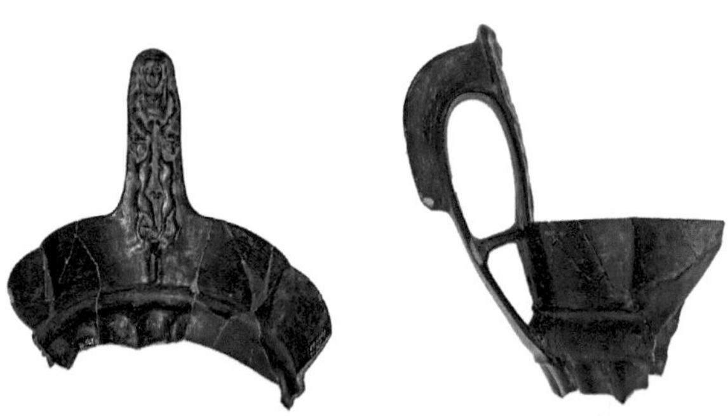

19. *Potnia theron* on the handle of a bucchero kyathos from Poggio Civitate (Murlo), PC 19710569.
Courtesy of the Poggio Civitate Archaeological Project.

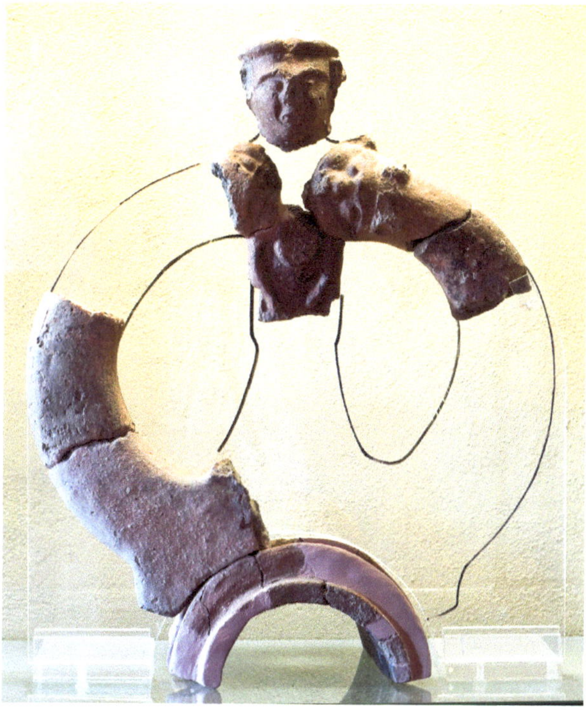

20. Acroterion in the form of a human figure flanked by felines. Poggio Civitate (Murlo), PC 19680553.
Courtesy of the Poggio Civitate Archaeological Project.

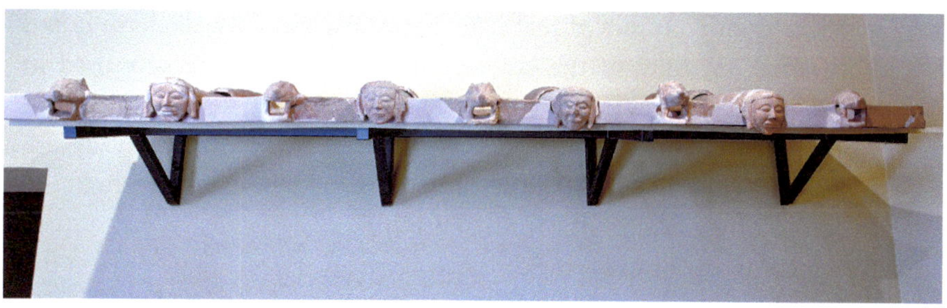

21. Lateral sima with alternating human and feline heads. Poggio Civitate (Murlo). Murlo Archaeological Museum, Murlo.
Courtesy of the Poggio Civitate Archaeological Project.

type's later popularity does not reflect a steady, uninterrupted development. Instead, coroplasts were looking *back* to earlier iconography, which by the 3rd/2nd century would have been fairly rare and would have looked decidedly old. In the case of the *potnia theron*, the choice of an archaizing subject was further underscored by the use of archaizing stylistic features such as swallowtail folds.

Like other architectural terracottas, the known *potnia theron* antefixes mostly lack secure stratigraphic indicators, and their dating relies primarily on stylistic comparisons. We can, however, at least confirm their general popularity during the 2nd century BCE, as many such antefixes are associated

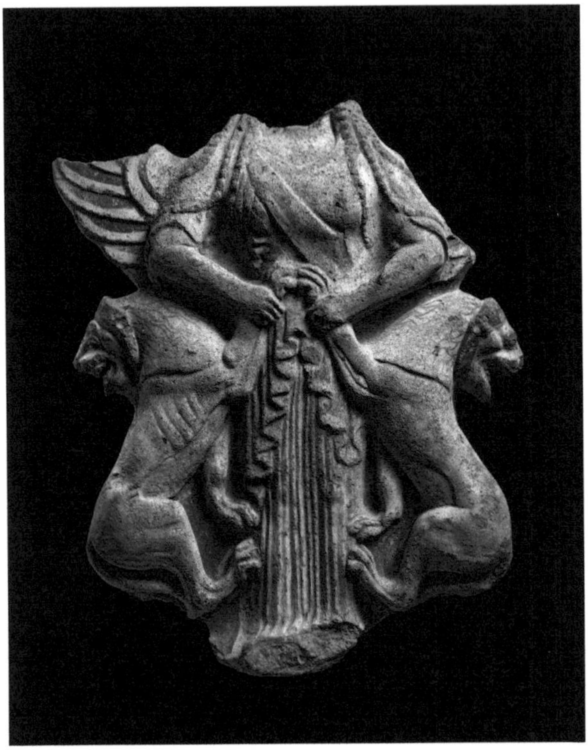

22. *Potnia theron* from Capua, late 6th/early 5th century BCE. London: British Museum.

archaeologically with temples of that date. Strazzulla and Comella have noted that *potnia theron* antefixes of the last centuries BCE were especially used in Latium and in Roman colonies and were comparatively rare in Etruscan areas.[49] Still, it is significant that *potnia theron* imagery was so widely diffuse in Archaic Etruria and that some of the earliest instances of its architectural use come from the Etruscan sites of Murlo and Pyrgi.

Even an incomplete list of sites with *potnia theron* antefixes dating between the 3rd and 1st centuries attests to their remarkable prevalence in central Italic temple architecture. They appear at Alatri, Anagni, Aquileia, Aquino, Ardea, Ascoli Piceno, Bologna, Caere, Camerinum, Campochiaro, Capua, Chieti, Civitalba, Colle S. Giorgio, Cori, Cosa, Firmum, Fregellae, Gabii, Jesi, Lanuvium, Luni, Marino, Minturnae, Monte Rinaldo, Nemi, Norba, Offida, Palestrina, Pietrabbondante, Pignataro Interamna, Porto Recanati, Quadri, Rome, S. Maria di Falleri, Schiavi d'Abruzzo, Segni, and Spello, among others.[50]

3.2.4 Strigilated Sima

3.2.4.1 Description

The vast majority of 3rd–1st century central Italic temples featured a sima with a row of long concave vertical strigils and a groove cut into the top for the insertion of a perforated cornice (Figure 23, lower half). The precise dimensions of these strigils vary, and some simas include a narrow lower register with additional decoration in relief or paint. The sima's vertical face is supported by hidden struts, and even in this technical feature variations can be detected among examples from a single site (Figures 24–25).[51]

While I consider the basic format of a sima with a large strigil course, made for attachment to a perforated cornice, as a broad recognizable category and a fundamental element of the "standard" temple kit of the 2nd century, it is nevertheless important to recognize the many compositional variations that do occur amongst preserved examples. At Cosa, for instance, eight different sima types with concave strigils are attested. Two of these are composed almost entirely of long vertical strigils, with rosettes in relief adorning the crown of one but otherwise lacking additional decoration.[52] Three subtypes include a strigil course at the top, which occupies at least half of the composition and is then cut off by a horizontal roll with a flat fascia below.[53] Traces of paint on this fascia suggest that it was decorated with a pattern, perhaps a meander, but in most cases

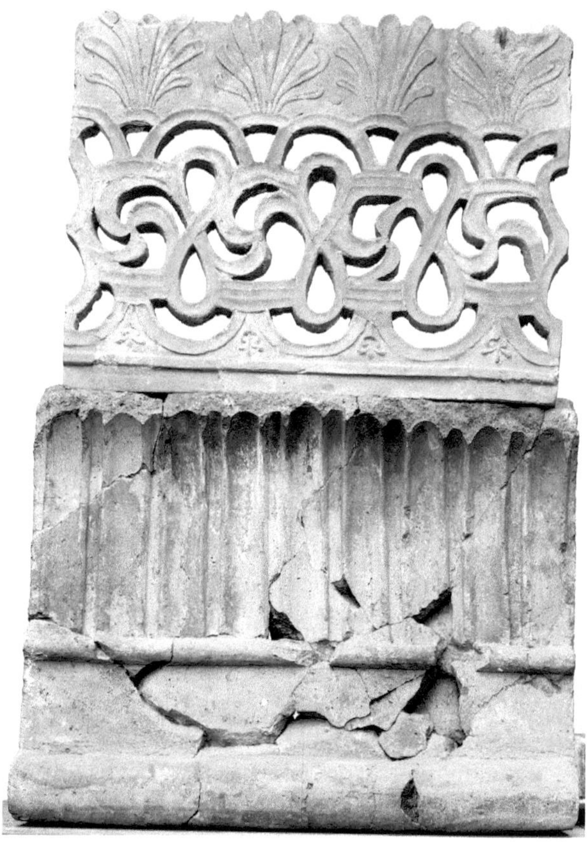

23. Strigilated sima (below) and perforated cornice with triskelia and figure-eights (above) from the tripartite temple in Minturnae's *area sacra*, 2nd century BCE.
Courtesy of the Penn Museum, image no. 26049 (detail).

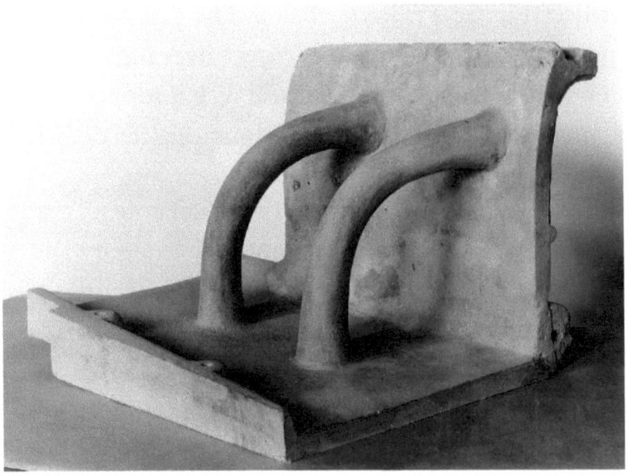

24. Strigilated sima from Minturnae with flying struts. Philadelphia: Penn Museum. Courtesy of the Penn Museum, object no. 32-36-3A.

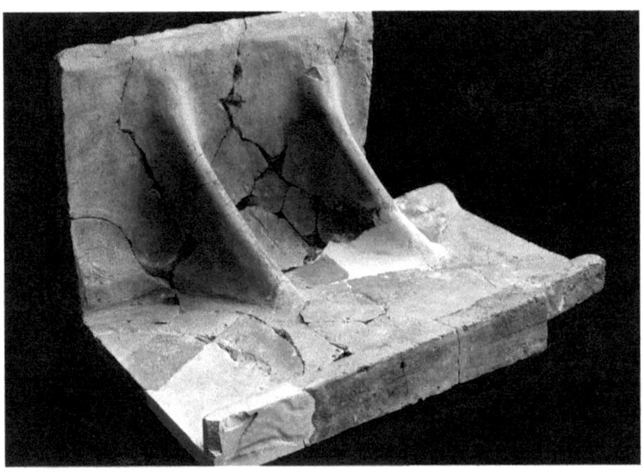

25. Strigilated sima from Minturnae with attached struts. Courtesy of the Penn Museum, image no. 26047.

the colors are insufficiently preserved to reconstruct the design with certainty. Three more sima subtypes from Cosa again have strigils at the top but molded decoration on the lower band.[54] The height of the strigil course varies widely in these examples and may occupy a majority, minority, or roughly half of the composition. Beneath it is a band of alternating lilies and roses, paterae and rosettes, or palmettes.

As in the case of the revetment plaques, the coloring of the strigils varies in the 3rd–1st century examples: they may all be a single color, alternate between two, or repeat several colors in sequence. At Cosa, for instance, one type includes only yellow strigils,[55] and another is described by the excavators as having orange strigils with blue, yellow, and red repeating in the spaces between them.[56] One version that appears in three different fabrics at Cosa features red strigils with white edges separated by black channels for two of the fabric groups and strigils alternating between red and dark purplish gray, again with white edges and black channels, for those using a third fabric but the same mold.[57] Greater polychromy is visible on other Cosan simas, for instance with strigils alternating yellow, green, red, and white from left to right.[58]

3.2.4.2 Development

Strigilated simas have a particularly complex history since the inclusion of a strigil register occurs in multiple forms and over many centuries. Charlotte Wikander has pointed to the Greek roots of Italic simas in general, which she argues were then modified and combined with local elements to create a "wholly Etruscan" version.[59] Earlier iterations feature strigils above a band of figural decoration. Wikander considers the 6th century an important moment of change, when a raised border was added along the sima's lower edge in order to increase its overall height and better meet the demands of the growing scale of temples in this period.[60] Figural motifs are largely left behind at this point, a trend that would dominate the decoration of strigilated simas for the next five hundred years.

Perhaps due to the iconographic poverty of this type, it is often acknowledged only in passing in discussions of Italic terracottas.[61] Like the other elements of the "standard kit," however, it is one of the most widespread and popular types on 5th–1st century BCE temples in central Italy. There is remarkably little change evident from site to site or century to century.[62] Where compositional variations do occur (for instance, in the height and decoration of the lower band), they seem not to reflect any clear chronological development, making it once again impossible to establish a linear typology.

The development of the strigilated sima can probably best be understood in relation to the perforated cornices that sat above them on the roof and that joined them directly via a groove in the sima's upper edge.

3.2.5 Perforated Cornice with Triskelia and Figure-Eights

3.2.5.1 Description

With the exception of acroteria, perforated cornices constituted the uppermost element of terracotta decoration on temple roofs. They were typically inserted into a supporting sima and are amongst the most intricate and delicate terracotta types (Figure 23, upper half). A row of three or four palmettes (each with five or more often seven petals) forms the upper edge, which is scalloped to follow the shape of their projecting leaves. The straight central leaf may be pierced for the insertion of a meniscus. Each palmette is usually supported by a small arc, which in turn rests upon a series of larger arcs below. In the center of the composition is a row of figure-eights, of which two or three are complete and the two on the edges cut in half for joining to the adjacent cornice with its own half-figure-eights. Between these are irregular circles formed by the edges of the eights and the mirrored arcs between them, with triskelia in the center. In some cases, additional inverted arcs appear below these, mirroring the plaque's upper zone but with a small downturned flower rather than a palmette between them. At the base is a flat band. Unlike all other elements of the terracotta temple "kit," the ribbons that form the eights and arcs are pierced so that empty space separates them, making the sky their true background rather than a terracotta base plaque. This feature makes the cornices more fragile than other elements but also more graceful and light. Given their terminal position on the rooftop, they would have been easier to replace than more hemmed in elements like simas.

Traces of color are only sporadically recorded, and the polychromy likely varied widely given the longevity of the type. An example from the Scasato I temple at Falerii Veteres, dated by Comella to the late 4th/early 3rd century, preserves the black-red-white palette that was common on earlier terracottas.[63] Five subtypes uncovered at Cosa display the expanded polychromy of the last few centuries BCE. Yellow seems to have been popular for the palmette leaves, bordered by white or black, or alternating with red palmettes.[64] At least two subtypes had yellow triskelia bordered by either red or green, one with red and yellow figure-eights and the other with only red.[65] Most examples from Cosa with color preserved on the cornice's lower edge reveal a black or dark gray-blue ground with a red fillet.[66]

3.2.5.2 Development

The development of the perforated cornice with triskelia and figure-eights can also be traced to the great temples of central Italy, particularly Etruria and Latium. Examples dated to the 5th century BCE have been found in Veii, Rome, and Orvieto (Figure 26), and it then appears in the 4th and early 3rd centuries at sites like Cerveteri, Falerii Veteres, Ardea, Segni, and Todi.[67] Like the *potnia theron* antefix, however, the use of this cornice does not seem to have been continuous – Strazzulla has suggested that it may have been abandoned at these earlier sites in favor of other types, only to be reintroduced in the 2nd century BCE on temples across central Italy.[68] While its use seems more occasional in the 5th and 4th centuries, it constitutes by far the most popular cornice type in the 2nd century, varying quite little from town to town and adhering closely to the original design. The fact that it appeared on sacred architecture already in the 5th century strongly suggests that its later revival may have involved a conscious act of referencing.

While the perforated cornice with triskelia and figure-eights is certainly the most widespread, other perforated cornice types are attested with some regularity on 3rd–1st century temples in central Italy. These too are usually derived from earlier types. Some feature rounded piercings, while a particularly popular group is perforated in a modified meander or swastika pattern (Figure 27). Variations in cornice type often appear alongside other elements of the "standard kit."

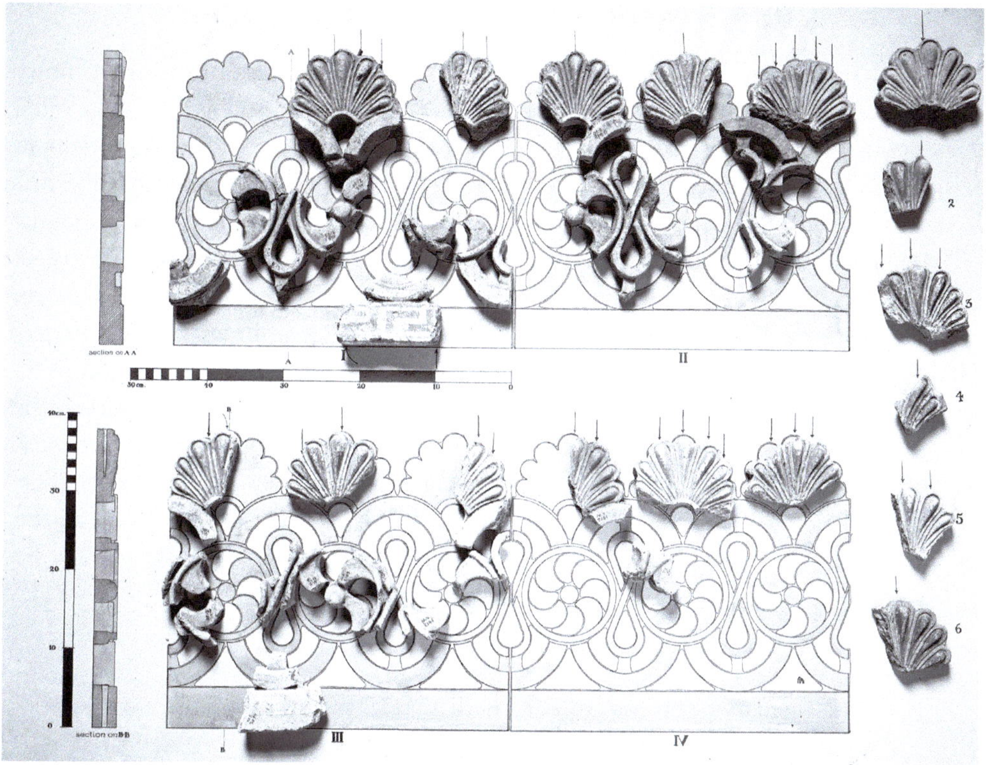

26. Perforated cornice with triskelia and figure-eights from Orvieto, 5th century BCE. Philadelphia: Penn Museum.
Courtesy of the Penn Museum, image no. 5901.

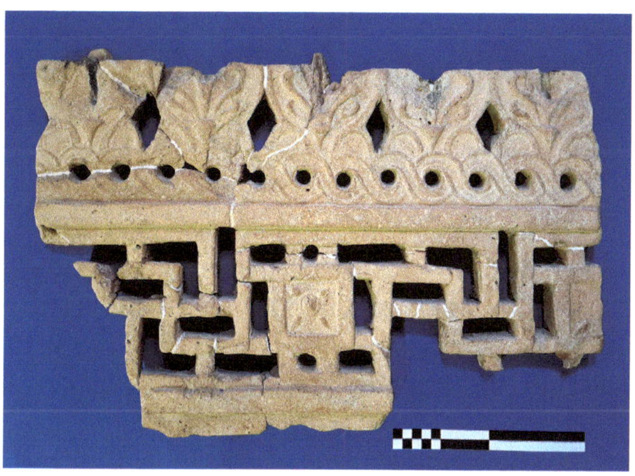

27. Perforated cornice from the Grande Tempio at Luni, late 2nd/early 1st century BCE. Luni: Museo archeologico nazionale di Luni.
Courtesy of the Direzione regionale musei Liguria.

3.3 USING THE "STANDARD TEMPLE KIT"

Elements of the "standard kit" appear on more temples of 3rd–1st century central Italy than are helpful to list here. The five types described above are often used all together as a complete set, whereas in other cases a particular element may be substituted by a less widespread version. It is important to emphasize that roof decoration was by no means limited to these five elements, and acroteria, pedimental sculpture, doorframe plaques, etc. were important parts of the overall design. The ubiquity and longevity of the "standard" types does, however, represent a phenomenon worth considering further. In order to better understand how and why the "standard kit" is used, it will be beneficial to consider a few of the many sites at which these terracottas have been found. Given the prevalence of these terracottas, any selection of sites is by definition arbitrary. The three discussed below are not necessarily emblematic of central Italic temples in general but have been chosen because they highlight different aspects of the "standard kit" and its use in the last centuries BCE.

3.3.1 Falerii Veteres – An Early Example

The sanctuary of Lo Scasato I at Falerii Veteres seems a good place to begin, as it may be one of the first temples, if not the first, to feature the "standard kit."[69] Annamaria Comella dates the temple's monumental phase, to which the majority of the surviving terracottas are attributed, to the late 4th/early 3rd century BCE.[70] The lack of archaeological data from Count Adolfo Cozza's excavations at Lo Scasato in the 19th century precludes certainty where the site's chronology is concerned, and Comella's analysis of the architectural terracottas must necessarily depend first and foremost on stylistic criteria. As we have seen, style is not always straightforward when it comes to these objects, and it is perhaps unsurprising that the same terracottas had previously been dated to the second half of the 3rd century by Taylor[71] and Andrén[72] and to the 2nd century by the Richardsons[73] and von Freytag Löringhoff.[74] Comella's meticulous study does, however, constitute the most thorough analysis of the material from Lo Scasato, as well as the most up to date inventory of comparanda. Her dates are therefore cautiously accepted here.[75]

Less disputable is the fact that the elements of the "standard kit" appeared all together in a single building phase at Lo Scasato.[76] Cozza's excavations uncovered, in the same general area and sharing a clay fabric as well as other technical features, revetment plaques with addorsed palmettes, revetment plaques with looped palmettes, *potnia theron* antefixes, strigilated simas, and perforated cornices with triskelia and figure-eights (Figure 28).[77] These elements did not constitute the sole decoration of the temple, as a range of additional elements have been assigned to different parts of the building in

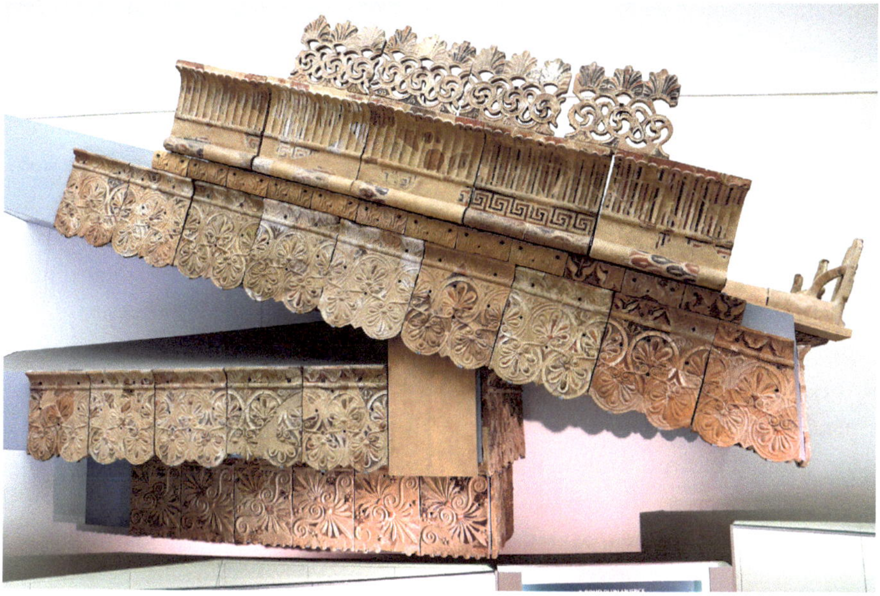

28. Architectural terracottas from the temple of Lo Scasato I at Falerii Veteres, showing elements of the "standard temple kit." Rome: Museo Nazionale Etrusco di Villa Giulia. Photo Wikimedia Commons (CC-BY-SA 4.0), used with permission of the Museo Nazionale Etrusco di Villa Giulia.

the same phase.[78] Again, if Comella's proposed chronology is correct, the Scasato I temple could be the earliest instance in which elements of the "standard kit" appear as a complete set on a temple roof. In the late 4th/early 3rd century, however, the combination of these elements was not yet standard. Their arrangement was not only innovative but would prove wildly influential.

The color palette of the Scasato terracottas has more in common with their predecessors than with the many versions that followed them. Except for the small yellow lanceolate leaves on both revetment plaques and the greenish or grayish blue color of the *potnia theron*'s wings, these terracottas are overwhelmingly dominated by black, red, and white. These are the traditional colors for central Italic architectural terracottas and the only that were used prior to the expansion of the palette in the second half of the 6th century. In the late 4th/early 3rd century, this restricted polychromy must have lent a somewhat old-fashioned air to the new building at Lo Scasato. Interestingly, the nearby and older Scasato II temple, which had been richly redecorated in the early 4th century BCE, featured a wide array of painted color including blue, yellow, and pink.[79] The explicit archaizing of the Scasato I temple's polychromy would have been even more obvious in this context.

In addition to their coloring, the designs of the Scasato I terracottas find close parallels on Etruscan temples in the immediate region. The major sanctuaries at Orvieto, Tarquinia, Pyrgi, and Cerveteri were all under 60 km distance from Falerii Veteres, easily walkable in two days or less. Veii could be reached in roughly eight hours on foot.[80] The geographic proximity of these sites suggests that commissioners and viewers would likely have been familiar with the region's major sanctuaries – a hypothesis amply supported by the appearance of the terracottas at Lo Scasato. Indeed, it almost seems as if individual decorative elements from these temples had been singled out and collected together for use on the new building. Both revetment plaque types appear in numerous fragments attributed to the early 4th century phase of Temple A at Pyrgi,[81] but the antefixes have heads of maenads and silens,[82] and no perforated cornice with figure-eights has been found.[83] At Punta della Vipera, where the terracottas are closely linked to those from Pyrgi (often even made from the same mold), we find the revetment plaque with addorsed palmettes as well as the strigilated sima used in the temple's second phase decoration, dated to the mid-4th century BCE.[84] The sima, however, is topped by a different type of perforated cornice, and the raking beams of the temple featured a revetment plaque with hanging palmettes and four-leafed flowers.[85] At Veii, the strigilated sima and perforated cornice with figure-eights both appear, but the revetment plaques with addorsed palmettes and those with looped palmettes are absent. Both plaque types as well as the perforated cornice have been found at Orvieto but did not necessarily belong to the same temple. A looped palmette plaque as well as a variation of the strigilated sima and perforated cornice – the former with a sea monster and the latter with a winged female added in relief – were found in the Vigna Parrocchiale area at Cerveteri.[86] The revetment plaque with addorsed palmettes is attested at Cerveteri's Manganello temple and in the late 4th/early 3rd century phase at Vigna Parrocchiale.[87] It is unclear whether the latter temple featured its four "standard" elements at the same time.[88]

Closer still to Lo Scasato, strigilated simas are attested at Falerii Veteres' Celle sanctuary, and revetment plaques with addorsed palmettes have been found at Celle, Vignale, and Scasato II, although these differ from the Scasato I examples in having a strigilated rather than floral cavetto. The perforated cornice with figure-eights and revetment plaque with looped palmettes are attested at Falerii Veteres only at the Scasato temples, and *potnia theron* antefixes have been found only in association with Scasato I (Figure 17).[89]

Four of the five elements that would come to constitute the "standard kit" were clearly well-known features of the religious landscape that surrounded Falerii Veteres at the close of the 4th century BCE. Conspicuously absent at these neighboring sites, however, is the *potnia theron* antefix.[90] Most 5th and 4th century antefixes in this region depicted alternating silen and maenad heads set within great elaborate shells. The fact that the *potnia theron* at Lo Scasato alternated with the male *despotes theron* might be seen as following loosely in this tradition, which took advantage of the male/female contrast to create a pattern of alternating colors across the roof's edge. At Lo Scasato, as on the earlier Etruscan antefixes, the male's red skin is juxtaposed with the light skin of the female. Beyond this broad aesthetic tendency, however, the two types have little in common. The Etruscan silens and maenads (if indeed those are the correct terms for them) are shown as isolated heads within a shell frame, while the *potnia theron* and *despotes theron* are full-body figures. Dionysiac allusions are vaguely apparent in the case of the silens and maenads, but the *potnia* and *despotes* images seem far more concerned with making explicit the divine power of the pair. This is clear in the inclusion of prominent wings, in the polos that the *potnia* sports, and of course in the posture of dominating rearing felines.

While the silen/maenad shell antefixes undoubtedly take pride of place in this region during the 5th and 4th centuries, one possible predecessor for the *potnia theron* may be identified in the late 6th century *potnia hippon* antefix attributed to the Venti Celle structure at Pyrgi (Figure 29).[91] The formal parallel is not exact, but the Pyrgi antefix does depict a full figure who grasps the rearing animals (in this case horses) that flank her. Wings are also present, and roughly in the same sector of the antefix as on the later *potnia theron*, but in the Pyrgi antefix they belong to the horses rather than the goddess. The

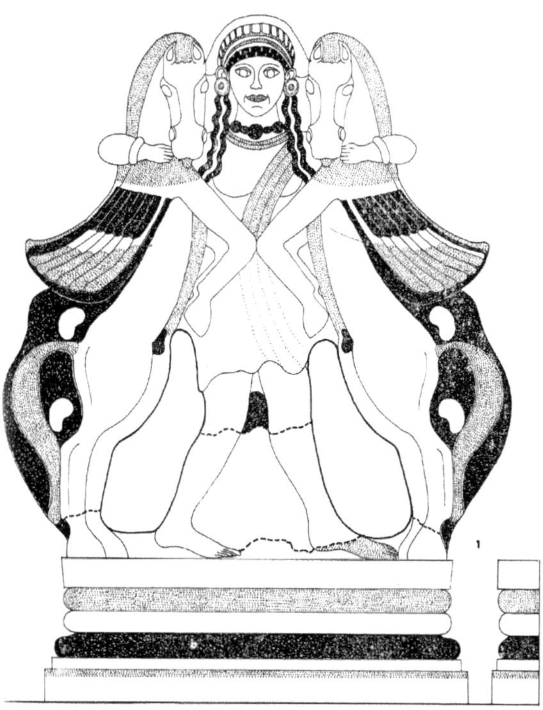

29. *Potnia hippon* antefix from Pyrgi. Image after *Pyrgi* 1970: 313, fig. 240.

discovery of a few bearded faces of this type show that the Pyrgi *potnia* was accompanied by a male counterpart.[92]

It is possible, though not provable, that a few of these antefixes still decorated the roof in the late 4th/early 3rd century. Given their vulnerability and exterior placement, antefixes seem often to have been used more eclectically than other architectural terracottas. Unlike simas or revetment plaques, which had to conform to the size of the architectural spaces they occupied, antefixes could really be of any size and shape so long as their base fit the form of the cover-tile. A single damaged antefix could therefore easily be replaced by an entirely different type, and indeed the variety of antefixes linked with single temples strongly suggests that numerous types stood concurrently on temple roofs. The *potnia hippon* is one of six full-figure antefix types attributed to the archaic Venti Celle building, which are technically and stylistically quite similar to a set of three head antefixes dated to the same phase that adorned the adjoining Temple B.[93] Given the general lack of evidence for later antefixes that could be attributed to the Venti Celle, an extensive overhaul of the Archaic versions seems not to have occurred.[94] Full-figure antefixes were rare on local temple architecture in the period between the Pyrgi examples and the later *potnia theron*. Their enduring presence at Pyrgi, especially when viewed facing their shell-type neighbors, would have drawn attention and amplified their appearance as ancient and physically time-worn.

Interestingly, a *potnia theron* antefix has also been attributed to the late 6th/early 5th century phase of the Capitolium in Rome, and versions of the same type appear to have been used on the temple for subsequent redecorations as well.[95] The similarity might simply relate to the presence at Falerii of itinerant artisans, but the result – that this same figure appeared on both temples – could also have been symbolically charged for certain viewers. If commissioners and/or viewers of the temple at Lo Scasato were aware of the *potnia theron's* presence on Rome's Capitolium, the placement of a *potnia theron* antefix alongside the old-fashioned terracotta types described above might even have been interpreted as an assertion of religious primacy. Recognizable elements from famous temples across the region were here gathered together in an arrangement which, to some, may have served to visually mark the religious centrality of Falerii.[96]

The remarkable decorative program at the temple of Lo Scasato most likely went up before the military confrontation of 241 BCE. Its construction would therefore have coincided with a moment of escalating tension between Falerii and Rome. The Faliscans had been allied with several Etruscan cities against Rome in the 4th century. Following a cessation of military action in 353 BCE, a new conflict broke out in 293, ending in another peace treaty.[97] When the Faliscans rebelled just over fifty years later, Rome emerged the decisive victor and (at a minimum) dramatically restructured Falerii. Doubts have recently been raised regarding the extent of Falerii Veteres' destruction, since at least some of the sanctuaries appear to have continued in use.[98] Still, the mid-3rd century was unquestionably a moment of major urban and political upheaval, with Falerii Novi founded in the valley below the old town.

Decisions regarding the temples of Falerii Veteres must be considered in the broader political context of these ongoing hostilities with Rome during the 4th and 3rd centuries BCE. Comella has suggested that the pedimental decoration of the temple at Lo Scasato emphasized Falerii's mythic history to send a clear anti-Roman message.[99] I believe that the non-pedimental terracottas also played a fundamental role. While the terracottas attributed to the 5th-century phase at Lo Scasato generally correspond to the types in use on other temples at Falerii Veteres, the late 4th/early 3rd–century decoration marks a clear break.[100] This was likely the last large-scale investment in religious architecture at Falerii Veteres before 241 BCE.[101] Instead of employing the established motifs already common to Falerii's temples, the designers of Lo Scasato I gathered together an assembly of architectural terracottas whose history at major regional sanctuaries stretched back centuries. In this context, it is also essential to note that these terracottas appear to have been produced at Falerii itself, meaning that we cannot attribute the appearance of these types to "chance" factors such as workshop availability or ease of importation.[102] They were manufactured deliberately for this temple, and their placement on the roof implicitly marks Falerii as *the* regional center – as the only site with a mythic and religious history so expansive that it encompasses and supersedes the great traditions of Etruria as well as Rome. One wonders whether the appearance of *potnia theron* antefixes on the new temple at Falerii Novi many years later might have been read by some as a sign of compliance with Rome and by others as an enduring marker of defiance.[103]

3.3.2 *Standard Kit, Local Cult – Gabii and Monte Rinaldo*

Excavations at the sanctuary of Juno Gabina at Gabii by the Escuela Española de Historia y Arqueología en Roma between 1956 and 1959 yielded hundreds of fragments of architectural terracottas, many belonging to elements of the "standard kit" (Figure 30). The excavators divided these into two principal phases – the first dating to the third quarter of the 2nd century, and the second to the first quarter of the 1st century BCE. A few terracotta types found at the site do not fit neatly into either of these categories. One is an archaic antefix, interpreted by Martín Almagro-Gorbea as evidence for an earlier structure on the site.[104] Campana reliefs, a floral antefix, and another cornice type likely belong to sporadic renovations of the 1st century BCE.[105] Fragments of antefixes with female and male heads (the latter interpreted as a young satyr) were also uncovered and dated generally between 150 and 100 BCE, although the

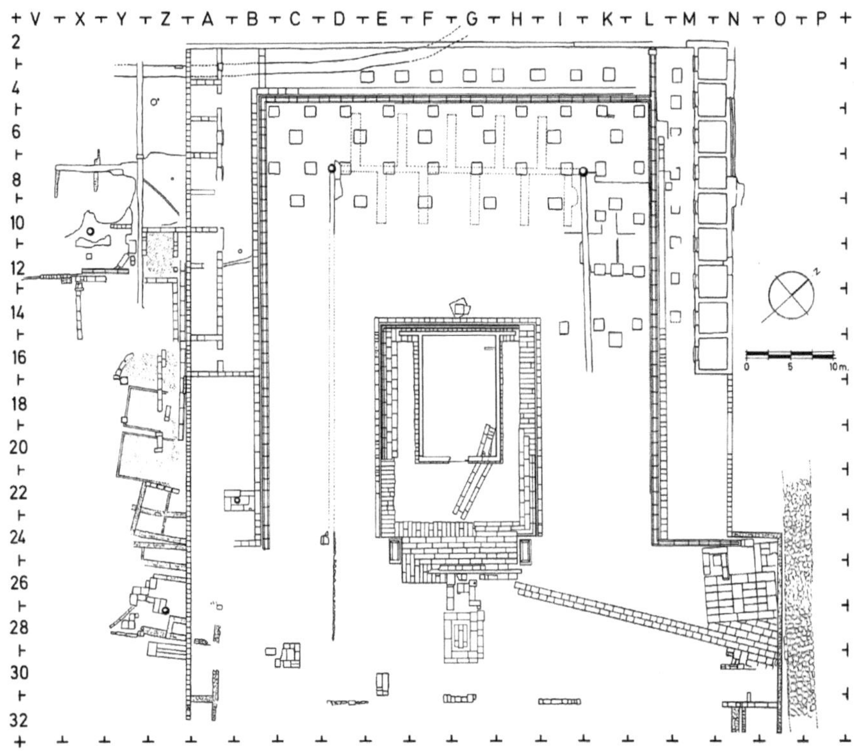

30. Plan of the sanctuary at Gabii at the conclusion of excavations conducted by the Escuela Española de Historia y Arqueología en Roma. Image after Jiménez in Almago-Gorbea 1982: 41 fig. 1.

excavators do not consider them part of the core decorative program for the first phase temple.[106] They may in fact have appeared on the roof along with the more numerous *potnia theron* antefixes – a phenomenon we have already observed elsewhere.

Both revetment plaque types of our "standard kit," as well as antefixes with *potnia theron*, occupied the temple roof in the 2nd century BCE. Surprisingly little evidence was uncovered for the appearance of the sima and cornice, but the meager fragments that were identified have led the excavators to reconstruct a strigiliated sima and a perforated cornice with a meander/swastika pattern.[107] The roof of the temple in this period would thus have featured nearly the full complement of "standard" elements – the only difference being the substitution of the slightly less widespread (though still popular) meander cornice for the cornice with figure-eights (Figure 31, I).

New versions of both revetment plaques as well as the *potnia theron* antefixes were used for the early 1st century BCE renovation (Figure 31, II). Of particular interest is the fact that the antefixes of this phase bear the inscription IVN on their base – presumably a reference to Juno (Figures 32–33).[108] Inscriptions are

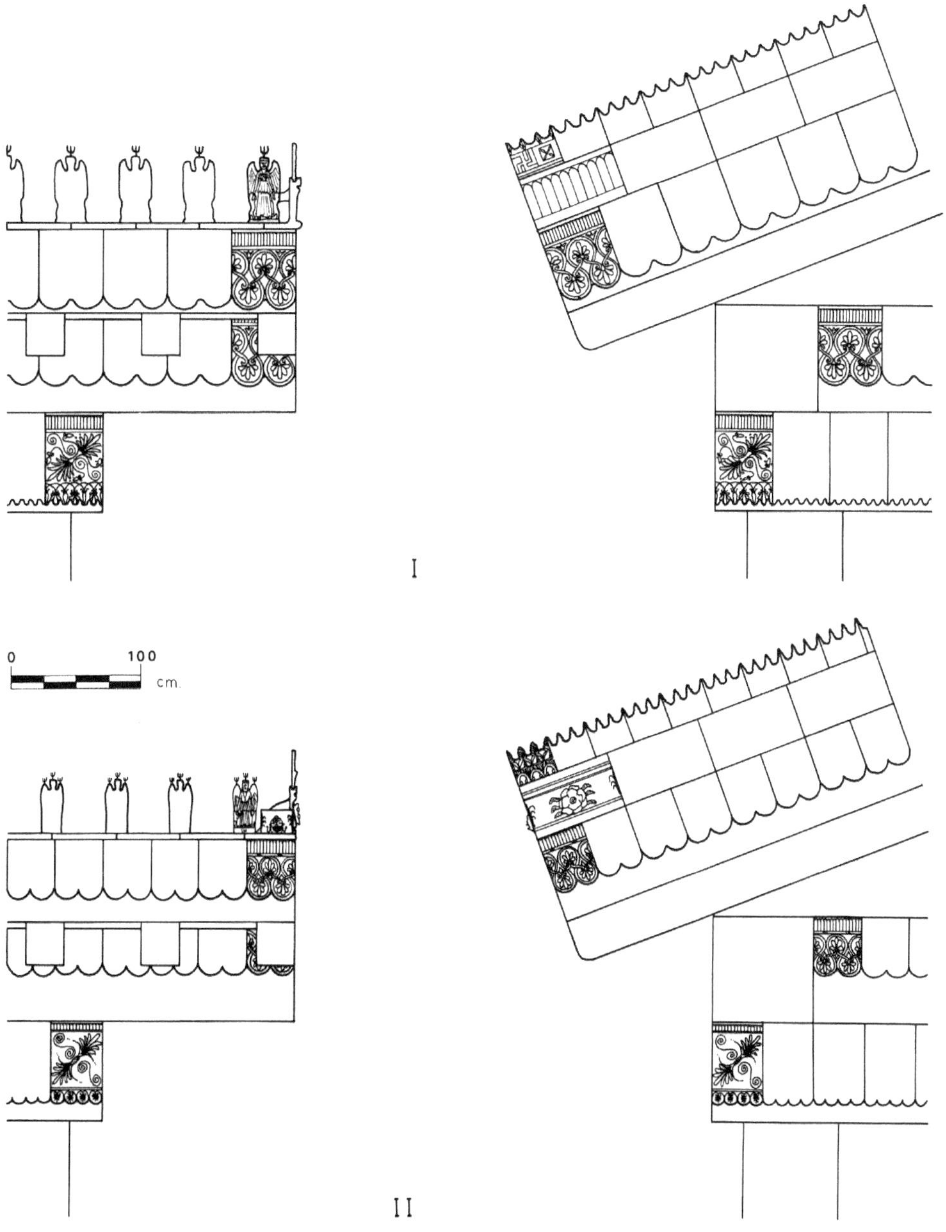

31. Phases I and II of the Temple of Juno at Gabii, as reconstructed by the excavators. Image after Dupré 1982: 190 fig. 17.

extraordinarily rare on architectural terracottas.[109] While the precise character of *potnia theron* seems rather flexible across time and space, she is often thought of as vaguely related to Diana/Artemis.[110] Indeed, in light of these antefixes and some structural features of the temple, Lora Holland has suggested that the Juno worshiped at Gabii "may have been rather Diana-like."[111]

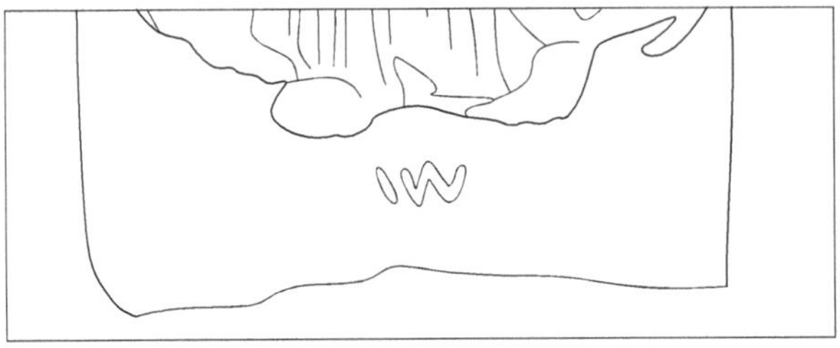

32. Detail of IVN inscription on a *potnia theron* antefix from Gabii. Drawing by Dallin Evans, after Dupré 1982 Pl. 27.8.

Later texts refer to Gabii as the city of Juno, suggesting an ancient and well-known cult to that goddess.[112] While there remains no irrefutable evidence that the 2nd-century temple excavated by the Escuela Española was dedicated to Juno, the inscriptions on the antefixes certainly suggest this as the most likely scenario.[113] In the context of "standard" terracotta elements in 3rd–1st century BCE central Italy, the explicit labeling of the *potnia theron* at Gabii is significant. By the time these antefixes were introduced at the site, they constituted one of the most widespread elements of temple decoration – appearing on buildings dedicated to a range of deities.

As will be discussed further in Chapter 5, the 3rd–1st centuries BCE represented a moment of renewed interest in local mythic history, which was often explicitly emphasized on temples. Johnston and Mogetta have noted the enduring symbolic power of Gabii's 5th-century destruction by Rome, exemplified by the anachronistic manner in which late Republican and early Imperial writers characterize the town as a sort of "archaic ruin" despite clear archaeological evidence for its prosperity in the mid-Republic.[114] The labeling of *potnia theron* antefixes at Gabii may, in some sense, be part of the same phenomenon and reflect the same intensified interest in the city's deep past and (fallen) religious authority. Taking a wildly popular figure such as *potnia theron* and identifying her explicitly with the ancient goddess of Gabii can be seen as a strong statement of religious primacy – a declaration that a goddess present across central Italy finds her true roots at Gabii alone.

This is certainly not the only site where "standard" elements are drawn into a local cultic framework. At Monte Rinaldo in the middle-Adriatic region of Picenum, the great 2nd-century temple featured most of the "standard kit" – with only the cornice swapped out for the still-popular version with swastikas and the raking beam enhanced by a series of beautifully worked high-relief plaques with doves amid vegetation (Figure 34). Interestingly, the revetment plaques with addorsed palmettes from this temple are modified so that an arrow replaces the central palmette stalk, transforming the image unequivocally into that of a thunderbolt (Figure 35).[115] This must be connected to the

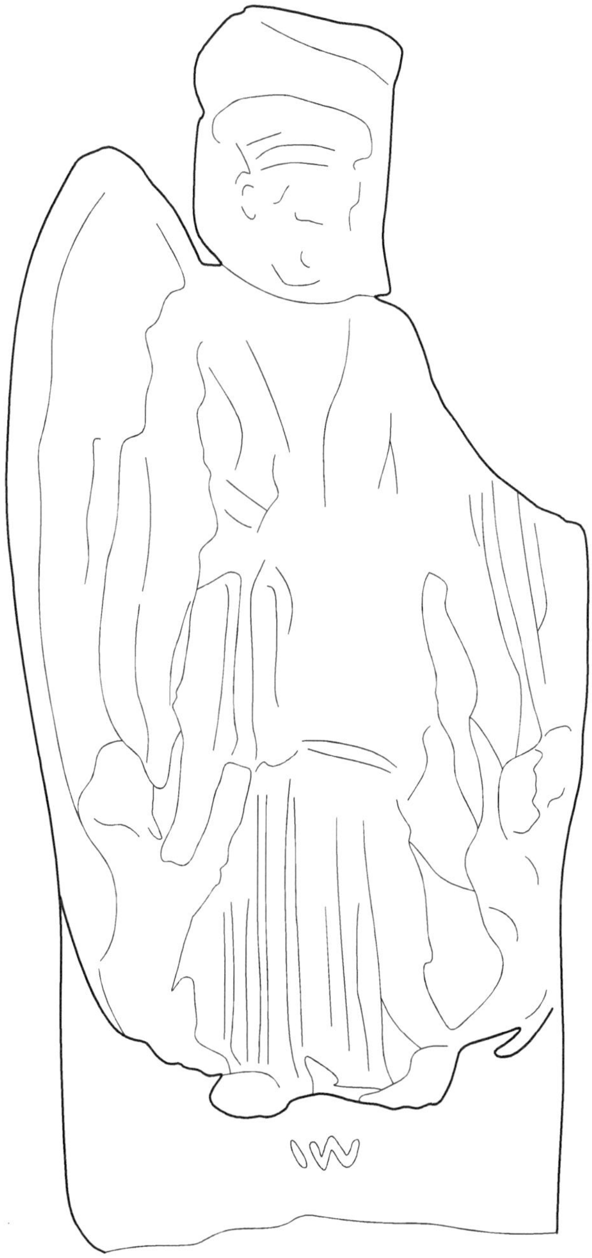

33. *Potnia theron* antefix with IVN inscription from Gabii. Drawing by Dallin Evans, after Dupré 1982 Pl. 27.1.

fact that the sanctuary was dedicated to Jupiter, as attested by a large number of inscribed votives that name him.[116] Once again, a "standard" element is given a local spin, minimally modified in order to highlight the specific nature of the cult. It is telling that Monte Rinaldo's architectural terracottas as well as the inscribed votives appear to have been produced locally.[117]

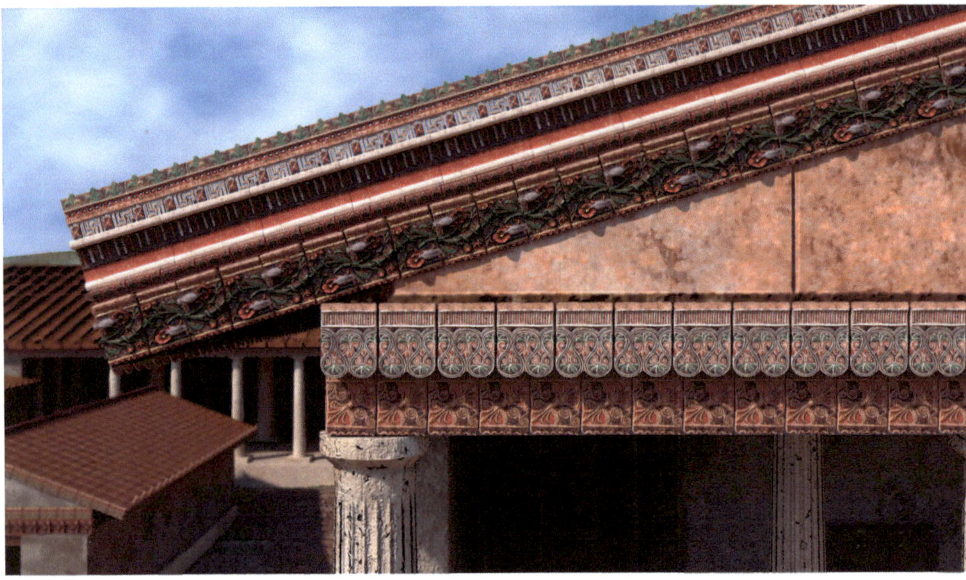

34. Digital reconstruction of the temple roof at Monte Rinaldo, with hypothetical color, 2nd century BCE. 3D model by Giacomo Mancuso, based on the study and reconstruction by Francesco Belfiori.
Image courtesy of F. Belfiori.

3.3.3 Minturnae – Valuing Continuity

Minturnae was founded as a Roman colony in 296/5 BCE at the mouth of the Liris river, on the modern border between Lazio and Campania. Much of the site was excavated by Jotham Johnson of the University of Pennsylvania during the 1930s. These campaigns revealed the foundations of several temples as well as a range of architectural terracottas, only a portion of which were published by the excavators. The history of the site and its terracottas will be treated in more detail in Chapter 4, but a note on the use of the "standard temple kit" at Minturnae is warranted here.

Johnson's excavations revealed the foundations of two pre-Imperial temples in the *area sacra* just north of the Via Appia.[118] The first was apparently destroyed by fire in the early 2nd century BCE, at which point the entire area was restructured to house a tripartite temple surrounded by a three-winged portico. Numerous fragments of architectural terracottas belonging to the "standard kit" were discovered in this area – some of them ritually buried, some used as fill for the early 2nd-century restructuring, and some found where they had apparently fallen from the building at a later point. Although the incompleteness of the excavation record presents some challenges in reconstructing these roofs, enough information does survive to enable a fair degree of confidence.

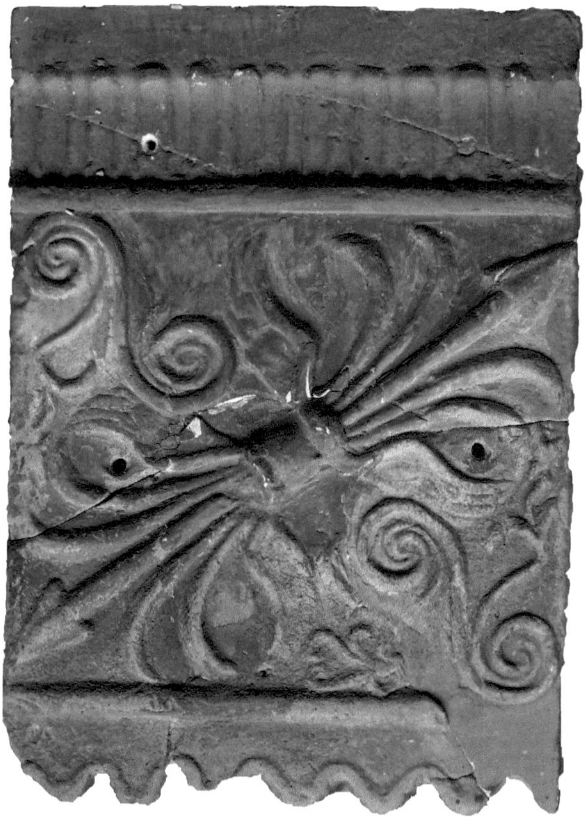

35. Revetment plaque with thunderbolts from Monte Rinaldo, Type L1 in Belfiori 2020a: 195 fig. 1.
Photo courtesy of Francesco Belfiori. Research project of the Soprintendenza ABAP per le province di Ascoli Piecno, Fermo, e Macerata and the Università di Bologna, in agreement with the Comune di Monte Rinaldo.

Due to their discovery in pits below the later portico, three roofing elements can be securely assigned to the *area sacra*'s earlier temple. These are: a revetment plaque with addorsed palmettes, a strigilated sima, and a perforated cornice with triskelia and figure-eights. Given the discovery of four subtypes of the revetment plaque with looped palmettes in this area (though not in the pits), it seems quite likely that this plaque also featured on the upper and raking beams of the early temple. This hypothesis is further supported by the frequent pairing of looped palmette plaques with addorsed palmette plaques in central Italy generally and by the lack of any other revetment plaque uncovered at Minturnae that could plausibly have filled this space. The other key element absent from the pits are antefixes. Two fragments housed in Minturnae's storerooms appear stylistically to be earlier than other excavated antefixes from the site, but each survives in only one poorly preserved example, and neither has a documented find-spot.[119] It is therefore difficult to associate them with this particular temple or even to suggest that they constituted an entire group rather than one-off replacements. A more plausible candidate is one of the three *potnia theron* antefix subtypes uncovered in Johnson's excavations of the *area sacra*. One subtype must be associated with the tripartite temple (see below) and another with the 1st century BCE Temple B. No documentation survives regarding the find-spots of the third, unattributed *potnia theron* subtype.[120] Based on the only published photo, it appears to be just slightly smaller than that of the tripartite temple. Stylistic features such as the down-curved shape of the figure's garment more closely resemble the *potnia theron* antefixes from the Scasato I temple at Falerii, dated to the late 4th/early 3rd century BCE (Figure 17). It seems likely, therefore, that the early temple at Minturnae's *area sacra* featured the full complement of "standard kit" elements.

Better documentation and a more helpful archaeological record make the reconstruction of the tripartite temple's roof a simpler matter. New subtypes of the revetment plaque with addorsed palmettes, the strigilated sima, and the perforated cornice with triskelia and figure-eights appear to have adorned this building, as well as revetment plaques with looped palmettes and *potnia theron* antefixes. Its pediment likely featured a scene of assembled gods and may have important implications for the identity of the deity worshiped here, as well as the broader symbolic message of the temple's decorative program. We will return to this point in Chapter 4 and keep our focus for the moment on the use of "standard" elements.

When the first temple burned down in the early 2nd century BCE, it seems to have been replaced by an entirely new structure in a new part of the *area sacra*. It is significant that this second temple was decorated in almost identical fashion to its predecessor, featuring the full complement of "standard" kit elements. The differences in style between these groups of terracottas are minimal and can only be determined by close examination of features such as the number of petals on a small flower or the direction of an s-spiral. The precise dimensions of each element also vary slightly.[121] While these differences aid in distinguishing one subtype from another, they are so subtle as to have been virtually invisible to ancient viewers.

What these differences do confirm, however, is that the terracottas used on these two temples could not have been made from the same molds. Duplicating the decorative program was therefore neither a cost-saving nor a time-saving measure. Instead, it speaks to a broader trend in archaism and stylistic conservatism in terracotta roofs during the last centuries BCE (see Section 3.5), in which "old-looking" designs were preferred and consciously preserved.

One final point about the "standard" elements of Minturnae's temples bears mention. As we have seen, elements of the "standard kit" belong to broadly recognizable types that span central Italy but vary in certain small details of

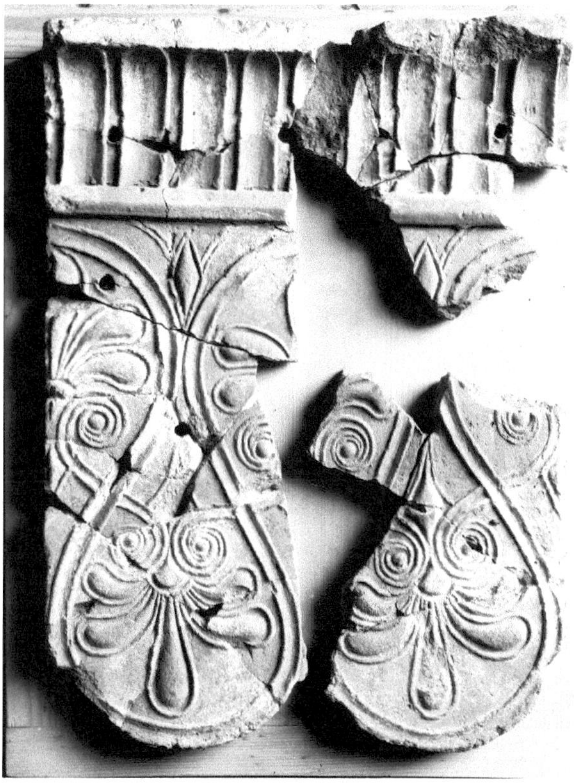

36. Looped palmette plaque from Minturnae's triple-cella temple.
Courtesy of the Penn Museum, image no. 26054.

their arrangement and style. The looped palmette plaques are among the most widespread terracotta types in the last three centuries BCE. It is therefore particularly interesting that the unique form they take at Minturnae is linked specifically to the pre-Roman Marica sanctuary that still stood in the marshy area just outside the town.[122] Valentina Livi has noted a precise correlation between the form of the palmette on the looped palmette plaques of the tripartite temple (Figure 36) and the palmette antefixes from the Marica sanctuary (Figure 37).[123] The specific rendering of the palmette is unique to these two examples and suggests a close relationship between the decoration of the Marica sanctuary and of Minturnae's tripartite temple in the 2nd century BCE. The palmette antefix itself directly imitates the earlier decoration of the Marica sanctuary, meaning not only that its archaic antefixes were still visible at the beginning of the 2nd century but that they were consciously emulated in the colonial-era iteration of the sanctuary as well as in Minturnae's urban "Roman" center. The fact that the form of this palmette was incorporated into a new composition, whereas the antefix itself was not copied, makes this visual quotation particularly intriguing. As at Gabii and Monte Rinaldo, even "standard" elements could thus contain specific and highly local references.

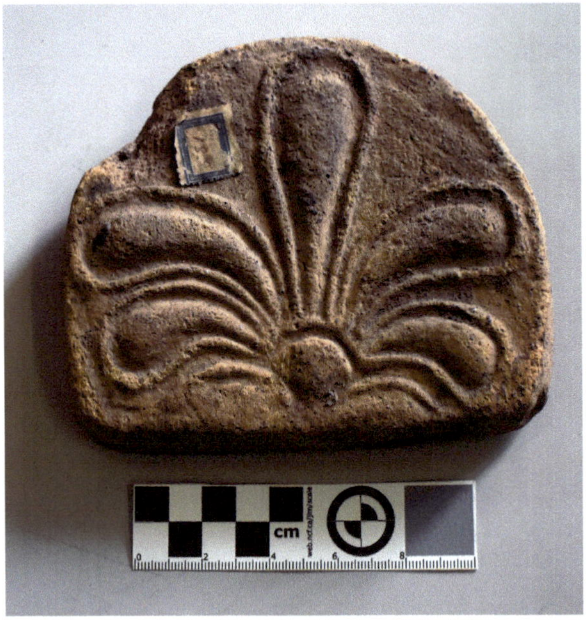

37. Palmette antefix from the Sanctuary of Marica at Minturnae. Naples: Museo archeologico nazionale di Napoli, inv. 176329.
Photo by author, published by permission of the Ministero della Cultura – Museo Archeologico Nazionale di Napoli.

3.4 ICONOGRAPHY AND MEANING

With five architectural terracotta types so widespread on religious buildings of the 3rd–1st centuries, we might justifiably ask *why* these were chosen and whether their particular iconography carried any special meaning. The only terracottas of the "standard temple kit" to feature figural decoration are the *potnia theron* antefixes. While the basic iconography of this goddess spans millennia, her precise religious connotations appear more fluid, and her identity and syncretism with other deities (such as Artemis and Astarte) have long been open to debate. In general, however, these analyses are in agreement regarding the strong religious potency of *potnia theron* in her early appearances. It is therefore odd that while many scholars consider her Archaic depictions as significant and symbolically charged, her frequent appearance on later buildings is characterized as "mere decoration," or, at best, as vaguely apotropaic.[124] The *potnia theron* antefixes inscribed IVN, discussed above in the context of the sanctuary of Juno Gabina at Gabii, directly contradict this notion. The Gabii antefixes attest not only to the enduring symbolic value of the *potnia theron* and her iconography but also to the possibility of associating the goddess with specific local cults. *Potnia theron*, of course, was not always linked to Juno in this period – she appears on temples dedicated to a wide range of gods. Her explicit labeling at Gabii may have been a way of claiming a widespread motif for a local goddess and her cult, implicitly declaring Gabii the true origin of *potnia* and her power. This would suggest a rather flexible attitude toward the well-known motifs of temple terracottas. Even ubiquitous types could be drawn into a local framework and its claims to ancient traditions.

The Gabii example is unusual but cautions us against dismissing *potnia theron* antefixes as ornamentation without religious meaning. As noted earlier, the *potnia*'s ancient connotations may have played a role in her popularity. The antiquity of her imagery was likely known, even if vaguely, and would have been underscored by the preservation of various heirloom items such as the bucchero pots and jewelry on which she appeared in the 7th and 6th centuries. The gap in her usage on antefixes further suggests a pointed archaism when she reappears in the late 4th or early 3rd century.

The other elements of the "standard temple kit" are dominated by vegetal motifs whose possible symbolic connotations are more difficult to pinpoint. Indeed, the role of plants and trees in Roman religion, particularly during the Republic, remains obscure. While we hear of sacred groves and landscaped sanctuaries – and there is archaeological evidence for such features – we can rarely be sure of their precise arrangement, let alone the species of plants they contained.[125]

Later authors comment more explicitly on the connection between plant life and cult worship. Pliny the Elder, for instance, has this to say:

> Haec fuere numinum templa, priscoque ritu simplicia rura etiam nunc deo praecellentem arborem dicant; nec magis auro fulgentia atque ebore simulacra quam lucos et in iis silentia ipsa adoramus. arborum genera numinibus suis dicata perpetuo servantur, ut Iovi aesculus, Apollini laurus, Minervae olea, Veneri myrtus, Herculi populus; quin et Silvanos Faunosque et dearum genera silvis ac sua numina tamquam e caelo attributa credimus.

> Once upon a time trees were the temples of the deities, and in conformity with primitive ritual simple country places even now dedicate a tree of exceptional height to a god; nor do we pay greater worship to images shining with gold and ivory than to the forests and to the very silences that they contain. The different kinds of trees are kept perpetually dedicated to their own divinities, for instance, the chestnut-oak to Jove, the bay to Apollo, the olive to Minerva, the myrtle to Venus, the poplar to Hercules; nay, more, we also believe that the Silvani and Fauns and various kinds of goddesses are as it were assigned to the forests from heaven and as their own special divinities.[126]

While tempting, it is difficult to read such precise associations between god and plant back onto pre-Imperial terracottas. Not only do we lack contemporaneous evidence for these connections, but the very appearance and use of plants on architectural terracottas cautions against such an interpretation. The plants of the "standard temple kit" are quite stylized and seem more concerned with pattern and form than with identifiers for marking particular botanic species. More importantly, the same types appear over and over again on temples regardless of the temple's dedicatee(s). The standardization of vegetal motifs on terracottas is thus at odds with the variety of deities worshiped in these temples.

Still, Pliny's general equation between flora and the antique rites of simple country places (*priscoque ritu simplicia rura*) is suggestive. It seems likely that some sort of ideological correlation, however nebulous, existed between floral motifs and religious architecture at least by the 3rd century BCE. In the case of temple decoration, the very adoption of the "standard" elements marks a decisive move toward floral imagery and away from the more figural representations (processions of warriors and chariots, large staring heads, etc.) that had characterized much of early Italic terracotta design. Indeed, the comparative *lack* of such figures on 2nd and 1st century terracottas has even prompted its characterization as "an age without images."[127]

As the now massive literature on floral motifs in the Augustan period demonstrates, however, non-figural imagery can still be rich in symbolism.[128] Its connotations need not necessarily be specific (i.e., laurel=Apollo), they can also be broadly suggestive or associative. Given the fact that terracottas of the "standard kit" appear to have been used almost exclusively for temples, at least before the 1st century BCE, it may be that their teeming vines and flowers reflect a more general association between religion and vegetal imagery. In other words, floral motifs were seen as particularly appropriate for the decoration of temples.[129]

It is perhaps telling that the adoption of these highly vegetated terracottas coincides chronologically with a period in which temple landscaping and sacred groves are increasingly attested archaeologically.[130] Whatever precise connotations certain plants did or did not carry, viewers entering many of these religious spaces would have been faced with a mass of vegetation – both real and fictive – that stretched from earth to sky. As we shall see in Chapter 6, the association between temples and plant motifs reaches its most explicit and self-conscious expression in the Augustan period, when the vegetal imagery of architectural terracottas is deployed to evoke the "ancient" religious landscape.

3.5 CONSERVATISM AND ARCHAIZING

As discussed above, no element of the "standard temple kit" was new at the moment of its 2nd century BCE spike in popularity. Each can be traced back to examples of the 4th, 5th, or even 6th century and was used on sacred buildings at famous central Italic sanctuaries, with a particular profusion in Etruria. Between the 3rd and 1st centuries BCE, they constitute the most popular and ubiquitous elements of architectural decoration in central Italy. The fact that these "standard" elements seem to have been associated specifically with religious architecture is fundamental to understanding their use and symbolic value.

We know archaeologically that the popular forms of the 2nd century were first developed centuries earlier, but would the designers and viewers of a given temple have been aware of this fact? The question of how long architectural terracottas could remain in place on a building was raised in Chapter 2 and has important implications not only for reconstructing roofs and their chronologies but also for considering whether viewers were conscious of the antiquity of these terracotta types and thus of the archaizing *act*. As noted earlier, Lawrence Richardson had hypothesized an average lifespan of twenty to twenty-five years for these objects, after which a roof's terracottas would need replacing.[131] Such short intervals, however, are insufficiently attested archaeologically, and there is growing recognition that terracottas must have remained in place far longer than previously thought. The first decorative phase of the Grande Tempio at Luni, for instance, appears to have lasted at least 150 years.[132] Rabun Taylor has demonstrated that the decoration of Temple B at Cosa likely remained more or less unaltered for over 250 years.[133] Indeed, many sites have yielded a relatively small number of terracotta types compared to the number of years in which the temples themselves were known to operate, suggesting that replacements occurred rather rarely. Barring a catastrophic event, the retention of terracotta decoration over several centuries was likely common practice.

When terracottas were damaged, attempts were made to replace individual pieces rather than the entire group. This would have been especially simple in the case of outer elements like antefixes and the notably fragile perforated cornices. In some cases, we also have examples of terracottas made from the same mold but with a different fabric. Molds must frequently have been kept after a building's decoration was completed and used subsequently to create identical replacements for damaged pieces.[134] This would certainly be a more cost-effective approach to temple upkeep, rather than replacing the entire roof decoration every few decades. The result is that many temples of the 3rd–1st centuries would still have featured terracottas designed at least one hundred years earlier.

Furthermore, examples of "ancient" terracottas would still have been visible on many older shrines. These were likely familiar to members of the local region, who would travel to specific sites for festivals and other rituals. The antique aura of these images would have been manifest not only in their style and their association with venerable religious sites but perhaps also in their physical dilapidation. The passage of time would have amplified their already antiquated appearance.

The fact that some elements of the "standard kit" were apparently *re-introduced* to temple architecture around the 3rd century BCE suggests that designers and commissioners were deliberately referencing these age-old elements of the sacred landscape. This is underscored by the extreme fidelity with which they mimic their predecessors and suggests a very high degree of consciousness in the archaizing process. The popular designs of the 2nd century BCE would have looked deliberately old-fashioned, as well as highly religious.

Once these "standard" elements were adopted on temples, they were rarely replaced by new versions. Even when we have evidence for large-scale renovations, we see a concerted effort to alter the appearance of a temple's decoration as little as possible. New versions of a revetment plaque with addorsed palmettes might be installed, but what is remarkable in these cases is how closely replacements imitate their predecessors even when they are made from new molds, as we saw in the case of Minturnae. There might be minor adjustments to the dimensions, to the form of the buds, to the ornamentation of the lower border, and so on. These differences, however, are far more visible to *us* than they would have been to ancient viewers. *We* line them up and compare them side by side, scrutinizing the style of a curve or delineation of a petal in search of chronological and typological clues. Such close comparison might have been feasible for the artisans working on the temple but would have escaped most viewers entirely. Rather, they would have seen a cleaner, less damaged replacement of the same roof element, decorated with the same basic design.

The habit of replacing damaged terracottas with nearly identical versions (whether from new or reused molds) is quite widespread and appears to have carried on for centuries. The tendency is eloquently illustrated by the sheer number of subtypes that survive from individual sites. At Cosa, for instance, eight distinct versions of the architrave revetment with addorsed palmettes are attested in the last two or three centuries BCE and eleven of the plaque with looped palmettes (Figure 38).[135] Minturnae has yielded two of the former and four of the latter, Luni four of the former and two of the latter, and Gabii two of each type.[136] This practice argues strongly against traditional assumptions regarding "Romanization" – namely the idea that colonies and smaller towns were trying to "keep up" with developments in Rome through their temple decoration. On the contrary, rather than efforts at innovation and modernization, we see communities going to extraordinary lengths to preserve as closely as possible the original appearance of their sacred buildings, which were themselves modeled on ancient examples.

The questions surrounding Roman "archaistic" sculpture, a topic of increasing interest over the last few decades, may provide a useful point of reference here.[137] It is now generally accepted that archaistic styles were viewed as

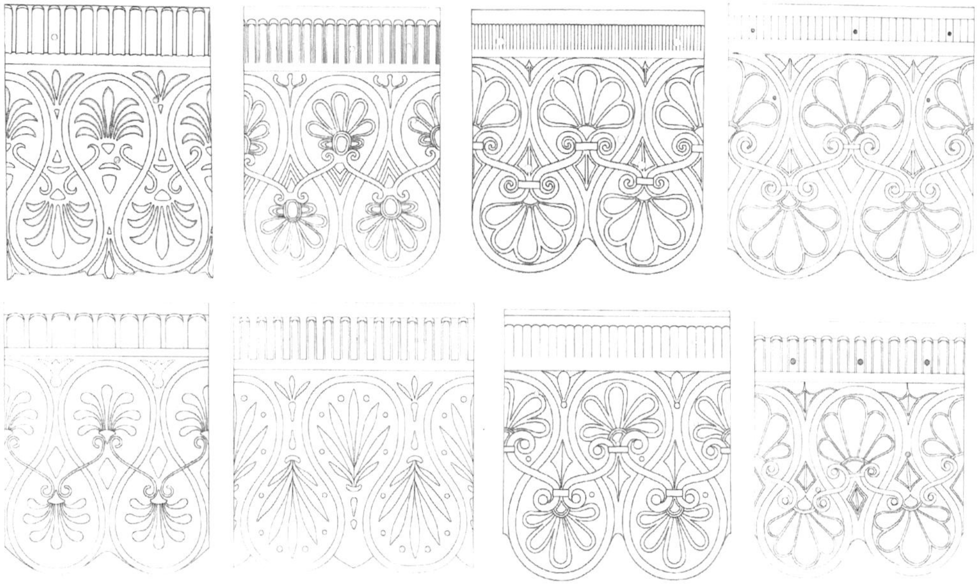

38. Eight of the eleven looped palmette plaque types from Cosa. From upper left, types C2:191, C2:192, C2:201, C2:213, C2:235, C2:236, C2:242, C2:257.
Courtesy of the American Academy in Rome, Cosa Archaeological Collection. Image compilation by Kelley Vernon.

particularly apt for religious contexts. Many Roman archaistic sculptures feature images of gods or worshippers, whose retrospective depiction seems to reinforce their timeless nature. This interest is amply attested in the Augustan period, when Campana reliefs and terracotta statues – archaizing for their material as well as their formal qualities – appear in the princeps' new Palatine complex.[138] As Christopher Hallett has rightly pointed out, however, the phenomenon cannot be chalked up to religious concerns alone.[139] After all, late Republican and early Imperial authors were similarly intent on deploying archaic words and on referencing their own revered predecessors. Quintilian explicitly pairs these trends, arguing that "age confers dignity" (*dignitas*) on ordinary words and commenting that Vergil's use of antique forms lent his poetry "that authoritative air of antiquity, which is impressive also in pictures."[140]

The vaguely "holy" nature of ancient images is similarly referenced by later authors. In describing a work supposedly crafted by Daedalus himself, Pausanias writes that such representations may be "strange to see but are nevertheless marked by a kind of holy (ἔνθεος) quality."[141] Age and religious authority are sometimes paired explicitly. We might think, for instance, of the argument in Cicero's *De Natura Deorum* (2.5) that belief is strengthened by the passage of the ages, or of Livy's (39.18.7) comment regarding the preferential treatment of "ancient" (*vetusta*) sites of Bacchic worship when the newer ones were being demolished.

While the particular connotations of archaizing styles will have differed depending on context and viewer, the general effect seems to have been one of added dignity, venerability, and religious potency. Indeed, these same qualities may account for the general appeal of "ancient" and "primitive" imagery that lingers up to the present – suggesting a paradoxical human desire to hold onto the past even (or especially) in the face of change.[142]

Hallett has suggested that the troubled years of civil war that culminated in the Principate may have produced a "longing for unchanging, absolute values" and thus the popularity of a style that itself "enacts continuity."[143] If we step outside Rome, we might make the same case for many Italic towns during the last centuries BCE. This, after all, was a period of sweeping political upheaval, in which once-powerful cities were losing their autonomy, territories were being annexed to Rome, and new colonies were springing up across a transformed and transforming landscape. In this context, images recalling the glory days of politically weakened groups may have carried special weight. Temples offered an ideal medium for asserting religious and cultural clout. They were arguably the most important of a town's buildings, were sited for maximum visibility, and seem generally to have been treated with veneration even by Roman conquerors.[144]

The speed of political change between the 3rd and 1st centuries, coupled with the special status of religious structures, may account for the tenacity with which central Italic sites held on to traditional forms in temple decoration. The resolute conservatism of architectural terracottas in this period is particularly evident if we compare them to their Archaic predecessors. Nancy Winter's *Symbols of Wealth and Power* tracks central Italic roofs between 640 and 510 BCE.[145] At nearly every site documented by Winter, roof decoration evolved considerably within the space of a little over a century. Mold-made decoration appeared at Poggio Civitate around 630 BCE, for instance, a development that would soon supplant the previous habit of painting on a flat surface.[146] New motifs, such as the guilloche, scale patterns, and anthemia developed c. 600–580 BCE, followed soon after by the introduction of figural scenes depicting rows of animals or warriors and chariot processions.[147] A diverse series of new motifs and figural designs emerged during the mid-to-late 6th century, including some floral imagery that foreshadowed the later "standard temple kit."[148] The speed of change in terracotta decoration over the 130 odd years before 510 BCE makes the archaizing and stubborn fixity of the four centuries that ensued all the more striking.[149]

Elements of the "standard kit" were intimately associated with temple architecture. By the 2nd century BCE, these must have carried a special religious charge, although this would have been generic rather than specific to particular deities or traditions. I would suggest that the particular potency of these images derived above all from their aura of religious antiquity.[150] Ancient shrines – some still operational, some crumbling – would have been well-known and venerated features of the landscape. An average viewer might not have been to Rome, but she would likely have visited local shrines for religious festivals. It seems hardly accidental that the "standard" elements of 3rd–1st century temple decoration are precisely those that decorated the most important central Italic sanctuaries on the eve of Rome's rise. Their peak in popularity is in the 2nd century BCE, when they appear on the temples of colonies as well as at nominally independent sites. By that point, these particular forms seem almost to have become synonymous with temples, as if they represented what a traditional temple *should* look like. Why even newly founded temples in Roman and Latin colonies should be crafted in deliberate reference to the religious landscape of conquered peoples is a question to which we shall return in Chapter 5.

NOTES

1 See Section 3.5.

2 Känel 2001: 33–37 first drew attention to the standardization of temple terracottas in the 3rd and 2nd centuries into a "canonical" system and highlighted their dependence on earlier prototypes. As he notes (52), this standardization goes hand in hand, somewhat paradoxically, with an increased use of hand-sculpted figural high reliefs during the same period.

3 In some cases they are even modified to represent a thunderbolt explicitly, see, e.g., the plaques from Monte Rinaldo in Section 3.3.2 and Figure 35.

4 For instance, the plaques from Orvieto's Belvedere temple (Andrén 1940: 183, II:45, tav. 70:231).

5 Most of these colors have since faded, but we are fortunate to have Jotham Johnson's description (Johnson 1935: 83–84) as well as a letter he wrote to Dohan dated December 13, 1931 (held in the Penn Museum archives), in which he describes being able to see ochre, red, magenta, and two shades of blue-green on the plaques.

6 UPM 32-36-7. The inventory number assigned to the fragment at Minturnae is too damaged to read with certainty, it may be 420114.

7 Minturnae inv. 26661/420113.

8 *Cosa II*: 178–179.

9 See, for instance, Richardson's description of a subtype attributed to the original decoration of Temple D: "The lowest pair of leaves of the palmette is red, the next blue, the next yellow, the center leaf is red, with the stems at either side yellow" (*Cosa II*: 194), or that of a plaque he assigns to the 5th period of decoration/2nd redecoration of the triple-cella temple: "The palmette leaves in the main field are alternately red and blue, there being sometimes three red leaves and four blue, sometimes four red leaves and three blue" (*Cosa II*: 280).

10 Red: *Cosa II*: 194, 280; Yellow: *Cosa II*: 218, 237; Blue: *Cosa II*: 246.

11 Strazzulla 1987: 151; Andrén 1940: CLVI , CCXXXVII.

12 Cristofani 1973: 237, n. 13.3; Strazzulla 1987: 151 and tab. VI.

13 Strazzulla 1987: 151 and tab. VI.

14 Strazzulla 1987: 151.

15 Andrén 1940: 141 n. 3, pl. 53:172; Strazzulla 1987: 151; Comella 1993: 50.

16 Strazzulla 1987: 151. For instance, on plaques from Cosa, Luni, Rome, Ardea, Lanuvium, Alatri, Minturnae, and Aquileia, among others (see Strazzulla 1987: tab. VI).

17 This and the previous plaque may not have always been locked into these exact positions, however. See, for example, the reconstruction in Carlucci 2004.

18 The ribbons seem often (though not always) to be painted white in these early examples, but the coloring of other elements varies considerably. Early examples with preserved paint include two types from Pyrgi (*Pyrgi* 210–211, 678) and Orvieto (Andrén 1940: 198 II:6, 199 II:7).

19 *Cosa II*: 214.

20 *Cosa II*: 243.

21 Black: *Cosa II*: 191, 214, 243; White: Cosa II: 235. Though not suggested by the excavators, it seems possible that this may also be the white ground.

22 *Cosa II*: 191.

23 *Cosa II*: 214.

24 *Cosa II*: 235.

25 *Cosa II*: 193.

26 *Cosa II*: 243.

27 Strazzulla 1987: 156–157 and tab. VII. An early 5th century plaque from Satricum shares some important similarities with this type, though it has an additional register in the middle, Carlucci 2021: 202–203 type LT.C.X, 536, fig. 243.

28 Strazzulla 1987: 157, contra the attempts by Arvid Andrén to do just that (Andrén 1940: CCXXXVI); see also Lawrence Richardson's objections to Andrén's typology: *Cosa II*: 214.

29 Strazzulla 1987: 157 and tab. VII.

30 E.g., at Cosa (*Cosa II*: 270–271) and Ardea (Andrén 1940: 445 no. IV:6); for another possible example, see Pensabene and Sanzi Di Mino 1983: 124, type 61 n. 220.

31 This distinction was first articulated by Andrén 1940: CLXXXIII, and esp. CCXXIX–CCXXX, and is followed in most discussions of *potnia theron* antefixes, e.g., Pensabene and Sanzi Di Mino 1983: 118–124; Strazzulla 1987: 120–124; Iaculli 2006; Belfiori 2020a.

32 Andrén 1940: CCXXX.

33 Recognized already by Andrén 1940: CLXXXIII.

34 Belfiori 2020a: 218–233.

35 Belfiori 2020a: 218, type A1.

36 Belfiori 2020a: 218.

37 Types A5 and A4, respectively. Forte et al. 1992: 219–221.

38 In this case, the *potnia*'s light skin may also be meant to differentiate her from her male counterpart, the *despotes theron*, whose skin is painted red on examples from Lo Scasato (Commella 1993: 64).

39 Taylor and Bradshaw 1916: 27; Comella 1993: 64.

40 For instance, at Praeneste (Andrén 1940: 377, IV:4, Pl. 226 n. 410; Gatti 1995: 102 fig. 35), Falerii-Lo Scasato (Comella 1993: 64–73, tav. 26b); and Colle S. Giorgio (Iaculli 1993: 52–54). A single fragment of a *despotes theron* antefix was uncovered at Monte Rinaldo (Belfiori 2020a: 231–233 type A8), suggesting that it may have been a single replacement rather than part of the larger planned decorative program. An early nod to this practice might be detectable in the 6th-century simas from Poggio Civitate (Murlo), Nielsen 1994: 65; Tuck 2006: 133; Tuck 2010: 213–214.

41 For instance, Barnett 1957: figs. 28 and 29b.

42 For *potnia theron* in Minoan, Mycenaean, and early Greek art, see Spartz 1962.

43 Damgaard Andersen 1996; Nielsen and Rathje 2009: 267–268; Tuck 2006: 132; 2010. Moore 2021 offers a discussion of *potnia theron* iconography in Etruscan contexts as potentially influencing, in turn, Celtic designs.

44 On the early development of the *potnia theron* in central Italy, see Damgaard Andersen 1996. On the bucchero, see Valentini 1969, 1970; Radet 1909: 25 ff. cat nos. 37–40, figs. 38–40.

45 Rystedt 1983: 54–56., figs. 28–30, pls. 28–30; Nielsen 1994; Tuck 2006: 132; Winter 2009: 114–116 no. 2.E.7.D; Tuck 2010: 213–215.

46 Winter 2009: 116–117 no. 2.E.8.
47 For Pyrgi, *Pyrgi* figs. 240.1, 241, 242, 244–250; Carlucci 2021: 117–118 type 1.IA, 293. For Capua, see Radet 1909 cat. 30 fig. 29; Koch 1912: 65–66, fig. 74, tav. XVI:2. Rescigno 1998: 332 notes some uncertainties regarding the actual use and placement of these *potnia theron* figures at Capua. For Rome, see Galluccio 2016: 273–278, type III.3.20; Carlucci 2021: 123–124 type I.IIIA.
48 Koch 1912: 65–68, Comella 1993: 64–73
49 Strazzulla 1987: 121, Comella 1993: 67–68.
50 Bibliographic citations for these are compiled in Comella 1993: 66–68 n. 114, with the exceptions of Bologna (Pensa 1983: 390–391), Camerinum (Frapiccini and Silvestrini 2016: 310–311), Firmum (Pupilli and Costanzi 1990: 54, cat. 157; Stortoni 2013: 291, fig. 4) Monte Rinaldo (Belfiori 2020a: 218–228, 233), Offida (Pignocchi 1996–1997: 218–220; Belfiori 2019: 127–130), Porto Recanati (Percossi Serenelli 2009: 472–474).
51 On the examples shown in figures 24 and 25, Johnson 1935: 78-9 and 81.
52 *Cosa II*: 188–189, 199–200.
53 *Cosa II*: 172–174, 209–210, 240 (considered a remake of the previous sima), 271–272.
54 *Cosa II*: 158, 254; *Cosa III*: 158.
55 *Cosa II*: 159.
56 *Cosa III*: 159.
57 *Cosa II*: 172–174.
58 *Cosa II*: 189.
59 C. Wikander 1993, esp. 88. See also O. Wikander 1994 on the development of the "Etruscan" sima in relation to influences from Magna Graecia and Campania in particular.
60 C. Wikander 1993: 90.
61 See, for instance, Comella's comment that the type is so diffuse over such a long period that attempting to list all examples would be a futile effort (Comella 1993: 45). For a general discussion, see Andrén 1940: CCXXXIII–CCXXXIV. Carlucci 2021: 151–173 carefully analyzes the central Italic simas dated between 510 and 460 BCE.
62 Also in examples of the so-called second phase, see Carlucci 2021: 153.
63 Comella 1993: 43–44.
64 Yellow leaves with white borders: *Cosa II*: 211; yellow leaves with black borders: *Cosa II*: 241; alternating yellow and red: *Cosa II*: 234.
65 *Cosa II*: 211, 241.
66 *Cosa II*: 211, 234, 241.
67 Strazzulla 1987: 141–148, tab V; Comella 1993: 43-4 type A1; Carlucci 2021: 246–247 type CT.B.V.
68 Strazzulla 1987: 142 and tab. V. An unusual version of this cresting from Nemi is rendered in bronze rather than terracotta (Andrén 1940: 384).
69 Carlucci (2020: 84) notes that its late 4th century BCE phase constitutes "quasi un modello per le associazioni di nuovi tipi decorativi e di modanature."
70 Comella 1993: 150–152.
71 Taylor and Bradshaw 1916.
72 Andrén 1940: 136–142.
73 *Cosa II*: 220, 307.
74 Von Freytag Löringhoff 1986: 242–245.
75 As they are in most current scholarship, see, e.g., Carlucci 2020. For a summary of previous opinions regarding the temple and the date of the terracottas, see Comella 1993: 27–39, 87–91.
76 This distinguishes the temple at Lo Scasato from other early sites, such as the Capitoline temple in Rome. All elements of the "standard kit" can be associated with various phases on the Capitoline hill, but they belong to different fabric groups and appear to have been used on the Temple of Jupiter and/or other temples on the hill at different times (Galluccio 2016; Carlucci 2021: 440–441; Hopkins 2022: 108). Pensabene has attributed examples of

all these types to the first phase of the Temple of Victory on the Palatine, dedicated in 294 BCE (Pensabene 2001: 94–100, 2017: 205–208, 250–272). These, however, come from scattered areas of the southwest Palatine, meaning that their date and attribution are hardly certain. In fact, the interpretation rests largely on their similarities with the material from Lo Scasato. It cannot currently be proved which are older, and I have chosen to discuss the Scasato material here due to its clearer cohesion as a group.

77 Respectively, Comella's type A5, A4, B1, A2, A1. These were mostly found in a layer of collapse around the temple (Cozza 1888; Comella 1993: 125–126).

78 Comella 1993. These include some revetment plaques whose precise location on the building remains unclear (for a summary, see Comella 1993: 224).

79 Carlucci 2004: 35.

80 In making these calculations, I am assuming the use of local roads. Travel across major state-funded roads is easier to track and as a result better-studied (for instance, the online tools furnished by ORBIS), but travel to and from major sanctuaries is well attested, and traces of smaller roads leading to these sites have in many cases been uncovered.

81 *Pyrgi* 208-15.

82 *Pyrgi* 195–203.

83 Strigilated simas are attested, but apparently lack slots for attaching a perforated cornice: *Pyrgi* 232; see also Ciasca 1959: 209–10 and fig. 62.

84 Stopponi 1979: 251–259.

85 Stopponi 1979: 253–254 g, tav. V, 1; 256 i, fig. 3.3.

86 Andrén 1940: 53–55, IV:1 and IV:2, pl. 19:60, fig. 21. For the looped palmette plaque, see Guarino 2010: 57–58, Lastra 19, dated to the late 5th/early 4th century BCE. More recent excavations at Vigna Parrocchiale have also uncovered fragments of perforated cornices without figural additions, e.g., Guarino 2010: 50 Cornice traforata 18, 97 Cornice traforata 34.

87 Manganello: Andrén 1940: 63, VI A:2, tav. 21:73. Vigna Parrocchiale: Guarino 2010: 72–77 lastra 23, 82–88 lastra 28, 93–97 lastra 33.

88 For a proposed classification by date, see Guarino 2010: 170–175. A single fragment of a *potnia theron* antefix has also been found at this site (Guarino's Antefissa 40) but seems to date later than the example from Lo Scasato.

89 The fragmentary remains from Scasato II are discussed in Carlucci 2004. Given the absence of several elements that undoubtedly formed part of the roof decoration (for instance, antefixes, hanging curtains, and tiles), it is unclear how closely the roof of Scasato I followed that of Scasato II.

90 A *potnia theron* antefix has been found at Cerveteri but almost certainly dates later than the Scasato example: Andrén 1940: 61, V:4, tav. 21:71; Comella 1993: 66–67.

91 *Pyrgi* 311–321; for the date, see also 402–405. These antefixes were initially attributed to Temple B. For a more recent analysis, with bibliography, see Carlucci 2021: 117–118, 292–293.

92 *Pyrgi* 317–321; Carlucci 2021: 293.

93 The shell antefixes feature heads of a maenad, silen, and "black" African: *Pyrgi* 332–346, 404–405; Carlucci 2021: 286. On the similarities, see Carlucci 2021: 292.

94 Restorations to Temple B and to the Venti Celle both seem to have been quite limited, see, e.g., Colonna 2000: 294.

95 Galluccio 2016: 273–278, type III.3.20; cf. p. 283 type III.3.28, p. 288 type III.3.34.

96 See recently Hopkins 2022 (esp. 109–110) on the "deep sociocultural entanglement" suggested by the striking similarities between terracottas at Rome and politically hostile areas like Falerii Veteres.

97 Livy VII.20.8, Livy X.45.4–8.

98 Biella 2020.

99 Comella 1993: 146–147, 226–227.

100 Comella 1993: 209.

101 See recently Carlucci 2020: 91, noting the evidence for limited continuity at some of Falerii's sanctuaries but at a considerably reduced scale compared to the major building projects attested for earlier phases.

102 Biella 2004: 338–340. Among other evidence, part of a mold for the perforated cornice with figure-eights has been uncovered at the Scasato sanctuary. On the discovery of molds and arguments for local production of ceramics at Falerii Veteres, see also Carlucci and De Lucia Brolli 2017; Carlucci 2020.

103 Drawings of the *potnia theron* antefixes from Falerii Novi, as well as the antefixes themselves, are unfortunately lost: Andrén 1940: 149.

104 Almagro-Gorbea 1981; Dupré 1982: 178, type VII:2l Carlucci 2021: 480–481.

105 Dupré 1982: 191–192.

106 Dupré 1982: 179–181, cf. fig.17 and the discussion of the decorative phases on pp. 189–192.

107 Dupré 1982: 153 cat. 143, p. 172 V:2-B, 189–91 and fig. 17:I.

108 Dupré 1982: 176–178, cat. VII:1B; lam. XXVII.8.

109 In central Italy, there are a few instances in which words in Etruscan were inscribed on architectural terracottas, usually with a stylus on the wet clay, e.g., at Arezzo (Andrén 1940: 277–278 n. VIII:8) and Bolsena (Andrén 1940: 209–210 n. II:2–II:5). There are also cases in which numbers are inscribed on the backs of terracottas, but these seem to be directions regarding placement on the roof rather than cult references. For a remarkable set of plaques from Fregellae with a large fragmentary inscription in terracotta, see Känel and Stangoni 2019: 112–113 and 118–119; Nonnis 2019.

110 *Potnia theron* appears in Homer (*Il.* 21.470) as an epithet of Artemis, and indeed the connection between the two deities seems to have been particularly pronounced in the Greek world. On *potnia theron* imagery in Etruria in relation to the worship of Artemis, see Nielsen and Rathje 2009, esp. 267–268.

111 Holland 2002: 15 n. 36.

112 Virg. *Aen.* 7.682–683; Sil. *Pun.* 12.537.

113 Johnston and Mogetta 2020: 109 n. 70 are cautious to accept this association, though it has long been assumed and has generally been accepted following the publication of the excavations in that area (Almagro-Gorbea 1982); e.g., Gabrielli 2003: 251; Rous 2010: 110–111.

114 Johnston and Mogetta 2020: 109.

115 Belfiori 2020a: 186–187, 194–199, cat. L1, fig. 1; Belfiori 2020b: 9 and fig. 5A. The comparanda for this modification are very limited and seem to be restricted to the region: Belfiori 2020a: 195–196.

116 Belfiori 2020b: 10 and fig. 5D.

117 Belfiori 2020b: 9–10.

118 The function of the foundations identified by Johnson as the *aedes Iovis* have been questioned (see Section 4.3.1) but there is in any case clear evidence for two distinct phases of Republican religious structures in this area.

119 Minturnae inv. 27769/419884 and 26728/420118.

120 Johnson 1935: 83 fig. 41, Antefix type 2.

121 The tripartite temple's decoration is not simply smaller than that of the earlier structure (Livi 2002: 29; 2006: 98). Some elements are smaller (i.e., the strigilated sima, which measures 48 cm in height for type 3, compared to 48.8 cm in height for type 1), some are larger (perforated cornice type 3 is restored at 42.5 cm x 56 cm, whereas type 1 is estimated at 38.3 cm in height and 54.8 cm in width,), and some are simply proportioned differently (i.e., plaque B type 1 measures 61 cm x 39 cm, while type 2 is 60 cm x 39.5 cm).

122 On the sanctuary, see Mingazzini 1938.

123 Livi 2006: 109–111; Livi 2019: 371, 375.

124 E.g., Damgaard Andersen 1996: 107.

125 Literary sources refer to both *lucus* and *nemus*, but there is debate amongst scholars as to how to interpret this nomenclature (e.g., Coarelli 1993: 47–48; Scheid 1993: 19; Hunt 2016: 148–150). For "sacred groves" at specific archaeological sites, see Coarelli 1987: 89–90; 1993: 48–51; Reggiani 1998: 36; Carroll 2010, 2017. For trees in cult contexts, see Hunt 2016: 266–291.
126 Pliny *NH* 12.3. Text and trans. Rackham 1945 (Loeb Classical Library), 5.
127 Rous 2010.
128 Among others, see Büsing 1977; Sauron 1982; L'Orange 1985; Kellum 1994; Castriota 1995; Cohon 2004; Maschek 2008a, 2008b, 2010, 2014; Caneva 2009, 2010; Pollini 2012; Cofer 2015; Crawford-Brown 2022.
129 Architectural terracottas with vegetal motifs were, of course, also used on non-religious architecture in 3rd–1st century BCE central Italy. Still, the preponderance of vegetal motifs on temple terracottas (e.g., on elements of the "standard temple kit") is noteworthy.
130 Coarelli 1993: 46–47, 48.
131 *Cosa II*: 169.
132 Forte et al. 1992: 189. For a similar situation at Tarquinia, see Cataldi 1985: 77.
133 Taylor 2002: 68–69.
134 Proposed already by Mengarelli, who considers the retention of molds an Etruscan habit (Mengarelli 1936: 71–72, further supported in this case by the fragments of matrices found at Caere: pp. 76, 81). See also Andrén 1940: CXIX.
135 Plaque with addorsed palmettes: *Cosa II*: 175, 177–179, 193–194, 202–203, 217–220, 237–238, 245–247, 260–262, 278–281. Plaque with looped palmettes: *Cosa II*: 175, 191–193, 201–202, 213–214, 235–237, 242–243, 257–258, 275–276, 292–293; *Cosa III*: 165–166. A variant of this type, in which every other palmette along the upper row is replaced by a head, occurs in five subtypes at Cosa: *Cosa II*: 215–216, 243–245, 259–260, 276–278, 288.
136 Minturnae: Johnson 1935: 81, 83–85. Johnson unfortunately did not publish the plaque with looped palmettes (it appears as fig. 16 in Johnson 1935) but refers to the four subtypes in passing in Johnson 1935, as well as in a letter to Dohan dated December 13, 1931, currently held in the Penn Museum archives. Luni: Forte 1991: R1–4, 19–33, 76–79, figs. 1–4; C1–2, 42–52, 80–82, figs. 6-7. Gabii: Dupré 1982: 141–147, 132–141.
137 For archaizing in stone sculpture, see Bulle 1918; Schmidt 1922; Ridgway 1977: 303–322; Zagdoun 1989; Fullerton 1990; Hackländer 1996; Perry 2005; Hallett 2005, 2012; Touchette 2015; and of course Hölscher 2004 for the semantic system that, he argues, governs Roman interpretations and adaptations of particular Greek styles.
138 For the connotations of archaizing styles in an Augustan context, see especially Zanker 1988: 243–245, Hallett 2012, 2018. This topic will be taken up in more detail in Chapter 6.
139 Hallett 2012: 91–95.
140 Quint. *Inst.* 8.3.24-5, trans. and text Russell (Loeb Classical Library): *Cum sint autem verba propria ficta tralata, propriis dignitatem dat antiquitas. Namque et sanctiorem et magis admirabilem faciunt orationem, quibus non quilibet fuerit usurus, eoque ornamento acerrimi iudicii P. Vergilius unice est usus. 'Olli' enim et 'quianam' et 'moerus'et 'pone' et 'pelligerent' adspergunt illam, quae etiam in picturis est gravissima, vetustatis inimitabilem arti auctoritatem.*
141 Paus. 2.4.5, trans. author's. Δαίδαλος δὲ ὁπόσα εἰργάσατο, ἀτοπώτερα μέν ἐστιν ἐς τὴν ὄψιν, ἐπιπρέπει δὲ ὅμως τι καὶ ἔνθεον τούτοις (text Jones, Loeb Classical Library).
142 For a broad art historical analysis of the phenomenon, see Gombrich 2002.
143 Hallett 2012: 95.
144 Even when towns were razed, Roman policy was typically to avoid harming temples for fear of divine retribution. The temples at Falerii Veteres, for instance, continued in use after the apparent destruction of the town.
145 Winter 2009.
146 For the roofs of these period, see Winter 2009: 49–142.
147 For the latter, Winter 2009 chs. 3–4.

148 For instance, the revetment plaque with floral decoration from Cerveteri, Winter 6.D.5 (Winter 2009: 463).

149 With the exception of some important innovations of the early "second phase," see Carlucci 2021 for changes between c. 510 and the first half of the 5th century BCE.

150 See also Känel 2001: 54–55 on the material of terracotta itself as carrying connotations of *pietas* in the context of temple architecture.

FOUR

LOCAL IDENTITIES AND LOCAL NETWORKS

Two Case Studies

4.1 INTRODUCTION

Even as the "standard temple kit" was gaining widespread popularity across central Italy, a concurrent trend sought to incorporate more unusual – specifically local – elements into temple design. This is particularly visible on architectural terracottas of the last three centuries BCE and speaks to the profound importance allotted to place and to local religious history. The emphasis on local elements must also be interpreted in the context of intercommunity competition so prevalent during this period. As the political landscape of Italy took new shape, once-proud towns found themselves suddenly powerless – subject to Rome's favor even if they remained nominally independent. It may be for this reason that local religious history took on added weight; it represented one of the only fields in which towns could compete with one another and with Rome itself.

The use of local-style architectural terracottas often occurs in conjunction with elements of the "standard" kit. We have already observed the religious and ancient connotations that these "standard" elements seem to have carried, and it is the goal of the present chapter to explore how the more unusual terracottas functioned in dialogue with widespread types in order to craft specific visual identities for communities. The two case studies presented here – the colonies of Cosa and Minturnae – are certainly not intended as a comprehensive demonstration of how architectural terracottas were employed in 3rd–1st century central Italy. Rather, they offer two close looks at how local traditions might be drawn on within a colonial context, in order to illustrate the complexity of temple roofs and their layered meanings. Any number of sites could serve here, but Cosa and Minturnae offer a particularly appealing pair for their Latin and Roman legal status, respectively, for their location north and south of Rome, and for their very different modern excavation and publication histories.

4.2 COSA

4.2.1 Overview of the Site

Cosa was founded as a Latin colony on an uninhabited hill overlooking the Tyrrhenian coast in 273 BCE in territory recently confiscated from Etruscan Vulci (Figure 39). This was a prosperous region endowed with natural ports as well as commercial links to the interior. From its inception, Cosa was inserted into a vibrant network of well-established and thriving Etruscan towns with long-standing traditions in terracotta production. Their monumental urban sanctuaries and rural shrines remained major features of the region's sacred

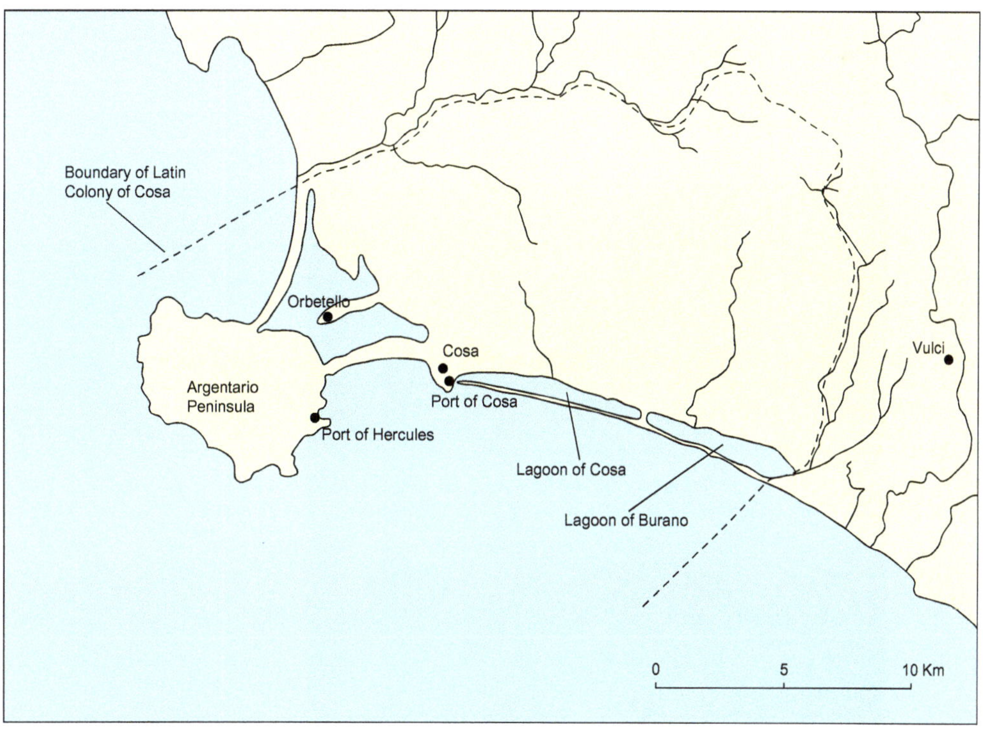

39. Map showing Cosa and its immediate surroundings.
Drawing by Dallin Evans.

landscape long after the founding of the colony. As we shall see, Cosa's architectural terracottas reveal close ties to examples from these sites, with many pieces deriving from the same workshops or even molds, suggesting a particularly close-knit network along the Etruscan coast between Punta della Vipera (Santa Marinella) and Talamone. At the same time, the appearance of several types popular at sites across Italy attest to Cosa's broader contacts with Latium and "Roman" Italy.

The colony's earliest history is notoriously problematic, since very few structures can confidently be dated to the period immediately following its foundation. Most prominent of the 3rd-century constructions is the large circuit of polygonal walls (Figure 40). It is possible that the space of the forum and the basic grid plan of the city were laid out in this period as well, although open questions remain in both cases, and the bulk of urban projects appear to date later (Figure 41).[1] Also assigned to the 3rd century BCE is the *curia/comitium* complex in the forum and a small square structure on the summit that has been a topic of debate for decades. Most recently, Rabun Taylor has suggested that this 7.5 x 7.5 m structure actually represents Cosa's first temple.[2]

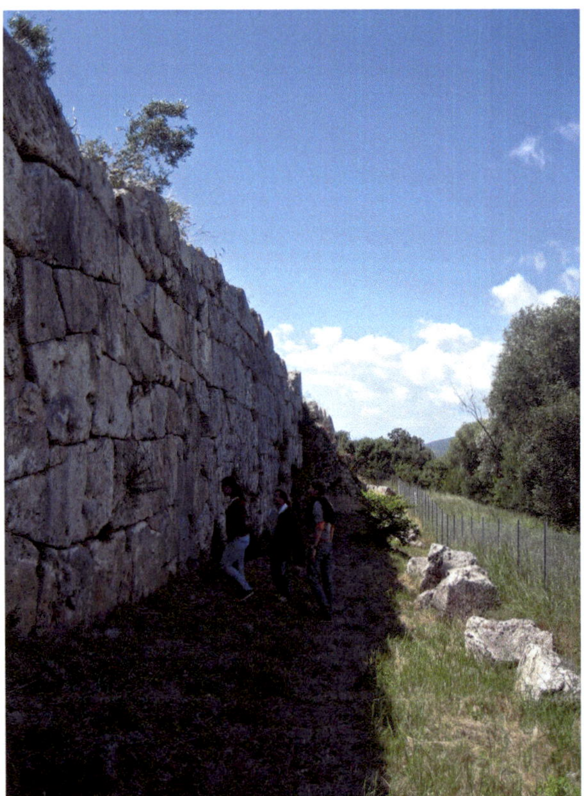

40. Surviving stretch of Cosa's circuit walls.
Author's photo, courtesy of Cosa Excavations.

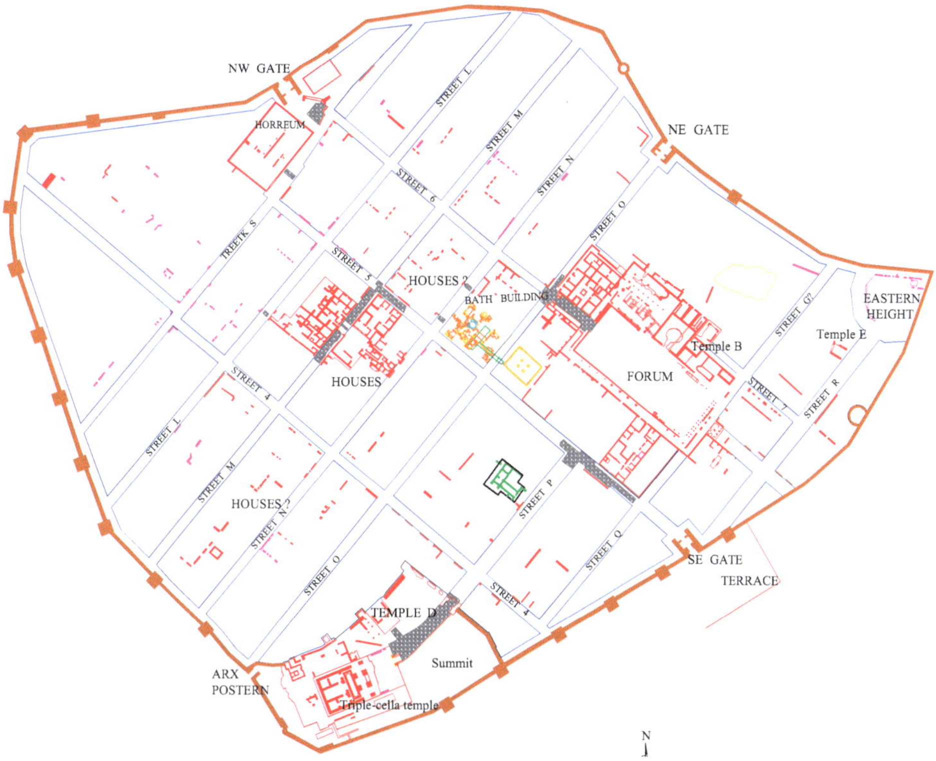

41. Plan of Cosa, current state (with projection of the streets following Brown). Courtesy of Cosa Excavations, key structures referred to in the text added by the author in bold.

It is noteworthy that no houses dating to the colony's early years have thus far been excavated.

We hear from Livy that the struggling town petitioned for a new supplement of colonists at the start of the 2nd century, which they were granted in 197 BCE.[3] This influx rejuvenated the colony and led to a great spurt in building activity. A group of large atrium houses was built around the forum, the curia was enlarged, and a basilica as well as a new forum temple ("Temple B") were installed.[4] Another temple seems to have been built on the Eastern Height around the same time, as well as the triple-cella temple and the smaller "Temple D" on the summit.[5]

A violent event affected at least part of the town sometime around 70 BCE, the best evidence for which comes from two houses near the site's current museum, northwest of the forum.[6] There are indications of destruction by fire in other areas of the site, but in most cases the date cannot be pinned down very precisely.[7]

Cosa seems to have undergone a period of urban renewal or possibly resettlement around the time of Augustus, and several building phases on the summit, in the forum, and in various houses are assigned to the late 1st century

BCE. The town suffered again in the mid-1st century CE, when an earthquake apparently destroyed the basilica and damaged the triple-cella temple. Post-Neronian Cosa has long been characterized as a town in decline, save for a brief reoccupation under Caracalla. Current excavations of the forum bath complex, however, have begun to alter this picture, and the town's imperial history is now being reconsidered.[8]

A dizzying number of architectural terracotta fragments have been uncovered since the inception of excavations at Cosa in 1948. Many were found in association with temples or sacred areas (on the summit, or around the foundations of Temples B, E, and the Port Temple), while others were reused for decoration in domestic contexts (i.e., the House of Diana) or as building material in non-sacred contexts during the Imperial period (i.e., in the bath complex). While the Cosa terracottas are for the most part quite well documented, especially compared to many other sites, not all have been published.

The problems with Lawrence Richardson's typology for the architectural terracottas from Cosa and the general dearth of stratigraphic indicators for these objects were discussed in Sections 2.2 and 2.3. Because the currently available evidence precludes certainty regarding their precise chronology, my concern here will not be to rewrite Richardson's attributions but to ask what new information this material can yield. Despite the problematic nature of the typology, Richardson did an immense service in meticulously cataloguing the many terracottas from Cosa. Rabun Taylor's fundamental reevaluation shed new light on this material and on terracotta roofs more generally.[9] While Taylor focused primarily on phasing and architectural reconstruction, my goal here will be to put Cosa's terracottas within their urban and regional context. As I will show, they have much to tell us about local networks and cultural exchange, as well as about broader urban aesthetics at a moment when Cosa's visual identity was being shaped.

4.2.2 Temple Roofs at Cosa – The Creation of an Aesthetic

4.2.2.1 Summit Temple 1

The fact that architectural terracottas were found sealed in the construction levels of the triple-cella temple indicates that a building of some kind preceded it on the summit. Given the similarity of these terracottas to those used on subsequent temples at Cosa and at other sites in central Italy, it seems quite likely that this early building was indeed a temple. Taylor has suggested that some of the terracottas used to line the cistern of the triple-cella temple may have also formed part of its decoration (Figure 42). Since, as he argues, the lining would have taken place late in the construction process, the colonists may have used "broken or excess terracottas . . . as bricks or even fill."[10] Rather

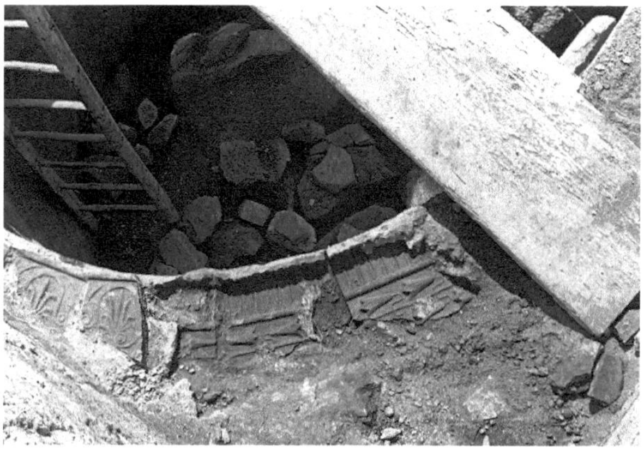

42. Pronaos of the triple-cella temple at Cosa, showing the cistern lined with architectural terracottas.
Courtesy of the American Academy in Rome, Cosa Archaeological Collection.

than wasting useable and comparatively expensive decorative pieces for construction, however, it seems more likely that any excess terracottas would have been placed in storage to serve as replacements in the event of subsequent damage to the roof. And while one or two broken terracottas might well have served as building material, evidence from other sites strongly suggests that the terracottas found in construction layers belong overwhelmingly to previous phases and that they were reused in this way due to their sacred nature as property of the god.[11] Furthermore, if the cistern is indeed contemporaneous with the temple, it would likely have been lined *before* the roof was completed in order to prevent water from being wasted.[12]

For these reasons, I would consider all fragments found in the construction layers and cistern lining of the triple-cella temple as candidates for the decoration of a preexisting structure on the summit. Theoretically, these should mostly belong to Summit Temple 1, although some may also have decorated Temple D, which is thought to pre-date the triple-cella temple by a few decades. The relevant architectural terracottas, along with their *Cosa II* attributions, are listed below. To distinguish one type from another, I use a modified version of the system employed by Taylor. Each terracotta type is thus identified by the volume in which it was first published (C2=*Cosa II*, C3=*Cosa III*, and so on), followed by the page on which discussion of it begins.[13]

- Shell antefixes with the heads of Minerva and Hercules (C2:154).
  - assigned to the "Temple of Jupiter" in *Cosa II*.
- Female head antefix (C2:285).
  - tentatively assigned to an early building on the summit in *Cosa II*, perhaps a "light wooden pavilion over the *auguraculum*."

- Revetment plaque with standing and hanging palmettes and lilies (C2: 161).
  - assigned to the "Temple of Jupiter" in *Cosa II.*
- Revetment plaque with crossed ribbons and flowers: two types (C2: 163).
  - assigned to the "Temple of Jupiter" in *Cosa II.*
- Revetment plaque with looped palmettes (C2:191).
  - assigned to Temple D in *Cosa II*, although one fragment was found in the construction level (IV) on the south side of the triple-cella temple.
- Revetment plaque with looped palmettes (C2:192).
  - assigned to Temple D in *Cosa II*, although one fragment was found in the construction level behind the wall of the triple-cella temple's cistern.
- Revetment plaque with looped palmettes (C2:213).
  - assigned to the triple-cella temple in *Cosa II*, despite the fact that two fragments were found in the construction level (IV) of the triple-cella temple.
- Perforated cornice with serpentine ribbon and circular piercings (C2:159).
  - assigned to the "Temple of Jupiter" in *Cosa II.*
- Perforated cornice with triskelia and figure eights (C2:240).
  - assigned to the 3rd period of the triple-cella temple in *Cosa II*, though one fragment was found in the construction level (IV) of the triple-cella temple, where according to Richardson it had "strayed."
- Sima with strigils above band of mirrored alternating lilies and roses (C2:158).
  - assigned to the "Temple of Jupiter" in *Cosa II.*
- Sima with strigils above a flat fascia (C2:172).
  - assigned to the "Temple of Jupiter" in *Cosa II.*
- Sima with strigils (C2:188).
  - assigned to Temple D in *Cosa II*, although one fragment was found under the floor of the triple-cella temple.
- Eaves tile with a meander pattern (C2:153/208).
  - assigned to the "Temple of Jupiter" and triple-cella temple in *Cosa II.*
- Eaves tile with egg and dart border (C2:185).
  - assigned to Temple D in *Cosa II* "on probability rather than proof"; the only fragment was found in the masonry of the walls of the triple-cella temple's cistern.

As Richardson suggests, some of these may reasonably be assigned to Temple D given the preponderance of fragments discovered in its immediate vicinity. This seems likely for revetment plaque C2:192 and possibly C2:191 (both of the looped palmette type), as well as for the sima with strigils (C2:188). The attribution of the eaves tile with egg and dart (C2:185) to Temple D has no archaeological grounding, as the only fragment was found in the triple-cella temple. Of the other variously assigned types, Richardson's assertation that the perforated cornice with triskelia and figure eights (C2:240) had "strayed" into the construction level of the triple-cella temple but really belongs to its third period of decoration (dated c. 100 BCE) cannot be maintained if this level is to be considered reliable. The same is true of the revetment plaque with looped palmette (C2:213), which Richardson assigns to the triple-cella temple's first phase despite the discovery of two fragments in the construction level.

We are thus left with two types of antefixes (C2:154 and 285), three types of revetment plaques (C2:161, 163, and 213), two types of perforated cornice (C2:159 and 240), two types of simas (C2:158 and 172), and two types of eaves tiles (C2:153/208 and 185). No two types of a single element are of precisely the same dimensions, and in several cases the differences are quite pronounced. For instance, the diameter of one antefix (C2:154) is 40–41 cm, whereas the other's (C2:285) is c. 29 cm. One of the perforated cornices (C2:159) is 31.2 cm high compared with the 53.1 cm of the other (C2:240), while the simas are of slightly different heights – one measuring 45.5 cm (C2:158) and the other 49 cm (C2:172).

The presence of two types of most elements in the construction level of the triple-cella temple suggests that two buildings, or two decorative periods of the same building, preceded it on the summit.[14] This is likely in addition to Temple D, which has already been plausibly assigned one or two revetment plaques and a sima, as well as the other terracottas attributed to its original decoration by Richardson. It was tentatively suggested in *Cosa II* that a small wooden structure may have stood on the early summit,[15] and based on this reexamination such a proposal seems quite likely.

In any case, we can be sure that besides Temple D, at least one more structure pre-dated the triple-cella temple on the summit. Where this temple stood, and to whom it was dedicated, are more problematic. Indeed, its presumed location has wandered about the summit in the more than half-century since *Cosa II* was published. The excavators originally envisioned it in the then-unexcavated area just south of the triple-cella temple, beneath the remains of a small medieval chapel.[16] Subsequent excavations in 1965 revealed that the presumed site was actually the result of 1st century BCE terracing work and located the early temple on the west slope of the summit instead. The living rock was said to have been worked in this area and to have yielded the plan of a c. 17 x 8 m building.[17] These excavations have never been fully published, however, and the cuttings in the rock have been questioned.[18] Taylor has since proposed that the only early temple on the summit is actually represented by the so-called *auguraculum* beneath the triple-cella temple – a c. 7.5 square structure oriented in alignment with the triple-cella temple's altar.[19] This seems the most likely explanation given the evidence currently available, but the gaps in the publication record and the thin stratigraphy of the summit makes it entirely possible that we are missing important indications of early structures on the site.[20]

Because we have no definite foundations, determining the chronology of the proposed building presents obvious challenges. It must have been built sometime between the colony's founding in 273 BCE and the construction of the triple-cella temple c. 175–150 BCE. The date of 240–220 BCE proposed in *Cosa II* is based on a stylistic interpretation of the architectural terracottas, coupled with the stated belief, discussed above in Chapter 2, that a major temple would not have been built during the First or Second Punic Wars.[21] Many scholars have since objected to this assumption and would rather place the temple close to the founding of the colony.[22]

Finally, we have the problem of its dedicatee. It has traditionally been described as the "Temple of Jupiter," but the criteria for this designation are extraordinarily tenuous. The reasoning is as follows: antefixes of Hercules and Minerva are associated with the temple, and because these two deities stand in direct genealogical relationship only to Jupiter, the temple must have been dedicated to him. These same antefixes were carefully removed from the temple c. 170–160 BCE, stored for ten to twenty years, and then placed on the roof of the "Capitolium" to reinforce the sacred connection between the two buildings.[23] This interpretation is problematic on many levels. First, we have no firm evidence that the triple-cella temple was a "Capitolium." Even if there was cult continuity between the two structures, then, it need not relate to the worship of Jupiter. Second, the claim that these same antefixes were reused on a subsequent building is speculative at best. As evidence, Richardson notes that they appear in multiple fabrics and that some examples were found at higher levels and were thus still in use on the roof of later buildings.[24] Multiple fabrics, however, often appear for the same terracotta type at Cosa and likely reflect nothing more than a replacement made from the same mould. Furthermore, practically every type excavated in lower levels on the summit was also found in late or surface contexts. Third, the iconography of antefixes is almost never related to the deity worshiped in the temple, as the widespread presence of maenads, satyrs, and *potnia theron* figures makes clear. The Minerva/Hercules pair is known from a range of earlier temples dedicated to neither deity, nor to Jupiter. The temple's dedicatee must therefore remain an open question.

4.2.2.2 Temples B and D

The attribution of architectural terracottas found in the forum to Temple B is fairly certain, as it appears to have been the only temple in the vicinity. Temple D's reconstruction is more disputable, however, as its proposed decorative elements were found all across the summit, in contexts also associated with the decoration of the triple-cella temple and Summit Temple 1. In general, terracotta types are assigned to Temple D in *Cosa II* if the majority of the fragments were found nearby. It should be emphasized that while sensible, this method is by no means infallible. When old terracottas were reused as fill or construction material, as seems frequently to have been the case on the summit, they could easily have been moved the few meters between Temple D and the triple-cella temple without compromising their sacred status. Indeed, fragments of nearly every type associated with Temple D have also been found in the construction or fill of the triple-cella temple.

The unpublished summit excavations of 1965–1968 yielded hundreds of fragments of architectural terracottas, which may alter the overall percentages of fragments found near Temple D versus near the triple-cella temple.[25] I rely here on the data published in *Cosa II* and on Scott's comments regarding the results of these later excavations.[26] It is certainly possible, however, that the decoration of Temple D will someday need to be rethought in light of these unpublished fragments.

Scott has convincingly highlighted the close connection between Temple D on the summit and Temple B in the forum – both of which he would date to the first quarter of the second century, immediately following the deduction of 197 BCE.[27] Several of the architectural terracottas attributed to these temples are remarkably similar to one another, as well as to those from nearby Talamonaccio.[28] Each of these roofs included revetment plaques with looped palmettes, shell antefixes with Bacchic themes (heads of Silens, Satyrs, or Maenads), and perforated cornices with circular piercings. While the roofs were not identical (Temple B, for instance, also had revetment plaques with crossed ribbons whereas Temple D had plaques with addorsed palmettes), they would have created a very similar overall effect.

The decorative programs of these temples are further linked by their pedimental groups, each of which show a lively mythological scene apparently rooted in the repertoire of Volterran urns.[29] Talamonaccio's is the most secure in terms of subject, with its famous depiction of the Seven Against Thebes (Figure 43). Emeline Richardson has proposed that the pediment of Temple B at Cosa showed the Recognition of Paris – a plausible but currently

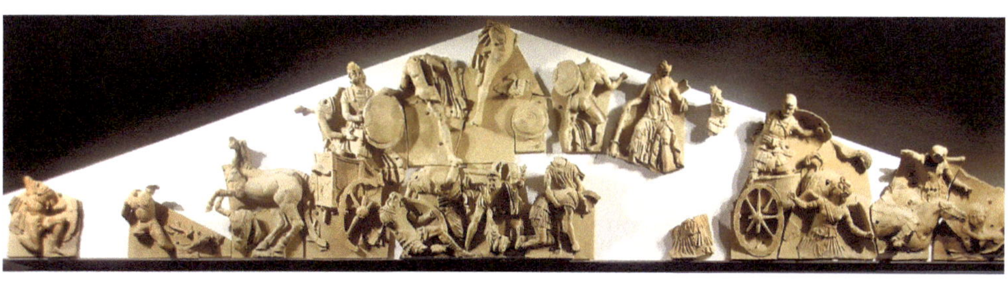

43. Pediment from the Talamonaccio temple showing scenes of the Seven Against Thebes. Florence: Museo Archeologico Nazionale di Firenze. Image: creative commons, https://en.m.wikipedia.org/wiki/File:Luni_pediment_group.jpg. Published with permission of the Museo Archeologico Nazionale di Firenze (Direzione regionale Musei della Toscana).

unprovable identification.[30] Ann Scott's analysis of as-yet unpublished finds from the summit has led her to suggest that Temple D's pediment may have shown the Sacrifice of Iphigenia, but this study has not yet appeared and therefore cannot fairly be evaluated.[31] Even if various interpretations might be offered regarding the precise subject and format of each pediment, it is at least clear from the surviving fragments that all three were of the "narrative mythological" type, characterized by animated figures in dramatic situations. This separates them importantly from the staid assembly or ceremony scene featured on the triple-cella temple's pediment.

If Taylor's analysis is correct, Temples B and D are also linked by the fact that they retained the bulk of their terracotta decoration for about two centuries and never underwent a major renovation. The case in strongest for Temple B, where insufficient terracottas have been found to reconstruct a second full decorative phase.[32] The fragments recovered from the vicinity of Temple D, on the other hand, seem to me to suggest not a full redecoration but rather a greater frequency of piecemeal repairs. Taylor accounts for the different subtypes of looped palmette plaques and perforated cornices by arguing that they decorated opposite pediments of the same temple.[33] Still, I would emphasize that such a situation more likely reflects repairs rather than original design. Revetment plaques would probably have been replaced as a group, as their sizes must match. It is also likely that perforated cornices would have been replaced along with their corresponding simas, as the two must fit together perfectly and the simas must be the same size. The presence of two subtypes of each of these could reflect a repair to one end of the building, perhaps associated with the elongating of Temple D's podium.[34]

Further support for this interpretation comes from the fact that the "original" set of Temple D's terracotta decoration, as outlined by Richardson, appears in three distinct fabrics.[35] Richardson suggests that these represent three workshops operating in tandem, but in the case of Temple D it seems much more likely that the different fabrics simply reflect subsequent repairs made using the same molds. Retaining molds in this way and making new elements as needed would in fact be the only plausible way to avoid redoing the entire roof every time a single element or area was damaged. Thus, the basic design of a roof could be retained for centuries, as indeed seems to be the case with Temples B and D.

4.2.2.3 The Triple-Cella Temple

The triple-cella temple on Cosa's summit was identified by its excavators as a Capitolium and ascribed to the worship of Jupiter, Juno, and Minerva. This designation is central to Brown's reconstruction of Cosa as a mini-Rome and has figured heavily in broader historical discussions of "Romanization." Most scholars have now abandoned the term, citing any lack of evidence for the structure's connection with the Capitoline triad.[36]

In fact, we have no firm evidence regarding the dedicatee(s) of this temple. The Minerva and Hercules antefixes can hardly be invoked in this context, as antefixes generally do not reflect the identity of the deity worshiped. It is enough to point out that antefixes very similar to these have been found at Talamonaccio, Tarquinia, and probably Punta della Vipera, and that even according to Richardson's reconstruction the subsequent phases of the triple-cella temple featured antefixes with the heads of Bacchus and Ariadne, as well as the *potnia theron*.

The unpublished summit excavations of the 1960s yielded fragments of a Hercules figure and of Ganymede with the eagle that have been variously described as acroterial statues,[37] columen plaques or beam-end sculptures,[38] and as perhaps "mounted against the open cresting."[39] These are usually attributed to the triple-cella temple but occasionally also linked to the so-called "Temple of Jupiter."[40] Because no details regarding their measurements, fabric, or excavation context have been published, little can be said definitively regarding their association with a particular structure.[41] The presence of Ganymede might suggest a connection to Jupiter but cannot be invoked as evidence that the full Capitoline triad was worshiped in Cosa's triple-cella temple.[42]

The temple's pedimental scene does, however, appear to have been an assembly or ceremony and might thus offer clues regarding the cult's dedicatee. Fragments of five life-size figures must have stood in the center of the pediment. Unfortunately, these are insufficiently preserved to enable a reconstruction or even an identification of the figures. They include a seated male, a standing nude male, two warriors in armor, and a female wearing a sandal. The presence of only one central female figure does, however, argue strongly against the hypothesis that the Capitoline triad was depicted in the center of the pediment.

Given the current state of evidence, the nature of the cult practiced in Cosa's triple-cella temple cannot be determined. Still, there is much to be gained from an examination of its decorative history. The following architectural terracottas have been assigned to this temple:

- Shell antefixes with the heads of Minerva and Hercules (C2:208, C2:232).
    - o A questionable attribution, described as a "remake" of the "Temple of Jupiter" type in different fabrics.
- Shell antefix of unknown design, possibly with the head of Hercules (C2:233).
- Antefixes with the heads of Minerva, Hercules, Bacchus (?), and Ariadne (?) (C2:252).
- *Potnia theron* antefix (C2:270).
- Revetment plaque with looped palmettes (C2:213).
- Revetment plaque with looped palmettes (C2:235).
- Revetment plaque with looped palmettes (C2:236).
- Revetment plaque with looped palmettes (C2:242).

- Revetment plaque with looped palmettes (C2:257).
- Revetment plaque with looped palmettes (C2:275).
- Revetment plaque with looped palmettes and heads (silen and maenad) (C2:215).
- Revetment plaque with looped palmettes and heads (young satyr and maenad) (C2:243).
- Revetment plaque with looped palmettes and heads (Silenus and Bacchus?) (C2:259).
- Revetment plaque with looped palmettes and gorgoneia (C2:276).
- Revetment plaque with addorsed palmettes (C2:217).
- Revetment plaque with addorsed palmettes (C2:237).
- Revetment plaque with addorsed palmettes (C2:245).
- Revetment plaque with addorsed palmettes (C2:260).
- Revetment plaque with addorsed palmettes (C2:278).
- Perforated cornice with triskelia and figure-eights (C2:210).
- Perforated cornice with triskelia and figure-eights (C2:234).
- Perforated cornice with triskelia and figure-eights (C2:240).
- Perforated cornice with triskelia and figure-eights (C2:255).
- Perforated cornice with triskelia and figure-eights (C2:272).
- Sima with strigils (C2:209 and C2:240).
- Sima with strigils (C2:271).
- Sima with palmettes (C2:224).
- Sima with strigils, paterae, and rosettes (C2:254).
- Perforated palmette acroterion (C2:256).
- Eaves tile with egg and dark border (C2:185).
    - Assigned to Temple D in *Cosa II*, though the only fragment was found in the masonry of the triple-cella temple's cistern.
- Door-frame plaque with palmettes and lilies (C2:220).
- Door-frame plaque with palmettes and lilies (C2:238).
- Door-frame plaque with palmettes and lilies (C2:247).
- Door-frame plaque with palmettes and lilies (C2:262).
- Ovolo molding with lesbian leaf (C2:212).
- Campana relief: youthful Bacchus with a satyr carrying an amphora (C2:297).
- Campana relief: Silenus supported by cupid with a dancing maenad (C2:297).
- Campana relief: bearded Bacchus with a dancing maenad (C2:298).
- Campana relief: Apollo citharoedus with Nike (C2:298).
- Campana relief: Perseus and Minerva (C2:298).
- Campana relief: Apollo and Hercules struggling over the tripod (C2:299).

Assigning decorative periods and phases to these fragments is complicated not only by their strong similarities in style and design but also by the generally consistent dimensions of the different types. The six subtypes of revetment plaque with looped palmettes, for instance, range in height only from 58.2 to 59.8 cm, and in width from 50.2 to 54 cm. While others vary more noticeably in size, the differences are never great enough to suggest a major renovation or altering of the building's overall aesthetic. Furthermore, in these cases there are generally only two principal groups of subtypes, each of nearly identical size. The perforated cornices with triskelia and figure-eights, for instance, display an *overall* range in height from 45.5 to 53.1 cm and in width from 47.6 to 55.5 cm. Two subtypes of this cornice (C2:210 and C2:272) match more closely, measuring between 45.5 and 46 cm in height and between 47.6 and 50 cm in width. A second group (C2:240 and C2:255) hovers between 51 and 53.1 cm in height and 52.5 and 55.5 cm in width. The revetment plaques with looped palmettes and heads have an overall height range between 56.4 and 59.8 cm and an overall width range from 47.9 to 59.5 cm, but similarities between subtypes suggest greater consistency. C2:215 and C2:276, for instance, are between 56.4 and 56.5 cm in height and between 54 and 54.4 cm in width. Similarly, the overall range for the revetment plaques with addorsed palmettes is 72.5–76.2 cm in height and 43.5–54 cm in width, while C2:245 and C2:260 range only from 75–76.2 cm in height and 43.5–45.6 cm in width. Perhaps the greatest discrepancy is in the size of the strigilated simas, which range from 47.4 to 61.9 cm in width. However, their heights vary only from 52 to 52.8 cm, a difference that is virtually negligible. Because they would have formed a continuous row of strigils when placed side by side, the difference in width would not actually have been visible from the ground, meaning that this alteration would have had no effect on the appearance of the roof.

It is possible that the subtypes of very similar measurements could in some cases have been used as single repairs, but the large fragment quantity of most of these subtypes suggests more sweeping replacements. Importantly, the full substitution of any series appears to have followed the general dimensions and design of the previous examples. The lack of good chronological markers and the strong similarity in design makes it difficult to prove the order in which these terracottas were introduced. We can, however, at least note the strong tendency toward conservatism and the general desire to retain the original appearance of the roof over the course of several hundred years. In this respect, the decoration of the triple-cella temple closely mirrors the traditional attitude already observed regarding Temples B and D. The major difference here relates to the style of the pediment, and it may be the case that the choice of a ceremony/assembly of gods over a mythological narrative served to highlight the triple-cella temple's status as the town's principal cult seat.

4.2.2.4 Temple E

Excavations in the 1990s revealed the foundations of a structure on the Eastern Height convincingly identified as a temple ("Temple E").[43] The extant foundations are of polygonal masonry, and measure 6.25 x 11.25 m. This makes the structure smaller than other temples at Cosa, though the style of the masonry is quite similar to that of Temple D. It is dated by its architectural terracottas and by an amphora fragment in its podium fill to the early 2nd century BCE.

Only thirteen fragments of architectural terracottas were found in association with Temple E, the area having been heavily disturbed as a result of medieval building activities and the effects of earthquakes.[44] Though sparse, these terracotta fragments do represent a full decorative program with the exception of acroteria, consisting of a satyr or maenad shell antefix, a strigilated sima, a perforated cornice with triskelia and figure-eights, a perforated cornice with serpentine ribbon and circular piercings, and a revetment plaque with crossed ribbons. Nearly all of these examples are a perfect match for terracottas used on the various temples of the summit or on Temple B in the forum. Temple E, however, does not replicate the decoration of any single Cosan temple but employs a selection of types from several of them.[45]

4.2.2.5 Port Temple

Perched on a rocky hill above Cosa's fishing lagoon, the Port Temple represents one of the least-understood structures associated with the ancient town. By the time Brown's team could study the site in 1950, most of the temple and its surroundings had been demolished due to quarrying activities. These works were set to continue, and the archaeologists therefore performed a one-day excavation to salvage as much information on the temple as possible.[46] Their efforts revealed a square cella of 8.88 m on each side, as well as scant remains of the east part of the pronaos and one anta.[47] The temple apparently lacked a podium and sat directly on bedrock.[48] Two building phases were visible, the first of which has generally been dated to c. 175 BCE, with a rebuilding in the first quarter of the first century BCE.[49] Unfortunately, no columns or other architectural features survived. Brown's reconstruction of four columns along the temple's façade is based on the plan of Temple D, which he considered closely related in plan and design to the Port Temple.[50] Given the scanty remains of the latter, however, any reconstruction of its plan or comparison with other temples must be considered highly speculative. Nor can the remains be reexamined, as modern quarrying activities have by now utterly obliterated the small temple. When McCann's team returned to examine the site in 1968, they could find no trace of the structure.[51]

Brown's team did, however, uncover more than 200 fragments of architectural terracotta decoration, and McCann's subsequent survey added a few more examples to this number. The vast majority of these fragments belong to revetment plaques with looped palmettes of a type attributed to Temple D on the summit.[52] Besides these, two fragments of a strigilated sima, one fragment of a revetment plaque with crossed ribbons, one fragment of a perforated cornice, one fragment of an antefix with a satyr's head (no shell), and two unidentified fragments probably from antefixes were also uncovered.[53] These belong to types associated in *Cosa II* with Temple D, Temple B, the triple-cella temple, and the so-called "Temple of Jupiter." As elsewhere at Cosa, it seems that the Port Temple's terracottas were not designed specifically or exclusively for it. Rather, at any given moment multiple temples in the town would have featured identical revetment plaques, antefixes, simas, or cornices, though none seem to have had full matching programs.

In addition to these elements, three fragments of pedimental sculpture can also be associated with the Port Temple – one excavated in 1950 and two found in McCann's survey. The former depicts the turned head of a helmeted warrior at approximately half-life-size.[54] Of the latter fragments, one cannot be identified (McCann tentatively suggests that it may resemble a feather or scale pattern), while the other preserves a small section of a draped female figure's torso at about one-quarter life-size.[55] Given her reduced size, she would likely have stood toward the corner of the pediment, while the warrior would have occupied a more central position.

McCann has compared these two figures to fragments from the Talamonaccio temple and has even suggested that Cosa's Port Temple similarly featured a pediment depicting the Seven Against Thebes, albeit executed by a different artist.[56] While not impossible, this hypothesis is quite difficult to support, as a helmeted warrior and draped female figure could belong to virtually any mythic scene. In the absence of additional fragments, we cannot identify the pediment's subject. The movement and twisting motion of the preserved figures does, however, place us firmly in the realm of the narrative/mythic pediment type, as opposed to the more staid ceremony/assembly type seen on Cosa's triple-cella temple. In this sense, it is broadly aligned with the kinds of pediments known from Cosa's Temples B and D, as well as Talamonaccio and other sites across Italy. As noted above, many of these seem to be closely connected to Volterran urns in terms of style and iconography.

Brown had suggested Portunus or Palaemon as the temple's dedicatee, while McCann argues for Neptune instead.[57] The architectural terracottas offer no help in this regard, as the pediment scene is too fragmentary to be reconstructed and the other examples belong to types associated with a range of different temples. No conclusive evidence currently exists for the identification of the deity or deities worshiped at the Port Temple, and the question must for now remain open.

4.2.3 Cosa's Local Terracottas

As the preceding overview has made clear, many architectural terracotta types appear on multiple buildings at Cosa. This implies a fair degree of visual continuity within the colony, at least in the realm of religious architecture. The strong similarities between Cosa's sacred buildings would have created the impression of a clear Cosan aesthetic. How this related to the religious landscape of the surrounding region is the topic to which we now turn.

The large corpus of architectural terracottas from Cosa suggests a complex network of interaction on several geographic scales. Every element of the "standard temple kit" has been found at the site – some in an impressive number of subtypes – indicating that Cosan temple decoration generally followed the broader trends of central Italy. A few terracottas reveal striking similarities with examples from sites south of Rome. One Cosan subtype of a perforated cornice with swastikas, for instance, closely matches a cornice from Ardea, while a version of the popular revetment plaque with addorsed palmettes from Cosa is so similar to an example from Lanuvium that Richardson believed they may have come from the same workshop.[58] These links are the exception, however, and may reflect the travels of itinerant artisans or one-off purchases from large workshops. In most cases, the style and details of even the "standard" types at Cosa closely mirror those of preexisting Etruscan sanctuaries in the region.[59] Shared workshops are likely in these instances. Other "standard" elements follow the type's general template but find no precise parallel at other sites. These may reflect a Cosan iteration of a widespread type.

The reliance on local networks is clearest when we turn to the more unusual elements of Cosa's temple decoration. A revetment plaque with crossed ribbons and flowers survives in two variations at Cosa, one from the summit (34 fragments) and the other associated primarily with Temple B in the forum (139 fragments – two fragments likely belonging to this subtype were found in the excavations of Temple E, and another comes from the Port Temple).[60] Both feature a thin cavetto decorated with stylized hanging flowers, below which is a main register consisting of large ribbons crossed in an x, from which a pair of flowers emerge symmetrically – one pointing up and the other down (Figure 44). Between the crossed ribbons is a large rosette. A row of hanging palmettes and lilies with looping stems occupy the register below, and the bottom of the plaque is finished with dentils ending in a crenellation.

The crossed-ribbon design finds parallels in other architectural terracottas from the region, especially in Etruscan zones, and appears on the decorative face of several urns from Volterra. In one example now in the Museo Guarnacci, a disembodied head wearing a Phrygian cap floats between the ribbons, in the space occupied by the large rosette on our Cosan examples (Figure 45).[61] Massa-Pairault has highlighted the similarities between these urns and the related terracotta plaques.[62]

Crossed ribbons also appear on architectural terracottas from Volterra, as well as at Bolsena, Sassi Caduti (Civita Castellana), Bettona, and Sovana just about 40 km from Cosa.[63] By far the closest parallels for the Cosa plaques come from the Ara della Regina at Tarquinia and the Punta della Vipera sanctuary at Santa Marinella, about 60 km southeast of Cosa on the Tyrrhenian coast.[64]

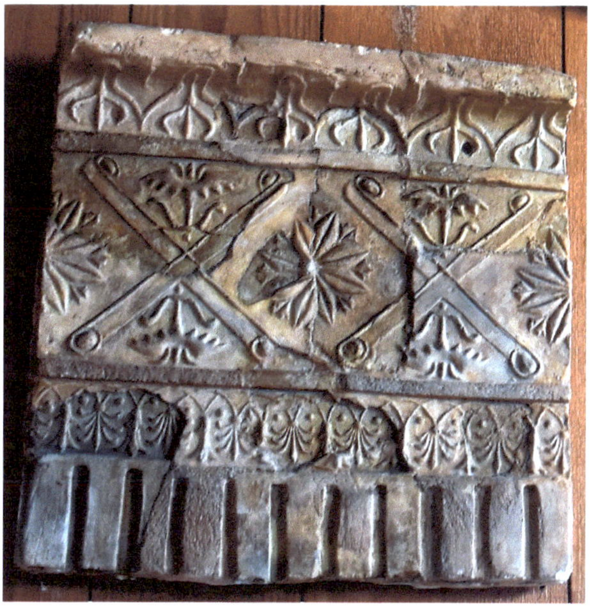

44. Revetment plaque with crossed ribbons and flowers, from Cosa.
Author's photo, courtesy of the Direzione Generale dei Musei della Toscana, Firenze.

The latter lacks a dentil register but otherwise differs in only minor details from the Cosan examples. Also from Punta della Vipera comes a very small version of this plaque, measuring only 17 x 12.5 cm., which may have decorated either a door or panels of the columen or mutuli.[65] Finally, a fragment from Talamonaccio attests to the use of a very similar type on its temple.[66] Its poor preservation excludes a confident reconstruction of all the plaque's registers, but the crossed ribbons are very similar to those of the examples cited above, though the Talamonaccio plaque would have been bigger than these others.

The most similar plaques are thus concentrated along the Etruscan coast between Santa Marinella and Talamone. Four sites in this zone have yielded closely related examples, suggesting a certain regional popularity for the type and perhaps even the movement of traveling artisans working within this coastal area. At the same time, the broader iconographic parallels, particularly at Volterra, suggest a more widespread use of the basic scheme especially in Etruscan areas during the 3rd and 2nd centuries BCE (Figure 46).

Other revetment plaques from Cosa suggest a similarly local point of reference. A plaque with standing and hanging palmettes and lilies may be compared to six sets of similar fragments from Tarquinia, one of which appears to be identical to the Cosan version.[67] Another revetment plaque is decorated with winged heads amid s-scrolls, and large hanging palmettes (Figure 47). Identical plaques, apparently from the same mold, have been found at the shrine in the Ponte Rotto necropolis at Vulci.[68]

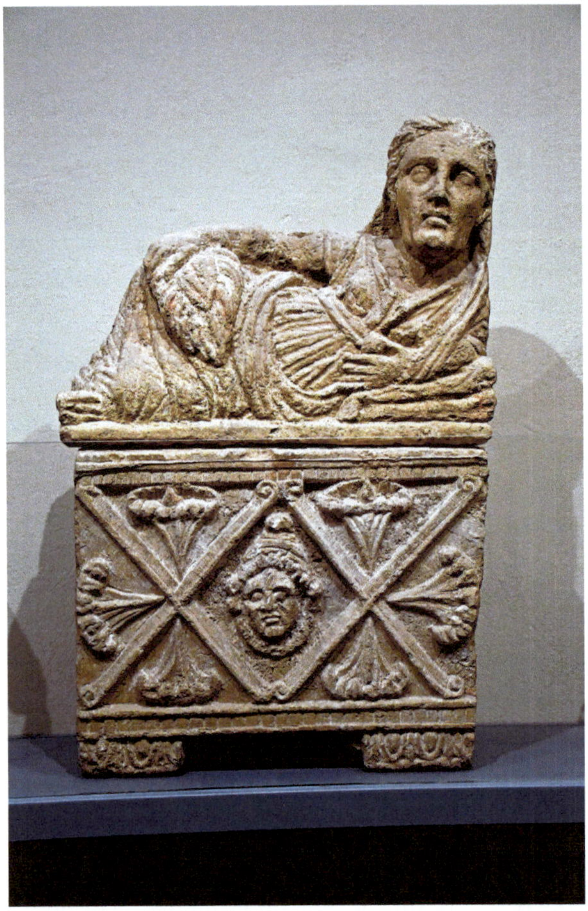

45. Funerary urn from Volterra with a design of crossed ribbons. Volterra: Museo Etrusco Guarnacci di Volterra, no. 41.
Courtesy of the Museo Etrusco Guarnacci di Volterra.

A pair of shell antefixes showing Minerva and probably Hercules is attested in five different fabrics at Cosa, making it one of the most widespread and reused types at the site (Figure 48).[69] The Minerva wears earrings and a necklace of pointed pendants and is identified by the tall Corinthian helmet resting on her head. The head of her male counterpart is instead crowned by a lion's mask, which is styled to look almost like a helmet itself. No definite fragment of the face is preserved, meaning that we cannot say with absolute certainty that he does indeed represent Hercules rather than a satyr masquerading as the hero – a type known from other examples.[70] Still, it would be odd to pair a satyr with Minerva except in a specific mythological scene, and the identification of the figure as Hercules seems reasonable.

We may immediately dismiss Richardson's claim that Hercules antefixes are unknown in Etruria and are popular only in Campania.[71] Important comparanda come from Etruscan sites close to Cosa, and the hero in general is quite

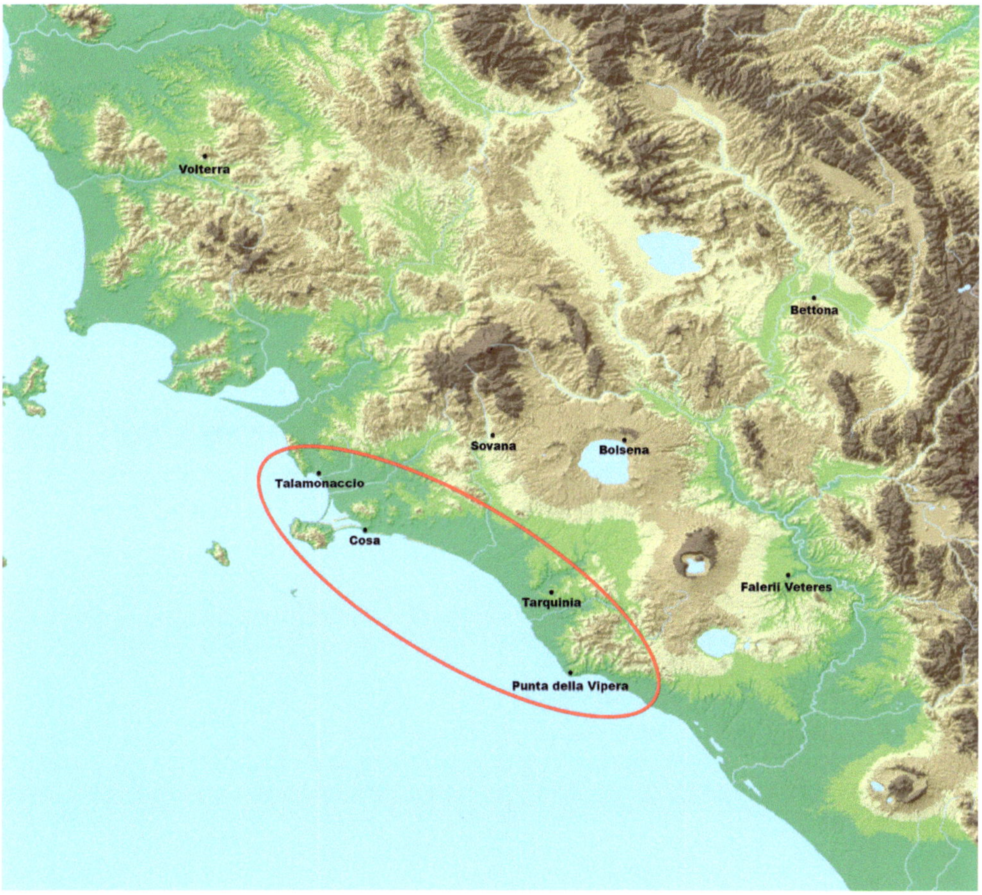

46. Map showing the distribution of sites with revetment plaques with crossed ribbons and flowers. The most closely related types come from the sites circled in red. AWMC: à-la-carte map, modified by Kelley Vernon.

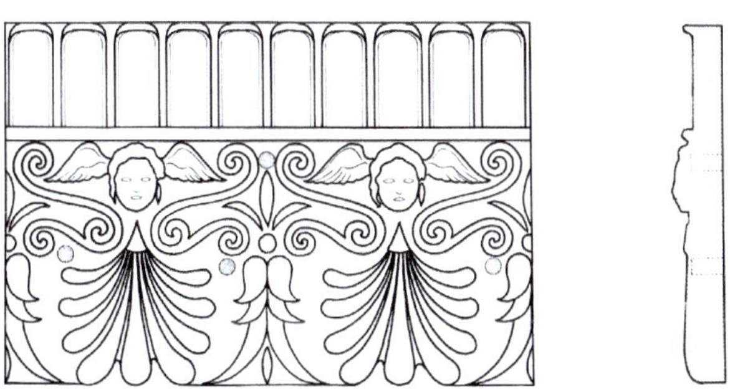

47. Revetment plaque with winged heads, s-scrolls, and hanging palmettes, from Cosa, type C2:286.
Courtesy of the American Academy in Rome, Cosa Archaeological Collection.

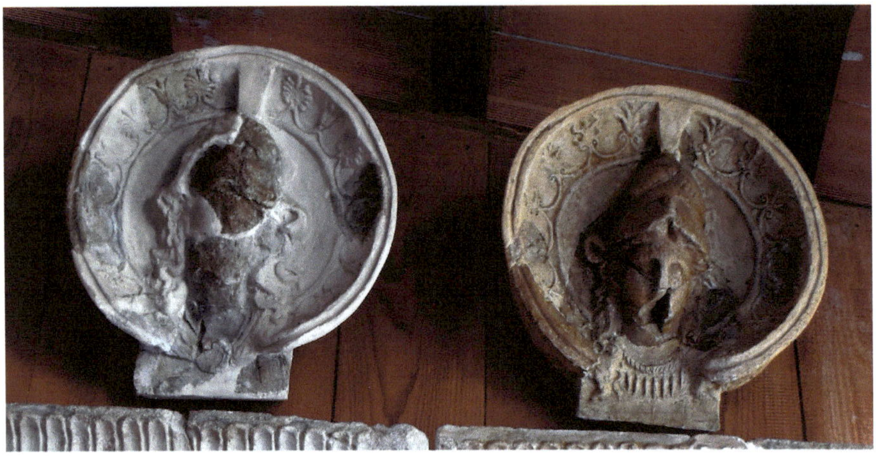

48. Shell antefixes with the heads of Hercules and Minerva, from Cosa.
Author's photo, courtesy of the Direzione Generale dei Musei della Toscana, Firenze.

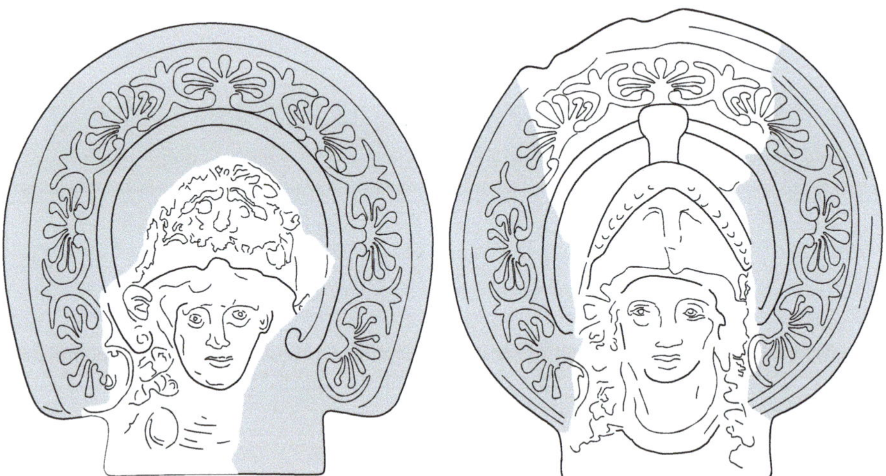

49 (A AND B). Shell antefixes with the heads of Hercules and Minerva, from Talamonaccio. Drawings by Dallin Evans, after von Vacano and von Freytag Löringhoff 1982 figs. 62 and 63.

popular in the region.[72] In fact, the same Minerva/Hercules pair appears on remarkably similar shell antefixes at nearby Talamonaccio (Figure 49a and b).[73] The Hercules here is beardless and sports the same helmet-like lion's head. The Talamonaccio Minerva is also closely related to the Cosan example, though her necklace lacks any pendants and is more reminiscent of a torque. Both are slightly smaller than their Cosan counterparts but are so close in design that they may even derive from the same workshop.[74] Fragments of an almost identical shell were also found at Punta della Vipera.[75] Although unfortunately no head was preserved, the similarity in the shell suggests that the same antefix pair may have been employed here. A Minerva antefix identical to the Cosan

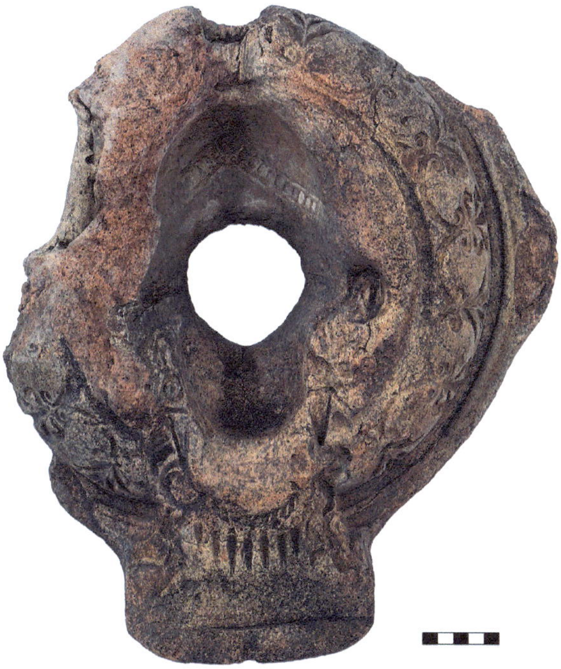

50. Mold for the Minerva head antefix type found at Musarna (Viterbo).
Photo courtesy of Vincent Jolivet.

example is said to derive from Tarquinia,[76] and a mold excavated at Musarna (Viterbo) near the Temple of Hercules appears to be an identical match for the Cosan Minerva (Figure 50).[77] Direct evidence for mold links is extremely rare in this period. In the absence of terracottas manufactured from this mold at Musarna, we are left to wonder whether Minerva antefixes were actually employed at the site or whether this single mold was damaged and discarded in transit. Musarna is almost 90 km due east from Cosa. Given the preponderance of Minerva/Hercules shell antefixes along the coast, it seems possible that the Musarna mold reflects the travels of artisans moving inland with some of their supplies.

Amongst the Cosan terracottas dated securely before 150 BCE (fragments were found under the floor of the triple-cella temple and in the fill under the floor of Temple D) is a sima with strigils in the upper register and a lower band adorned with alternating lilies and roses in mirror image, which emerge from a central horizontal roll (Figure 51).[78] The basic design of lilies repeated or alternating with roses is fairly frequent on Italic (especially Etruscan) terracottas, with comparable examples known from Talamonaccio, Orvieto, Arezzo, Perugia, Selvasecca, Lake Trasimeno, Falerii Veteres (Civita Castellana), and Ardea.[79] That the design relates to Etruscan artisans is further supported by the discovery of simas with alternating lilies and roses at a

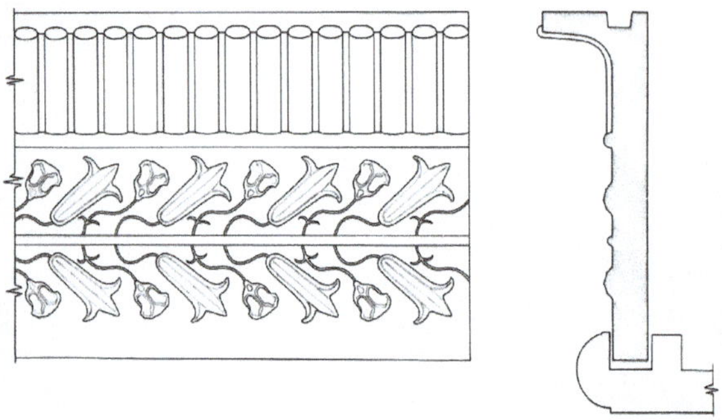

51. Sima with strigils above a register of lilies and roses, from Cosa, Type C2:158. Courtesy of the American Academy in Rome, Cosa Archaeological Collection.

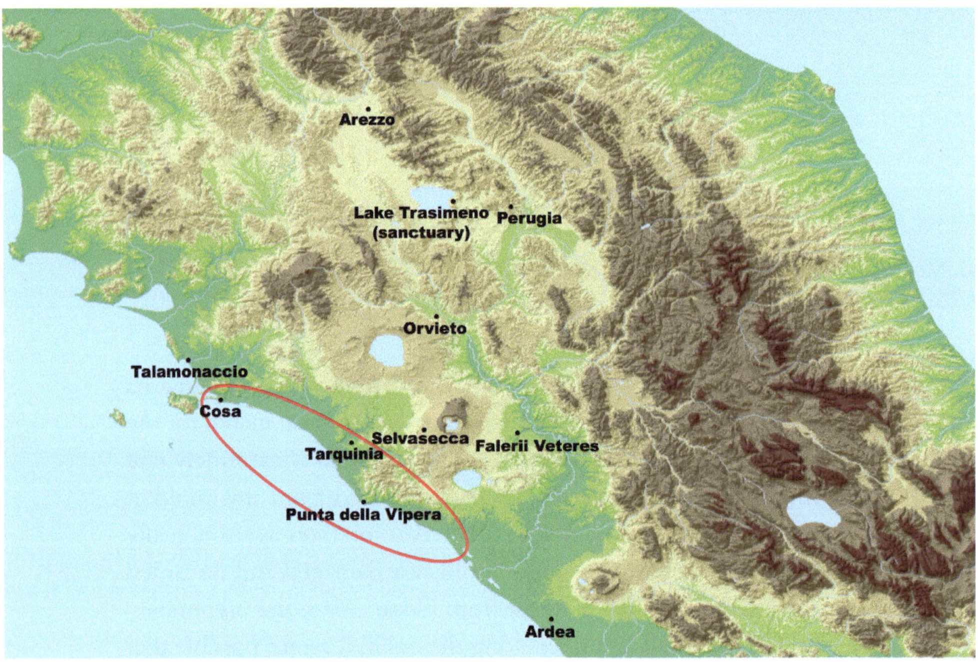

52. Map showing the distribution of terracottas with a design similar to that of C2:158, with the most closely related examples circled in red. AWMC: à-la-carte map, modified by Kelley Vernon.

sanctuary at Lake Trasimeno, dated to the late 3rd century BCE.[80] These simas have been linked to tile fragments whose borders are inscribed with Etruscan letters, apparently used an as aid for placing the pieces in the correct position on the roof.

Still, the closest parallels for the Cosa sima's precise design and for its placement below a row of strigils come from Tarquinia and Punta della Vipera (Figure 52).[81] Both sites have yielded more than one subtype of the

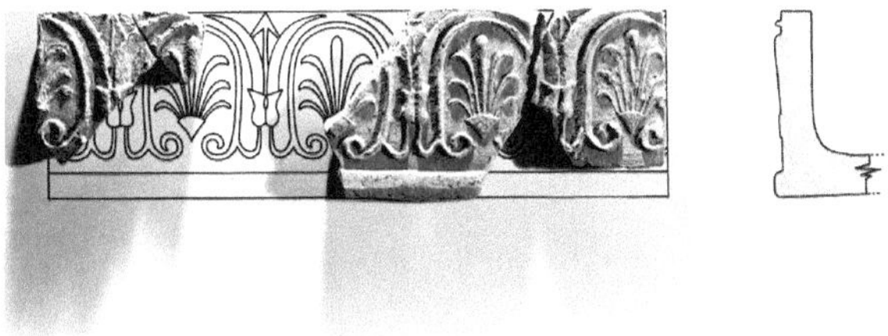

53. Small sima with palmettes, from Cosa, Type C2:224.
Courtesy of the American Academy in Rome, Cosa Archaeological Collection.

same design, suggesting that the original sima was copied for use on a subsequent building or phase.

A small sima, only 14 cm in height, is attested by twenty-six fragments from Cosa's summit (Figure 53).[82] It has no groove for the insertion of a perforated cornice above and is the only type to lack a register of strigils entirely. Richardson assigned it to the compluvium of the triple-cella temple due to its reduced size, although he notes that its association with that structure "is not entirely beyond question, since most of the large fragments come from the vicinity of Temple D."[83] No fragment was found in a stratigraphic context that could provide any chronological indicators, and it remains one of the more enigmatic terracotta types from Cosa.

The very existence of a compluvium on the triple-cella temple has been sharply questioned, and it is difficult now to accept Brown's reconstruction of the roof.[84] This sima may have adorned a smaller building on the summit, perhaps Temple D, the precursor to the triple-cella temple, or another unknown structure.

Its design consists of a row of palmettes inscribed in ribbons ending in a simple curl toward the base. Stylized flowers stand vertically between the palmettes, their central petal pointed upwards like an arrow. A nearly identical example, slightly larger than the Cosa sima, has been found at Tarquinia.[85]

Three subtypes of perforated cornices from Cosa feature a row of palmettes at the top, with a large central register occupied by circular piercings connected by a continuous serpentine ribbon (Figure 54).[86] This type was used on the summit as well as on Temple B in the forum: identical examples of one subtype were found in both areas, and one set from the forum appears to be a second generation version of a type from the summit.[87] These subtypes find their closest comparanda at Tarquinia and Talamonaccio. In fact, one subtype (C2:189) is apparently identical to cornices from both these sites, again attesting to the strong relationship between Cosa's terracottas and those of its Etruscan neighbors.[88]

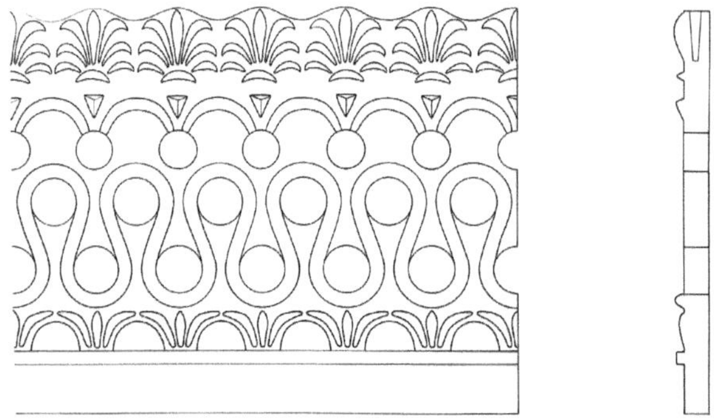

54. Perforated cornice with serpentine ribbon and circular piercings, from Cosa, Type C2:189. Courtesy of the American Academy in Rome, Cosa Archaeological Collection.

4.2.4 Cosa and Local Networks

Three sites have stood out in the preceding discussion as consistently offering close comparanda for Cosa's non-"standard" architectural terracottas: Talamonaccio, Punta della Vipera, and Tarquinia. It will be worth considering the history and terracotta traditions of each of these, in order to better understand the local networks in which Cosa participated and the ways in which viewers might have perceived the town's temple terracottas.

The links between architectural terracottas at Cosa and Talamone have long been recognized, and the two towns lie only 20 km apart above neighboring ports. The Talamonaccio hill was occupied already in the late Bronze Age and is amongst the most strategic locations on the coast, close to natural ports and with sweeping views of the plains and sea. In fact, the very siting of Cosa mimics Talamonaccio in this regard.

The ancient town of Telamon likely included an earlier temple on the lower hill of Bengodi, where a fragmentary antefix and sima with a painted meander pattern dating to the late 6th or 5th century BCE were found.[89] Little is known of this area, however, and archaeological documentation regarding ancient Telamon is, unfortunately, generally lacking.[90]

Pot sherds dating to the 13th/12th centuries BCE were found on the Talamonaccio hill in the area of the later temple, attesting to the site's early use.[91] Little evidence is preserved between the early 6th and 4th century, but the Bengodi terracottas suggest that this does not represent a true gap in occupation. High quality pottery is particularly abundant from the second half of the 4th century BCE, when the town appears to have flourished anew. A group of architectural terracottas from the site has also been dated to this period and may represent the first iteration of the Talamonaccio temple.[92]

In the absence of stratigraphic indicators, the precise phasing of the temple remains problematic. Based on stylistic and historical criteria, von Vacano and von Freytag Löringhoff date the installation of the famous pediment to c. 150

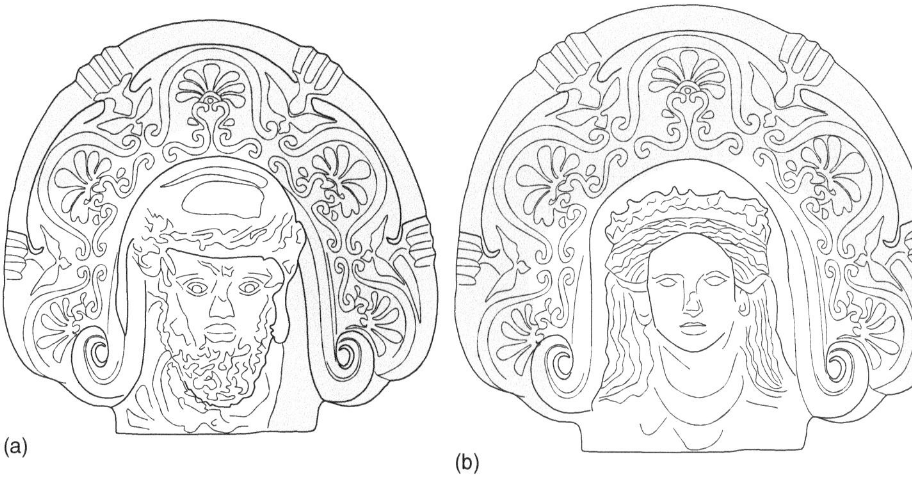

55 (A AND B). Shell antefixes with heads of a silen and maenad from Talamonaccio. Drawings by Dallin Evans, after von Vacano and von Freytag Loringhoff 1982 figs. 46 and 47.

BCE (Figure 43).[93] It is worth stressing that this date cannot be proved based on the evidence currently available and that it relies in large part on the problematic Cosa chronology. The temple seems to have been destroyed by fire around 100 BCE and was not rebuilt.[94]

Many of the architectural terracottas from the Talamonaccio temple are closely related to examples found at Cosa (e.g., Figures 48–49), and some even appear to derive from the same workshop. There are also, however, strong links between many of Talamonaccio's terracottas and earlier examples from Orvieto, and it is possible that the town served as something of an intermediary in the spread of certain motifs to Cosa.[95] The shell antefixes from Talamonaccio with busts of a silen and maenad are dated to the second half of the 4th century BCE (Figure 55a and b) and thought to derive from similar examples of the late 5th century BCE from Orvieto (Figures 56–57).[96] The same basic motif is then picked up in modified form at Cosa a century or two after its appearance at Talamonaccio, by which time it must have seemed decidedly old-fashioned.[97] As these antefixes and other terracotta elements show, the decoration of the Talamonaccio temple was firmly rooted in the traditions of Etruscan religious architecture in each of its phases. The strong visual similarities between it and Cosa would have served to emphatically insert the new colony into the sacred landscape of its Etruscan neighbors.

Another site with which Cosa's terracottas are closely linked is Punta della Vipera, about 60 km south of Cosa along the Tyrrhenian coast. The foundation of the temple is typically dated to the third quarter of the 6th century BCE on the evidence of antefixes and Greek vases found in the vicinity. The sanctuary seems initially to have stood in open countryside, unattached to a known habitation site before the Roman period.[98] It was, however, less than

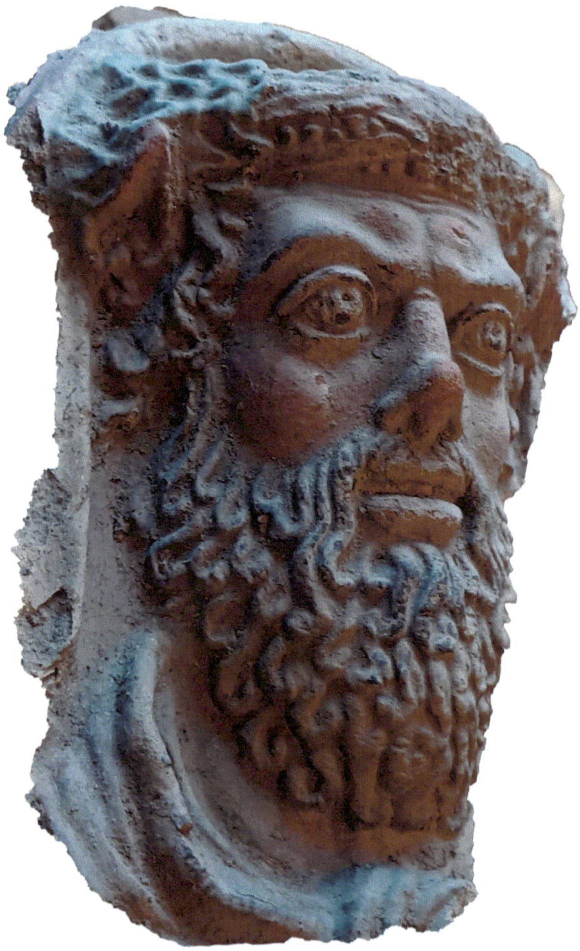

56. Fragment of a shell antefix (most of shell missing) with head of a silen, from Orvieto's Belvedere Temple. Orvieto: Museo Claudio Faina di Orvieto.
Courtesy of the Museo Claudio Faina di Orvieto.

15 km northwest of the major coastal sanctuary at Pyrgi, and the terracottas from these sites are strongly linked. In its proposed mid-4th century phase, for instance, Punta della Vipera's strigil-shell antefixes and revetment plaques with hanging palmettes and flowers come from precisely the same molds as those at Pyrgi.[99] Numerous additional terracottas are nearly identical in certain features of their decoration, even if they derive from separate molds.[100]

The terrain around the Punta della Vipera sanctuary had been heavily disturbed prior to the initiation of excavations, and no stratigraphic indicators are preserved following the temple's proposed 4th-century phase.[101] Torelli and Stopponi's chronology is thus based primarily on style (including comparisons with Cosa) together with interpretations of historical events.[102] The problems with the former method have already been amply discussed. The

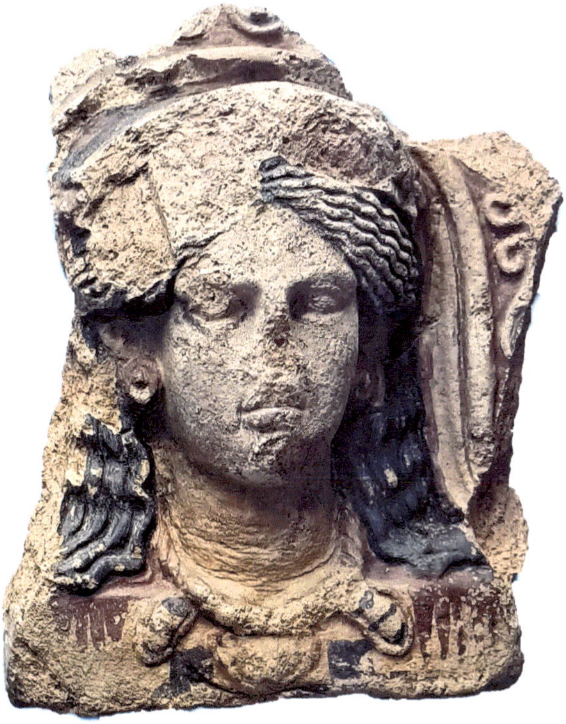

57. Fragment of a shell antefix (most of shell missing) with head of a maenad, from the area sacra di Cannicella, Orvieto. Orvieto: Museo Claudio Faina di Orvieto.
Courtesy of the Museo Claudio Faina di Orvieto.

historical considerations urged by Torelli are unfortunately equally unconvincing in this case. He relates the redecoration of the temple to the founding of the Roman maritime colony of Castrum Novum. The similarities between its and Cosa's terracottas would thus reflect the Roman identity of both. The date of Castrum Novum's foundation, however, is debated.[103] Furthermore, the style of the terracottas is in both cases firmly rooted in the architectural traditions of the local Etruscan region and reflects an uninterrupted development. In the absence of clear evidence to the contrary, there is no reason to assume that something common to local Etruscan architecture in the 4th century suddenly becomes "Roman" in the 3rd century, particularly when it appears on a sanctuary used without interruption from the Archaic period onward.

The final site with which Cosa's terracottas share an intimate and persistent connection is Tarquinia. Here too archaeological data is patchy, as the vast majority of known terracottas related to the Ara della Regina sanctuary were excavated by Romanelli in 1938 and went undocumented stratigraphically.[104] Two Archaic temples (Temple I and Temple II) were incorporated into the massive 4th century structure, known as Temple III or the "Temple of the

Winged Horses."[105] The architectural terracottas belonging to this phase bear strong links to examples from the Belvedere temple at Orvieto as well as from Selvasecca, and the three sites were likely part of the same local production zone.[106] Maria Cataldi has argued that Temple III never underwent a major roof redecoration, with the majority of terracotta elements remaining *in situ* for the entire life of the building, and additional elements being replaced piecemeal as necessary.[107] She does, however, note a group of repairs united by a common fabric that she dates to the early 3rd century based on comparisons with the so-called "Temple of Jupiter" at Cosa and to a lesser extent with Phase III at Punta della Vipera.[108] Richardson had already noted the close ties between some of Cosa's terracottas and those found in the Romanelli excavations – many of which seem to derive from the same workshop or perhaps even the same mold. The date of these pieces cannot be proven, but they may well suggest a shift or expansion of Tarquinia's trading network in the 3rd century BCE toward a more coastal orientation. Given its long history and prominence in the region, it is quite possible that many of these designs spread to Cosa and Punta della Vipera directly from Tarquinia.[109]

The fact that Cosa's closest connections in terms of architectural terracotta decoration are with Talamonaccio, Punta della Vipera, and Tarquinia is particularly suggestive when the sites are viewed on a map (Figure 58). With the exception of Tarquinia, these sanctuaries are located on each of the three

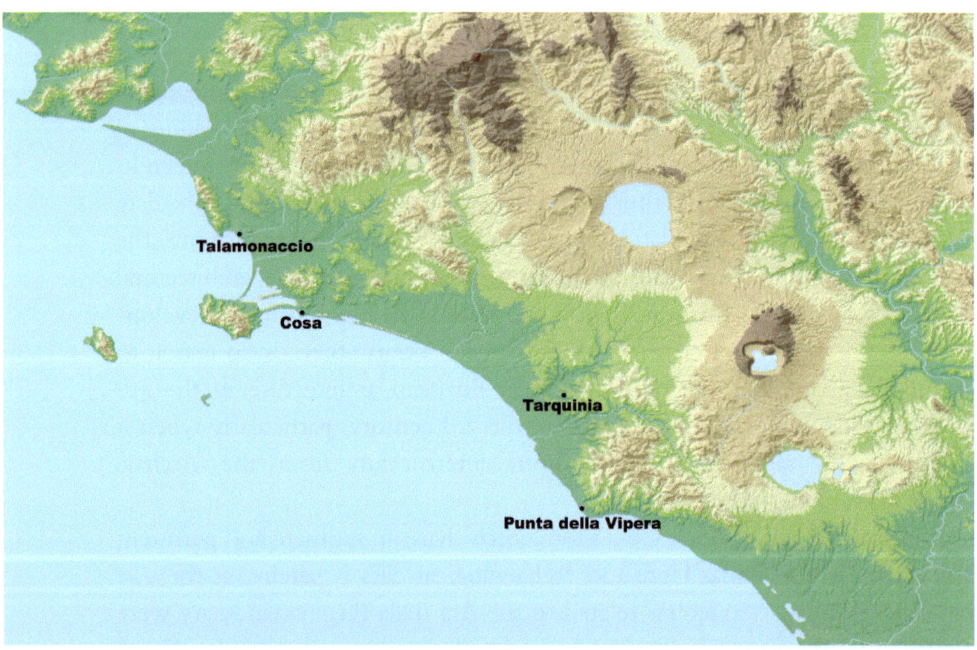

58. Map showing the sites with which Cosa's architectural terracottas have the most in common: Talamonaccio, Tarquinia, and Punta della Vipera. AWMC: à-la-carte map, modified by Kelley Vernon.

protected promontories along this section of the Tyrrhenian sea. These would have been the most convenient stopping-points for ships traveling up or down the coast and strongly suggests that molds, terracottas, or artisans may have been moving by sea in this region during the 3rd and 2nd centuries BCE. While the evidence of shipwrecks is insufficient to prove such a hypothesis, the fact that these towns were apparently trading primarily with their closest sea neighbors (*not* their closest neighbors by land) makes it likely that oversea movement played a major role in local trade networks. This would be logical, as commercial transportation was significantly cheaper by ship than by land.[110]

However these terracottas traveled, their ultimate effect was to create a common visual aesthetic on the temples of the local region. No two temples would have looked exactly the same, but the overall similarities would have been readily apparent to viewers. This is noteworthy given the very different legal statuses of these locales. While Rome had successfully defeated the Etruscan polities of this zone in the early 3rd century BCE, its subsequent interference would have been felt differently in different areas. Cosa was, of course, a Latin colony, and unlike its trading partners was thus associated with the conqueror. We know that territory was confiscated from the old Etruscan polities of the region following their defeat, particularly the desirable tracts of land along the cost. There is, however, no sharp change in the material culture of Talamone, Punta della Vipera, or Tarquinia following Roman conquest, and the pre-Roman shrines of these locations appear to have gone unharmed and to have continued as core features of the religious landscape.[111] As noted above, the foundation date of Castrum Novum (a maritime colony) near Punta della Vipera is debated and in any case need not have impacted the legal status of the Punta della Vipera sanctuary itself, which lay outside its bounds. Talamone appears to have retained a fairly high degree of autonomy even after the expansion of Roman power in the region and, as far as we can tell, a strong Etruscan identity. While Latin begins to appear on inscriptions in the surrounding towns, the epigraphic record from Talamone is entirely in Etruscan for the 3rd and 2nd centuries.[112] This is particularly significant given its close physical proximity to Cosa.

The religious architecture of this region expresses no obvious moment of "Romanization." On the contrary, the purportedly "Roman" town of Cosa seems to have consciously shaped its sacred structures in relation to the preexisting traditions, aesthetics, and iconographies of its neighbors. The reasons for this will be explored further below, but here it is worth noting not only that new and old temples across the region would have *looked* similar as a result of such practices but also that certain figures and deities were particularly ubiquitous. The satyr and maenad pair so popular on Etruscan antefixes, for instance, peered from the roofs of several Cosan temples as well. The heavy presence of Minerva and Hercules at Cosa also had strong iconographic and religious links to the local landscape. The Punta della Vipera sanctuary seems to have been dedicated to Minerva, and she appears on architectural terracottas across the region, including on an antefix from Bolsena in which she is identified by name (*Mera*) in Etruscan.[113] A shrine to Hercules/Hercle is attested at Vulci as well as a terracotta head of the hero,[114] and an image of Hercle and the hind appears among the terracotta decoration of Veii's Portonaccio temple.[115] A Hercules/Hercle shrine has also been uncovered at Musarna and may be associated with the mold of a Minerva antefix found nearby (Figure 50). Closer to home, the early "Deposit A" on Cosa's summit included pottery dedicated to Hercules, and the town itself sat just above the Portus Herculis.[116] Given the prominence of Hercules and Minerva (Hercle/Menrva) at nearby sites, the use of this pair may have served to integrate Cosa into its surroundings, and to subtly imply that the ancient gods of the region favored the new town and recognized it as a significant sacred site.[117]

Visual evocations of the local religious landscape extend to other aspects of Cosan temple design as well. The triple-cella temple, its most important and by far most prominent structure, was fitted with an "archaizing" molding at the base of the podium – the so-called "Etruscan" round molding (Figures 59–60).[118]

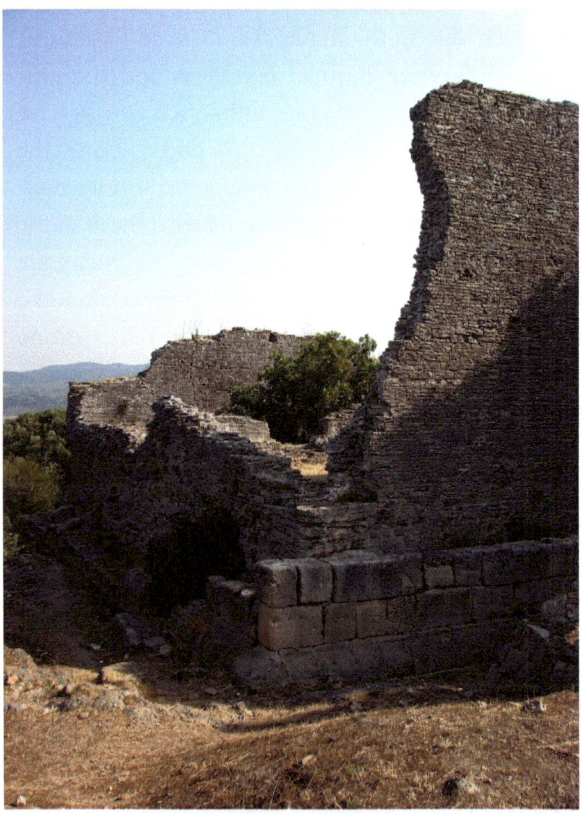

59. Cosa's triple-cella temple, current state.
Courtesy of Cosa Excavations.

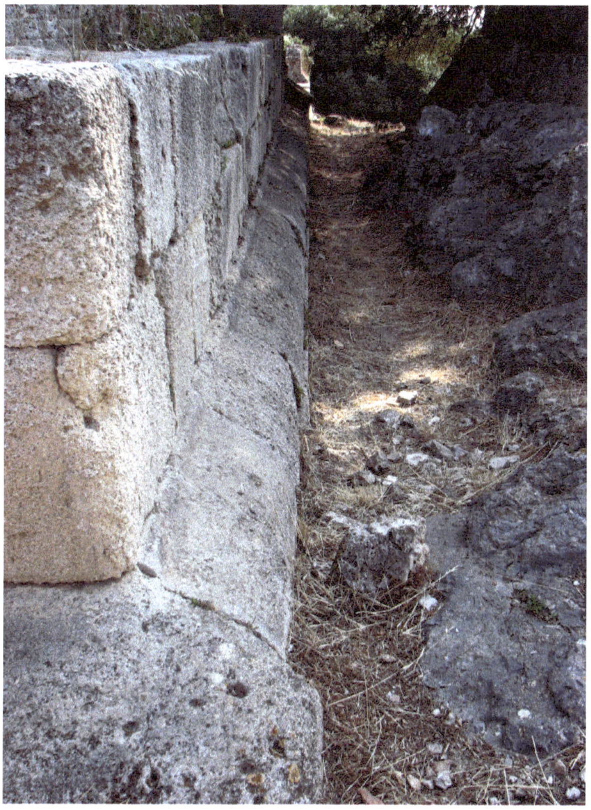

60. Detail of Cosa's triple-cella temple showing the "Etruscan" round base molding. Courtesy of Cosa Excavations.

Moldings of this type were widespread throughout the region, including at the major sanctuaries of Tarquinia, Pyrgi, and Vulci, whose links with Cosa have already been noted.[119] While the chronology of podium moldings is itself fraught, these other examples appear to pre-date the Cosan version at least by a couple of centuries.[120] Its inclusion at Cosa would not only have linked the triple-cella temple to the surrounding landscape architecturally but would also have lent it a distinctly old-fashioned air. Both effects would have been strengthened by the choice of building material, which offered yet another opportunity for local referencing: the purplish tuff stone that characterizes so much of Vulci's architecture was used across Cosa's sacred summit for temple stairs, columns, and even altars.[121] Architectural features such as material and molding thus worked alongside the roof terracottas to create an overall effect of venerable antiquity that would have been immediately readable to local viewers.

4.2.5 A Cosan Visual Identity

The arrival of 1,000 new colonists in the early 2nd century BCE resulted in a flurry of construction activity at Cosa, often involving experiments with new building technologies using lime mortar.[122] As Marcello Mogetta has recently and persuasively argued, much of this likely involved colonial labor and relied on the expertise of previous inhabitants and/or rural settlers.[123] This urbanistic push would have been critical for the "creation of a new communal identity" at Cosa.[124]

The construction of Temples B, D, and E in this same period, and their furnishing with remarkably similar terracotta decoration, nicely aligns with this broader urban picture. There appears to have been no strong desire to differentiate these temples through their decoration – the individuality of particular structures was evidently less important than the visual consistency of the town as a whole. The similarities in architectural decoration unified and codified the town's sacred landscape, creating an implicit dialogue between inter-visible as well as more isolated religious buildings at Cosa.

Those responsible for temple construction and upkeep in the colony appear to have gone to great lengths to maintain the overall aesthetic of Cosa's sacred buildings once it had been established. Of the more than twenty discrete antefix types found at the site, for instance, only one (the *potnia theron*) features a full-bodied figure (Figure 61).[125] A paltry nine or ten fragments of this type have been uncovered, suggesting that while this model was available, it never became a major decorative element on the town's temples. By contrast, the vast majority of Cosa's antefixes are head antefixes, with and without framing shells (Figure 48 and 62, among many others). It is probably not a coincidence that head antefixes are by far the most popular antefix type at nearby Etruscan sanctuaries, with a history stretching back centuries. The fact that the *potnia theron* is attested at Cosa, and attested so scantily, strongly suggests that the overwhelming prevalence of head antefixes was indeed intentional.

The reuse of similar or even identical elements on multiple temples in the town further reminds us that non-pedimental terracottas cannot be used to identify the deity worshiped in any given shrine. With their pointedly old-fashioned designs, these terracottas signify not a specific cult but rather a shared religious identity visually expressed. They imply status, antiquity, and piety.

As we have seen, many of the motifs popular at Cosa derive directly from the immediate geographic landscape – from the temples of Cosa's conquered Etruscan neighbors. The choice to use these elements cannot be attributed simply to the availability of local artisans working in their local styles, as Cosan temples also featured elements of the "standard kit," terracottas linked to more distant sites like Ardea, and some examples that are apparently Cosan inventions. This points to a high degree of deliberate choice in the design of these roofs. Why a new colony should actively incorporate (and thus promote) the visual language of its defeated enemies is a question to which we shall return in Chapter 5.

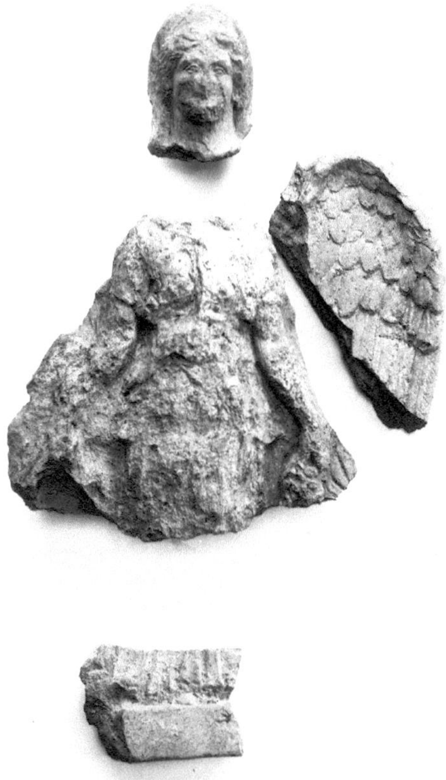

61. *Potnia theron* antefix, from Cosa, Type C2:270.
Courtesy of the American Academy in Rome, Cosa Archaeological Collection.

4.3 MINTURNAE

4.3.1 Overview of the Site

Minturnae was founded as a Roman colony in 296/5 BCE at the mouth of the Liris river (Figure 63). The original town was likely designed on a rectangular *castrum* plan and enclosed by walls of polygonal masonry.[126] This area has never been fully excavated, however, and little can therefore be said of its appearance or precise layout.[127] Another set of opus quadratum walls in tufo probably belong to a late 3rd century expansion of the town, after it outgrew the relatively confined perimeter of the early *castrum*.[128] By this time, small shops and perhaps a temple had already been constructed outside the original wall circuit.[129] Both the *castrum* and the later expansion were laid out with direct reference to the Via Appia, which bisects Minturnae to serve as the city's *decumanus maximus* (Figure 64).[130]

A large portion of the site was excavated by Jotham Johnson of the University of Pennsylvania between 1931 and 1933. His excavations focused

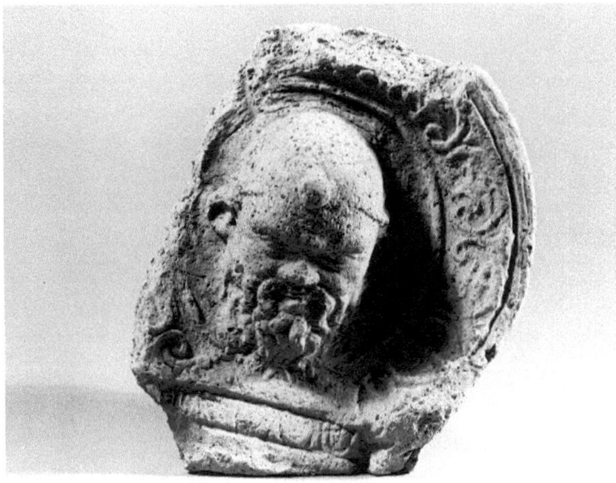

62. Silenus shell antefix attributed to Temple B, from Cosa, Type C3:156. Courtesy of the American Academy in Rome, Cosa Archaeological Collection.

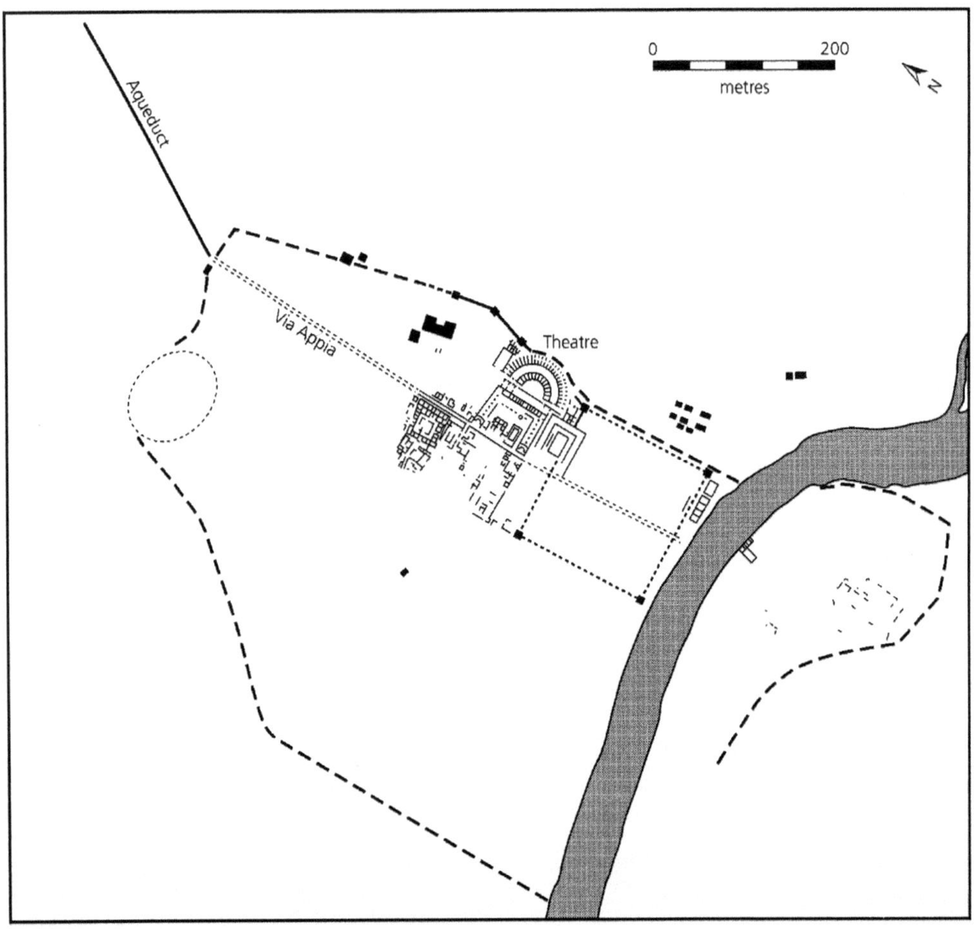

63. Plan of Minturnae showing the Via Appia, Liris river, area excavated by Johnson (theater, *area sacra* and forum), and the mostly unexcavated *castrum* area to the east. Image after Laurence, Cleary, and Sears 2011 fig. 6.4.

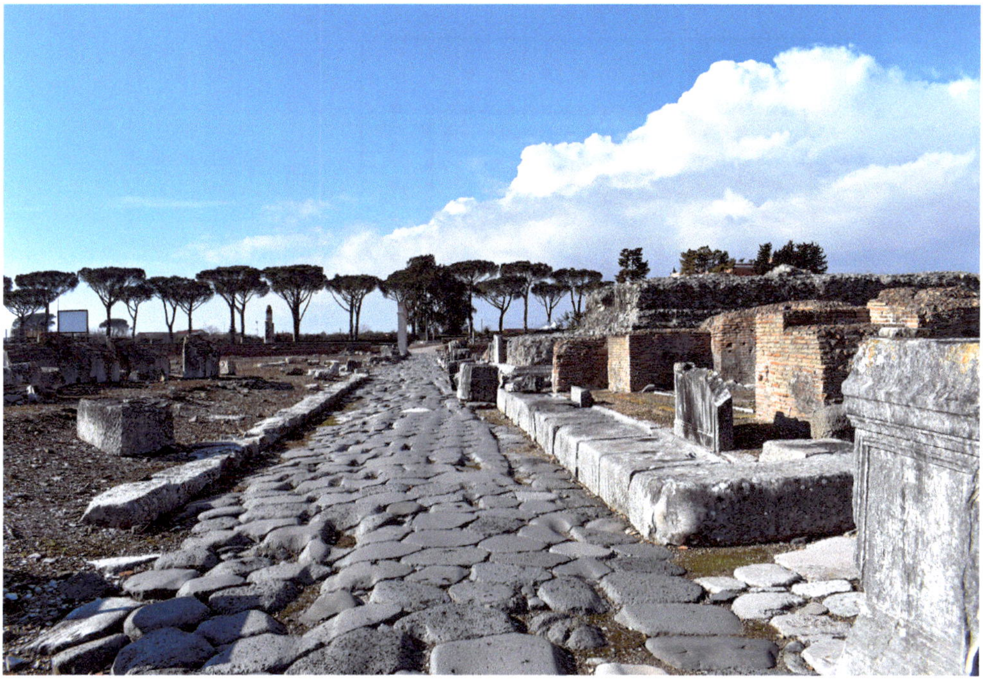

64. The Via Appia at Minturnae. Author's photo, printed by kind permission of the Direzione Regionale Musei Lazio – Comprensorio Archeologico e Antiquarium di Minturnae e Ponte Real Ferdinando – Minturno (LT).

primarily on the area just west of the original *castrum* and revealed an *area sacra* and forum, north and south of the Via Appia, respectively.[131] In the southwest corner of the *area sacra*, Johnson uncovered the foundations of a rectangular structure in *tufo grigio*, measuring 17.85 m x 8.68 m.[132] He identified this as the *aedes Iovis* – an appellation based on two references in Livy, who mentions a Temple of Jupiter at Minturnae that was struck by lightning in 207 BCE and again in 191 BCE.[133] Johnson found no evidence of fire or destruction that could be related to the earlier incident. However, Livy's second assertion does gain support by the presence of a fire-damaged coin hoard below the foundations of the three-winged portico, dating between 200 and 190 BCE. The *tufo grigio* structure may well be the early *aedes Iovis*, but it should be emphasized that no archaeological evidence links the extant foundations with the worship of Jupiter, and the structure itself may not even have been a temple.[134] The earliest area of the colony is scantily known, and the *aedes Iovis* might well lie within the walls of the early *castrum*.[135]

Following the fire in the early 2nd century BCE, the *area sacra* was restructured to include a three-winged portico surrounding a temple with a tripartite plan (Figure 65). Oddly, the temple was placed off-center in relation to the portico and the portico itself is of uneven proportions, with the north and east

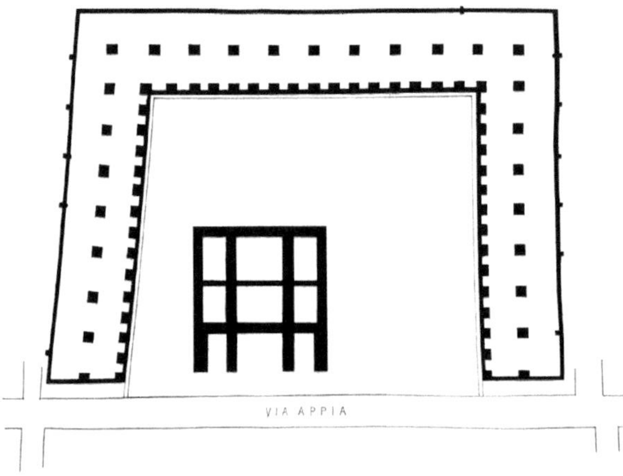

65. Minturnae's *area sacra*, showing the remains of the tripartite temple and the three-winged portico.
Courtesy of the Penn Museum, image no. 26377.

wings meeting at a 91.5-degree angle, while the west wing is set off from the north by 96 degrees. While the reasons for these peculiarities remain unclear, the contemporaneity of the structures is supported by the building materials and by finds in the foundation levels of both structures.[136] The temple and its framing portico adjoin the Via Appia so closely that one could practically have stepped from the road to the temple's front staircase (Figure 2). The buildings of the *area sacra* are thus sited for maximum visibility: anyone traveling along this major artery, which stretched from Rome to Capua, would have had no choice but to see them.[137]

Recent studies have tended to reject the traditional identification of Minturnae's tripartite temple as a "Capitolium." Not only is the reconstruction of the ground-plan questionable, but there is no archaeological or literary evidence to suggest that Minturnae had a cult dedicated to the Capitoline triad (or indeed to any other triad combination).[138] It is now increasingly recognized that tripartite temples and Capitolia are not synonymous – there are examples of tripartite temples that are certainly not Capitolia, as well as known Capitolia that lack a divided interior.[139] Vitruvius describes a tripartite division as an architectural standard for Tuscan-style temples, with no reference whatsoever to the type of cult worshiped within.[140] Furthermore, no connection can be convincingly established between a town's colonial status and the presence of a Capitoline temple, particularly before the Empire.[141] Evidence for the dedicatee of Minturnae's tripartite temple will be discussed below, but for now it is important to stress that its ground plan alone offers no clues in this regard.

The *area sacra* and much of the town's urban center was restructured in the mid-1st century BCE, following a large-scale fire and perhaps connected with

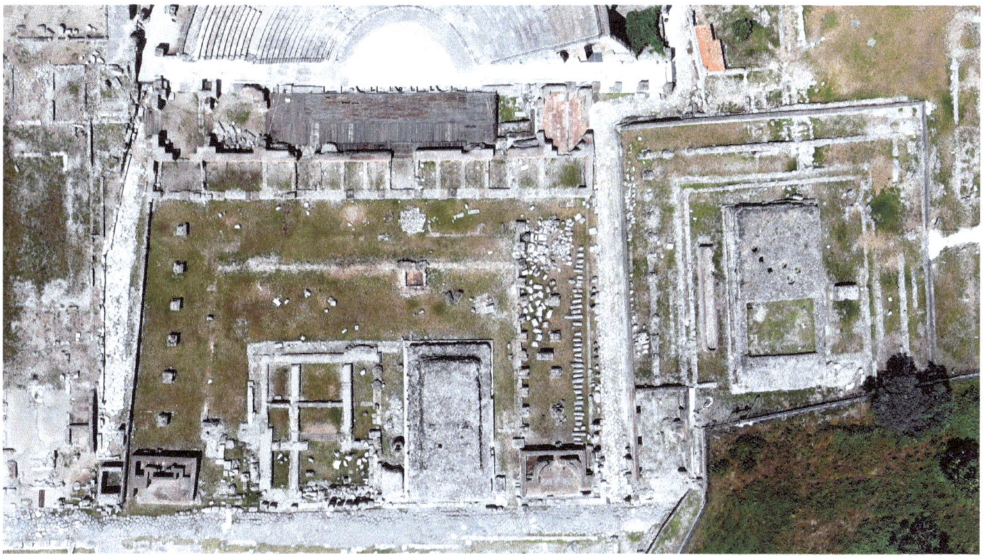

66. Aerial view of Minturnae's *area sacra* (left), Temple B and its portico (right) with the remains of the polygonal castrum wall running through it. Image by Nathanael Tavares, printed by kind permission of the Direzione Regionale Musei Lazio – Comprensorio Archeologico e Antiquarium di Minturnae e Ponte Real Ferdinando – Minturno (LT).

the arrival of new colonists under Caesar and/or Augustus.[142] The three-winged portico and tripartite temple were rebuilt in stone atop the same foundations, and at some point toward the end of the Republic a sacred well was installed just east of the tripartite temple and filled with architectural terracottas from the previous phase.[143]

A new Ionic temple ("Temple B") was constructed east of the old *area sacra*, measuring 22.46 m x 12.92 m and built of tufo, travertine, and opus reticulatum.[144] It straddled the polygonal wall of the early *castrum*, demonstrating clearly the obsolescence of this perimeter by the early Empire (Figure 66). Temple B was also surrounded by a three-winged portico and fronted the Via Appia, linking it visually with the earlier tripartite temple (see Section 4.3.4). A marble slab inscribed to the divine Caesar and referencing the *Lex Rufrena* was found near the temple.[145] This inscription, together with Temple B's building materials and its architectural similarities to the temple of Divus Julius in Rome, led to its traditional interpretation as a temple to the Divine Caesar.[146] The recent discovery of a coin dating to 11/12 CE in the core of the terrace may complicate this identification.[147] The temple seems to have been planned as part of a larger urban project that included a monumental structure south of the Via Appia, newly excavated and identified as an Augusteum.[148] Based primarily on the presence of water features around Temple B, Giovanna Rita Bellini has suggested that it was in fact dedicated to Venus Genetrix.[149] We shall return to this question below (see Section 4.3.2).

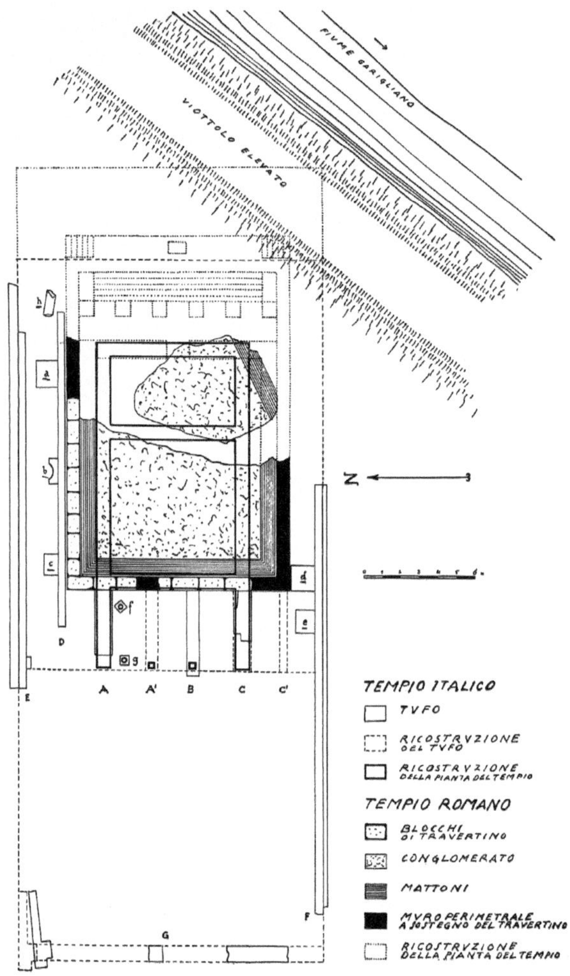

67. Plan of the sanctuary of Marica at Minturnae. Image after Mingazzini 1938, pl. 45.

Minturnae underwent substantial urban renovations during the early Principate. A new temple was added ("Temple A," probably of Tiberian date), and the town received a large theater just north of the *area sacra* as well as a basilica and the monumental structure identified as an Augusteum. Soon after, the town was further enriched by nymphaea, an aqueduct, a bath complex, a macellum, a curia, and an amphitheater which has been located but never excavated.[150]

It is important to note that the Auruncan sanctuary of Marica, in use at least from the 6th century BCE, lies less than 2 km from Minturnae's forum (Figure 67). It was apparently rebuilt or restored several times during the last few centuries BCE and retained its role as one of the region's most important cult sites even after Roman conquest. Plutarch's account of Marius' flight at Minturnae attests to the enduring fame of Marica's sacred grove.[151] He notes that it was forbidden to carry anything out of the grove once it had been carried in, suggesting not only that the ancient rites of Marica were still adhered to in Marius' day but that they were known even in Plutarch's time. Its close proximity to Minturnae's urban center means that the Sanctuary of Marica must also be considered as integral to the town's visual landscape, and as a structure with which the town's residents would have been intimately familiar. The large number of votive offerings that post-date the Roman conquest further attest to the sanctuary's enduring importance after the establishment of the colony.[152]

Of particular relevance to the present study are the numerous high-quality architectural terracottas found at the Marica sanctuary. Many are comparable to contemporaneous examples from Capua and attest to Minturnae's role as a leader in terracotta production at least from the 6th century BCE.[153] There is some uncertainty as to their precise phasing and placement, and it has been suggested that the Marica sanctuary may have consisted of more than one structure.[154] The surviving fragments include simas with strigils, revetment plaques with palmettes, painted eaves tiles, as well as antefixes with Daedalic female heads, female heads with a nimbus (Figure 68), gorgons, as well as

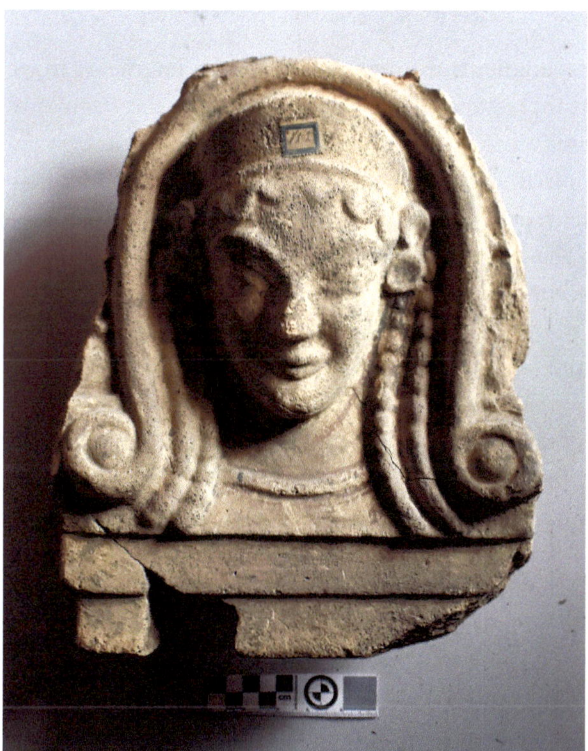

68. Late Archaic antefix from the sanctuary of Marica at Minturnae.
Naples: Museo archeologico nazionale di Napoli. Photo by author, published by permission of the Ministero della Cultura – Museo Archeologico Nazionale di Napoli.

several versions of palmette antefixes.[155] This last type appears to have been particularly significant for the visual character of the Marica sanctuary, as it was imitated in the 2nd century BCE phase as well.[156] Architectural terracottas are attested at Marica's sanctuary into the 1st century CE, further attesting to its enduring importance even after the founding of the colony.[157]

4.3.2 "Standard" and Specific: The Pediment of the Tripartite Temple

As we saw in Chapter 3, Minturnae's tripartite temple as well as its predecessor in the *area sacra* appear to have been equipped with the full array of "standard" terracottas. These well-known types would have been familiar to viewers from across central Italy and may have endowed the temples with a sense of legitimacy and antiquity, asserting the new colony's role within the broader religious landscape. At the same time, a number of specifically local referents ground the terracotta program within its local setting. We have already noted the incorporation of the palmette type from the Marica sanctuary onto the "standard" looped palmette plaques of the new tripartite temple (Figures 36–37). Its prominent pedimental sculpture may similarly have contextualized the temple for viewers within a specific geographic and historical context.

As with many terracotta pediments from central Italy, the fragments from Minturnae defy straightforward restoration. Approximately 300–400 fragments of terracotta statues were discovered during Johnson's excavations in a large pit along the east flank of Temple B. These remained almost entirely unpublished until Valentina Livi's 2022 report cataloguing some of the more securely identifiable fragments.[158] The observations offered here are based on my own study of the few surviving fragments in storage at Minturnae and the archival documents and photos held in the University of Pennsylvania Museum archives, taking into account Livi's new publication.[159]

The archival photos show the statues as reconstructed soon after excavation. The statues themselves are largely lost, making the photographic documentation all the more precious. In several cases, however, surviving fragments can be matched to a corresponding photo and thus aid in determining the size of the original piece.[160]

The extant fragments can be divided into at least two groups based on clay fabric.[161] Two fragmentary figures belong to the first group, which likely showed a scene of assembled gods.[162] The second and larger group comprises a minimum of four figures but probably several more.[163] Calculations based on the preserved fragments allow us to roughly estimate the height of these figures and thus their relative placement within the space of the pediment. Figure 69 offers a tentative reconstruction of how these figures might have been arranged. The largest figure should have occupied the center – a standing,

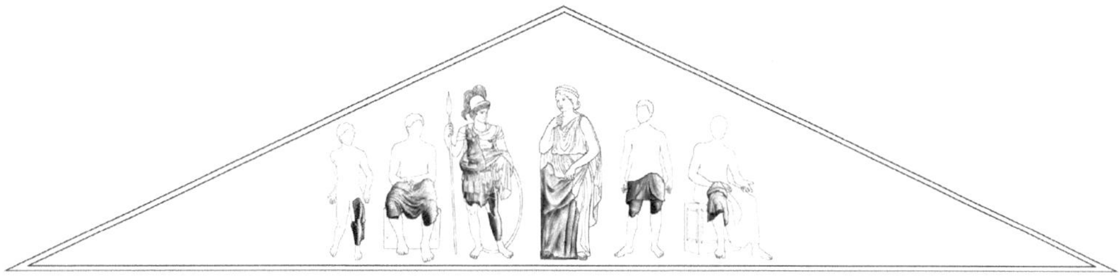

69. Possible arrangement of terracotta statues on the pediment of Minturnae's tripartite temple.
Illustration by Jennie Anderson.

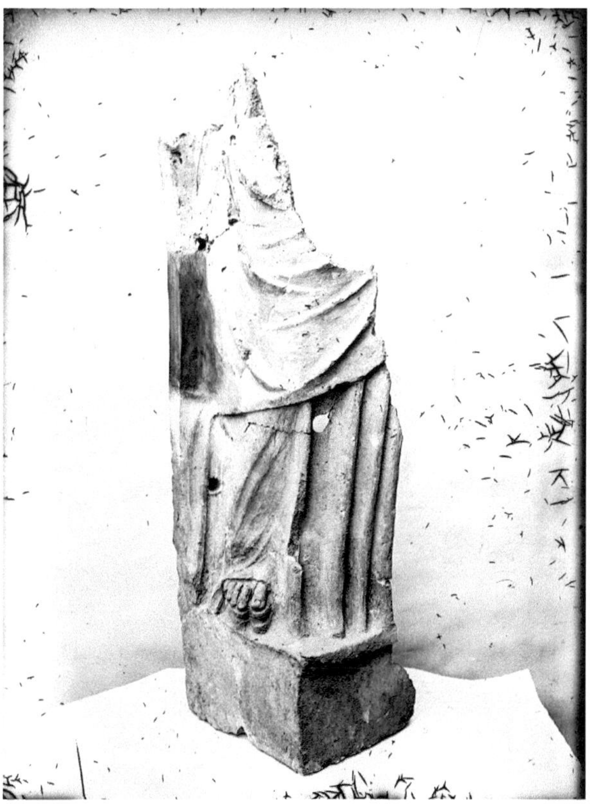

70. Fragments of a terracotta pedimental statue from Minturnae of a female figure as restored (incorrectly) soon after excavation.
Courtesy of the Penn Museum, image no. 29114.

draped female figure, reconstructed (certainly incorrectly) in an archival photo held by the University of Pennsylvania museum (Figure 70).[164] Unfortunately, nothing survives of her head or of any identifying attributes, but if she stood centrally in the temple's pediment we can reasonably assume that she represents a deity.[165] Flanking her would have been two standing male figures. One wears military dress (Figure 71) and the other a garment falling just above the

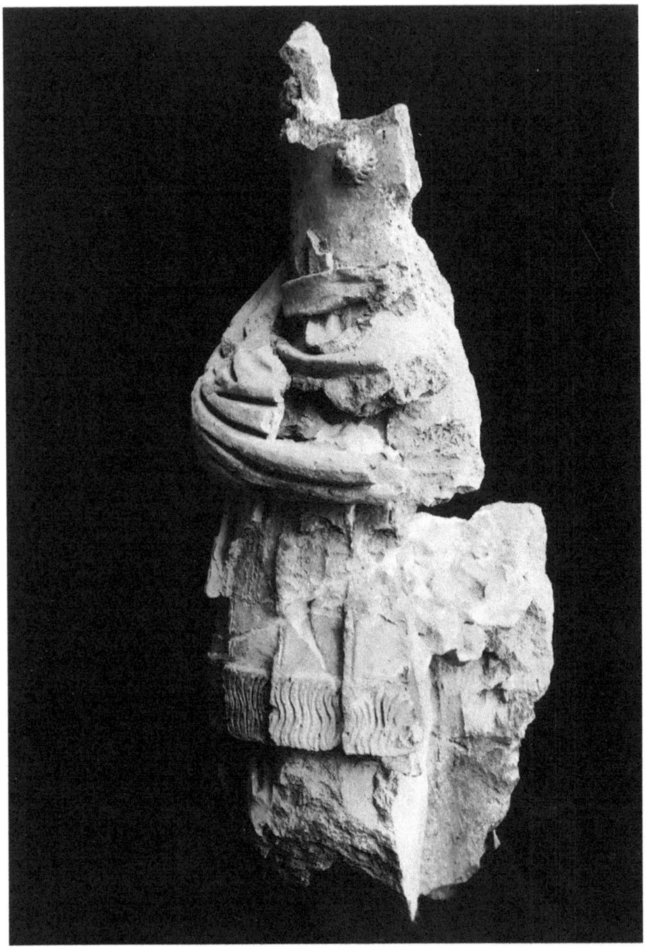

71. Fragments of a terracotta pedimental statue from Minturnae of a male figure in military dress as restored soon after excavation.
Courtesy of the Penn Museum, image no. 26022.

knees.[166] Beyond them, moving toward the pediment's corners, we find two seated figures, one on each side. At least one is male.[167] Smaller standing figures may have appeared on either side of these, as attested by a preserved leg with drapery visible in another photo and surviving in two fragments.[168] Many of the smaller fragments preserved in storage but not shown in the archival photos might possibly belong with this group (including fragments of hair, a hand holding drapery, an animal foot that might have decorated the base of a seated figure's chair, etc.), but they cannot be securely assigned at present due to the complicated history of the fragments' movement and mixing following their excavation.

Most 3rd–1st century terracotta pediments from central Italy show either a lively mythological scene (e.g., Figure 43), or a more staid representation of

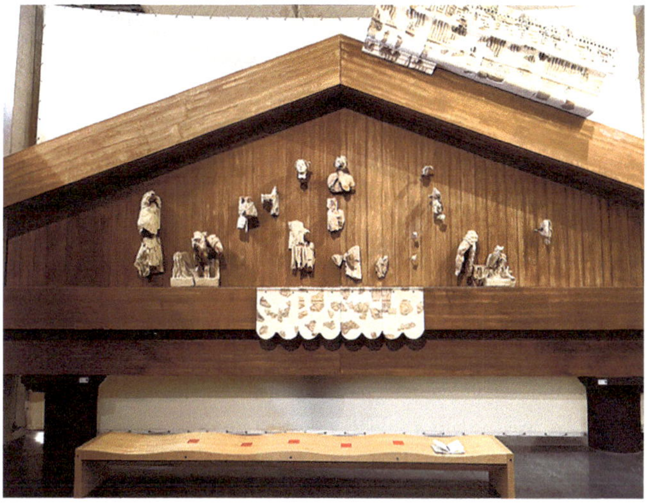

72. "Pediment of Apollo" from the area of the Civitella, Chieti. Chieti: Museo Archeologico Nazionale "La Civitella."
Photo by Alexander Ekserdjian, published by permission of A. Ekserdjian and the Ministero della Cultura, Direzione regionale Musei Abruzzo.

assembled gods (e.g., Figure 11). Given the static poses of the Minturnae figures, it seems quite probable that we are dealing with a pediment of the latter type. The Minturnae group might thus be compared with the pedimental statues from Cosa's triple-cella temple, and indeed many of the individual figures are quite similar.[169] The Via di San Gregorio pediment is also analogous, and like the other two includes a standing male figure in military dress. In all three cases, the central figures are roughly life-size, though at Cosa the corner figures are of considerably reduced dimensions.[170] Further comparanda include pedimental groups of standing and seated gods at Nemi and Ardea ("Castrum Inui") and three pediments at Civitella di Chieti (Figure 72).[171] All are dated to the 2nd century BCE, which aligns well with the Minturnae chronology.[172]

It is likely that this larger pedimental group originally decorated Minturnae's tripartite temple. Although the fragments were found beside Temple B, there is currently no evidence for an earlier phase of that temple, and the only known remains date to the early imperial period. The tripartite temple seems to have been the only temple standing in the vicinity during the 2nd century BCE. The deposition of the pedimental sculptures in a pit near Temple B would thus suggest that that sector was considered part of the same sacred precinct.[173] The statues themselves are fairly large compared to other examples of Italic terracotta pedimental statuary, though similar sizes are attested at Cosa's triple-cella temple and on the Via di San Gregorio pediment. They therefore ought to belong to a large temple, and the dimensions of Minturnae's tripartite temple seem adequate.[174] The two fragments of different clay might belong to a restoration of this pedimental group, or to another building of similar or slightly reduced dimensions.

The problematic correlation between a temple's pedimental decoration and its primary cult is well-known, particularly when the decoration shows a scene from myth. If the Minturnae group does depict an assembly of gods, however, we can reasonably expect the figures to relate in some way to the type of cult practiced in the temple. Since the central figure appears to have represented a female, the temple was likely dedicated to a goddess.[175] This in itself argues strongly against the traditional interpretation of the tripartite temple as a Capitolium. Were this the case, we would expect to find Jupiter in the center, flanked by Juno and Minerva.[176] Instead, the pediment seems to have featured a female deity surrounded by primarily male figures. This also calls into the question the common identification of the tripartite temple as a later iteration of the *aedes Iovis*. As discussed above, our only evidence for a temple of Jupiter at Minturnae comes from two attestations in Livy, both of which refer to events early in the life of the town. Because the earliest area of the colony remains mostly unexcavated, we should not rule out the possibility that the *aedes Iovis* stood within the original *castrum* area and that the temples of the *area sacra* are unrelated to the worship of Jupiter.

The fragments themselves certainly point in this direction. The figure in military dress who likely stood beside the central goddess closely resembles known depictions of Mars (Figures 11 and 73), suggesting that our focal deity may in fact be Venus.[177] A cult of Venus is well attested epigraphically and archaeologically at Minturnae.[178] One of the magistrate inscriptions found reused in the podium of Temple A specifically references her cult.[179] A small marble base with a dedication to Venus was found at Minturnae between the theater and the Garigliano river. It is dated to the late 3rd or early 2nd century BCE, making it quite an early example of marble being used for this type of dedication in Italy.[180] Several fragmentary statues of Venus, two of which have been identified as Venus Marina, were found in excavations of Minturnae's theater and in the vicinity of Temple B.[181] In addition, the underwater excavations of Dominic Ruegg yielded twenty-six bronze and lead clamshells, interpreted as votive offerings to Poseidon and Venus, as well as votive metal figurines of Venus.[182]

Interestingly, the importance of Venus at Minturnae seems heavily linked to the preexisting cult of Marica – the two goddesses having been in some way assimilated. Marica is a marshy goddess closely connected to water and the sea. Venus' oceanic birth may have offered an appealing parallel, and the goddess is also known as a patron of navigation.[183] Indeed, the clamshell votives, and perhaps the Venus Marina statue type as well, suggest a predominantly maritime character for the goddess' worship at Minturnae.[184] The apparent link

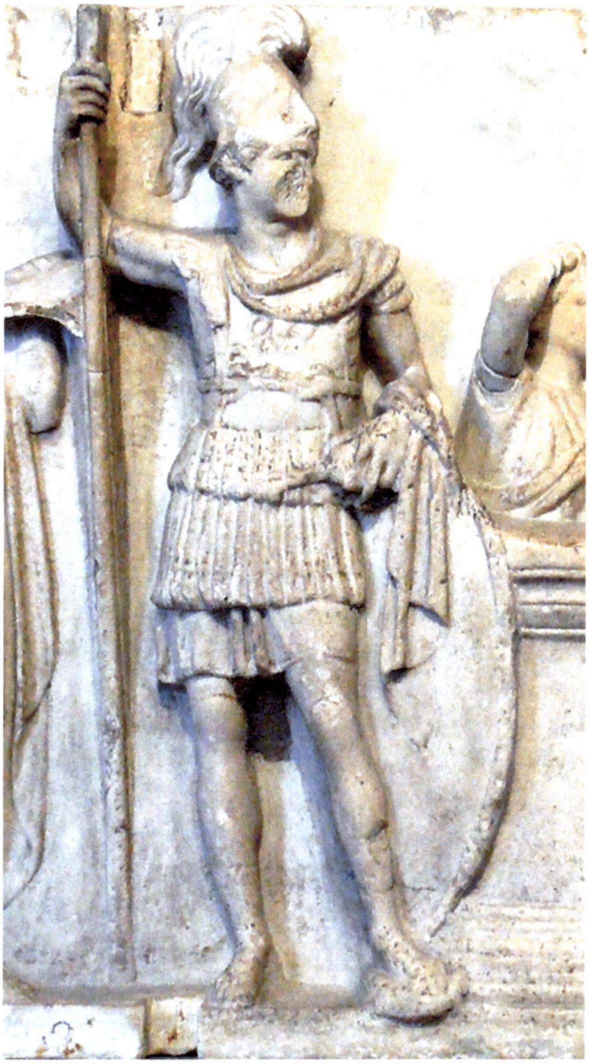

73. Figure usually identified as Mars, from the so-called Altar of Domitius Ahenobarbus. Musée du Louvre, Paris.
Image: Wikimedia Creative Commons.

between Marica and Venus is confirmed by Servius, who reports that an "Aphrodite Pontia" (i.e., Venus Marina) was worshiped alongside Marica (*ad. Aen.* VII, 47):

> Dicunt alii per Maricam Venerem intellegi debere, cuius fuit sacellum iuxta Maricam, in quo erat scriptum ΠΟΝΤΙΗ ΑΦΡΟΔΙΤΗ.

> Others say that Venus should be understood for Marica; she had a shrine near Marica's, on which was written "Maritime Aphrodite."[185]

We thus have certain evidence of a cult of Venus at Minturnae from at least the early 2nd century BCE, if not before. As noted above, Bellini has recently suggested that Venus was worshiped in Temple B. The fact that no pre-Imperial phases for Temple B have been identified complicates this hypothesis, since Venus was worshipped at Minturnae several centuries earlier. The evidence of the pedimental statuary makes it more likely, in my opinion, that the tripartite temple was dedicated to Venus. The widespread attestations of Venus' cult at Minturnae imply a long-standing structure integral to the town's religious life, and the tripartite temple was just that.

The Romans were careful not to destroy the sanctuary of Marica after conquering the region, and in fact they built the new colony of Minturnae just beside it. The connection between Marica and Venus may have offered an ideal opportunity to bridge the gap between the Auruncan and Roman cult centers – with Venus functioning as a newer, Roman complement to the ancient Auruncan goddess who still occupied an important role in the region. In this case, the use of the palmette type from Marica's temple on the "standard" looped palmette plaques of the new tripartite temple may be viewed as a directed visual reference – symbolically charged, while at the same time almost playful. The pedimental and non-pedimental architectural terracottas of the tripartite temple worked in tandem to root the new structure in the preexisting religious landscape, presenting a harmonious image of Minturnae that easily encompassed both its recent colonists and Marica's ancient rites.[186]

4.3.3 *The Pi-shaped Portico's Local Program*

The three-winged portico that surrounded the tripartite temple represents the other major structure in Minturnae's *area sacra* during the last two centuries BCE. Like the temple it framed, the portico was also decorated with an eye-catching terracotta program. Its architraves were sheathed with a revetment plaque featuring two rows of nine-leaf palmettes in mirror image on its principal register, separated by horizontal s-spirals (Figure 74).[187] A short strigilated cavetto tops the plaque, below which is another short register with curving floral motifs. The bottom of the plaque is lightly scalloped to follow the projecting tips of the downturned palmette leaves. Parallels for this plaque were unknown at the time of excavation, though an apparently identical fragment has since been identified at the Monte d'Argento cult site about 3 km from Minturnae.[188] Further comparanda have also been found at Fregellae, a close trading partner of Minturnae's with which it was linked by the Liris River. Although at Fregellae the plaque's upper row is embellished by heads alternating with the palmettes, or in one case by the unusual inclusion of a terracotta inscription, the dimensions and style are so close that the versions from both sites likely derive from the same workshop (Figure 75).[189]

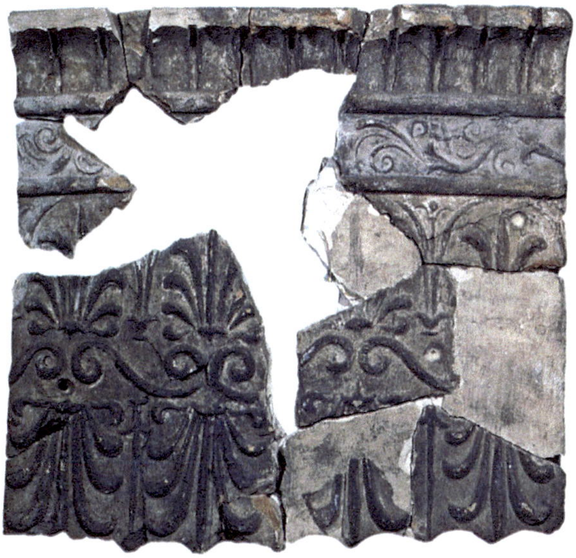

74. Revetment plaque attributed to Minturnae's triporticus. Philadelphia: Penn Museum.
Courtesy of the Penn Museum, object no. 32-36-6.

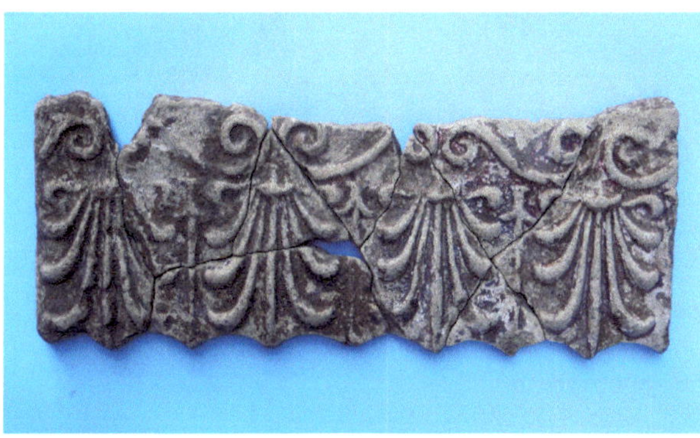

75. Fragment of a revetment plaque from Fregellae, closely related to a version from Minturnae.
Courtesy of the Ministero della Cultura – Soprintendenza Archeologia, Belle Arti e Paesaggio per le province di Frosinone e Latina. Photograph courtesy of Rudolf Känel.

Above the revetment plaques, a pair of alternating antefixes stood at the edge of the portico's roof (Figure 76). Both represent full standing figures. On the first type, a mostly nude male plays a syrinx and wears only boots, a lion's skin, and perhaps a low polos. His horns, pointed ears, and musical occupation suggest a silen or satyr, while his prominent musculature and lion's skin tied at the chest are more reminiscent of Hercules. Either large wings or an oddly billowing garment frame this unusual figure.

This antefix appears to be firmly rooted in the local region. At least eight examples of this type have been found at the Sanctuary of Aesculapius at

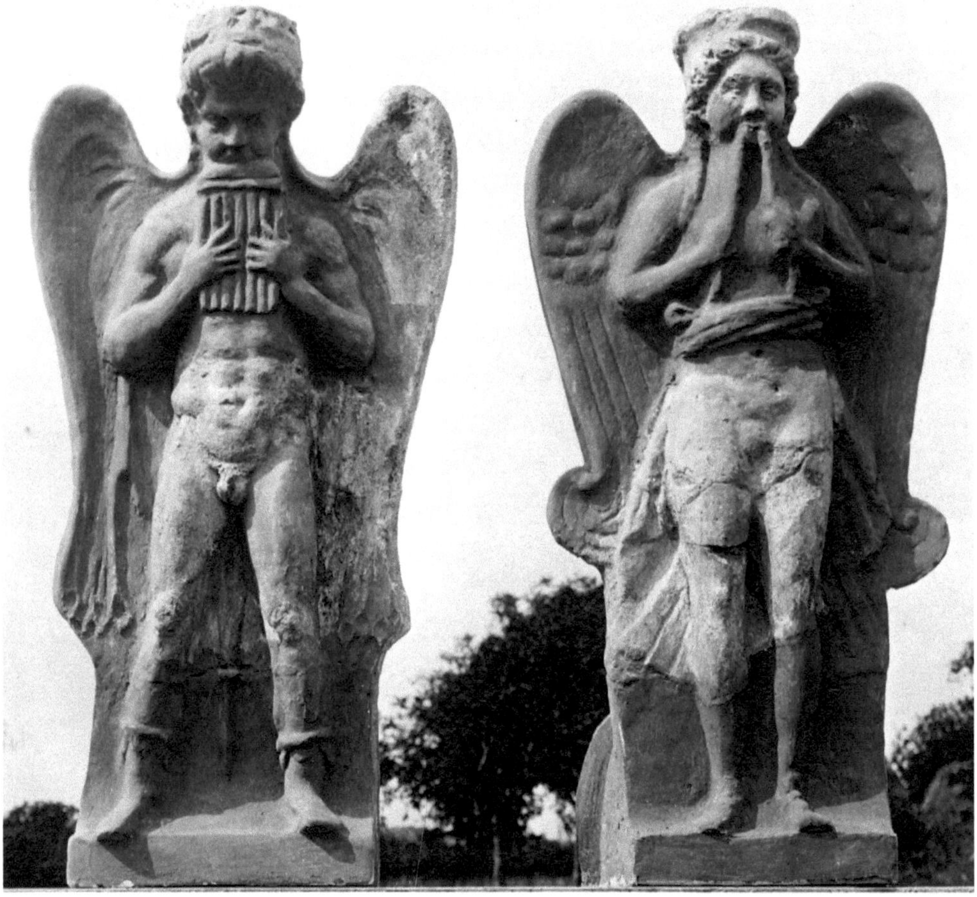

76. Antefixes of a satyr playing a syrinx and a winged flute-girl, attributed to Minturnae's triporticus.
Courtesy of the Penn Museum, image no. 26036.

Fregellae (Figure 77).[190] These are typologically very similar to the Minturnae version, although smaller in their dimensions.[191] A similar antefix from Capua may date to the first half of the 3rd century and thus be among the earliest iterations of the type.[192] It is quite similar in all respects to the Minturnae piece, except for the treatment of the hair and beard. Interestingly, both include the detail of the lion's tail that hangs down between the figure's legs. A final fragment almost identical to that from Minturnae was found at Aquinum but is now lost.[193] Aquinum is just about 15 km from Fregellae. This unusual antefix type seems therefore to have circulated only within a close geographic region during the 3rd and 2nd centuries BCE.

The syrinx-player would have alternated with another antefix, this one depicting a winged female playing a double-flute.[194] She too is mostly nude, with only a thin garment tied above her navel and hanging down behind her.

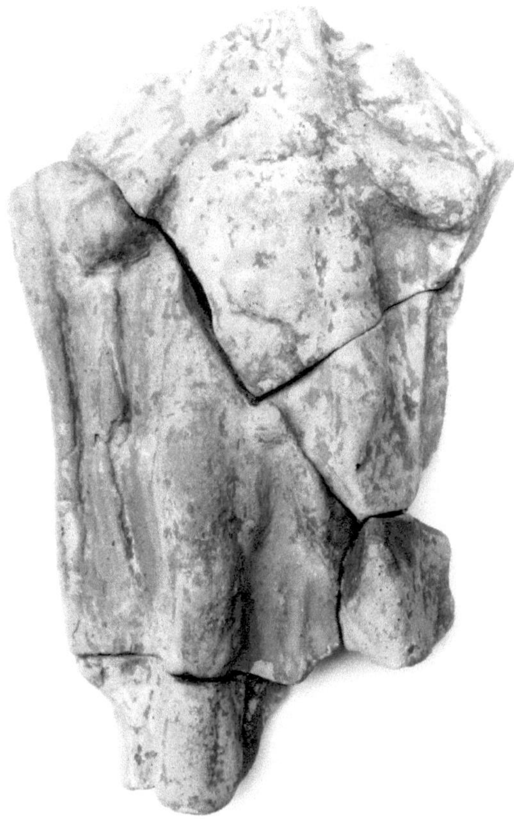

77. Antefix of a satyr playing a syrinx from Fregellae, closely related to a version from Minturnae.
Courtesy of the Ministero della Cultura – Soprintendenza Archeologia, Belle Arti e Paesaggio per le province di Frosinone e Latina. Photograph courtesy of Rudolf Känel.

While versions of this type are known at a wider range of sites, most differ markedly from the Minturnae example.[195] Not surprisingly perhaps, the closest comparanda come once more from the Sanctuary of Aesculapius at Fregellae.[196]

The three securely attributed elements of the triporticus' decoration are thus distinctly local in character. Each finds comparanda at nearby sites, but is virtually unknown beyond the region. It is important to note that the area of southern Latium/northern Campania had a long and venerable tradition in architectural terracotta production, with Minturnae and Capua standing out as leaders in terracotta technology and design already in the 6th century BCE.[197] The evidence of architectural terracottas strongly suggests that Roman colonization did not disrupt preexisting ties within the region but simply added new sites (such as Fregellae) to a still active network (Figure 78).[198] Indeed, many of the 3rd–1st century BCE architectural terracottas from

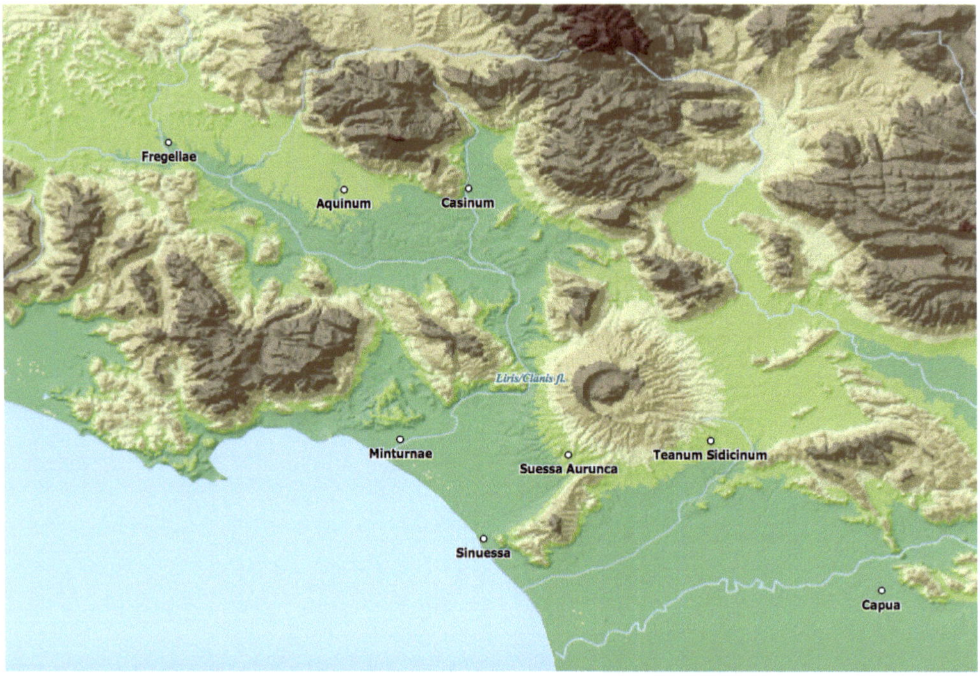

78. Map showing the area around Minturnae, including the sites with which Minturnae's architectural terracottas have the most in common from the Archaic period through the founding of Roman colonies in the region. AWMC: "À-la-carte" map.

Minturnae display close similarities with examples from sites to the south and east – often the very same sites with which links can be detected in the pre-Roman period. An unusual vegetal antefix (perhaps a stylized pinecone?) likely dating to the 2nd century BCE is attested in identical form only at Minturnae and the Loreto sanctuary at Teanum Sidicinum (Figure 79).[199] The architectural terracottas from these two sites are closely linked beginning in the Archaic period, suggesting a strong continuity in local networks. Similarly, the endurance of Minturnae's age-old bond with Capua is attested by the presence of similar simas at both sites even after Roman colonization.[200] Alongside the use of "standard" elements on Minturnae's temples, therefore, we have consistent evidence for a parallel reliance on the terracotta traditions of the local region.

That "local" pieces formed the bulk of the triporticus' decoration may be significant. The eccentricity of its architectural terracottas would have been highlighted when viewed in juxtaposition with the tripartite temple, which it surrounded on three sides. The temple drew conservatively from the most widespread and archaizing elements of terracotta architectural decoration, featuring the same "standard" types that had graced the preceding temple in the *area sacra*, as well as numerous temples across 2nd century central Italy.

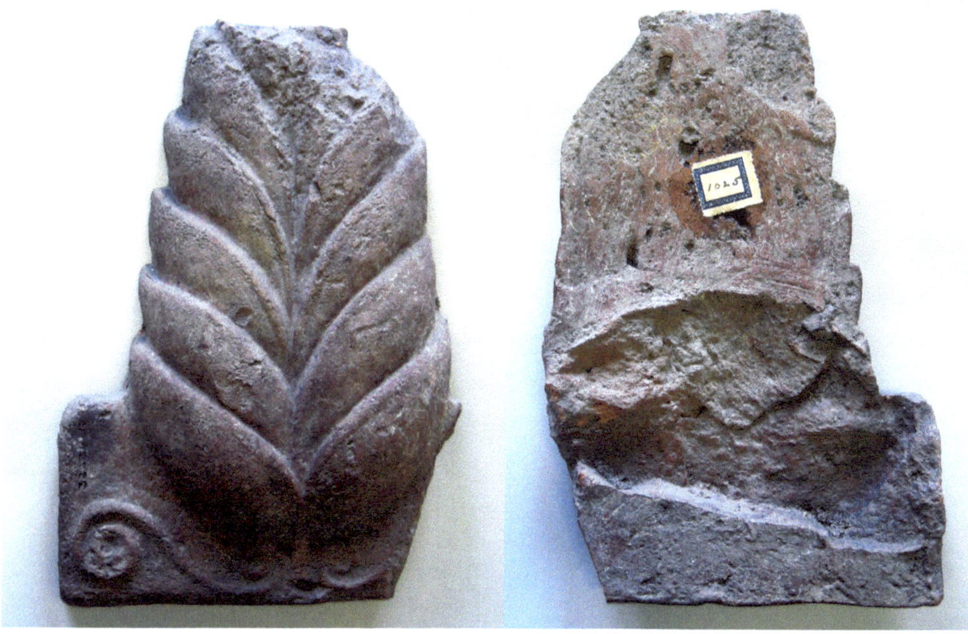

79. Vegetal antefix from Minturnae seen from the front and back. Philadelphia: Penn Museum.
Photographs by author. Courtesy of the Penn Museum, object no. 32-36-13.

While the terracotta decoration of the temple and triporticus is quite different, the two programs are in clear dialogue with one another. The basic pose of the *potnia theron* and the portico antefixes, for instance, are quite consistent. Each features a frontal, standing figure wearing a *polos* and framed by prominent wings or drapery. Their physical proximity invites comparison between the two roofs, and the differing forms of the antefixes likely speaks to the function of each building. On the triporticus, a pair of mostly nude musician figures demarcates the performative space around the temple (Figure 80), while the still and somber *potnia theron*, with her ancient religious connotations, formed the sole repeating element around the temple's edge (Figure 81). The visual hierarchy would have been highlighted by the varying heights of these antefixes, with the *potnia theron* on the temple's roof hovering well above the level of the portico's syrinx- and flute-player. While the latter were symbolically and physically *below* the *potnia theron*, they would nevertheless have been closer to viewers and thus easier to see.

Here as elsewhere, elements of the "standard" kit were apparently considered particularly suitable for temples. The triporticus at Minturnae offered a space for innovation and for the display of distinctly local iconography. It is significant that the triporticus literally encases the temple, forming a local frame through which the temple is presented to viewers. This effect would have

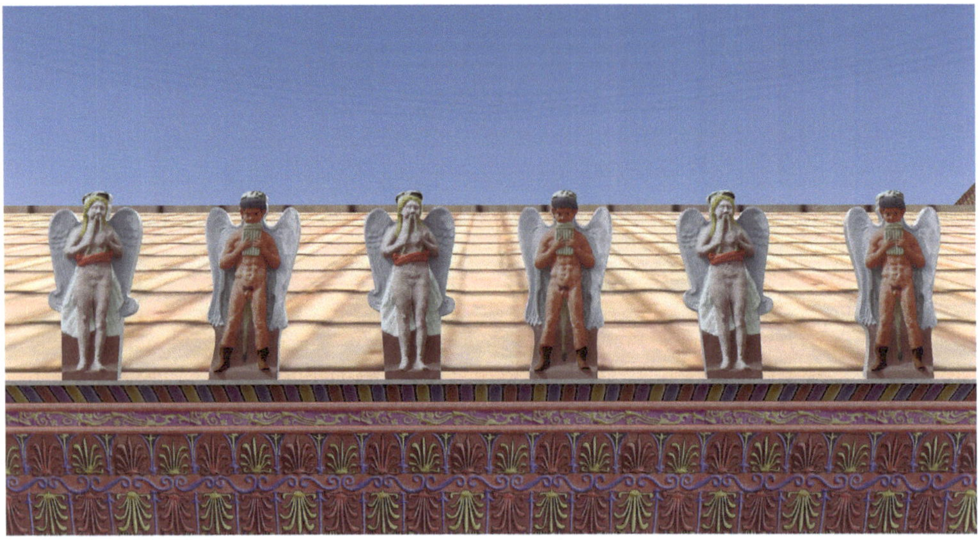

80. Digital reconstruction of the decoration of the triporticus at Minturnae. Restored colors based on surviving traces as well as Johnson's description from the moment of excavation. The antefixes retained less color, and the reconstruction of their polychromy is thus more speculative than that of the revetment plaques. Reconstruction by Indiana University's Virtual World Heritage Lab and Flyover Zone Productions in consultation with the author.

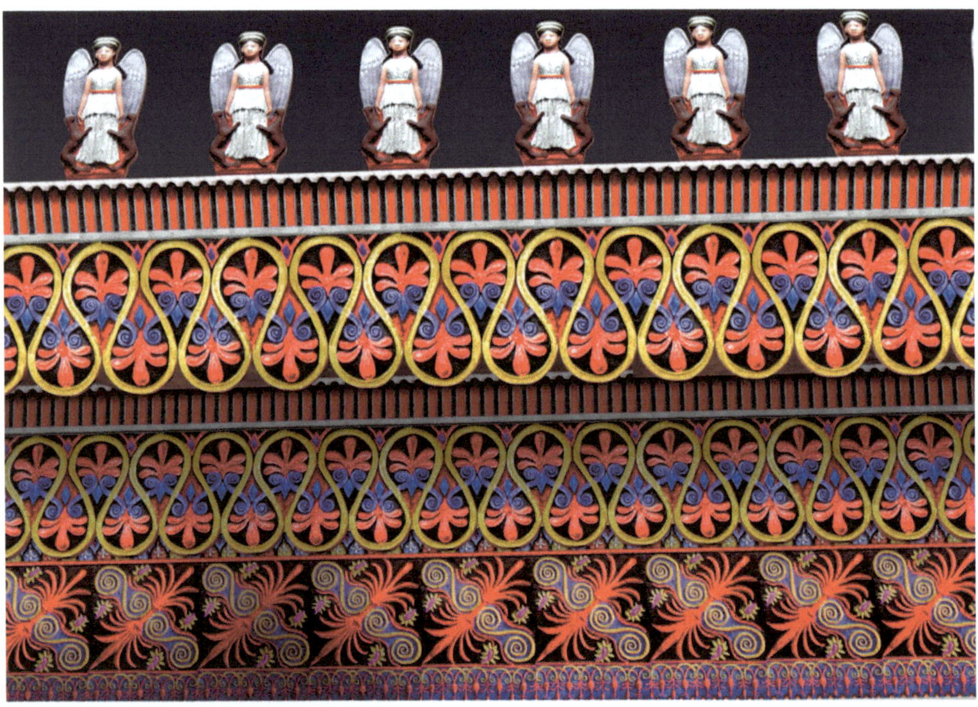

81. Digital reconstruction of the decoration of Minturnae's tripartite temple. Restored colors based on surviving traces as well as Johnson's description from the moment of excavation. Only the coloring of the *potnia theron* antefixes is mostly speculative, as the preserved traces of color were comparatively few. Reconstruction by Indiana University's Virtual World Heritage Lab and Flyover Zone Productions in consultation with the author.

been heightened by the likely appearance of Venus in the center of the pediment, whose presence pointedly recalled the ancient Marica sanctuary just down the road and implied the seamless incorporation of this local cult into the new colony's religious identity. As we have seen, the Marica sanctuary was a fundamental feature of Minturnae's sacred landscape well into the period of the empire and may even have been intervisible with the *area sacra*.

It is worth emphasizing that the combination of "standard" and local elements on the buildings of the *area sacra* must have been deliberate. Not only do the temple and triporticus belong to the same construction phase, but their architectural terracottas appear to be of identical, local manufacture. Analysis of terracotta samples pertaining to both structures revealed that they belong to the same petrographic group.[201] This means that the choice of whether to use more traditional, "standard" forms, or the more experimental designs of the local region, was not dependent on importation or availability – it was a *choice*. The same artisans could and did make both, in the same place.

4.3.4 Archaizing Antefixes at the Dawn of the Imperial Period

Minturnae's Temple B was built in the early imperial period just 60 m east of the tripartite temple and mirrored its predecessor by fronting the Via Appia and being surrounded by a three-winged portico. Being a later structure, however, Temple B was built of tufo, travertine, and opus reticulatum, making terracotta ornamentation functionally unnecessary. Over thirty fragments of *potnia theron* antefixes were nevertheless found flanking the temple's ruins and appear to have constituted part of its original decoration (Figure 82).[202] That the Minturnese chose to add terracotta antefixes to a building that did not require them is noteworthy. The choice of *potnia theron* is particularly significant, as it would have visually linked Temple B with the tripartite temple of the *area sacra*, which by this point would likely have been the colony's oldest and most important cult building. The decision to retain terracotta antefixes suggests that these were seen as integral features of the town's sacred architecture. Their inclusion would also have given the new Temple B a somewhat old-fashioned appearance, setting it firmly within the tradition of Minturnae's temples.

Given the general similarities between the tripartite temple and Temple B (both set within a three-winged portico and facing the Via Appia) as well as the presence of *potnia theron* antefixes on both roofs, the latter seems almost to have been fashioned as a slightly smaller version of the former. The visual comparison between the two temples would have been inescapable for viewers moving along the Via Appia. If the tripartite temple was dedicated to Venus, as I have suggested above, the traditional interpretation of Temple B as dedicated to Divus Iulius would nicely explain this visual quotation. It was designed on a

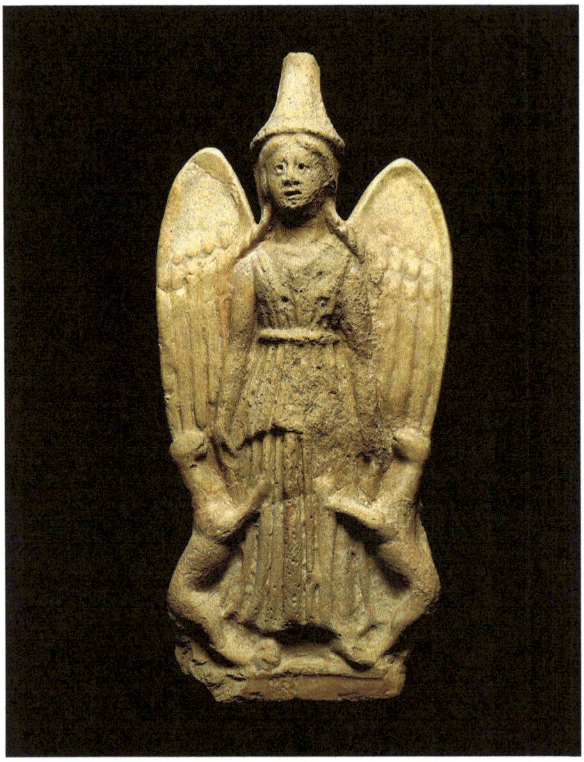

82. *Potnia theron* antefix from Temple B at Minturnae. Philadelphia: Penn Museum. Courtesy of the Penn Museum, object no. 32-36-14A.

respectfully smaller scale but with explicit visual reference to the nearby temple of his patron deity.

Either way, the inclusion of structurally unnecessary terracotta antefixes on this late building speaks eloquently to the enduring symbolic power of terracotta decoration. A similar situation appears to have occurred elsewhere at Minturnae as well. A large rectangular structure referred to tentatively as Temple L by Johnson remains poorly understood, due in part to extensive damage caused by explosions in 1943 or 1944.[203] It sits south of Temple B across the Via Appia and seems to have been part of the Augusteum complex. While the precise nature of the building remains uncertain, the preserved remains do suggest two distinct phases during the imperial period, which are attested by plentiful segments of opus latericium as well as opus mixtum.[204] Campana reliefs with Nilotic scenes were discovered in this area (Figure 83), as well as at least one terracotta antefix with a palmette, bucrania, and wreaths (Figure 84a and b).[205] If this structure is indeed a temple, it would be a fairly late instance in which terracotta decoration is retained. As on Temple B, these terracottas would have served a purely decorative function. Long after Minturnae's architects had moved to stone and concrete

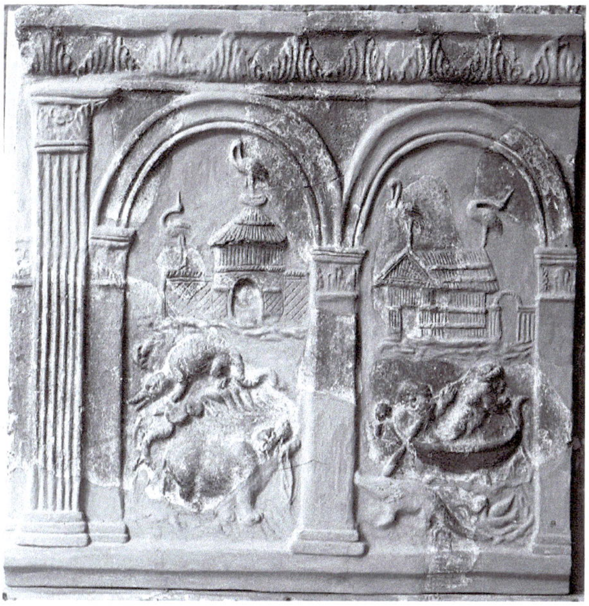

83. Campana relief with Nilotic Scene, from Minturnae. Philadelphia: Penn Museum.
Courtesy of the Penn Museum, object no. 32-36-15.

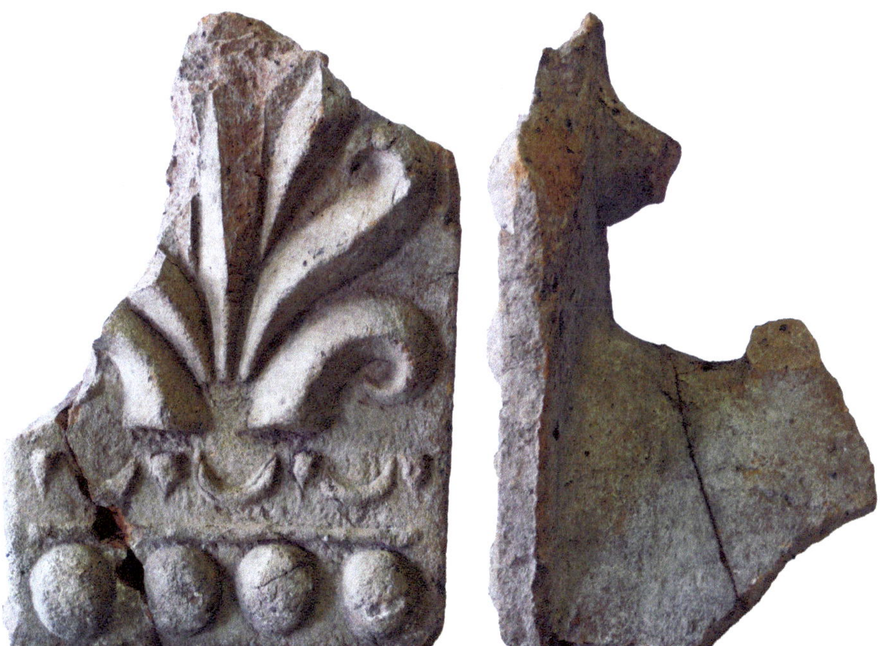

(a) (b)

84. (A AND B) Antefix with palmette, bucrania, and wreaths, from Minturnae. Philadelphia: Penn Museum.
Photographs by author. Courtesy of the Penn Museum, object no. 32-36-10.

construction, then, the aesthetic and symbolic value of terracotta remained important for the town's visual identity.

4.3.5 A Minturnese Visual Identity

The above discussion has touched on only a few examples of the numerous architectural terracottas that survive from Minturnae. Several points regarding the broader corpus can nevertheless be made. It is clear that Minturnae played a major role in architectural terracotta production over an extended chronological period. The importance of the Marica sanctuary endured well beyond the installation of the Roman colony nearby, and the evidence of architectural terracottas suggests that many of the preexisting local artisan networks remained active through the close of the millennium.

Many of the terracottas from Minturnae are characterized by an archaizing or retrospective quality. Indeed, every new generation of temples seems to have consciously referenced the last: the 2nd century palmette antefixes of the Marica temple imitating the Archaic versions, the colony's tripartite temple referencing both its predecessor in the *area sacra* as well as the Marica temple, and finally Temple B reviving the *potnia theron* antefixes from the temples of the *area sacra*. The last instance eloquently illustrates the symbolic power that terracotta still retained for Minturnae's visual and religious identity, even after it had become structurally irrelevant.

The precise forms of architectural terracottas could also be adapted and combined to create new effects. The interplay between temple and portico decoration visible in Minturnae's *area sacra*, for instance, illustrates the complex ways in which terracottas could be read or reinterpreted depending on their context. The tripartite temple featured all elements of the "standard temple kit," but these were presented in the distinctly local frame of the three-winged portico. Careful viewers might also have caught the explicit reference to the distinctive palmette antefixes of the Marica sanctuary, and most viewers would have recognized the connection between Venus and Marica.

As at Cosa, we see a careful curation of elements from both the local religious landscape and the wider repertoire of central Italic terracottas. Common and uncommon elements are adopted, adapted, and combined in new ways, revealing a remarkable blending of styles and types from north, east, and south. The result is a series of terracotta roofs that, taken together, can only really be described as "Minturnese." This unique combination defined a visual identity for the colony and allowed it to assert its status and religious role in the local region as well as in central Italy more broadly. Once established, the decorative style of Minturnae's temples was closely adhered to, augmenting the sense of antiquity and continuity that these terracottas were designed to project.

4.4 MAKING SENSE OF THE EVIDENCE

The architectural terracottas from Cosa and Minturnae suggest complex networks of interaction and adaptation operating at multiple scales. In both cases, elements of the "standard temple kit" are paired with distinctly local types. This combination of elements effectively serves to distinguish the sacred architecture of one town from another, while at the same time asserting its participation in the broader religious landscape of central Italy.[206] As has been stressed above, the blending of types and styles appears to be highly deliberate, and this is important for our understanding of the role of architectural terracottas in this period. The evidence could be examined from any number of perspectives, but issues of manufacture, competition, and religion merit particular consideration here. We will then turn to the broader colonial context in Chapter 5.

First, the logistics of manufacture. The question of fixed versus itinerant workshops was raised in Chapter 1 and bears revisiting in light of the data presented above. As we have seen, the current evidence argues strongly against the singular models of fixed *or* itinerant artisans. Both systems must have operated concurrently though varying in degree based on a host of factors – supply and demand, ease of travel to certain areas, geographical or temporal concentrations of commission opportunities, workshop structure and size, local availability of resources and demands on these resources for other types of production, and of course the needs and preferences of makers, patrons, and communities. A single model is simply inadequate to describe the multiple configurations of architectural terracotta production in central Italy. While our evidence *from* workers and workshops is lamentably patchy, the terracottas themselves attest to the movement of some artisans over long distances as well as to the more circumscribed geography of others. Examples of the former include the appearance of remarkably similar terracottas at sites like Cosa and Ardea, or the Minerva mold at Musarna, which seems to match antefixes from Cosa (Figure 50). At the same time, many terracottas from Cosa and Minturnae attest to specifically local trade networks, with closely related examples appearing only at sites within the local region. Mold-links are evident, for instance, between some of the terracottas from Fregellae and Minturnae, and the fact that the types themselves seem limited to this area has led to the suggestion that Fregellae's mold-made terracottas were produced locally, whereas the hand-made elements are likely the work of traveling artisans.[207]

Although the very existence of the "standard temple kit" suggests shared approaches amongst artisans over a considerable geographic and temporal expanse, its actual use reveals a more nuanced picture that reinforces the idea of simultaneous fixed and itinerant workshop structures. Some elements of the "kit" appear in identical or near-identical forms at far-flung sites (indicating movement), while others reveal in their details a close-knit local network (indicating a fair degree of geographic fixity). Yet others are sufficiently distinctive to suggest manufacture for a specific site and construction event. In other words, multiple manufacture models are apparent even in the case of "standard" elements.

The input of traveling as well as locally based artisans must therefore be recognized as crucial components of the resulting roofs. John Hopkins has recently discussed the complex realities of copresence in the case of earlier building activity in Rome, and the evidence of 3rd–1st century terracottas suggests that such collaborative processes extended at least through the close of the millennium.[208] Regardless of whether or not copresence was "readable" to viewers gazing up at a finished roof, the physical presence of diverse workers, whether at the moment of initial construction or during later repairs, would have been inescapable. These workers would, after all, have required room and board. They would have been seen walking through town and working at the construction site. They likely made use of local workshop facilities such as kilns and sought local expertise to identify sources of high quality clay and other materials. As Hopkins rightly emphasizes, the copresence of diverse workers inevitably influenced the technical, aesthetic, and iconographic features of the terracottas they produced, meaning that any broad characterization we might make of temple architecture in this period is as much about workers and interaction as it is about physical place.[209]

Political and economic rivalry offers a second lens for interpreting the terracotta evidence. The Late Republic has often been characterized as an age of competition – between individuals, communities, towns, and so on.[210] This extends to the religious landscape as well, not only because sanctuaries bolstered the prestige of their associated urban centers but also because sanctuaries must often have been in direct competition with one another. Benjamin Rous has interpreted the numerical decline and spatial concentration of cult places beginning in the 2nd century in terms of a market model, arguing that the "essential keys to success for any cult place in the late republican period were an advantageous location and the number and importance of the services on offer."[211] While many factors must have contributed to local attitudes toward sanctuaries as well as to their survival, it seems likely that inter-sanctuary and inter-polity competition played some role. This was a period of dramatic transformation in central Italy. As political and military power coalesced ever more definitively around Rome, once-proud towns were left with few means of asserting their importance. Religious architecture, which was couched at least superficially in the vocabulary of piety rather than insubordination, may have offered an ideal means of emphasizing local prestige without endangering political accords.

A striking feature of the use of local and regional referents in architectural terracottas is that they appear at colonies as well as at nominally independent sites. This too bears on the question of competition. Colonies were typically planted on recently confiscated land, in areas with deep and proud religious traditions. Politics and religion were never independent entities in ancient Italy, and asserting the cult importance of new settlements must therefore have been a major concern. This may partly explain the incorporation of local styles on the architectural terracottas of new buildings: for power messages to be understood in a local context, they had first to be *readable*. We have seen that Cosa's temple terracottas were intimately linked to those of the surrounding region and display a sustained reliance on traditions from local Etruscan religious architecture. Many terracottas occur in multiple subtypes at Cosa, and conscious efforts seem to have been made to establish a recognizable visual identity for the town's temples and to preserve this aesthetic following any renovations. Similarly, at Minturnae, the proximity of the colony's tripartite temple to the ancient sanctuary of Marica demanded a careful approach to roof decoration. Through a combination of local and more widespread types, paired with direct references to Marica's temple, Minturnae's *area sacra* was presented as fundamental to the religious landscape of the local region – as sharing in and surpassing the Auruncan religious tradition.

All this, of course, must be considered in light of the fact that temples were first and foremost sacred structures.[212] While the competitive political dimension may have mattered greatly for some members of the community, most would have understood these temples primarily in terms of religion – as places designed to honor the gods and secure their protection. Again, both the "standard temple kit" and the more local elements fit comfortably into this framework. I suggested in Chapter 3 that the stubborn conservatism of the "standard kit's" elements was likely due to their association with notions of antiquity and religious tradition, which rendered them particularly appropriate to temple architecture. The terracottas discussed in this chapter, while more uncommon, also derive predominantly from the preexisting religious architecture of the local region. In both cases, we see a desire to forefront religious piety in terms of longevity and tradition and to reference sacred structures within the broader urban (or extra-urban) landscape through visual cues.

Manufacture, politics, and religion, then, were all core components contributing to the appearance and reception of these objects, both at the moment of creation and later as they actively shaped a community's visual landscape from their perch on a temple roof. To interpret these architectural terracottas from one perspective alone would be to oversimplify our evidence and to deny the multifaceted nature of their creation and their role as social meaning makers. In the specific case of 3rd–1st century terracottas, however, there is an additional element that urges more focused attention: the historical context of colonization. Indeed, it is the transforming landscape of central Italy in this period that makes these objects particularly precious as cultural documents, and that distinguishes them from their predecessors and successors. To better understand how these terracottas shaped meaning, we must account for the colonial situation and the humans that inhabited it. Who planned and interacted with these terracottas, and how did the colonial context shape that interaction? What might these objects have signified to patrons, artisans, inhabitants, or passersby? Why were "old"-looking terracottas chosen for new colonies? And finally, how does all of this relate to processes of group identity formation in colonial contexts? These are the questions to which we now turn.

NOTES

1 See Sewell 2005, 2010: 25–33 for a re-analysis of the town plan and the placement of the early forum. For a recent discussion of Cosa's building phases and technologies, see Mogetta 2019, Mogetta 2021: 195–205.

2 Taylor 2002, and see Section 4.2.2.1.

3 Livy 32.2.7 and 33.24.8. Their initial request of 199 BCE was denied.

4 The town's street plan may date to this period as well (Fentress 2000: 17–18). As Bradley 2006: 162 puts it, "the whole creation of the urban infrastructure seems linked to the reinforcement of the colony at this point." On building during this period, see Mogetta 2019, 2021: 195–205 on Cosa specifically and 181-231 for the broader colonial context.

5 As noted in Chapter 2, I use "summit" to refer to the area traditionally called the "arx," "Summit Temple 1" for the earliest temple in this area, and "Triple-Cella temple" for the large 2nd century temple referred to in previous scholarship as the "Capitolium."

6 The House of the Treasure and the House of the Skeleton, discussed in detail in *Cosa IV*.

7 For chronological uncertainties, see Section 2.3.

8 Scott et al. 2015; De Giorgi et al. 2019. A more detailed chronological analysis will appear in the full excavation publication.

9 Taylor 2002.

10 Taylor 2002: 70.

11 Glinister 2000.

12 The precise dating of the cistern remains problematic, and there is no firm evidence that it was built or lined simultaneously with the temple. I owe these observations to Ann Glennie, who recently reexamined this material (Glennie 2022).

13 This is simply an expansion of Taylor's system (Taylor 2002: 59) to allow for the inclusion of multiple Cosa volumes, rather than *Cosa II* alone. For instance, "C3:160" would refer to the perforated cornice described in *Cosa III* beginning on page 160.

14 The presence of three (or four, if we include C2:191) types of revetment plaques is consistent with this suggestion, as most buildings employ two revetment plaque types at once – one on the architrave and one on the raking beams.

15 *Cosa II*: 284.

16 *Cosa II*: 19–24; Scott 1992: 91.

17 Scott 1992: 92.

18 E.g., Taylor 2002: 78. Scott 1992 gives a very summary account, as does Brown 1967.

19 Taylor 2002: 78.

20 Noted too by Taylor, who remarks that foundations on the summit were generally set on the living bedrock, and could thus "easily be removed without a trace" (Taylor 2002: 69).

21 *Cosa II*: 165, 21, and see Section 2.2.
22 Strazzulla 1977: 42–43; Taylor 2002: 69; among others.
23 *Cosa II*: 21–22. For criticism of this logic, see Taylor 2002: 66; and Bispham 2006: 97–98.
24 *Cosa II*: 154, 208–209.
25 Excavation notebooks in the archives of the American Academy in Rome attest to the large quantity of recovered terracottas, referred to mostly in passing. A full tabulation and analysis of these fragments remains a desideratum for future work on Cosa.
26 Scott 1992.
27 Scott 1992.
28 "Talamonaccio" refers to the hill just outside of Talamone and is the site of the famous temple with the Seven Against Thebes pediment (see below).
29 Scott 1992: 94.
30 *Cosa III*: 167–182.
31 The theory is referred to only briefly in Scott 1992: 94.
32 *Cosa III*: 154–166; Taylor 2002: 68–69.
33 Taylor 2002: 72–73.
34 *Cosa II*: 111–118. Taylor also acknowledges this as a clear possibility but wishes to stress the fact that the two pediments "would never have been seen in juxtaposition," and therefore do not need to match (Taylor 2002: 73). In my opinion, the different perforated cornices of Temple B may also reflect a repair rather than the original design.
35 *Cosa II*: 184–185.
36 E.g., Bispham 2006: 100; Quinn and Wilson 2013.
37 Strazzulla 1985: 98.
38 Bruno 2001: 74; Bispham 2006: 100.
39 Scott 1992: 97.
40 For the latter, see Bruno 2001: 74.
41 The initial note regarding their discovery consists of a short paragraph in which they are described as "of large size" (Brendel 1969: 232).
42 Bispham 2006: 100. The only good comparandum for this piece in terms of subject is a plaque from Populonia, which comes from a triple-cella temple but is dated to the late 1st century BCE or early 1st century CE (Megale 2007).
43 *Cosa V*: 29–30.
44 *Cosa V*: 221.
45 *Cosa V*: 217–222.
46 *Cosa II*: 143.
47 *Cosa II*: 143–144. Brown reports that "the entire forepart of the temple almost up to the front wall of the cella was found to have been already gouged away."
48 *Cosa II*: 45.
49 *Cosa II*: 204; McCann 1987: 131.
50 *Cosa II*: 144–145; McCann 1987: 129.
51 McCann 1987: 131.
52 207 such fragments were found in 1950 (*Cosa II*: 204), and 4–5 during McCann's survey (McCann 1987: 134–134, LT1-LT5).
53 *Cosa II*: 204.
54 *Cosa II*: 330–332.
55 McCann 1987: 129, 135–136, LT6-LT7 and fig. VI-11.
56 McCann 1987: 129–131, 136.
57 *Cosa II*: 145; McCann 1987: 132–134.
58 The perforated cornice with swastikas is subtype C2:290 at Cosa. For the Ardea version, see *Cosa II*: 291 and Andrén 1940: 450 no. III:1. The revetment plaque with addorsed palmettes is subtype C2:278 at Cosa. For the comparison with examples from Lanuvium, see *Cosa II*: 281.
59 Känel 2001: 130 also draws attention to the prevalence of terracotta types common in southern and central Etruria on Cosa's "Temple of Jupiter."

60 *Cosa II*: 163–164, 204; *Cosa III*: 162–163; *Cosa V*: 219–220.

61 Museo Guarnacci no. 41.

62 Massa-Pairault 1973: 101–104.

63 The motif appears at these sites on architectural terracottas of various types. Volterra: Andrén 1940: 250 no. 7, pl. 85 fig. 301; Bolsena: Andrén 1940: 213 no. III:1, pl. 77 fig. 265; Sassi Caduti: Andrén 1940: 119 n. III:3, pl. 45 fig. 146; Carlucci 2020: 88–89, fig. 3c; Bettona: Andrén 1940: 266 n. 4, pl. 88 fig. 317; Sovana: Andrén 1940: 226 n. 24, pl. 81 fig. 283.

64 Ara della Regina: Romanelli 1948: 253 fig. 40, Cataldi in Colonna 1985: 74–75 n. A9; Punta della Vipera: Stopponi 1979: 263 f.; tav. X, 1–2 and fig. 6.2.

65 Stopponi 1979: 263 g; tav. X, 3 and fig. 6.3. The larger plaque, by comparison, measures 35 x 31 cm.

66 Von Vacano and von Freytag Löringhoff 1982: 57 and Figures 50–51.

67 C2:161. For the Tarquinia plaques: Romanelli 1948: 252–253, figs. 39–40; Andrén 1940: 71 nos. II:9 and II:10, pl. 22, figs. 76–77.

68 C2:286. For the Vulci plaques: Andrén 1940: 217 no. III:2, pl. 79 fig. 275; Bonamici 1992: 129-30, 133–134 and tav. IVa, who would identify the female heads as representing Medusa. It should be noted that neither of the two fragments from Cosa come from a datable context, complicating Bonamici's statement that they provide a point of reference for the Ponte Rotto examples (Bonamici 1992: 134).

69 *Cosa II*: 154–157, 208–209, 232–234.

70 A bearded male face of similar style and fabric was assigned by Richardson to this type, but he notes that the association is not certain (*Cosa II*: 155). For satyr antefixes with the attributes of Hercules, see, e.g., Andrén 1940: pl. 10 no. 33, pl. 51 no. 164, pl. 68 no. 223, pl. 87 no. 310, as well as the example from Minturnae discussed in Section 4.3.3.

71 *Cosa II*: 157; cf. Bispham 2006: 97, "it is clear that they have nothing in common with Campanian types."

72 For Hercules/Hercle imagery at Etruscan sites, see, e.g., Mastrocinque 1993. Scott 1992: 93 has emphasized the Latin connotations of Hercules, but the hero's long history in Etruria seems to me just as significant in this context. On this question, see also Massa-Pairault 1985b: 119 and Bispham 2006: 102.

73 Von Vacano and von Freytag Löringhoff 1982: 61–63.

74 *Cosa II*: 157.

75 Stopponi 1979: 261, fig. 5.2, tav. IX, 1.

76 Museo archeologico nazionale di Firenze inv. 75214. Richardson reports that "according to the inventory of the museum it was bought from a dealer in Corneto-Tarquinia in 1892 and was reported to come from the ancient city of Tarquinii. It is possible that it actually comes from Cosa, but there is no real reason to doubt the dealer's word" (*Cosa II*: 156). As he notes, the general similarities between terracottas from Cosa and Tarquinia make a Tarquinian origin for the antefix perfectly reasonable.

77 Jolivet and Lovergne 2011.

78 C2:158.

79 For these comparanda, *Cosa II*: 159, Stopponi 1979: 263 n. 103. Söderlind 2006: 119 fig. 11.4 dates the Selvasecca fragment to the first half of the 4th century BCE. Fragments with lilies deriving from the same matrix as that used for the simas of Orvieto's Belvedere Temple were found in 2001: Stopponi 2006: 216 fig. 20.17 and n. 52.

80 Bruschetti 1992: 320–321 and tav. II, a, b, tav. III, a, b; and p. 322 for the date.

81 Tarquinia: Romanelli 1948: 252 fig. 39; Andrén 1940: 70 no. II:6, pl. 22 figs. 76 and 78. Punta della Vipera: Stopponi 1979: 261–263, fig 5.4–6, tav. IX, 4–5.

82 *Cosa II*: 224–225.

83 *Cosa II*: 224.

84 See the arguments in Fentress 2000: 21–22.

85 Romanelli 1948: 252 fig. 39, upper left corner.

86 *Cosa II*: 159–160, 189–191; *Cosa III*: 160, 161–162.
87 *Cosa III*: 161–162.
88 Von Vacano and von Freytag Löringhoff 1982: 71; *Cosa II*: 190–191. Additional examples from Tarquinia, pictured in Romanelli 1948: fig. 40, are also closely related.
89 Cappelli 1930; Andrén 1940: 238; von Vacano 1985: 166; Carlucci 2021: 431–432.
90 The primary archaeological documentation for Telamon comes from the hurried excavations conducted by Vivarelli in 1876, and the subsequent gathering of finds between 1888 and 1892, in which individual find-spots went unrecorded. Limited excavations in 1962–1964 and 1969 yielded new elements, but by this time the archaeological record was too damaged to be meaningfully salvaged (Ciampoltrini 1985: 115; von Vacano and von Freytag Löringhoff 1982: 54; von Vacano 1985).
91 Von Vacano and von Freytag Löringhoff 1982: 29.
92 Von Vacano and von Freytag Löringhoff 1982: 29–30, 54–60, nn. 1–15.
93 On the pediment, see Section 5.3.2.
94 Von Vacano and von Freytag Löringhoff 1982: 30.
95 See, e.g., von Vacano and von Freytag Löringhoff 1982: 59, 63, 71, 73.
96 Von Vacano and von Freytag Löringhoff 1982: 54–55. Identical or near-identical versions of the same types have been found in several areas around Orvieto, in particular at the Via S. Leonardo temple (Andrén 1940: 162, I:6 and I:7, pl. 62: 201 and 202. The latter, for instance, is identical to an antefix from the area sacra di Cannicella shown here in Figure 57: Andrén 1940: 190, II:5, pl. 71: 237). Versions of these antefixes also belong to later phases at Orvieto.
97 Several shell antefixes with alternating male and female heads are known from Cosa. Silen and maenad shell antefixes were found in the excavations of Temple B in the forum (C3:156), while shell antefixes with the heads of a maenad and young satyr (C2:174, 186, 187), as well as a pair with Minerva and Hercules (C2:154, 208, 232), appear in various versions on Cosa's summit. Fragments of framing shells attest to the existence of several other versions of the basic type, although the identity of the figures is not always known (e.g., C2:233, C2:157, C3:164).
98 Torelli 1967: 343.
99 Stopponi 1979: 252, 256.
100 Stopponi 1979 *passim*. The closest similarities are with phase III of Temple B at Pyrgi.
101 Torelli 1965: 125; 1967: 343. Official excavations at the site were initiated in the 1960s, thus *after* the publication of *Cosa II*.
102 Torelli 1967: 343.
103 Part of the issue is distinguishing *which* Castrum Novum our sources are referring to. On this problem and the relevant evidence, see Torelli 1967: 343–344 and n. 30.
104 Romanelli 1939, 1948. The work of the Tarquinia Project has, however, greatly helped to clarify the stratigraphic picture of this area: see the overview in Bonghi Jovino 2010, esp. 174–176 for the Ara della Regina.
105 Bonghi Jovino 2010: 174–176.
106 Andrén and Berggren 1969; Cataldi 1985: 77; de Grummond 2001–2002: 17.
107 Cataldi 1985: 77.
108 Cataldi 1985: 77.
109 Cataldi 1985: 77. On the many roads around Tarquinia connecting it with the surrounding region, see Harari 1997.
110 Laurence 1999: 95–108; Terrenato 2019: 233.
111 On continuity in the region's material culture following the founding of Cosa, see Bruno 2001.
112 Ciampoltrini 1985: 116; Ciampoltrini and Rendini 1992: 987–988; Ciampoltrini 1995b: 298; Ciampoltrini 2011: 22; Celuzza 2002: 171.
113 Torelli 1965: 126; for the Bolsena antefix: Andrén 1940: 209, II:2, pl. 78:266; de Grummond 2006: 148–149, pl. II.

114 Gazzetti 1985: 62; Buranelli 1992: 145–146 and tav. II.

115 Mastrocinque 1993: 58.

116 Bispham 2006: 95. For Deposit A, see Taylor 1957: 75–91.

117 Hercules/Minerva may have been a particularly apt choice for Cosa, as the pair is also attested on architectural terracottas in Latium and central Italy going back to the 6th century BCE (at Rome, Caere, Pyrgi, Satricum, Veii, and possibly at Velletri and Caprificio as well: Lulof 2000; Winter 2009: 377–381, 466–468). While the subject is similar, these are acroterial statues featuring full bodied images of the pair. They thus follow a different line of development than the local head antefixes immediately surrounding Cosa.

118 Meritt and Edlund-Berry 2000: 21, 88, XXV, 1; Edlund-Berry 2008: 444. The so-called Etruscan round molding is by no means limited to Etruscan areas and is attested in Roman, Latin, Umbrian, and Samnite architecture as well: Edlund-Berry 2022.

119 Edlund-Berry 2022: table 1.

120 For a recent discussion of moldings and their chronology, including the current limitations of our knowledge, see Edlund-Berry 2022. Podium moldings offer a particularly intriguing body of comparative evidence when considering architectural terracottas, given the ways in which both have been tied up in assumptions regarding "Romanization" despite their widespread use across central Italic religious architecture, including in areas beyond Rome's direct control. Like temple terracottas (especially the elements of the "standard kit"), these moldings tend to follow a recognizable format but differ from site to site in their details. As with the terracottas, this may suggest a combination of local and traveling artisans (Edlund-Berry 2022).

121 *Cosa II*: 32, 67, 74, 81, 83, 115. Vulci tuff was also used in the forum area, see, e.g., Cosa III: 19, 110, 217–218, 226.

122 Mogetta 2019, 2021: 195–205. Fentress and Perkins 2016: 381 ff. note that the supplement of 197 BCE also appears to mark the beginning of stone domestic architecture at Cosa. On the importance of the early 2nd century BCE phase for Cosan religious architecture, see also Scott 1992.

123 Mogetta 2019, esp. 261 on local knowledge as "a crucial prerequisite for the selection of sources of building materials, especially the volcanic sands and the stratified sandstone."

124 Mogetta 2019: 241 and *passim*. The "initial emphasis on public projects . . . would have been instrumental in defining the new, common identity and purpose between the colonists and the previous town inhabitants" (Mogetta 2021: 203).

125 *Cosa II*: 270–271.

126 Coarelli et al. 1989: 49–50. The polygonal masonry walls are 2.70 m thick. Johnson identified them as part of the pre-Roman settlement (Johnson 1935: 1–2), but they are now more commonly dated to the earliest phase of the Roman colony. In this case, the preexisting Auruncan settlement may have sat on a nearby hill, perhaps on the site of modern Minturno (Coarelli et al. 1989: 50).

127 Excavations in this area have only recently been undertaken by the Soprintendenza, and most of the material uncovered thus far is of Imperial date or later: Bellini 2006 and especially Bellini 2021.

128 Coarelli et al. 1989: 50.

129 For a discussion of Minturnae's "urban" and "periurban" development, see Goodman 2016.

130 On the importance of major roads in Roman urban planning, see Laurence 1999, with specific reference to Minturnae's layout at pp. 151–156. As Laurence puts it, "the general pattern at Minturnae is clear. We find a spatial situation which emphasizes the need to display the glory of the town to travelers" (Laurence 1999: 154).

131 Johnson refers to the area north of the Via Appia as the Republican Forum and the section to its south as the Imperial Forum.

132 Johnson 1935: 16. He notes that this is roughly 60 x 30 Roman feet.

133 Livy 27.37, 36.37.

134 For a summary of doubts regarding the structure's association with the *aedes Iovis*, see Bolder-Boos 2011: 119.

135 Livy (XXXVI, 37) associates the *aedes Iovis* and *tabernae* with the forum, but the exact extent of Minturnae's Republican forum remains unclear.

136 The installation of a three-winged portico framing a temple has often been discussed in relation to the "monumentalization" of central Italic sanctuary sites in the 2nd century BCE. Similar situations are known at sites like Gabii, Praeneste, Tibur, and Fregellae, see, e.g., Rous 2010.

137 On Minturnae's urban center as designed to be visible to travelers along the Via Appia, see Laurence 1999: 151–154.

138 Coarelli et al. 1989: 52; Livi 2006: 97; Kosmopoulos 2021: 302. Johnson (1935: 24–25) provides several possible reconstructions of the ground-plan. Bolder-Boos (2011: 120, 126) suggests that the original Capitolium may have been inside the *castrum* area and was then moved when the town expanded. She cites (119–120) the tripartite temple's position along the *decumanus maximus* as being particularly appropriate for a Capitolium, but given the wide variation in temple placement during this period and the lack of supporting evidence, this seems to me insufficient to retain the traditional identification. For a recent discussion of Italic temple podiums with internal grid structures in relation to seismic activity and damage prevention, with reference to Minturnae, see Diosono et al. 2022.

139 Barton 1982: 260 notes that Capitolia are "often, but not necessarily, physically divided into three longitudinal divisions." The temple at Pietrabbondante, for example, has a tripartite division but is certainly not a Capitolium. Other examples include the temple of the Dioscuri at Cori and the temples at Veii, Lanuvium, and Ardea. For a discussion of this problem with further examples, see Bispham 2006: 100; Quinn and Wilson 2013: 130–131.

140 Vitr. *De arch.* 4.7.2.

141 A recent survey of this debate can be found in Quinn and Wilson 2013; other important studies include Bianchi 1950; Barton 1982; and Bispham 2006; cf. also Stek 2009.

142 The Augustan colony is better attested than the Caesarian predecessor, but neither can currently be proved with absolute certainty. Hyginus Gromaticus provides the only literary evidence for the Augustan colony, while the Caesarian colony is attested only in Pseudo-Frontinus. Johnson 1935: 9 discusses the evidence for both, for which he finds archaeological support. See also the recent findings presented in Bellini 2021.

143 Johnson 1935: 29–36; Livi 2006: 98 and n. 33. This complicated deposit, identified by Johnson as a bidental, also includes a late Imperial addition.

144 This temple has never been fully published. It is briefly discussed in Johnson's 1940 Pauly-Wissova entry, esp. pp. 478–480; see further Mesolella 2012: 152–160; Ferrante, Lacam, and Quadrino 2015: 98–100; Kohlberger-Schaub 2015; Kosmopoulos 2021: 300–301; Bellini 2021.

145 The inscription reads: DEIVO IULIO / IUSSU POPULI ROMANI / E LEGE RUFRENA.

146 This suggestion was first put forward by Johnson 1935: 5–6 (see also Johnson 1940: 478–480). Brian Rose offered further arguments for the identification in a paper entitled "The Penn Museum and the Excavations at Minturnae," delivered at the American Academy in Rome on February 22, 2018. Kohlberger-Schaub believes the evidence of the statue base is insufficient to link the temple with the worship of the divine Caesar (Kohlberger-Schaub 2015: 155–156).

147 Bellini 2021: 12.

148 Bellini 2021: 11. On the Augusteum, see the contributions of G. Murro and L. Di Siena in Bellini 2021.

149 Bellini 2021: 11. For the water features, see also Manderscheid 2015, 2021.

150 For detailed discussions of Minturnae's buildings and urban development, see Johnson 1935; Coarelli et al. 1989; Bellini and von Hesberg 2015; and Bellini 2021. Useful summaries of the historical, epigraphic, and archaeological evidence from Minturnae can

be found in Bolder-Boos 2011: 101–127; and Ferrante, Lacam, and Quadrino 2015: 87–130. Lackner 2008: 121–125 discusses the development of the forum.

151 Plut. *Mar.* 39.4.

152 Most are documented in Mingazzini 1938; for a summary, see Livi 2006: 111–113; Bolder-Boos 2011: 122–127. The Marica sanctuary is mentioned in literary sources into the late 4th century CE.

153 Barletta 1996; Rescigno 1998.

154 Barletta 1996: 41; Livi 2006: 111; 2019: 375.

155 Rescigno 1998: 336–347.

156 Livi 2006: 109–111. See Section 3.3.3.

157 On terracottas from the Marica sanctuary dating between the 2nd century BCE and 1st century CE, see Livi 2019.

158 Livi 2022. Johnson mentioned the deposit and published a single photo in Johnson 1933b: 15, tav. VIII fig. 9, and Erika Harnett drew attention to the existence of the statues in 1998 (Harnett 1998: 104 n. 19). Many of the fragments are discussed in Crawford-Brown 2019b. As Livi notes, only those fragments that can be matched with archival photos taken at the time of Johnson's excavation can be securely attributed to this deposit, as the fragments were later moved and mixed with fragments from other areas (Livi 2022: 153).

159 My initial findings were presented in Crawford-Brown 2019b and have been updated here based on further study and Livi's article.

160 For a discussion of the surviving fragments, see Crawford-Brown 2019b: 210–224; Livi 2022. It is my understanding that Livi will soon publish a more comprehensive study of the fragments.

161 Johnson refers to five different types of clay and firing in a letter dated September 11, 1931, but five groups are not currently distinguishable for the fragments that survive in storage at Minturnae. This corpus is clearly incomplete, and its study is further complicated by the fact that large gobs of restorer's glue (the restorations themselves have since been undone) cover the breaks of most fragments, making it difficult to analyze the clay fabric. It is thus possible that more than two groups are represented by the extant fragments, though a fair degree of uniformity is suggested by the overall similarities in scale and style. Based on Livi's observations, the surviving fragments represent at least three pediments (Livi 2022: 176 n. 69).

162 Penn ar. Photos 26027 and 26023, showing the crossed feet of a draped female figure and the torso and legs of a semi-nude male figure seated on a throne. Fragments of both figures are currently held in on-site storage at Minturnae: Crawford-Brown 2019b: 216–218; Livi 2022: 158–164.

163 Securely part of the same fabric group are the fragments shown reconstructed in Penn ar. photos 26022, 26024, 26025, 26028, 26031, and 29114. Livi (2022: 170 cat. 6 and 168 fig. 26) notes a few minor differences in the fabrics of the fragments that match photos 26030 and 26032, but they seem to me generally consistent with this larger group (on the surviving fragments, see Crawford-Brown 2019b: 211–216, 219; Livi 2022). Many of the smaller fragments found in storage at Minturnae, as well as the figures shown in archival photos but not located on site, could also belong to this group.

164 Minturnae collection photo #29114. On this figure, see Livi 2022: 171–173 cat. 9.

165 Interestingly, heads and attributes are missing for all figures, a phenomenon Livi connects with the nature of their ritual deposit, Livi 2022: 176–177.

166 Penn ar. photos 26022 and 26032. It is possible that the leg shown in Penn ar. photo 26024 belongs to the figure in military dress (photo 26022), but this cannot be confirmed. It is included very tentatively in the reconstruction presented here. On these fragments, see Livi 2022: 164–167 cat. 3 and 170 cat. 7.

167 Penn ar. photo 26025, see Livi 2022: 168 cat. 4. The other, shown in photo 26028, is identified by Livi (2022: 173 cat. 10) as belonging to a female figure but seems to me too

fragmentary to identify with certainty and has therefore been left intentionally ambiguous in the reconstruction here.

168 Penn ar. photo 26030. On the fragments, see Livi 2022: 170 cat. 6.

169 *Cosa II*: 332–367; Scott 1992: 96–97; Torelli 1999: 132.

170 Cf. the discussion in *Cosa II*: 364–365.

171 For Nemi, see Moltesen 2009; for Castrum Inui: see most recently Rossi 2018 and Torelli 2018: 502–503, with previous bibliography; for Civitella, see Liberatore 2006. Further comparanda for the individual statues are provided in Livi 2022.

172 Livi 2022 also settles on a 2nd century BCE date for the Minturnae figures based on the known comparanda.

173 For analogous situations at other central Italic sanctuaries, see Glinister 2000.

174 The foundations of the tripartite temple at Minturnae are 18.6 m x 17.82 m, and the pedimental sculptures are all roughly life-size. The figures of the Via di San Gregorio are only slightly under life-size, and the pediment is thought to have spanned c. 14 m (Moltesen 2009: 361–362).

175 For examples in which the deity (or his/her attributes) to whom a temple is dedicated is shown in the center of the pediment, see Kaderka 2018: 281. On the placement of such images as urging comparative viewing alongside cult statues, see Ekserdjian 2023; esp. 20–23.

176 As in the relief showing the Capitoline Temple in the Palazzo dei Conservatori in Rome (MC 0807). For the "traditional pattern of a seated Iuppiter flanked by Minerva (on his right) and Iuno (on his left)," see Barton 1982: 260.

177 A similar figure in military dress, identified as Mars, appears on the Via di San Gregorio pediment (Ferrea 2002: 153–154 and cat. nn. 21–29; Kaderka 2018: 83–84). For related depictions of Mars, see *LIMC* II Ares/Mars. Torelli has argued for the identification of one of the seated female figures on the pediment from Temple A at Castrum Inui with Venus (most recently Torelli 2018: 502–503 with previous bibliography. On the figure, see also Rossi 2018: 346), but this figure is also quite fragmentary and lacking sure attributes. The two differ obviously in that the Minturnae example is standing (as appropriate for the pediment's central figure) whereas in Torelli's reconstruction for Castrum Inui she would be a seated observer.

178 See the overview in Bolder-Boos 2011: 110–112.

179 Johnson 1933a: n. 8. Ferrante in Ferrante, Lacam, and Quadrino 2015: 128.

180 Solin 1999: 400–401 and fig. 8; Coarelli 2008: 106; Ferrante in Ferrante, Lacam, and Quadrino 2015: 127.

181 Adriani 1938: n. 10; cf. Coarelli et al. 1989: 63 n. 5, who reference another statue preserved in the Zagreb Museum. Erika Harnett also discusses these statues: Harnett 1986: 70–71, cat. A10 and Z4.

182 Ruegg 1995: 21–22 (clamshells), 17–20 (figurines, including at least one Eros).

183 Coarelli 2008: 106.

184 The interpretation of the Venus Marina type itself remains somewhat debated, but the goddess' maritime character does seem to be emphasized by the occasional inclusion of a dolphin at her side; *LIMC* II, 65–67 (Venus Marina); Becatti 1971, esp. 24–38; Harnett 1986: 70–71. The Minturnae examples are both damaged. One seems to have included an Eros at the goddess' side, while the bottom of the other type is not preserved at all, making it impossible to ascertain whether or not she was accompanied by a dolphin (Harnett 1986: 70–71).

185 Text Thilo and Hagen (Teubner 1881), author's translation.

186 Interestingly, Gaetano Ciuffi records the discovery at Marica's sanctuary of a small bronze statuette of Mars dating to the 6th century BCE, suggesting that he was already worshipped in some form by the Aurunci (Ciuffi 1854: 72; Bolder-Boos 2011: 113, 124). The early pairing of a Mars-like figure with Marica might have further underscored the connection with Venus, who appears to be accompanied by Mars on the pediment.

187 Johnson 1935: 87–88.
188 Livi 2006: 105.
189 Känel 2010: 264, abb. 3; Känel and Stangoni 2019: 112–113, 118–119; Nonnis 2019. I thank Rudolf Känel for kindly sharing information and detailed measurements for the Fregellae plaques. On the relationship between Fregellae and Minturnae, see also Crawford-Brown 2019c.
190 Coarelli et al. 1986, esp. G. Manca de Mores and M. N. Pagliardi's discussion of the architectural terracottas: pp. 51–52, tav. XXVI 1, 5. While the colony of Fregellae was founded in 328 BCE, the Sanctuary of Aesculapius seems to date no earlier than the second quarter of the 2nd century BCE. Because the entire area was ravaged by the Romans in 125 BCE, terracottas from the Aesculapius temple are generally dated between 175 and 125 BCE. The two types are thus roughly contemporary in date as well.
191 The Minturnae version is reconstructed to a height of 54 cm, vs. the 34 cm suggested for the Fregellae examples. A few additional antefixes of this type are of uncertain provenance: Pensabene and Sanzi Di Mino 1983 no. 230 (= Inv. 295737), tav. LX, and no. 1010 (= Inv. 115429) tav. LX ("Dono Banca d'Italia, forse da Civita Castellana"), and a fragment now in Munich is listed in Andrén 1940: pl. 159 n. 545. The details (as far as one can see from the published photo) and the dimensions of the first of these precisely match those of the Minturnae type. Given the known dispersal of objects from Minturnae, it seems quite possible that this unprovenanced example may derive from the site.
192 This antefix is held in a private collection, and unfortunately is unpublished and undocumented. I thank Rudolf Känel for alerting me to the existence of this antefix and for sharing information on it. The connection between the terracottas of Minturnae and Capua is particularly striking, as it extends back into the Archaic period.
193 I thank Marco Germani for providing information on this piece.
194 Johnson 1935: 86–87.
195 A draped figure from Luni (Forte et al. 1992: 191) and a nude figure (possibly male?) flanked by amphorae from Tortoreto (*NS* 1896, 513 fig. 2) offer vague comparanda. Closer comparisons may be made with fragments from Praeneste (on display in the museum) and Capua (Koch 1912: 68 no. P 663 and Plate XVII 2), as well as with three pieces of unknown provenience catalogued by Pensabene and Sanzi Di Mino (Pensabene and Sanzi Di Mino 1983 nos. 227, 228, 229).
196 Pagliardi in Coarelli et al. 1986: 51 and Tav. XXVI 4. More recently, a fragment of this type was found in a closed stratigraphic context in domus I.7 at Fregellae, confirming a date in the 3rd century BCE. The fragment will soon be published by Rudolf Känel in *Fregellae. Le domus a est del Foro*, ed. F. Diosono et al., as cat. no. 137. I thank Dr. Känel for sharing information on this important fragment.
197 Barletta 1996; Rescigno 1998.
198 Crawford-Brown 2019c.
199 Minturnae: University of Pennsylvania Museum inv. 32-36-13. Teano: Museo archeologico di Teanum Sidicinum inv. 292456.
200 For architectural terracottas as evidence of enduring local networks in this region, see Crawford-Brown 2019c.
201 These samples were taken and analyzed by the author at the University of Pennsylvania in the spring of 2015. For the full petrographic report, see Crawford-Brown 2019b, Appendix 1. A summary of the findings is provided in Crawford-Brown 2019a: 196–198.
202 Johnson 1935: 90.
203 Bellini 2021: 17.
204 Bellini 2021: 17. The structure is referred to only twice in Johnson's publication, though here too he notes the brickwork: Johnson 1935: 7 and 77.
205 For the Campana reliefs, see Johnson 1934: 17. This antefix type survives in one nearly complete example in Philadelphia (University of Pennsylvania Museum inv. 32-36-10) and several smaller fragments in the Minturnae storerooms. The find-spot of the

Philadelphia example, the only one for which a provenience is recorded, is listed as Temple L. It seems quite possible that the unrecorded fragments come from the same area. On these terracottas, see also Livi 2002: 34.

206 Similar processes detectable across the "Hellenistic" and "Roman" Mediterranean have been fruitfully analyzed in terms of universalization and particularization – the former indicating processes by which elements originally attached to a specific culture take on a new role in a larger system and the latter to elements of the broader system applied and contextualized in a local context. See, in particular, Witcher 2000; Versluys 2013, 2015; Ricci 2019.

207 Pedacchioni 2019: 41–42. On the evidence of itinerant artisans for hand-modeled terracottas from Fregellae, see Känel 2019.

208 Hopkins 2024.

209 Hopkins 2024; see in particular 46–52 on the copresence of diverse workers in terracotta as necessarily unbinding these objects from political designations regarding states or territories.

210 This phenomenon has been most consistently described in relation to Roman elites, e.g., Wiseman 1985: 3–19; Rosenstein 1990; Hölkeskamp 1993; Flower 1996; Stolle 1999; Patterson 2000: 29–52; Bleckmann 2002; Keller 2004, 2007; Farney 2007; among others. In relation to material culture evidence, see, e.g., Welch 2006; Rous 2009, 2010, 2011; Vermeulen 2021; among others. For factional competition in relation to the archaeological record for the 4th and 3rd centuries BCE, see also Muccigrosso 1998; Terrenato 2019; Davies 2020.

211 Rous 2009: 76.

212 On colonization and religion in central Adriatic Italy during this period, see recently Belfiori 2022.

FIVE

INVENTING HISTORY, INVENTING IDENTITY

5.1 INTRODUCTION

The preceding chapters have traced several trends regarding the appearance and diffusion of central Italic temple terracottas during the last three centuries BCE. These objects reveal a persistent tendency toward archaism and conservatism, which is true for elements of the "standard temple kit" as well as for many of the more locally specific types. Antiquity, or at least the visual evocation of antiquity, was apparently prized over innovation. Furthermore, the particular interpretation of antiquity inherent in these roof programs is often intimately bound to the surrounding landscape and to preexisting traditions in local religious architecture. The logistics of manufacture, questions of politics and rivalry, and the overarching religious nature of temple decoration have each been singled out as core elements of these objects' social meaning. It should be stressed that such meanings would never have been static but must have changed over time and from person to person. Patrons, artisans, and viewers, for instance, would necessarily have experienced these terracottas in different ways and would have attached to them a highly personal set of connotations. In the case of the 3rd–1st century, moreover, all these factors must be considered against the historical backdrop of widespread colonization in Italy.

The present chapter highlights this colonial context and explores its implications for interpreting the evidence of architectural terracottas. It considers the people who inhabited colonial spaces and who interacted with architectural terracottas in these settings. It focuses, in other words, on the broader problems of who, how, and why. Who was responsible for the design of these terracotta programs? Who viewed them, and how might a viewer's background have impacted interpretation? How did new settlers use temple architecture to insert themselves into the local landscape? Why did they rely on archaizing and local designs, and why was an *old* aesthetic deemed necessary for *new* colonial communities?

Addressing these questions necessarily involves consideration of broader historical and theoretical issues from colonization practices, to identity formation, to the maintenance or even invention of cultural memory within communities. As I will argue, the ethnic and cultural heterogeneity of most colonial communities during the 3rd–1st centuries meant that there was no clear-cut visual culture to import. It had to be actively constructed, and religious architecture offered a particularly appealing medium. Because they survive so copiously, temple terracottas offer one of our clearest windows into processes of identity formation and tradition invention during the tumultuous centuries in which Rome consolidated its power in Italy.

5.2 MIXED POPULATIONS, MIXED VIEWERS

5.2.1 Peopling Colonial Temple Architecture: Patrons, Artisans, and Viewers

In order to consider larger questions concerning identity, cultural memory, and the invention of tradition, we must first establish whose we are discussing. Three major categories are at play: the people who commissioned and oversaw the construction of temples, the workers hired to build them, and the people who viewed and interpreted them once they had been built.[1] Our evidence is dishearteningly scanty regarding the first group. Local magistrates are generally thought to have played the leading role in public construction works in colonies, in which case they acted (at least nominally) on behalf of the wider community.[2] This local elite seems often to have included members of the indigenous population. Russell T. Scott has suggested, for example, that persons of Etruscan extraction were likely among those responsible for the building boom in 2nd century BCE Cosa, and similar arguments have been made for building projects in Latium and Campania.[3] While many such projects may have had a "communal" flavor, with magistrates acting on a local *Senatus Consultum*, this was not always the case.[4] An inscription on an altar at Gabii preserves the cognomen Cethegus, presumably related to the aristocratic family of the Cornelii Cethegi (Figure 85).[5] It is thus possible that the entire sanctuary complex at Gabii is a product of private munificence. In reality, the situation must have varied over time and from town to town.[6] When epigraphic attestations are lacking, it is generally impossible to pinpoint who

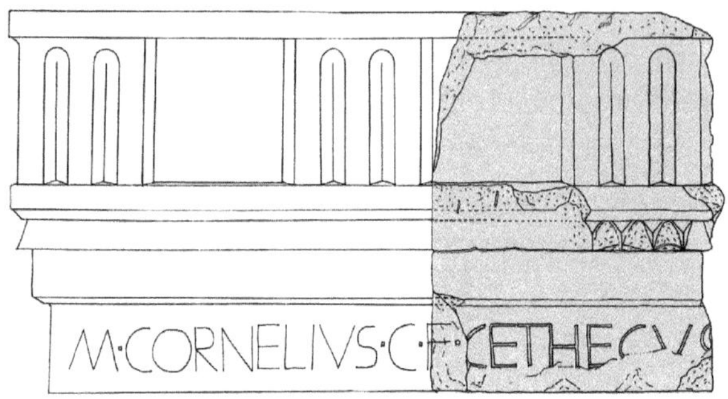

85. Inscription from the altar at the Temple of Juno at Gabii, as reconstructed by the excavators. Image after Coarelli in Almagro-Gorbea 1982: 126 fig. 1.

precisely was responsible financially or legally for the construction of a specific temple or restoration phase.

Still, some general observations can be drawn from the surviving evidence. Perhaps most significant is the fact that local elites, who seem to have taken a leading role in post-conquest constructions, were not necessarily part of a "Roman" culture – if such a thing can even be defined. The epigraphic and funerary evidence suggests a strong continuity in the presence of local elites within their communities before and after Roman conquest.[7] Indeed, Nicola Terrenato has argued that they played a fundamental role in the negotiation of conquest and in many cases saw their wealth and status increase substantially as a result.[8] While some physically relocated to Rome, the majority seem to have stayed put and to have maintained their roles in local power structures while acting as intermediaries with Rome and with elites of other regional polities.[9] They were the holders of wealth and power in most post-conquest communities and were likely responsible for the commissioning and financing of large-scale architecture in these contexts.

It is hardly surprising, then, that local patrons would have commissioned works consistent with pre-Roman local styles in religious architecture. Many other features of material culture remained relatively unchanged, and there is no obvious reason why local elites should have sought out temple decoration types with which they themselves were unfamiliar or that carried some sort of overt "Roman" referent.[10] This would mirror the better-studied situation regarding public cults established in new colonies. Rather than following a "Roman" or standardized model, these appear to have been heavily dependent on local practices and the loyalties of commissioning magistrates.[11] We shall return to this topic shortly.

Now, however, there is still the question of how much direct oversight the commissioner had when it came to details of architectural decoration.[12] Here too there was likely considerable variation – we can imagine cases in which patrons took a relatively hands-off approach after initial discussions and, conversely, instances in which the appearance of a deity on a pediment or the iconography of an antefix was carefully negotiated between patron and artist. Perhaps the best way for us to attempt to understand patrons' intentions is by examining their choice of artisans, since that crucial selection was presumably at their discretion. Artisans and workshops would have had a fairly well-established style and worked in the forms and traditions with which they were most familiar. Patrons probably saw examples of their work before hiring them, either on completed temples or through smaller samples. In other words, whether or not patrons cared to discuss the precise appearance of palmettes on revetment plaques or the choice of square or circular piercings on cornices, they surely had a general sense of what they were getting into in terms of style and overall aesthetic. It is significant, therefore, that the workshops most often hired in 3rd–1st century BCE central Italy worked in a highly archaizing style. The frequent and close similarities between the architectural terracottas of colonial temples and those of preexisting religious sites further suggest that patrons must have been aware of these connections and consciously chose to formulate their new temples on a traditional local model.

It is also noteworthy that patrons commissioned works from both local and itinerant artisans. This suggests that there was nothing inherently incongruous, at least from a patron's point of view, in asking an artisan from outside a given community to design the forms that would come to represent it visually. Such a practice is unsurprising when we consider the long history of architectural terracotta production in central Italy. As discussed earlier, itinerant artisans appear to have played a fundamental role from the beginning (see Sections 1.5.7 and 4.4). This is borne out by the striking similarities in temple terracottas from different towns (whether or not they were politically allied) already by the 6th century and is reflected in the later anecdote about Vulca being called to Rome from Veii to work on the Capitoline temple. We have seen in Chapters 3 and 4 how the terracotta evidence from the 3rd–1st centuries strongly suggests a situation of mixed local and itinerant artisans.

The limited evidence thus suggests that both the patrons who financed new temples in post-conquest contexts, as well as the artisans who built and decorated them, would have been "mixed" groups. A strong local element is clear in both cases, but this operates in conjunction with a deep involvement in the political, economic, social, and artistic developments of central Italy – an involvement that reflects the movement of people and not only of ideas. Patrons and artisans had plentiful options from which to choose as they set about designing a new temple roof. In almost all cases, they opted to forefront local traditions while still utilizing the popular archaizing types that would have been readable to a broad central Italic viewership.

Regardless of patrons' or artisans' intentions, once these terracottas were in place on a temple roof they would have actively begun to shape a town's visual character and would have been subject to interpretation by those who viewed them. Indeed, the majority of people who interacted with these terracottas probably had little or no say in the decision-making processes. They would nevertheless have been the key agents in how such objects were *received* and in what they came to signify for communities.

Who were these viewers? The question is particularly complicated in the case of colonies. Studies over the last decades have challenged traditional assumptions regarding the cultural homogeneity and Roman identity of colonial populations in the Republic.[13] Instead, Roman colonial processes clearly resulted in diverse outcomes and were often more "ad hoc" than previously presumed.

Even Edward Togo Salmon, who laid out the traditional interpretation most forcefully and influentially in anglophone scholarship, recognized the potential for mixed populations in colonies. While he considered early colonists to primarily have been Roman citizens, he notes that the Roman citizen body itself "was not composed exclusively of ethnic Romans or even of speakers of Latin" after 338 BCE.[14] In several cases, we have explicit literary evidence for the enrollment of former enemies in a new colonial foundation. Antium, for instance, was founded as a Roman citizen colony in 338 BCE, and Livy states that the defeated Antiates were allowed to enroll in the new colony and were even granted citizenship, though they were no longer allowed to possess warships.[15] In the case of Ardea, the senate chose to enroll a much larger proportion of Rutulians than Romans in the new colony.[16] Strabo describes Ariminum, founded as a Latin colony in 268 BCE, as an Umbrian settlement that had received (δέδεκται) Roman colonists, again suggesting a mixed population.[17] Paestum offers another famous example, in which the colonists and indigenous populations apparently used both shared and separate areas of the same city.[18] The diversity of potential colonists appears to have increased following the Second Punic War, with all Italian allies likely eligible.[19]

Most would now agree that Republican colonization did not operate on a single model or produce a single outcome. Procedures were adapted to particular circumstances and goals, and we likely cannot speak of a sweeping colonial policy until well after the Social War. What is increasingly clear is that the populations of Republican colonies were rarely, if ever, ethnically or culturally uniform.

Furthermore, we must remember that besides the "official" settlers of a colony (those formally enrolled as colonists by the Roman government), persons of other legal status could, and apparently did, reside in colonial territories. They are often referred to generically as *incolae*, and the precise nature of their legal rights will have varied over time and place. Many would likely have been members of the conquered population who continued to farm their ancestral lands even after these had technically become *ager publicus*.[20] *Incolae* might also include migrants from other parts of Italy, especially in the case of prosperous colonies where opportunities for trade and financial gain were plentiful. As Saskia Roselaar has shown, although the nature of the surviving evidence often renders it difficult to confirm the legal status of *incolae* or to chart their presence with the chronological precision we would like, there can be no doubt that persons other than the official colonists formed a considerable component of the population in most colonial territories.[21]

This was also an environment of extensive mobility.[22] Seasonal and temporary migration for employment intensified in the 3rd and 2nd centuries, and many people seem to have voluntarily relocated in search of better opportunities in more prosperous towns. Livy, for instance, reports that in 177 BCE the Samnites and Paeligni complained that 4,000 families had left their lands to settle at Fregellae.[23] This implies that, as in so many cases, Fregellae's period of maximum urban development coincided precisely with an increase in its inhabitants' diversity. Such influxes of new colonists or migrants would have underscored the need to assert (or create?) a recognizable colonial identity.

Just as with patrons and artisans, then, we must imagine a diverse group of viewers who interacted with temple terracottas on a regular basis, and whose prior experiences colored their interpretation of the roofs they gazed upon. We can identify no singular "culture" or "identity" for any of the three groups under discussion. The meanings connected to these architectural terracottas must similarly have been highly variable and flexible, changing over time and from person to person. Any referent is unlikely to have been exclusive, and it is clear that neither patrons, artisans, nor viewers were operating from an exclusively or even primarily "Roman" perspective. Instead, they were negotiating the necessities of specific local situations. Whether for tactical reasons or because it was simply what they knew best, they anchored their temples to the religious landscape of the local region, while simultaneously engaging in a broader visual language that was readable to multiple constituents. It is crucial that in interpreting these objects we bear in mind the diversity of the groups by whom and for whom they were made.

5.2.2 *Colonial Populations at Minturnae and Cosa*

To consider in more concrete terms how the ethnic or cultural makeup of colonial populations might impact our reading of architectural terracottas, it will be useful to return once more to the two case studies presented in Chapter 4. Minturnae and Cosa offer a fruitful comparison in this regard, as they were technically of different legal status – Minturnae founded as a Roman citizen colony in 296/5, and Cosa as a colony of Latin right in 273. This means that at least in the towns' initial stages, the Minturnese colonists were much smaller in number and retained their Roman citizenship. Cosan settlers, by contrast, were substantially more numerous and were likely drawn from more diverse population groups. Any Roman citizens enrolling as colonists at Cosa would have lost that citizenship upon settling in the new town.[24]

As we have seen, the earliest phases at Minturnae are poorly known archaeologically. It nevertheless seems clear from the preserved sections of wall that the original town was quite small and that it soon proved insufficient for the needs of its inhabitants. The rapidity of its expansion is somewhat at odds with Livy's claim that both Minturnae and nearby Sinuessa had difficulty in attracting new settlers at the time of their foundation in 296 BCE.[25] At least by the early 2nd century BCE, Minturnae had outgrown its original walls and expanded in all directions along the Via Appia. It is possible that the town's prosperity reflects an influx of new settlers, many of whom may not have been Roman citizens. A large number of non-Roman names are attested epigraphically at the site.[26] Some may belong to the colony's early occupants, while others could have migrated in search of financial opportunities as Minturnae grew into a commercial center. The town was, after all, well connected by land thanks to the Via Appia, to the interior via the Liris River, and to sea trade through its port (Figures 63, 78).[27] Roselaar has noted that "the presence of non-Romans is strongest in the colonies that developed into important trade centers" – of which Minturnae constitutes a clear example.[28]

While business-minded settlers would presumably have arrived later, there is substantial evidence for the persistence of local populations at Minturnae from the very founding of the colony. The continued status of the Marica sanctuary as a major regional cult center has already been discussed, and it seems that both colonists and the indigenous population visited and worshiped at Marica's sacred grove.[29] Also of interest is a drawing of Hyginus preserved in a manuscript now in the Vatican, which shows the walled city of Minturnae and the land divisions just outside its gates (Figure 86).[30] On the right, a grid plan is labeled *assignatio nova* – the regularized land divisions assigned to new settlers. The open area on the left, however, is described as *ager adsignatus per professiones*, meaning land assigned to the *veteres possessores* who were allowed to remain on their land.[31] This problematizes Livy's claim that the Aurunci were annihilated by the Romans.[32] The archaeological and epigraphic evidence strongly suggests that the local population largely persisted in the area around Minturnae and that at least by the 2nd century BCE many had been incorporated in some fashion into the population of the expanding town.[33] As noted above, the architectural terracottas attest to a high degree of continuity in regional commercial networks even after Roman conquest. Minturnae's coroplasts appear to have been in close contact with a range of neighboring groups, both Roman and indigenous, and many were likely of local origin themselves.

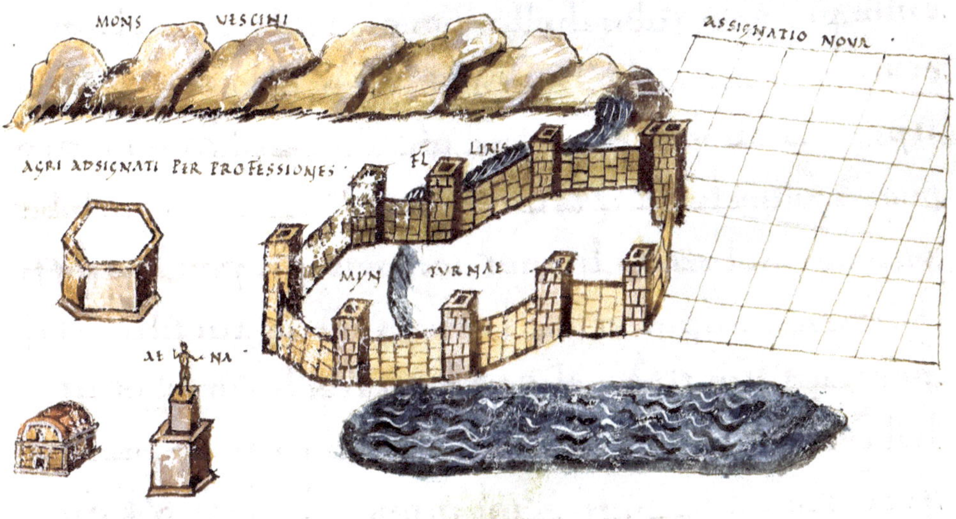

86. Drawing of land divisions around Minturnae, Vat. Palat. Lat. 1564, f. 88r. Vatican: Biblioteca Apostolica Vaticana.

The situation at Cosa, founded just over two decades later in confiscated Etruscan territory, appears quite different at first glance. Latin colonies are generally thought to have been open to all Latins, not only Roman citizens, and Cosa's initial group of settlers would thus have been considerably more diverse than Minturnae's, besides being numerically larger. The precise ethnic makeup of early Cosa is of course difficult to pinpoint given our lacunose evidence. Erdkamp has argued that before the Hannibalic War, most settlers of Latin colonies would have been veterans from the Roman army.[34] As already noted, there is also substantial evidence that non-Roman allies as well as local elites may have been granted land and have been included in new colonial foundations, sometimes as *incolae* rather than as "official" colonists. Bradley suggests that the paucity of specific literary references to mixed populations is simply "because ethnically mixed colonies were seen as unremarkable in a central Italian context."[35] Latin colonies were meant to function as autonomous (albeit allied) entities and likely drew from a range of populations inside and outside of Rome.

In the specific case of Cosa, there is some evidence for the marginalization of the local population at the moment of the colony's founding, as well as the destruction of nearby towns like Ghiaccioforte and Doganella.[36] Orbetello, on the other hand, appears to have survived at least initially despite being an old Etruscan town extremely close to Cosa.[37] Rather than a full "ethnic cleansing" of the region, Roman intervention seems to have functioned more as a large-scale restructuring, and certain areas clearly retained a strong Etruscan presence.[38] Talamone, whose temple terracottas are so closely mirrored at Cosa, seems to have remained almost defiantly Etruscan. Indeed, local pottery types continue to be used in the period immediately following Roman conquest, and Etruscan is the only language attested epigraphically at the site until the 1st century BCE.[39] The proximity of these sites is noteworthy – Talamone lies roughly 25 km up the coast from Cosa and would have been readily reachable in less than half a day's walk.

Whatever the precise ethnic makeup of early Cosa's colonists and *incolae*, the town did not flourish in the 3rd century. Few structures can be dated to this period, and we hear from Livy of the colony's population struggles. Due to their dwindling numbers, the Cosans requested a new supplement of settlers in 199 BCE, which they were finally granted in 197. It is to this period that the vast majority of Cosa's temples and urban infrastructure is dated.

Livy notes specifically that anyone was free to join the group of 1,000 new colonists sent to Cosa in 197 BCE provided he had sided with Rome during the Hannibalic War.[40] This means that we are dealing with a potentially wildly diverse group of settlers in early 2nd-century Cosa – the period that came to define the town architecturally and urbanistically.[41] Colonists could have come from communities and ethnic groups across Italy, as well as from neighboring Etruscan towns and the surrounding countryside. Since the local censors were likely responsible for recruiting new colonists, we might imagine an increased Etruscan presence in 2nd-century Cosa.

Just as at Minturnae, therefore, it is impossible to speak of a unified "Latin" let alone "Roman" culture during the period of Cosa's flourishing. The phenomenon of mixed populations seems to have been one of the central features of Republican colonial practice. The implications of this cultural heterogeneity have not been adequately considered in studies of architectural terracottas, but I believe it is fundamental for understanding the motivations behind their design as well as how they were perceived by viewers in the last centuries BCE.

5.2.3 Interaction and Religion

Whether they arrived at the moment of foundation or as part of a later supplement, our evidence clearly indicates that new colonists did not live in isolation, shut within their walled cities. Rather, they traded actively with their neighbors and inserted themselves into preexisting commercial networks that were in turn bolstered and expanded by the construction of new road systems.[42] They also appear to have sought out information on local cults and shrines and in many cases to have molded their own religious identities to fit the mythic and religious history of the surrounding landscape.[43]

As Marion Bolder-Boos has shown, most known tutelary deities in Roman colonies founded before the 1st century BCE can be traced back to preexisting local traditions.[44] Luna, for instance, seems to have been chosen as the colony of Luni's tutelary goddess precisely due to her role in the Ligurian pantheon.[45] The importance of Jupiter Anxur at Terracina predates the Roman settlement and dates back to the Volscian phases.[46] A similar situation is attested for the three colonies founded by C. Gracchus in 123–122, and probably for the earlier cases of Ostia and Venusia.[47] As we saw in Chapter 4, there is strong evidence that a cult of Venus or Venus Marina was introduced at Minturnae during the Roman period specifically because of the goddess' association with the Aurucan Marica, whose sanctuary still dominated the coastal area just outside the town.[48]

Bolder-Boos argues that such practices helped to integrate the local population and thus reduce the risk of rebellion, consolidating Roman power in newly-conquered territories:

> The continuation of the role of the old tutelary deities must have sent a clear message to the conquered peoples, namely that the Roman colonists had won these gods' approval. The tutelary deities had not failed in their duty to their cities, but placed them under the care of the Romans; hence, their protection was transferred to the new rulers.[49]

Viewed in this light, the strong conservatism of temple architectural terracottas is perfectly logical. If the colonists wished to incorporate and adapt preexisting cults in the region, they had to ensure that their efforts were recognizable. Architectural terracottas offered the ideal medium, as they could *visually* reference these earlier shrines and hence the deities to whom they were dedicated. As we have seen, architectural terracottas could be retained on temples for several centuries, meaning that numerous pre-Roman examples would have been visible on sanctuaries across the region at the time of a new colonial foundation. It would thus have been relatively simple for new settlers to create these visual links, and for local viewers to recognize them.[50]

The specific cases of Cosa and Minturnae reflect this, and a sustained dialogue with local traditions in religious architecture is readily visible in their terracottas' iconography and style. The emphasis on Minerva and Hercules antefixes at Cosa, for instance, must be understood against the backdrop of these figures' widespread popularity on antefixes and in cults across the region's indigenous sanctuaries.[51] The repeated use of these antefixes at Cosa, where they are reproduced in five distinct fabrics, is particularly significant when we recall that the *potnia theron* antefixes so popular elsewhere never really caught on at the site. Local references through figural representations like these would have been bolstered by the close iconographical and stylistic similarities that many of Cosa's architectural terracottas bear to examples from nearby Etruscan temples. We might think, for instance, of the revetment plaques with crossed ribbons and flowers (Figure 44), which find close parallels at Tarquinia, Punta della Vipera, and Talamone, and whose basic composition is mirrored in plaques and even urns from a range of sites within the broader region. The same is true for the simas with lilies and roses (Figure 51) and the perforated cornices with circular piercings (Figure 54), among many other examples. These local links are most visible in the case of "non-standard" elements, but it is important to remember that although terracottas of the "standard temple kit" are attested at many colonies in central Italy, they *also* appeared on non-Roman indigenous sanctuaries, where in many cases their age and physical dilapidation would have been evident. Even "standard" elements, then, could have a local referent for certain viewer groups. Architectural features of the temples, such as the use of Vulci tufo or the so-called "Etruscan" round molding, must have furthered the effect, as would the appearance and themes of pedimental sculptural groups, which at Cosa seem often to have followed trends popular on contemporaneous Etruscan urns.

At Minturnae, the explicit equation of Venus Marina with Marica similarly signifies a desire to tie colonial cult practice to local religious environments. It is noteworthy that the ancient shrine of Marica was maintained and even repaired following the foundation of the colony. Religious imperatives (nothing could be carried in or out of Marica's sacred grove) as well as structural concerns (the unstable marshy terrain) precluded the construction of a town directly adjoining Marica's sanctuary, but Minturnae's urban planners seem to have laid out their colony as close to it as was feasible. The very siting of the colony thus reflects a need, or at least a desire, to integrate the new foundation within the preexisting religious landscape.

As we have seen, Minturnae's architectural terracottas similarly evoke its regional context. At a micro level, references to Marica's sanctuary are detectable in the unique form of the looped palmette plaques from Minturnae's tripartite temple, and the likely appearance of Venus on the pediment would have announced the connection more forcefully.[52] The three-winged portico that surrounded the temple was decorated with a series of terracotta types that seem specific to the local region, including the unusual syrinx-playing satyr who is attested first at Capua.[53]

The heterogeneity of the colonial populations at both Cosa and Minturnae presumably means that the interpretation of these terracottas would have varied depending on the background of any given viewer. Just as with patrons and artisans, we cannot presume a singular point of reference for all who gazed upon these temple roofs, and this has important implications for how we understand the overall effect and reception of these objects. First of all, the notion that Rome constituted the single or even primary point of reference for most viewers can immediately be dismissed. As we saw in Chapter 2, there is no evidence that any of the architectural terracotta motifs employed at colonies in central Italy originated in Rome or that they were considered in any way

"Roman" during the 3rd and 2nd centuries BCE. Furthermore, most of the people who viewed and interacted with them had likely never been to Rome, whereas they would have been familiar with the sanctuaries of the local region, to which they would periodically have traveled for various festivals and rituals. Such viewers were well equipped to draw connections with the local religious landscape, both in terms of the deities worshipped and in how their associated cult structures *looked*. For those new to the region and less familiar with its cult places, there was still much that was recognizable in the decoration of colonial temples. The use of "standard" elements not only drew fledgling colonies into the broader orbit of central Italic cult but endowed new temples with an air of antique venerability. This must have served an important legitimizing function in the eyes of *all* viewers, who could recognize familiar signs of religious solemnity and thus read these new temples as the timeless and stately religious symbols that their planners doubtless desired them to be. Temples played a particularly central role in community cohesion and identity – because of their associations with the divine, because of their regular use in ritual events, and because they were typically among the largest and most lavishly adorned buildings in a town. Whereas long-established polities had a deep religious and architectural history to work with, the appearance of temples in colonies must have been particularly crucial for creating the visual identity of a *new* community. The specific circumstances of colonial foundations demand that we read the architectural terracotta evidence in a slightly different way for this period. Beyond their potential political and religious implications, these objects document a moment in which new group identities were actively being formed as a result of colonization. This leads us to ask how such identities get created in the first place, and how visual culture – like architectural terracottas – operates in these processes.

5.3 SHAPING IDENTITY

5.3.1 Cultural Memory and Colonial Identities

The role of collective memory in the construction of group identities has prompted fruitful analyses of Roman literature and material culture in recent decades.[54] Still, such studies often ignore the pre-Augustan period, and surprisingly little attention has been paid to cultural memory in the context of Roman colonization within Italy.[55] Colonial foundations offer a particularly rich avenue for memory studies, as they are by definition *new* communities seeking some form of social cohesion in the context of a wider precolonial landscape. What constitutes collective or cultural memory in a new foundation is never obvious and seems in many cases to have required active creation on the part of residents. Examining the role of cultural memories in Italic colonies brings us into direct confrontation with questions of group identity formation and the invention of tradition, shedding new light on the material remains these colonists and their neighbors left behind.

Modern discussions of collective memory emerge primarily from the work of Maurice Halbwachs beginning in the 1920s.[56] Reacting to the strong individualism of Freudian theory in particular, Halbwachs proposed that memory as a phenomenon does not only occur in single persons but is shared by groups.[57] His work established the categories of "social" and "collective" memory and further emphasized the critical point that memory is far from static or uniform but represents a plurality of memories simultaneously occurring and evolving even within single groups. Halbwachs' *mémoire collective* was further expanded and refined by Jan and Aleida Assmann, who use "cultural memory" in reference to memories of the distant past (especially stories of origins) and "communicative memory" to describe memories transmitted by more direct communication and concerning more recent history.[58] Memory studies by now embrace a wide range of disciplinary perspectives and have benefited from the incorporation of new research in neuroscience.[59] Following the influential contributions of Hobsbawm and Ranger (*The Invention of Tradition,* see below) and Pierre Nora (*Les lieux de mémoire*), a number of studies have also examined the role of memory in modern European nation-building.[60]

Before approaching the role of memory in colonies like Cosa and Minturnae and asking how architectural terracottas might be expressive of memories and memory-formation, a few basic principles and definitions ought to be articulated. In what follows, I use "cultural memory" in the sense of Assmann, as a more specific subset of Halbwachs' *mémoire collective*:

> Cultural memory is a form of collective memory, in the sense that it is shared by a number of people and that it conveys to these people a collective, that is, cultural, identity.[61]

It is distinguished from "communicative memory," however, in that it is oriented specifically toward historical/mythical time – it refers to events that did not occur in the lifetime of living or recent persons. Cultural memory thus "claims to be valid for very large mnemonic communities (religious groups, societies, and so on)" and concerns "the way of remembering chosen by a community, the collective idea of the meaning of past events."[62] Critically, memory and memory-formation also involve forgetting and are kinetic and dynamic in nature.[63] When we say "memory," we are really talking about a constantly evolving *set* of memories.[64] Because of this, definitions and conceptions of cultural memory must necessarily be malleable themselves,[65] and expressions of what we call cultural memory can come in many forms. Following Karl Galinsky, we might say simply that cultural memory "denotes an ensemble of cultural traditions and practices and their manifestations in a variety of media, such as text, art, cult, and festival," and the ways in which these are chosen, remembered, and interpreted by a community.[66] In the context of the present study, it is also worth emphasizing the critical role that place plays in memory formation. Henri Lefebvre has scrutinized the ways in which space itself represents a social product and is thus inextricably entangled with politics and power.[67] Studies of place and space, particularly in contemporary societies, were greatly spurred by Pierre Nora's monumental *Lieux de mémoire*.[68] For Nora, *lieux de mémoire* constitute not only specific physical locations but also the sets of human practices, beliefs, and experiences with which these places are associated, and which give them meaning.

Despite the wide-ranging theories surrounding these concepts, all would agree that cultural memory and *lieux de mémoire* play a critical role in social cohesion. They enable individuals to identify with particular groups, as well as to differentiate themselves from others. As Roth has noted, "the importance to define and express one's identity . . . increases with the amount of contact one has with others."[69] He sees the sharp rise in contact during the mid-Republic as triggering an increase in the importance of regional identities. Certainly, the need to articulate identity must have been strong in Republican colonies. The colonial population itself comprised people recently thrown together, living in an unfamiliar place and surrounded by a conquered group that was not only "other" but potentially hostile as well. If the expression of specific cultural memories was an exigency, an equally great problem must have been how and where to identify them. In other words, what "memory" bound together a newly formed group of colonists?

5.3.2 Memory, Invention, and the Visualization of Identity

Hobsbawm and Ranger's 1983 edited volume was the first to explicitly theorize the concept of *The Invention of Tradition*. The various contributions focus primarily on the British Empire between the 18th and 20th centuries but offer conceptual frameworks that are broadly applicable to a range of historical situations. As Hobsbawm notes in his introduction, "there is probably no time and place with which historians are concerned which has not seen the 'invention' of tradition."[70] The phenomenon, he argues, is more likely to occur during periods of rapid societal transformation, for instance those covered in his volume. The last three centuries BCE arguably offer an equally dramatic moment of political and social change within central Italy, and similar instances of "invented tradition" should therefore come as no surprise.

In the face of innovation and change, Hobsbawm notes the tendency to make certain aspects of life appear "unchanging and invariant."[71] A particular historical moment is usually chosen in order to achieve this, drawing a visual or conceptual bridge between past and present. He offers the example of the British parliament building, which was rebuilt in the 19th century in a Gothic style.[72] The parallel with Cosa's temples, decorated with terracottas in the style of centuries-old sanctuaries of the region, is striking. In fact, the very processes of Republican colonization compare in unexpected ways with certain features of modern European nation-building. A markedly heterogenous group with different customs, myths, and dialects/languages is suddenly lumped together and given a group identity – the "French," the "Cosans." Such categories are necessarily constructed, even if they attain real significance over time. In order to acquire a true meaning, however, a common set of mutually recognizable identity markers must be created and accepted by the members of that group. This is where invented traditions prove particularly expedient. As Hobsbawm argues, "all invented traditions, so far as possible, use history as a legitimator of action and cement of group cohesion."[73] Invented traditions actively construct group identities, which are just as essential for the development and solidity of Republican colonies as modern nation-states.

In fact, it has been suggested that central Italy between the 4th and 2nd centuries BCE witnessed a sudden renewal of interest in local myths and foundation stories, many of which seem to have been unknown or at least relatively unimportant in the centuries prior.[74] Perhaps the best example occurs at Rome itself, where the city's Trojan origins become more extensively and systematically emphasized.[75] The public emphasis on Rome's mythological roots revolved on an idea of deep antiquity that not only legitimized its growing power but also offered its citizens a coherent narrative of their own identity.[76] An interesting feature of the Rome–Troy connection is that it seems to have been actively fostered at Ilion as well and to have endured throughout the period of the Empire.[77]

The same motivations and mechanisms that prompted Rome's "re-discovery" of its Trojan roots may have applied to smaller central Italic cities as well. The primary difference, of course, is that Rome would come to dominate these areas in so absolute a fashion that other foundation legends soon slipped into irrelevance and even extinction. Still, it seems clear that the trend in promoting local myth extended far beyond Rome between the 4th and early 1st centuries – precisely the period of its major military expansion in the region. Erich Gruen has explained the Trojan origins trend at Rome by suggesting that "the fable of Troy served Rome in two fundamental ways: it gave her a place in the cultural milieu of the Greek world – and, by the same token, it announced her distinctiveness in that world."[78] The same general principle might be applied to other Italic towns promoting a local origin myth during this period. Doing so simultaneously offered both membership and distinctiveness within the broader Mediterranean world but, more importantly, within the newly emerging Roman world.[79]

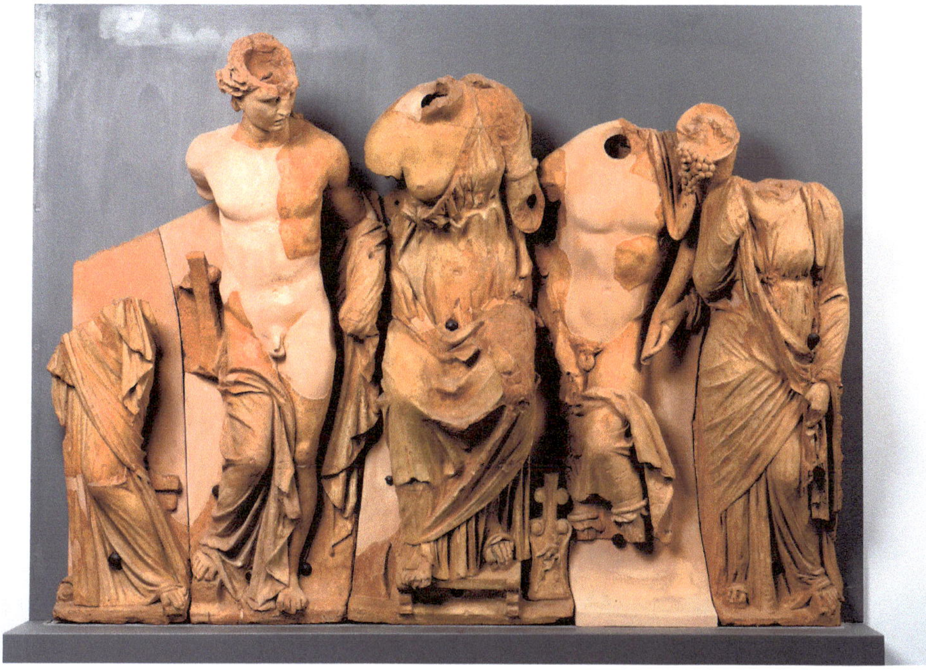

87. Terracotta pedimental relief from the Grande Tempio at Luni, with the goddess Luna at the center. Florence: Museo Archeologico Nazionale di Firenze. By permission of the Museo Archeologico Nazionale di Firenze (Direzione regionale Musei della Toscana), all rights reserved.

This interest in local foundation myths is particularly visible on temple pediments. An intriguing example comes from Luni, founded as a Roman colony in 177 BCE. The *Grande Tempio* appears to have been dedicated to the goddess Luna, who as we have seen was chosen specifically for her importance in the local Ligurian pantheon.[80] She also seems to have occupied the central position on the temple's pediment (Figure 87).[81]

Yet another of Luni's temples may have featured a pedimental scene with a similarly local orientation. Strazzulla has reconstructed the scattered sculptural fragments as a pedimental group depicting episodes from the myth of Telephus.[82] If she is correct, this pediment reflects an intriguing adaptation of local myth. Telephus was a major figure in the mythic history of nearby Pisa, his son Tarchon being identified in some accounts as the town's founder.[83] Part of Pisa's territory had been ceded to Luni at the time of the latter's foundation, resulting in subsequent territorial disputes.[84] The use of Telephus imagery on a temple at Luni would thus have been a sharp statement of primacy, effectively claiming a local myth for Luni rather than Pisa.[85] Luni's temples, like those at Cosa, were also adorned with a range of archaizing architectural terracottas drawn directly from a well-established regional

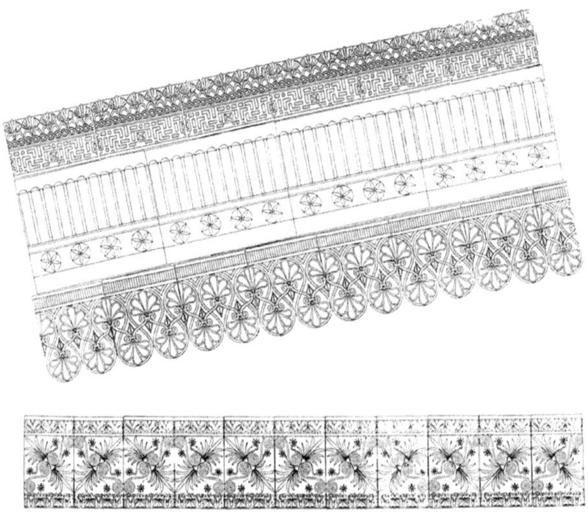

88. Reconstruction of the original decoration of the Grande Tempio at Luni. After Forte et al. 1992 Tav. XVI.

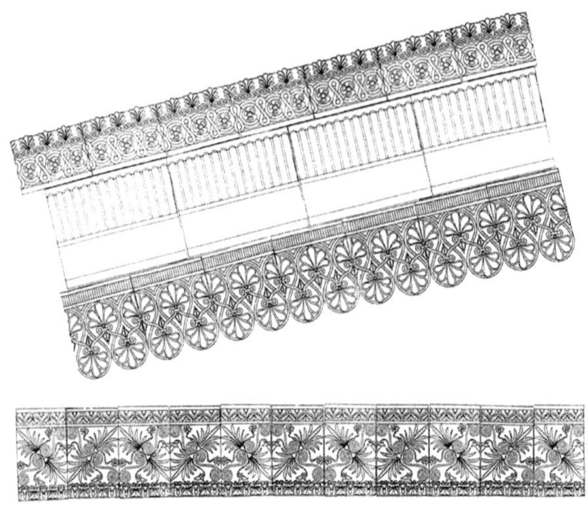

89. Reconstruction of the original decoration of the "Capitolium" at Luni. After Forte et al. 1992 Tav. XVII.

repertoire (Figures 88–89).[86] The combined pedimental figures and other terracottas would thus have served to mark Luni as *the* ancient, established cult center for its region – even if, in reality, it was a relatively new town.

A similar situation may be observed on the Talamonaccio pediment near Cosa, whose north side, facing the sea, was decorated with episodes related to the Seven Against Thebes (Figure 43). The myth had already been popular in Etruscan cities for centuries, appearing on the famous plaque from Temple A at Pyrgi (Figure 90), as well as on a significant number of smaller moveable objects such as mirrors, urns, vases, gems, etc.[87] In fact, it is estimated that

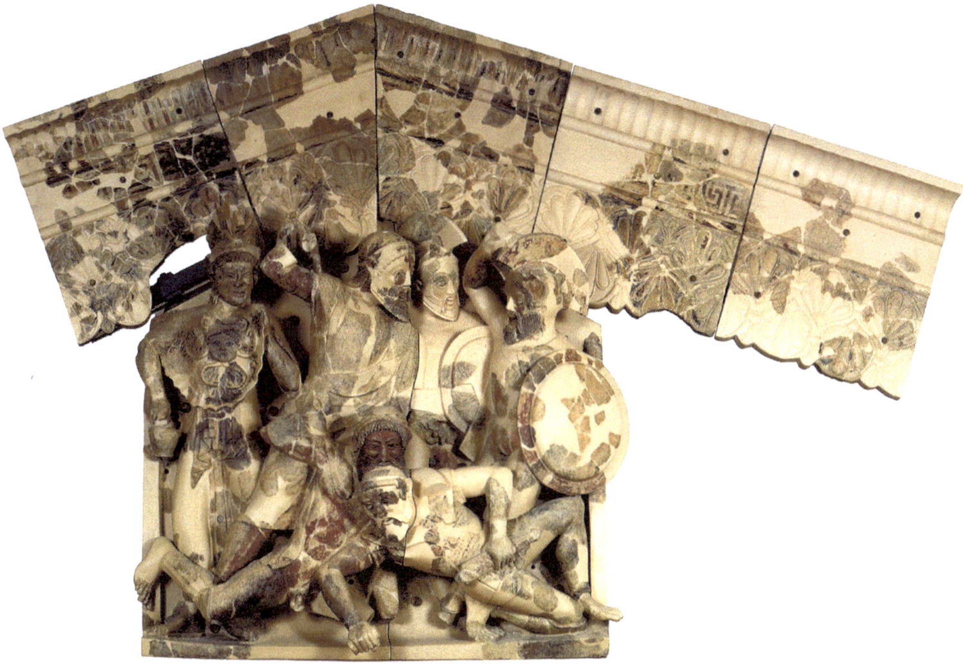

90. Pedimental relief plaque from Temple A at Pyrgi showing scenes of the Seven Against Thebes. Rome: Museo Nazionale Etrusco di Villa Giulia, inv. 146094.

20 percent of the urns from the Etruscan sites of Volterra, Chiusi, and Perugia show scenes from this saga.[88] Jocelyn Penny Small has demonstrated that these different towns each tended to depict distinct mythic moments related to the Seven Against Thebes, and with varying iconography.[89] For example, Chiusine urns show quadrigas and the attack on the walls but not Oedipus.[90] Urns from Perugia show Oedipus between his sons but never the engulfment of Amphiaraus.[91] The latter scene does appear at both Chiusi and Volterra but is shown differently at each site.[92] In Small's view, the diffusion of these scenes on Etruscan urns suggests that artisans from each town traveled to Talamone to see the pediment or that they had access to copies depicting it.[93] I would argue that it is more likely the opposite – that the Talamonaccio pediment reflects either a gathering of preexisting imagery from the surrounding region or that the coroplasts and urn manufacturers were working from similar models which have not survived. The first suggestion is supported by the varied portrayals of particular scenes in different towns. If the artisans were all imitating the Talamonaccio pediment, we should instead expect a consistent mode of representing each scene, one that matched its representation on the pediment.

We lack firm chronological markers that might indicate with certainty which examples of this scene were produced when. The urns and pediment seem to belong roughly to the same period of the late 3rd–2nd centuries BCE and likely signal a broader regional interest in this myth. It is possible that the frequent similarities in subject matter on pediments and urns at this time reflects a common source in local theatrical performances.[94] This would explain the sudden surge of interest in particular myths, as well as the varying modes of depicting certain scenes. In the case of the Seven Against Thebes, however, a 3rd/2nd century trend potentially prompted by the world of theatre would also have gained traction due to the myth's ancient significance in the region.[95] Furthermore, if by this period such scenes were generally relegated to smaller, movable objects (urns, mirrors, vases), then their representation on a large-scale temple pediment might serve to implicitly root the myth in a particular local sanctuary and thus to claim the tradition itself.

Such an assertion may have been further reinforced by the temple's other decorative elements. Several fragments of pedimental sculpture have been found that cannot belong to the Seven Against Thebes scene. The presence of nymphs, dolphins, and a ship suggests a marine theme, and the group also included the head of an old man with a flowing beard that appears to be wet. Giulio Ciampoltrini places these pieces on the temple's opposite pediment and relates the scene to the Argonaut cycle, specifically the prophecy of Glaucus.[96] More recently, Strazzulla has suggested that two additional heads belong to the same cycle and should be identified as Hercules and Orpheus.[97] Talamone claimed Telamon as its founder, the hero having reportedly established the town on the Argonauts' return trip.[98] The inclusion of this myth would thus have constituted a conspicuous promotion of local history, all the more evocative given the temple's position overlooking the sea, which would further have invited a site-specific reading. If the scene did indeed relate to Glaucus and the Argonauts, its pairing with the Seven Against Thebes would serve to tie the latter to Talamone's mythic history as well.[99]

Site-specific interpretations of myth must have been strengthened by the frequent performance of ritual beside and inside these temples. Our knowledge of pre-Imperial ritual practice is quite lacunose, and most literary sources date later. Still, whether or not we can identify particular rituals or ceremonies, we can be quite sure that they occurred. Local rituals likely operated along broadly similar lines as some of the better documented Roman festivals, many of which were specifically related to origin myths and strongly tied to particular places.[100] Ritual performance is a mode of memory production and must have played a critical role in the validation of mythic traditions (or invented mythic traditions) in 3rd–1st century central Italy as well.[101]

In addition to pedimental sculpture, many of the more unusual architectural terracottas that adorned these sanctuaries seem designed to suggest the performance of religious ritual as well as the specific nature of the cult. The

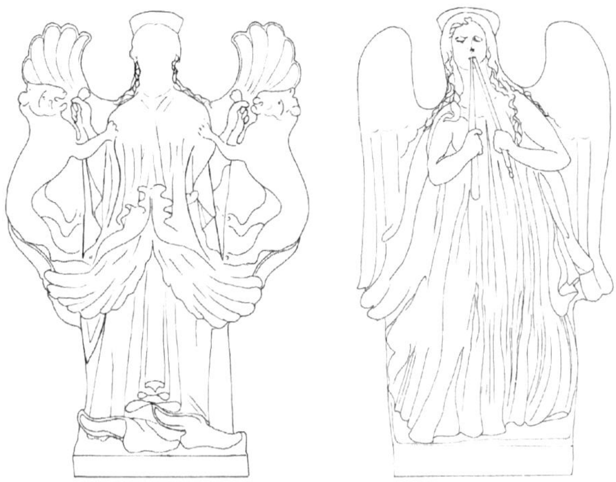

91. *Potnia theron* and flute-player antefixes from Luni. Image after Forte et al. 1992 tav. XIII.

syrinx-playing satyr and winged flute-girl antefixes from Minturnae were positioned atop the triporticus that surrounded the temple on three sides, thereby demarcating the physical space in which rituals were performed (Figures 65, 80). Perhaps it is not by accident that these lively figures are among Minturnae's most locally specific architectural terracottas in terms of iconography. With instruments at their lips, they would have appeared as active participants in the religious ceremonies taking place around the temple.

Musical antefixes also appear on the Grande Tempio at Luni, where a clothed and winged female figure playing a double-flute (Figure 91, right) alternates with a *potnia theron* (Figure 91, left) and an antefix depicting a female leaning on a pillar (Figure 92).[102] The pose of the latter is known from votive terracottas but appears only at Luni as an antefix. On the votives, she is usually thought to represent Diana, which may explain the architectural adoption of this figure on a temple likely dedicated to Diana-Luna.[103] The antefixes' iconography would thus serve to advertise and define the nature of the local cult. The *potnia theron* that appeared alongside them was similarly drawn into a local framework here.[104] Whereas the IVN inscriptions at Gabii presented a widespread image in terms of the local cult of Juno (see Section 3.3.2), the *potnia theron* at Luni unequivocally evoked Diana and her association with the eponymic Luna. This combination is a graphic expression of the inventive processes of identity formation that were taking place in new colonies across Italy in this period. The antefixes drew on preexisting imagery and reorganized it for a new context. It is significant that flute-girl antefixes stood alongside these others, as they evoked the performance of ritual around the temple and thus rooted the cult and its (recent) traditions in physical space.

Distinctive antefixes from Nemi reveal a similar desire to visually proclaim a local cult's importance. Unlike at Luni, however, no forced accommodation

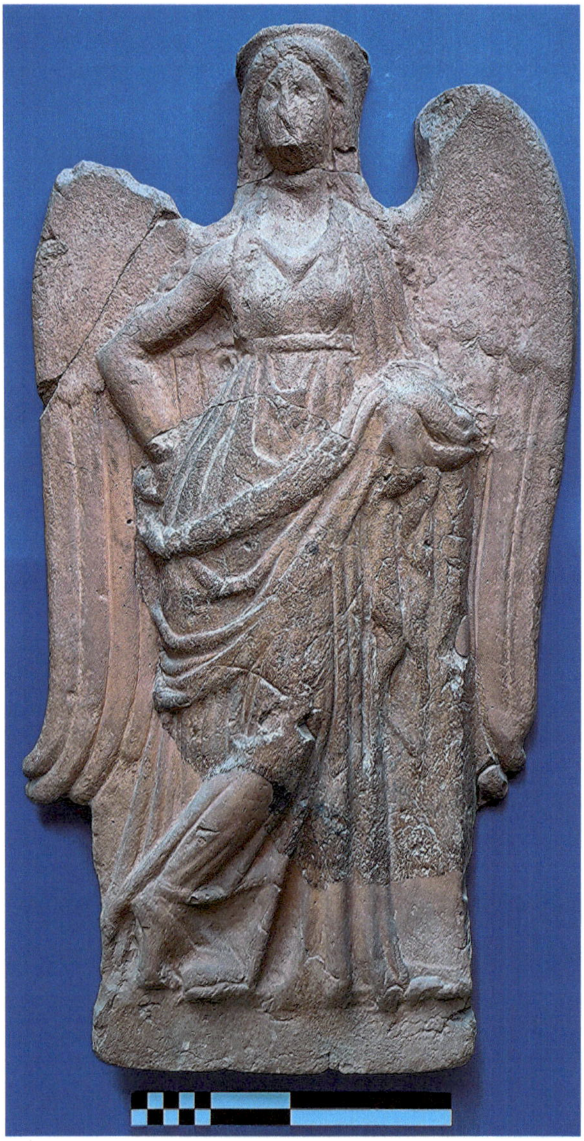

92. Antefix from Luni with a female figure leaning on a pillar. Luni: Museo archeologico nazionale di Luni.
Courtesy of the Direzione regionale musei Liguria.

for new or old deities was needed. Diana's sanctuary at Nemi was amongst the oldest and most famous in Latium. Evidence for ritual activity goes back to the 15th century BCE on the upper terrace, while votive material dating to the 7th/6th centuries BCE has been uncovered in the area where the main temple would later be built, probably in the late 4th or early 3rd century BCE.[105] *Potnia theron* antefixes have been assigned to the first iteration of the temple, and a number of antefixes with "Bacchic" themes (satyrs and maenads) similarly

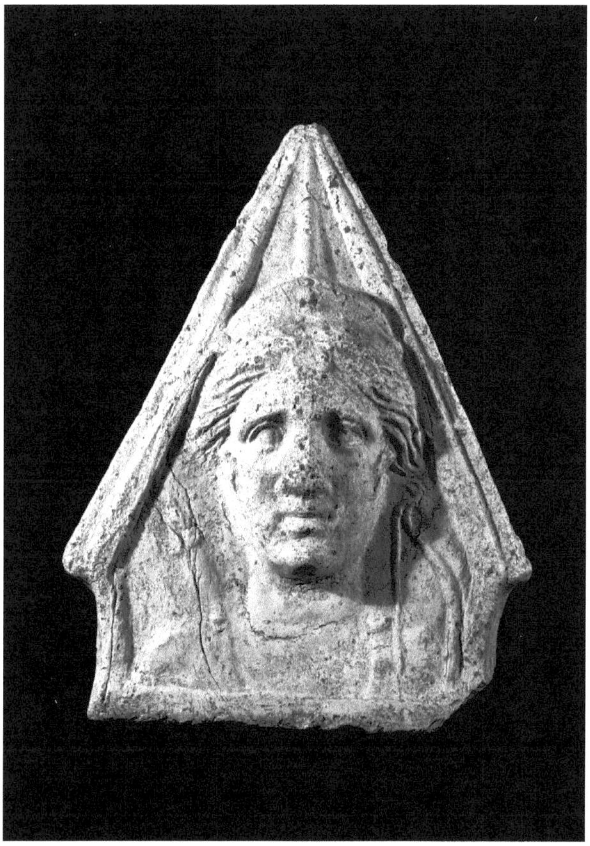

93. Triangular antefix with Diana, from Nemi. Rome: Museo Nazionale Romano, inv. 62644. Courtesy of the Ministero della cultura – Museo Nazionale Romano. Photo by Giorgio Cargnel and Luciano Mandato.

predate the later monumental phase.[106] None of these are unusual, and comparanda for their form and iconography can be found at Falerii Veteres, Caere, Rome, and other central Italic sites. It is not until the monumentalizing of Nemi's sanctuary in the 2nd and 1st centuries BCE that we see terracotta decoration used to visually distinguish the cult. Two new antefix types are introduced, both with an unusual triangular shape from which the head of Diana stares out (Figures 93–94).[107] On one type she is crowned by a crescent-shaped diadem and flanked by a quiver and bow, whereas on the other she is devoid of attributes. The stratigraphy at Nemi and the attribution of terracottas to particular buildings is complicated by the chaotic and undocumented nature of the excavations by Lord Savile and then the Orsini family in the late 19th century. These triangular antefixes are, however, generally thought to have decorated the portico, which would not only have made them highly visible given the portico's extensive length, but would almost have given the impression that they were presiding over the temple and the cult activity taking place before it.[108] In any case, it hardly seems accidental that these unique antefixes

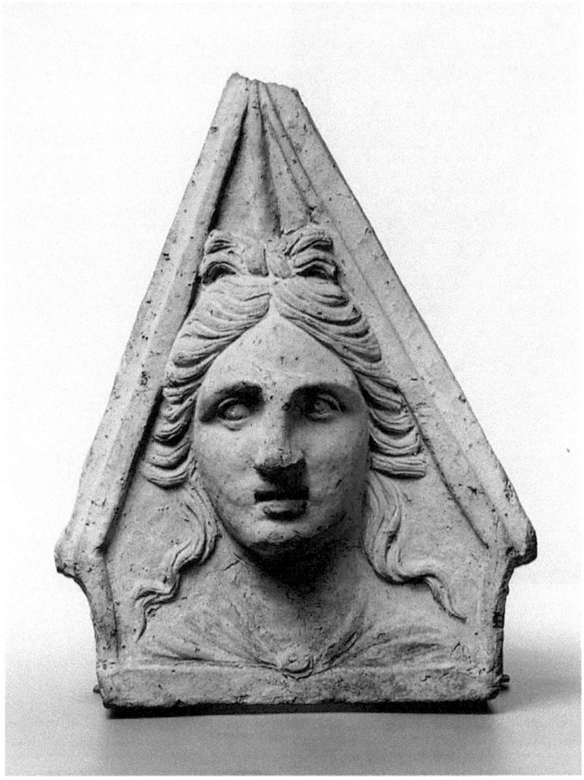

94. Triangular antefix with Diana, from Nemi, IN 1522. Ny Carlsberg Glyptotek, Copenhagen. Courtesy of the Ny Carlsberg Glyptotek, Copenhagen.

should be installed precisely when the sanctuary's importance was being asserted through a monumentalizing reorganization and when towns across Italy were vying to highlight the antiquity and exceptionality of their sanctuaries and mythic histories.

Such site-specific assertions of local roots are visible across central Italy in the last centuries BCE, regardless of a town's legal status. We have noted this phenomenon at nominally independent sites like Talamone and Nemi, where an emphasis on mythic history could be seen as an assertion of traditional religious identity in the face of Rome's expanding political power. The same desire to claim antiquity, however, entails a very different process when the town involved is a newly founded colony. In these cases, the promotion of "local roots" necessarily reflects a careful massaging of visual vocabularies to serve a particular end. This is evident in the emphasis on Luna and Diana on one temple at Luni, and, if Strazzulla's interpretation is correct, in the choice of Telephus for another pediment from the same site. The use of Hercules and Minerva imagery at Cosa seems similarly connected to the importance of these divinities at preexisting Etruscan sites in the region.[109] Their appearance at the Latin colony might have served to implicitly insert it into the local religious landscape, claiming the town's connection in its own right to these divine protectors. At Minturnae, some of the Roman colony's revetment plaques were modeled directly from those of the nearby Auruncan Marica sanctuary.[110] I have further suggested that the town's tripartite temple may have been dedicated to Venus, and that she likely appeared at the center of its pediment.[111] This would have created a clear link with the earlier cult of Marica at Minturnae.

Such acts indicate a conscious reshaping of tradition. They supply newly founded colonies with something they fundamentally lack – *history*. Local histories and especially mythic histories were central to the communal identities of Italic towns, and it is no coincidence that these were being emphasized anew precisely during the periods of Luni's, Cosa's, and Minturnae's urban development. Inventing or reshaping pre-Roman local histories and displaying them on a colony's temples offered an ideal solution to the mythic and historical deficiency inherent in new foundations.[112] Through religious visual markers like architectural terracottas, towns could not only assert their belonging within a region but could provide a communal identity, a cultural memory, to an otherwise incoherent collection of inhabitants.

The heterogenous composition of the patrons, artisans, and viewers who commissioned, created, and interacted with these terracottas is thus fundamental to their appearance but also to their broader role. The terracottas defined and signified a communal identity that was certainly not Roman but that was also not exclusively local. Their layered referents reflect the diversity of the groups involved in their production and reception. Just as these individuals represented multiple overlapping identities, so too did the terracottas participate flexibly in the local and broader central Italic religious landscape. The realities of colonization during the last three centuries BCE lent new meaning to these objects and endowed them with new symbolic potential. Groups both recent and long-standing were in search of defined collective identities – an exigency spurred by the political and territorial reorganizations that made this period so tumultuous. More than ever before, temple terracottas could be used to symbolize communities. They supplied the missing element to developing colonies, furnishing a visual identity that was geographically specific, religiously recognizable, and – perhaps most significantly – that *appeared* less flimsy and inchoate than the thrown together colonial community might actually have been.

NOTES

1 See recently Maschek (2022) on the important distinction between the "expert knowledge" of the builders and the "vernacular knowledge" of commissioners and how these knowledge systems impact intent and perception during and after the building process.

2 Cébeillac-Gervasoni 1990: 714–715; Lomas 1997: 27–29; Coles 2009: 119–120 and passim; Rous 2009: 74–75; 2010: 87. For the involvement of commissioners in the temples of new colonial foundations, see Coles 2009: 136–143. For a discussion of censors' involvement in public building projects in mid-Republican Rome, see Bernard 2018: 118–158. For patronage in Roman architecture more generally, see Stamper 2005: 38–39 (for the Republic), Anderson 2014, Wescoat 2015.

3 Scott 2019. See also Carroll 2010 and Rous 2010.

4 Rous 2010: 150–151. An inscription from Venusia (*CIL* I^2, 402 = *ILLRP*, 691) shows that local senates had the power to declare a space sacred or public. Inscriptions from other Latin colonies demonstrate the involvement of the local senate in public building projects, e.g., at Paestum (*CIL* I^2, 1682 = *ILLRP*, 636), Firmum (*CIL* I^2, 1921 = *ILLRP*, 594), and Aquileia (*CIL* I^2, 2197 = *ILLRP*, 487 a). On these, see Laffi 1983: 64–65.

5 Coarelli 1982b: 125–130.

6 Cébeillac-Gervasoni 1990; Rous 2010: 115.

7 Cébeillac-Gervasoni 1983, 1996; Terrenato 2019: 208–211. See also Bernard 2019b on the case-study of Brundisium.

8 Terrenato 2019.

9 Terrenato 2019: 208–211.

10 On the overall lack of major change detectable in the areas surrounding new colonies, see Terrenato 2019: 219–226.

11 Coles 2009; Bolder-Boos 2011; Terranato 2019: 224.

12 On this question in relation to terracotta roofs from Archaic central Italy, see Lulof and Smith 2017.

13 Fentress 2000; Bispham 2006; Bradley 2006; Pelgrom 2008; Roselaar 2011; Tarpin 2014; Laffi 2017; among others. On ethnic identities in ancient Italy more generally, see the fundamental study of Bourdin 2012.

14 Salmon 1969: 174 n. 65.

15 Livy 8.14.8. *Et Antium nova colonia missa, cum eo ut Antiatibus permitteretur, si et ipsi adscribi coloni vellent; naves inde longae abactae interdictumque mari Antiati populo est et civitas data.*

16 Livy 4.11.

17 Strabo 5.1.11. τὸ δὲ Ἀρίμινον Ὄμβρων ἐστὶ κατοικία, καθάπερ καὶ ἡ Ῥάουεννα: δέδεκται δ' ἐποίκους Ῥωμαίους ἑκατέρα.

18 Greco 1988: 82, 80 fig. 1; Pelgrom 2008: 344.

19 Roselaar 2010: 75–76, with bibliography; Roselaar 2011: 529–530, 543; Erdkamp 2011; Laffi 2017; Lomas (2017: 278) describes colonies with mixed populations as "an important mode of integration between Romans and other Italians."

20 See the discussion in Terrenato 2019, with reference to recent archaeological work demonstrating that "the existing farming landscape was mostly unaffected by the political transformation" (216–219, quote at 217).

21 Roselaar 2011.

22 See esp. Erdkamp 2008; Erdkamp 2011; Bourdin 2012: 551–589; Laffi 2017; Isayev 2017.

23 Livy 41.8.8.

24 Cf. Cicero's remark on Romans willingly changing city and becoming citizens of their new town (*Balb.* 28.): *multi etiam superiore memoria cives Romani sua voluntate, indemnati et incolumes, his rebus relictis alias se in civitates contulerunt.*

25 Livy 10.21.10.

26 Roselaar 2011: 544.

27 The Liris river does indeed appear to have been navigable in antiquity: Ruegg 1988: 210, Ruegg 1995.

28 Roselaar 2011: 547.

29 Bolder-Boos (2011: 123, 126–127) sees the Republican-era repairs to the Marica sanctuary and the surge in votive offerings as evidence that great attention was paid to the goddess

even after the colony's establishment, and as suggesting that Marica's sanctuary was cared for just as the colony's main temples were.

30 Vat. Palat. Lat. 1564, f. 88r.

31 Tarpin 2014: 184 and n. 163.

32 Liv. 9.25: *nullus modus caedibus fuit, deletaque Ausonum gens.*

33 On the persistence of indigenous populations, see Tarpin 2014, esp. p. 184 for the unlikelihood that conquered groups were exterminated as later literary sources sometimes assert. Roth 2017: 299 notes for the case of Minturnae specifically that the "separation of Roman settlers and locals . . . must have ceased to be a reality as soon as the town on the Via Appia started to prosper." Bolder-Boos 2011 (126–127) also notes the epigraphic presence at Minturnae of what are likely Auruncan names.

34 Erdkamp 2011.

35 Bradley 2006: 174.

36 Fentress 2000: 12–13. Excavations and field surveys in the ager Cosanus since the 1970s have yielded a wealth of information on settlement patterns and demographic change in this area. For a summary of these results, see Fentress and Perkins 2016: 387–397.

37 Ciampoltrini 1995b.

38 Of course, this is not meant to downplay the fact that even a large-scale "restructuring" would certainly have entailed grave and widespread acts of violence. On the brutality of Roman expansionism, see recently Roymans and Fernández-Götz 2019 and Fernández-Götz, Maschek, and Roymans 2020.

39 Ciampoltrini and Rendini 1992: 987–988; Ciampoltrini 1985: 116; Ciampoltrini 1995b: 298; Ciampoltrini 2011: 22; Celuzza 2002: 171.

40 *Cosanis eo die postulantibus ut sibi colonorum numerus augeretur, mille adscribi iussi, dum ne quis in eo numero esset qui post P. Cornelium et Ti. Sempronium consules hostis fuisset.* See also Erdkamp 2011: 114 on this passage, noting that supplements to colonies in general were likely not comprised of veterans. Laffi 2017: 53–54 interprets this passage to mean that the new settlers were drawn exclusively from Italian allies.

41 On the 2nd century as characterizing Cosa urbanistically also in terms of building technologies, see recently Mogetta 2019 and Mogetta 2021: 195–205.

42 On "Roman" roads building on preexisting networks and functioning primarily as modes of elite movement, both at a local/regional level and between their hometowns and Rome, see recently Terrenato 2019: 230–236. Sea traffic would also have been a major avenue for movement and especially trade.

43 Similar practices may in some cases be observed within the urban layout of new colonies. It has been suggested, for instance, that certain unusual features of Falerii Novi's design were deliberately intended to echo that of Falerii Veteres (Millett 2007; Laird 2016: 200). Whether these anomalies reflect an act of subversion/assertion of Faliscan identity on the part of the conquered population, or whether they were undertaken by the victorious Romans themselves, is more difficult to determine.

44 Bolder-Boos 2011, 2014. See also Coles 2009.

45 Bolder-Boos 2014: 284–285.

46 The precise location of this temple is debated, and many would now reject its association with the monumental terraced structure on the Monte S. Angelo. On the Colle S. Francesco, another of its hypothesized locations, votive offerings have been found dating from the pre-Roman phases into late Roman times, which would fit well with the apparent continuity of Jupiter Anxur's worship at Terracina. On the temple and questions over its placement, see Coarelli 1982a: 328–332; 1987: 113, 123–127; Bolder-Boos 2014: 286–287.

47 Bolder-Boos 2014: 281, 287–288. The Gracchan colonies are Colonia Minervia Scolacium, Colonia Neptunia Tarentum, and Colonia Iunonia Carthago. The prominence of Vulcan at Ostia has been variously explained, but it may relate to a nearby archaic sanctuary of Vulcan (Meiggs 1960: 342; Pellegrino 1986: 296–297). The Latin colony of Venusia might owe its name to the presence of an important Venus cult in the region (Torelli 1995:

150–154). Torelli further considers it likely that "a large indigenous element" would have been included amongst the colonists (152). The persistence of the cult of the two Fortunae at Antium well into Roman times indicates a similar situation (Bolder-Boos 2014: 288).

48 Section 4.3.2.

49 Bolder-Boos 2014: 289.

50 See Maschek 2022: 156 for the idea of a "horizontal system of meaning," in which features of a building could be related by viewers "to other buildings and structures which constituted the world of those who perceived them." As Maschek emphasizes, these meanings would never have been stable over long periods of time. On the multilayered meanings of 5th and 4th century BCE architectural terracottas in Rome, and how they interacted with the city's other buildings temporally and geographically for viewers, see Hopkins 2022.

51 On this and the following examples, see Section 4.2.3.

52 On the pediment, see Section 4.3.2.

53 See Section 4.3.3.

54 Important in spurring this trend were Walter 2004 and Gowing 2005. Diefenbach 2007 is another major contribution, although with a later chronological focus. For the performative qualities of Roman memory practice from a literary perspective, see Farrell 1997. Karl Galinsky's *Memoria Romana* project, initiated in 2009, has led to great strides in Roman memory studies across the empire and into the Christian period. Besides a number of conferences and individual studies, the project has now produced three edited volumes covering a broad geographic and chronological range (Galinsky 2014; Galinsky and Lapatin 2015; Galinsky 2016). Flower 2006 addresses Roman practices of forgetting as a feature of memory construction, particularly in a political context. For architecture as a tool for managing civic memory during the late Republic, see Davies 2018, as well as Popkin 2016 on Roman triumphs in particular. Popkin 2016: 11–22 offers a useful overview of memory studies in relation to Rome, and see more recently Popkin 2022 and Popkin and Ng 2022.

55 Most studies of memory in the Roman world have focused on the period of the Empire, and many on the Second Sophistic in particular. For instance, Alcock 2002; Galli and Cordovana 2007.

56 In particular, Halbwachs 1925, 1941, 1950.

57 A different but related approach to "social memory" with a more specifically art historical point of reference was developed around the same time by Aby Warburg.

58 Assmann 1995 (first published in German in 1988), 2010, 2011 (first published in 1992).

59 Attempts to reconcile this broad range of disciplinary perspectives, methodologies, and theoretical approaches include Olick and Robbins 1998; Erll and Nünning 2010; Olick, Vinitzky-Seroussi, and Levy 2011, as well as the journal *Memory Studies*, launched in 2008. For the application of advances in neuroscience, see Tulving and Craik 2000; Markowitsch 2010. See also Connerton 1989 on the performative and bodily qualities of social memory.

60 For a discussion of these works and their impact, see Olick and Robbins 1998: 117 ff.

61 Assmann 2010: 110.

62 Erll 2011: 32.

63 Beiner 2018 offers a recent in-depth discussion of "social forgetting." While he focuses on Northern Ireland, his analysis has relevance for a broad range of historical situations. For deliberate forgetting in a Roman context, see Flower 2006 and Davies 2018.

64 For this reason, James Wertsch prefers the term "collective remembering" to "collective memory" (Wertsch 2009: 119).

65 The concept has also been defined in extremely broad terms, for instance, as "the interplay of present and past in socio-cultural contexts" (Erll 2010: 2).

66 Galinksy 2015: 2.

67 Lefebvre 1974.

68 Nora 1984; see also Nora 1989. For the "spatial turn" in recent scholarship, and the often jumbled use of terms like "space" and "place" as applied in a range of humanistic disciplines, see Jerram 2013.
69 Roth 2013: 108.
70 Hobsbawm 1983: 4.
71 Hobsbawm 1983: 2.
72 Hobsbawm 1983: 1–2.
73 Hobsbawm 1983: 12.
74 Massa-Pairault 1992: 217–220; 1999: 545; Strazzulla 2007: 146 ff. See also Gabba 1982: 36–38. The tendency of elites in Late Republican Rome to emphasize their ethnic roots might be considered part of the same broader interest in origin, see Farney 2007.
75 Perret 1942; Galinsky 1969; Poucet 1985; Gruen 1990: 5–33; Roller 1999: 263–285; Rose 2002; 2008: 98–102.
76 E.g., Gruen 1992: 6–51.
77 Rose 2015: 141–149.
78 Gruen 1990: 20.
79 See, for instance, the arguments in Colivicchi 2008 regarding the "Greek-like image of Ancona's ruling class" (45) during this period.
80 Bolder-Boos 2014: 282–285; and see Section 5.2.3.
81 Bolder-Boos 2014: 283–284.
82 Strazzulla 1992: 172–183. On the unusual dimensions and arrangement of these figures, which she describes as a sort of continuous pedimental frieze, see pp. 179–180. Her identification of the pediment's subject is based on iconographic similarities between the figure of a kneeling boy (identified as Orestes) and the various other figures with known images of Telephus scenes. The unusual female figure with an aegis and exposed breast is identified by Strazzulla as Telephus' wife Hiera. She suggests iconographic parallels with Volterran urns, as well as with Pergamene models. On these fragments, see more recently De Tommaso, Paribeni, and Sorge 2011.
83 Lycophron *Alex.* 1242–1245 names Tarchon and Tyrensus/Tyrrhenos as the children of Telephus. Servius *ad Aen.* 10.179 (= *HRR* fr. 45), citing Cato's *Origines,* identifies Tarchon as the founder of Pisa. Tarchon is also credited with the foundation of Tarquinia by Steph. Byz. s.v. Ταρχώνιον. For a discussion of Pisa's origins and potential textual problems related to the Catonian attribution, see Briquel 1991: 249–276. The Telephus myth was known to the Etruscans by the 4th century BCE and appears on various mirrors, vases, and funerary urns (Briquel 1991: 200 ff.).
84 Livy 45.13.10.
85 In Strazzulla's view, the promotion of Telephus also emphasized a common mythic origin with Rome, thus serving a peacemaking role (Strazzulla 1992: 182–183). See also Strazzulla 2007: 151.
86 Frova 1973; Forte 1991; Forte et al. 1992.
87 Ronzitti Orsolini 1971; Small 1981; Colonna 2000: 311–325; Krauskopf 2000; also *LIMC* VII Septem esp. 46–53. The longevity of the myth in this region argues against the idea that the Talamonaccio pediment reflects Roman propaganda following the defeat of the Gauls (e.g. Cristofani 1981a: 41; Carandini 1985: 52).
88 Nijboer 1991: 24.
89 Small 1981.
90 E.g., *LIMC* VII Septem 50.
91 E.g., *LIMC* VII Septem 49.
92 Small 1981: 168–169; *LIMC* I Amphiaraos 40–44.
93 Small 1981: 167–168.
94 On the relationship between the imagery on Etruscan urns and evidence for Etruscan theatrical performances, see Nielsen 1993; 2004.

95 Scenes related to the story of the Seven Against Thebes are known from Etruscan sites already in the 6th century BCE (Krauskopf 2000).

96 Ciampoltrini 1995a. Philostratus *Imagines* II.15 includes a description of the prophetic Glaucus meeting the Argonauts. For Glaucus' iconography, *LIMC* IV s.v. *Glaukos (I)*, 271 ff.

97 Strazzulla 2007: 149–150.

98 Diod. Sic. IV 56.6 (citing Timaeus) = *FGrHist* 566 F 85.

99 Strazzulla 2007: 150. Ciampoltrini suggests that both scenes are evocative of oracle and prophecy and that the Talamonaccio temple itself may have served an oracular function (Ciampoltrini 1995a: 73–74).

100 E.g., the *lusus Troiae*, the Lupercalia, and the rituals related to the temple of Magna Mater. See also Scheid 2012 on festivals in the Forum Boarium, and Smith 2012 on the *feriae Latinae*, as well as Scullard 1981; Bispham and Smith 2000.

101 Brandt and Iddeng 2012: 6–8. See also Moser 2019 on memory and the performance of religious ritual in central Italy, and Graham 2021 on religion as lived experience.

102 Forte 1991: 87–92, 101; Forte et al. 1992: 191.

103 Forte et al. 1992: 199, 217–218.

104 Forte et al. 1992: 191, 215–216.

105 Ghini and Diosono 2012: 119; Diosono and D'Angelo 2019: 397.

106 Diosono and D'Angelo 2019: 399–404.

107 Blagg 1983: 33; Pensabene and Sanzi Di Mino 1983: 114–117 nos. 187–191. Känel 2000: 136; Diosono and Plebani 2013: 168, 170–172.

108 Coarelli has further suggested that the unusual triangular form of these antefixes may relate to Diana's worship as *Trivia* or *Diana triplex* at Nemi, and her triple role as hunter, protector of birth, and chthonic deity (Coarelli 1987: 169; Ghini and Diosono 2012: 119).

109 See Section 4.2.3.

110 See Section 3.3.3.

111 See Section 4.3.2.

112 As Cifani has argued, "urban monuments . . . play an essential role as public landmarks in the construction of a collective memory, and among these, religious sanctuaries were privileged places of collective and political identity" (Cifani 2018: 391).

SIX

REFRAMING AND REMEDIATING

Architectural Terracottas in Augustan Rome

6.1 INTRODUCTION

The preceding chapters have emphasized the heavy symbolic charge of temple terracottas in the last centuries BCE, focusing in particular on their archaizing tendencies and their often explicitly local points of reference. As we have seen, terracottas were powerful tools for communal identity in the turbulent context of Roman expansion and colonization within Italy. But how did they function once absolute Roman domination was assured? More specifically, how were centuries-old traditions in architectural terracotta translated to the new political reality within Rome itself?

The present chapter takes up these questions, exploring the fundamental shift that these objects and their connotations underwent with the dawn of the Imperial period. It is significant for the history of Italic architectural terracottas that their last major period of use (albeit on a reduced scale) coincides roughly with the Augustan Principate. During this time, terracotta decoration was gradually abandoned as the widespread exploitation of the marble quarries at Luni opened up new architectural possibilities across the Italian peninsula (Figure 95).

As Rome transformed materially, visually, and politically, Octavian/Augustus was scrupulous in his attempts to present innovation in a frame of tradition. Artisans played a major role in achieving this through visual culture. Architectural terracottas did not disappear overnight but were reworked and

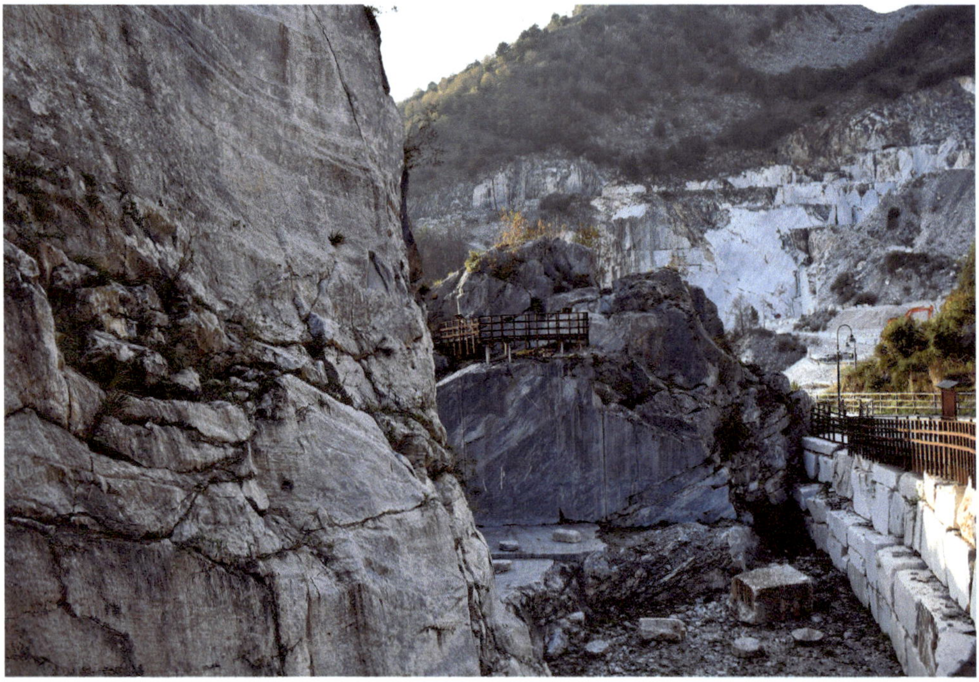

95. View of the marble quarries at Luni (modern Carrara), with ancient quarrying marks visible in the foreground (left) and modern quarrying activities being carried out in the background. Author's photo.

reframed for a new urban context. The so-called "Campana reliefs" were introduced sometime in the 1st century BCE and gained particular popularity under Augustus. These retained the traditional material of terracotta, and in some cases the same vegetal motifs that had graced Italic temples for centuries. Images of plants and vines were isolated and reframed into new compositions, often placed in relation to divine figures. The figural elements of the reliefs – which are primarily what distinguish Campana reliefs from their forbears – are rendered in a neo-Attic style, so that the style, form, and material work together to create a strongly retrospective result. In this inventive combining of disparate archaizing elements, the Campana reliefs are entirely new and fully in line with the broader Augustan ideology.

The present chapter first summarizes some key features of Campana reliefs and looks in particular at a subset dating mostly to the 1st centuries BCE and CE, especially around the time of Augustus. These reliefs, which privilege motifs drawn from traditional temple terracottas and place them at the center of the composition, usually in relation to vaguely defined deities, offer the clearest representation of the ways in which the symbolic value of vegetal motifs from terracotta shifted under the Principate. The vines and flowers that had once covered temples across Italy now became numinous evocations of an idealized and bucolic religious antiquity. I then consider the ways in which the material of terracotta, long a mainstay of Italic architecture, took on added connotations due to its increasing conspicuousness amid Rome's new stone constructions. That this contrast was noticed by viewers at the time is made clear by our surviving literary sources, who explicitly frame stone as a luxurious and fundamentally foreign material compared to the traditional Italic medium of terracotta. Finally, I turn to a key legacy of architectural terracottas in the Early Empire – the remediation of traditional vegetal motifs into stone.

The following discussion is therefore intended as something of an epilogue to the history of 3rd–1st century temple terracottas as agents of identity formation in the context of Roman expansion. By the same token, reflecting on the early imperial reception of these objects offers new modes for understanding many of the themes that have run through this study. The vast corpus of Campana reliefs, despite receiving increased attention in recent years, is in need of detailed and dedicated further research. What follows is in no way comprehensive but is meant instead to pick out certain significant features of these objects (particularly in their earlier iterations) and to relate them to their terracotta predecessors. What emerges from this analysis furthers several of the arguments presented thus far in relation to "traditional" temple terracottas. These include: a sustained interest in archaizing, especially in relation to religious images; a gathering and adapting of older forms into new compositions and arrangements as part of identity construction; and a flexible and kinetic quality to the symbolic overtones that terracotta decoration takes on in different places and historical situations. The following discussion will focus on reliefs from Rome itself, in part because it is in Rome that we see most clearly the impact of the new Augustan political context, but also because the manner in which these objects were employed at Rome further undercuts the traditional directionality arguments that I have repeatedly challenged in relation to the earlier material. Rather than symbolizing something specifically "Roman," the iconography, style, and even material of these reliefs evoked, in an Augustan context, a broad and highly idealized notion of *Italic* religious tradition. The local connotations these objects had held were now subsumed into a fictionalized historical trajectory that led unswervingly to the pious Augustan present.

6.2 CAMPANA RELIEFS: A NEW FORM IN OLD CLOTHES

Around the time that the exploitation of the Luna marble quarries was rendering traditional terracotta revetments obsolete, a new type of architectural terracotta was introduced in Italy. The so-called "Campana reliefs" take their modern name from Giovanni Pietro Campana, who collected numerous examples and published the first major discussion of the type in 1842.[1] They are attested in private houses, funerary buildings, temples, and public structures from the 1st century BCE to early 2nd century CE and appear to have been particularly popular under Augustus.[2] While grouped together in modern scholarship, what precisely constitutes a "Campana relief" is not always entirely straightforward, and many examples defy clearcut categorization.[3]

In general, these reliefs were produced in large series using molds, often in the same facilities in which bricks, roof tiles, and/or amphorae were being manufactured contemporaneously.[4] They are thus emblematic of the booming construction industries that characterized the first centuries BCE and CE, with single manufacturers churning out vast quantities of finished products that were then shipped and employed at sites across the region. Rome is often assumed to be the primary production center, but there is no firm evidence to support this, and examples have also been found across central Italic sites like Cosa, Gabii, and Falerii Veteres (Sassi Caduti), as well as outside of Italy in Southern France, Spain, and Greece.[5]

Many Campana reliefs were used in a similar manner as traditional revetment plaques, simas, or crestings – the plaques nailed to wooden beams and the crestings fastened to the simas.[6] The placement of "attachment plaques," on the other hand, is a topic of ongoing debate.[7] They may have been fixed to simas and functioned like traditional crestings, but many appear instead to have been mortared directly into interior walls.[8] The size of all these types was fairly standardized, with revetment plaques usually measuring 50 cm high x 46 cm wide (or 32 cm x 27 cm in later examples), simas hovering around 22 cm high x 44–48 cm wide, and crestings and attachment plaques varying in height but typically 44–48 cm wide.[9] Naturally, there were exceptions to this.[10]

The dating of Campana reliefs is at least as fraught as that of earlier architectural terracottas. This is partly due to their limited chronological span but above all to the unfortunate fact that most known examples come from large private collections and lack any type of archaeological documentation. In the cases in which Campana reliefs are excavated from well-documented contexts, stratigraphy is of limited help since such contexts are of course secondary – representing a collapse layer or a deliberate deposition that may have occurred long after the reliefs were manufactured. Stamps and inscriptions aid in some cases but are most helpful for the later examples.[11] The bulk of Campana reliefs are therefore dated primarily based on stylistic criteria. Given their archaizing stylistic tendencies, precise dates must be viewed with extreme caution.

Still, some general observations may be made regarding the iconography of Campana reliefs in the first century of their use. Although considerable variation exists in terms of composition and theme, most of the earlier reliefs may be broadly grouped into two categories: those depicting a specific mythological scene or at least recognizable mythological characters and those whose imagery is somewhat vaguer – featuring abundant vegetal imagery and/or showing apparently divine figures who lack precise attributes.[12] Examples of both groups are known from documented archaeological contexts, and seem to have been popular between the 1st century BCE and early 1st century CE.

Among these are the over 600 fragments of Campana reliefs uncovered during excavations of Cosa's summit.[13] Richardson assigned them to the last phase of the triple-cella temple, while Strazzulla suggested that they may have adorned a portico instead.[14] Either way, the summit was a dedicated religious area, and the archaeological context suggests a date no later than the end of the 1st century BCE.[15] The fragments belong to six discrete relief types, all of which show mythological subjects. Bacchic themes appear on three of the types (Figure 96), while the others show Apollo Citharoedus with Nike, Perseus presenting Medusa's severed head to Minerva, and Apollo and Hercules struggling over the Delphic tripod.[16] Versions of the latter two types are also known from Rome and elsewhere (Figures 97–98).[17]

Identifiable mythic scenes and personages such as these are typically shown in an abbreviated composition, with a small number of figures (often only two or three) occupying most of the relief.[18] They are executed in a neo-Attic style and tend toward heraldic composition, swallowtail folds in the drapery, and

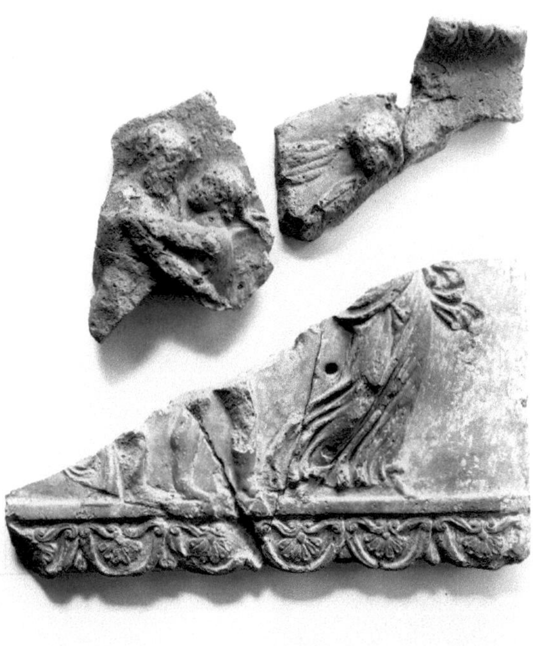

96. Campana relief showing Silenus, cupid, and a dancing maenad, from Cosa, Type C2:297. Courtesy of the American Academy in Rome, Cosa Archaeological Collection.

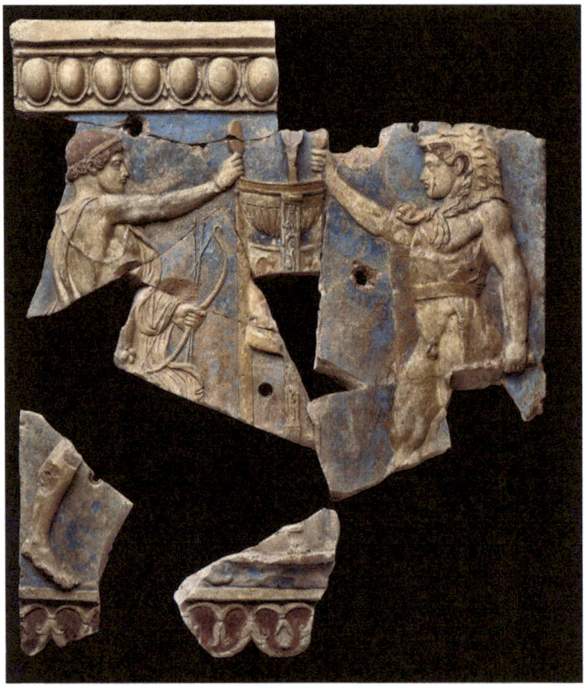

97. Campana relief from the Palatine hill in Rome, showing Apollo and Hercules struggling over the Delphic tripod. Rome: Museo Palatino. By permission of the Ministero della Cultura – Parco Archeologico del Colosseo.

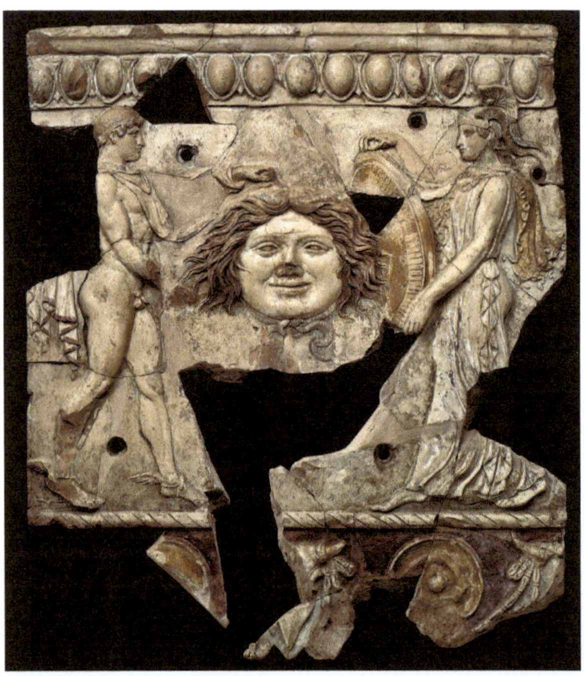

98. Campana relief from the Palatine hill in Rome, showing Perseus and Minerva flanking Medusa's severed head. Rome: Museo Palatino. By permission of the Ministero della Cultura – Parco Archeologico del Colosseo.

figures shown in a tiptoe stance.[19] The composition is staid and the style decidedly retrospective.

Most of these reliefs are framed above and/or below by a decorative floral band. This too marks a break with tradition, as mythological scenes in earlier temple decoration had generally been limited to the pediment, while floral and vegetal motifs appeared on elements such as revetment plaques and cornices. By setting a mythological scene between floral bands, Campana reliefs in a sense combined these two decorative elements into a single compositional space. The use of floral frames on these plaques may be part of a broader aesthetic interest in framing, a phenomenon seen most clearly in Roman wall painting of this period.[20]

Campana reliefs of the second group differ from the first in that they defy straightforward identification with specific myths or personages and usually feature a high proportion of vegetal imagery in the central scene. On a plaque from Ardea, for instance, a head floats amid a mass of flowers and scrolls.[21] Other versions of this relief are known, but the identity of the figure is never obvious (Figure 99). The placement of a floating head amid impossible foliage suggests a divine presence, however vaguely defined. A similar situation occurs on a plaque from Sassi Caduti (Falerii Veteres), where wings signal the

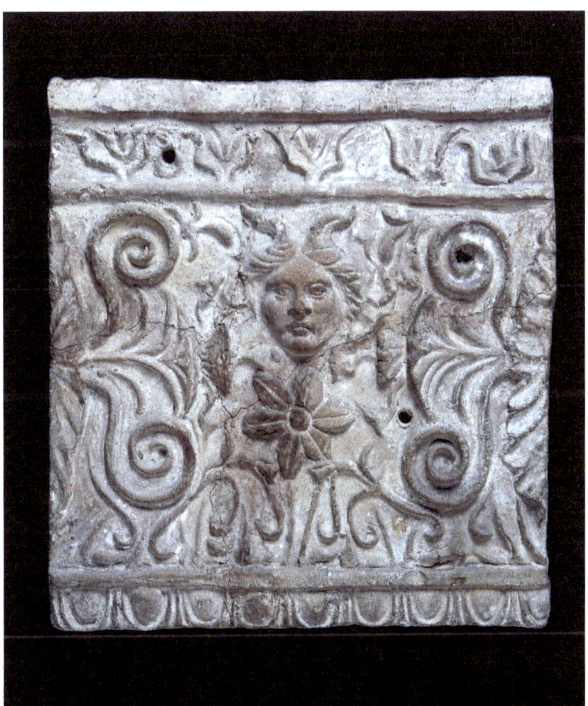

99. Relief with a floating head amid vegetal motifs. Paris: Musée du Louvre, S821. © RMN-Grand Palais / Art Resource, NY.

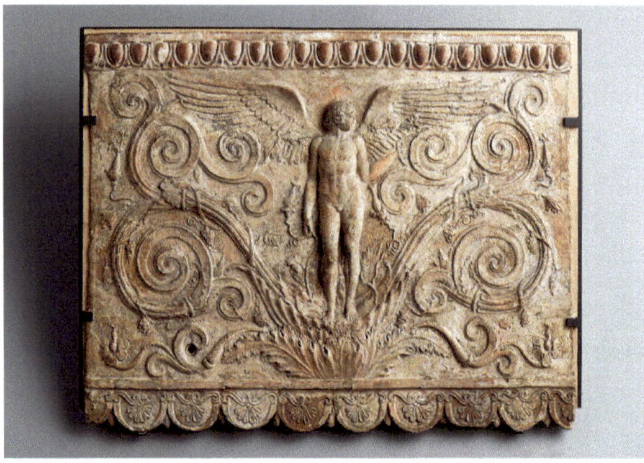

100. Campana relief of a nude divinity emerging from a plant. Paris: Musée du Louvre, CP3850.
© RMN-Grand Palais / Art Resource, NY.

nonhuman nature of the flute-player who stands perched on the scrolling vines of a plant that winds conspicuously through the composition.[22]

The same theme of an ambiguous divine figure amid swirling vegetation occurs in numerous variations and appears to have been particularly popular around the time of Augustus. Often, the human form merges directly with a plant or is centrally placed as if itself a flower or bud. On a relief type in the Louvre and known also from the Palatine Hill in Rome, a nude winged male figure emerges from an acanthus (Figure 100).[23] Branching s-spirals surround him symmetrically on both sides. He turns left to gaze at one and clasps it with his left hand, while the fingers of the hanging right hand graze a vine that creeps up vertically at his side. A similar motif appears on another relief showing a clothed and heavily archaizing winged female figure, who stands centrally atop an opening plant and grasps curling vines with both hands (Figure 101). A lotus with palmette emerges from her head like a crown, so that she is physically encased on all four sides by vegetation. Compositionally, she recalls the *potnia theron* antefixes of the "standard temple kit" (cf. Figure 17), but it is significant that on the Campana reliefs it is the world of plants, rather than animals, over which she presides.

While the figures in these examples inhabit vegetated space, some reliefs show humanoid figures as literally merged with plants. In one type, filled almost entirely with a remarkable range of vines and flowers, the central bud opens into a female face as if her neck were a stalk and her head a flower (Figure 102).[24] Other reliefs show a child-like figure, presumably the baby Dionysus, emerging from acanthus and grape vines which rise up to encase him (Figure 103).[25] So profound is the fusion of human and plant forms that the acanthus here replaces the figure's legs entirely. A similar situation occurs on another relief in which two figures flank a floating head with the horns of

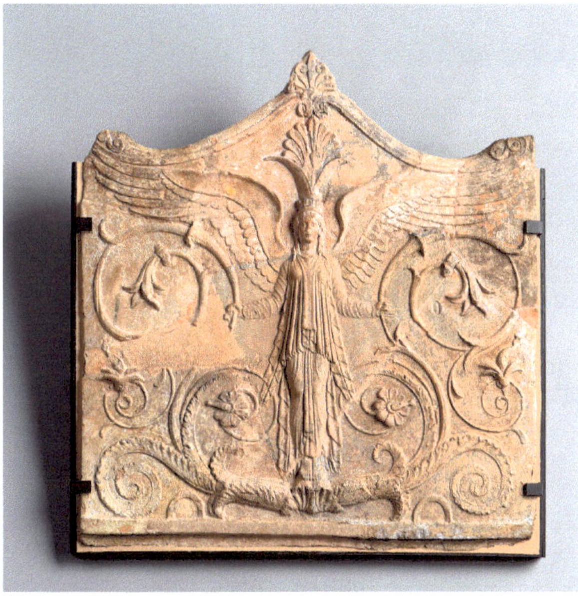

101. Campana relief of a divinity in archaizing style amid vines. Paris: Musée du Louvre, CP3845;S886.
© RMN-Grand Palais / Art Resource, NY.

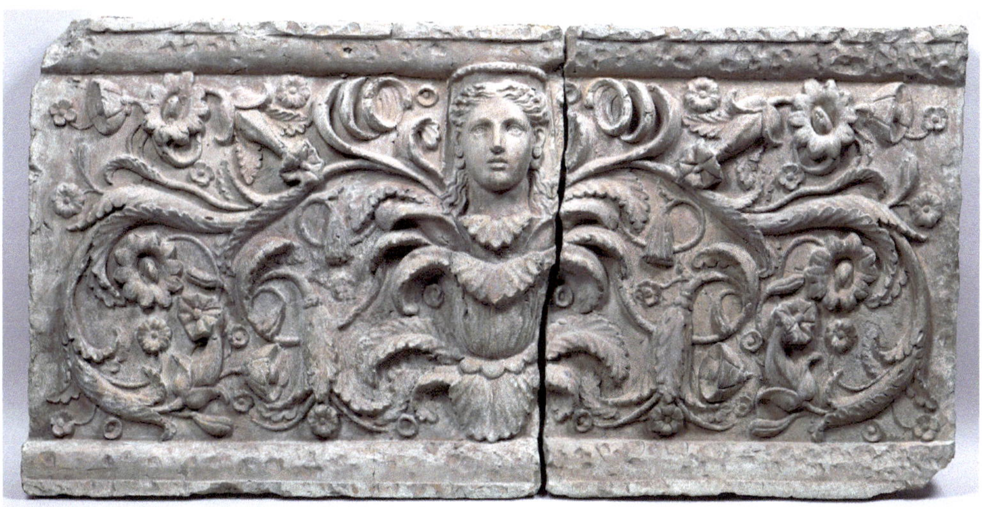

102. Relief with a female head amid vegetal motifs. Paris: Musée du Louvre, CP3874.
© RMN-Grand Palais / Art Resource, NY.

Jupiter Ammon.[26] The flanking figures have short tails like satyrs but are winged and with acanthus emerging from their waists in place of legs. Even the figures' wings curl, as if they too were on the verge of becoming vines.

This interest in combined human-plant figures can be traced directly to temple terracottas showing the so-called *donnafiore*.[27] Like the later Campana reliefs, the figure's legs have been replaced by curling vines, and her dress

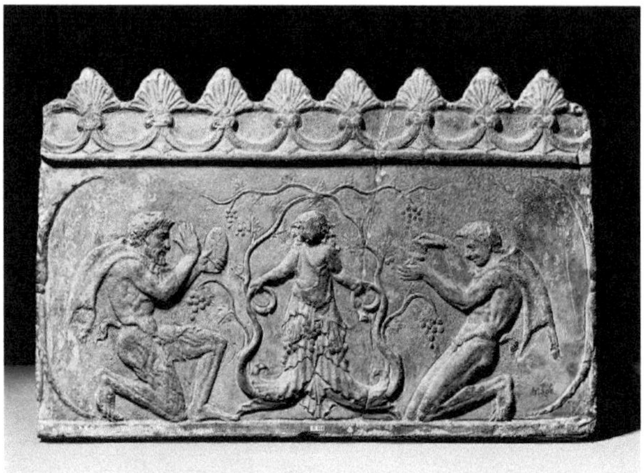

103. Relief with a figure (the infant Dionysus?) emerging from acanthus and grape vines. London: The British Museum.

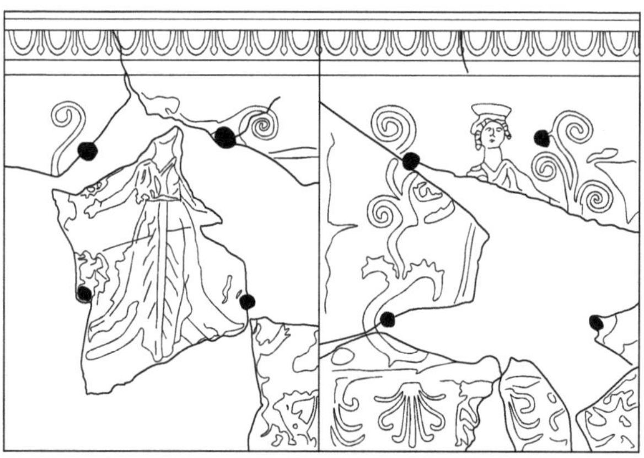

104. Plaques showing the *donnafiore* from Temple B at Pietrabbondante, second half of the 2nd century BCE.
Drawing by Dallin Evans, after Strazzulla 2006 fig. 3.8.

sometimes takes the form of a downturned leaf (Figure 104). She is iconographically linked to the *potnia theron* but foreshadows the Campana reliefs in that she grasps vines rather than animals.

Indeed, much of the vegetal imagery employed on Campana reliefs of the non-mythologically specific category derives directly from traditional temple terracottas. As we saw in Chapter 3, terracottas of the "standard temple kit" feature a disproportionate botanic emphasis, their surfaces covered almost entirely by the swirls and curls of vines (Figure 12). S-spirals and palmettes stand out as particularly recurrent motifs, dominating the composition on both revetment plaque types (Figures 13–15). S-spirals cover the Campana reliefs as well, encircling the humanoid figures or even held by them. Palmettes emerge

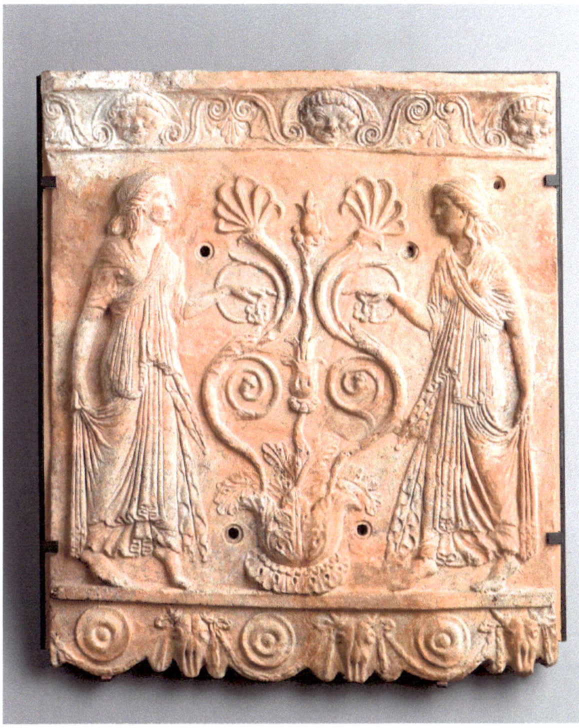

105. Campana relief with female figures in archaizing style flanking a plant. Paris: Musée du Louvre, S756.

from a figure's head or at the top of a central plant. Rows of palmettes appear frequently at the top or bottom of all types of Campana reliefs (e.g., Figures 96, 100, 103), protruding into space just as they had above traditional perforated cornices (Figures 23, 26).

The retention and indeed the reinvention of these vegetal motifs highlights the profound debt of Campana reliefs to earlier temple terracottas. But whereas these designs had long constituted the decorative focus of temples – their swirls repeating ad infinitum across the length of a roof – they are now isolated and emphasized within entirely new compositions. Paired with the vague but religiously evocative winged or floating figures, these vines take on an almost numinous quality. This is even made explicit in some cases. An Augustan plaque shows an acanthus opening into a central plant framed by two archaizing female figures who move toward it with a hand outstretched (Figure 105).[28] The vertical vegetation occupies the position sometimes reserved for a candelabrum or other cult object, as if the plant itself had now become the object of worship.[29] The palmettes at the top lean toward each approaching female figure, heightening the sense of interaction between the human and botanic. On another relief, a pair of female figures sit lightly on the scrolling vines that surround them and turn to face a central plant growing

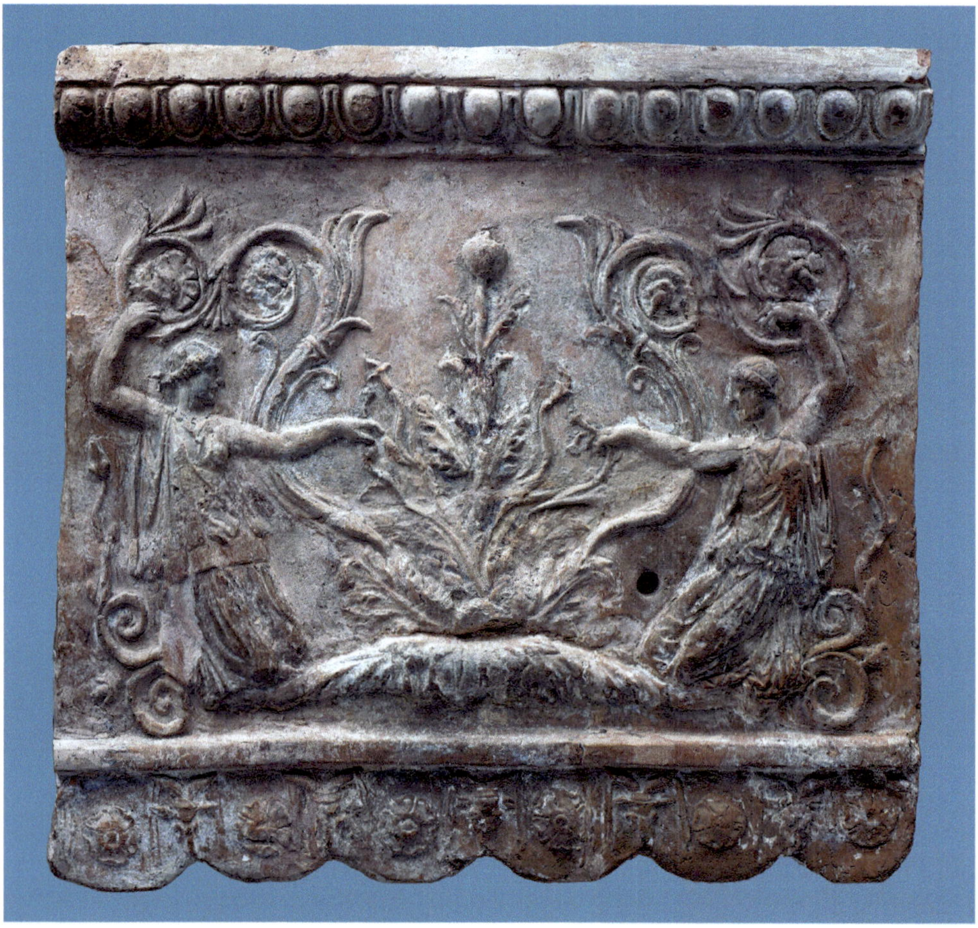

106. Relief with kneeling female figures amid vegetal motifs. Paris: Musée du Louvre, CP3847.

from an acanthus and ending in mirrored palmettes.[30] The same theme is expressed even more dramatically on another type, in which the female figures kneel on the plant's base and raise their arms as if witnessing (or evoking?) the plant's divine response (Figure 106).[31] Their reduced size compared to the plant further emphasizes its power. Floral spirals hang over their heads as well as before and below them.

The introduction of Campana reliefs into Roman architectural decoration signals an intriguing visual paradox: these reliefs were unquestionably new and innovative, while at the same time strongly archaizing in both their iconography and material. The neo-Attic style they so frequently employed evoked ancient traditions, calling to mind famous examples of classical Greek architectural decoration or votive statuary. But unlike their Greek forbears, these reliefs were rendered in terracotta. At a moment in which Italic marble was for the first time readily available and was being incorporated eagerly into Roman art and architecture, the use of terracotta for these reliefs is significant. Terracotta, after all, was the traditional material of Italic temple decoration – the material of the sacred.[32] In some sense, then, the clay material can be seen as rooting the neo-Attic style in Italic tradition. The double archaism of material and style drew on ancient visual stereotypes of the sacred, resulting in a new form that claimed antiquity even as it innovated.

The change in the treatment of traditional vegetal motifs is also significant in this context. As architectural terracottas were increasingly replaced by stone revetments, it seems almost as if these vegetal motifs came to stand in for the temples they had once decorated. By placing this familiar vegetation alongside archaizing numinous figures – all executed in the old-fashioned medium of terracotta – the Campana reliefs explicate an Augustan presentation of the idealized religious past. As we shall see, this reframing of vegetal motifs from traditional temple decoration is translated into the medium of marble during the Augustan period as well.

6.3 TERRACOTTA IN A MARBLE LANDSCAPE

Augustus' notorious statement that he found Rome a city of brick and left it a city of marble underscores the seriousness with which architectural materials were approached but also downplays the reality that for centuries marble and terracotta cohabited within the urban landscape.[33] This had already begun with the introduction of imported Greek marble into Rome, and we know of several manubial temples built or revetted in marble by the close of the Republic. Q. Caecilius Metellus erected Rome's first all-marble temple to Jupiter Stator between 146 and 131 BCE.[34] The temple's deliberate placement inside a quadriporticus of stuccoed peperino and alongside the Temple of Juno Regina with its local stone would have drawn further attention to the novelty and prestige of its marble material.[35] Lucius Mummius constructed a temple to Hercules Victor soon after, likely to be identified with the so-called Round Temple on the Tiber (Figure 107).[36] Though its foundations and core are of tufo and travertine, the Round Temple is revetted entirely in Pentelic marble. Other marble architectural remains are attested during the late Republic, but such constructions would have been an exception before the Augustan period.[37] As Maggie Popkin has argued, the choice of materials in Roman triumphal architecture closely followed notions of decorum.[38] Different building materials were deliberately placed side by side in order to contrast one another and to emphasize the appropriateness of each material for its architectural or sculptural use.

Before the opening of the Luni quarries, however, one connotation was common to all uses of marble – its foreignness as a material.[39] This could of

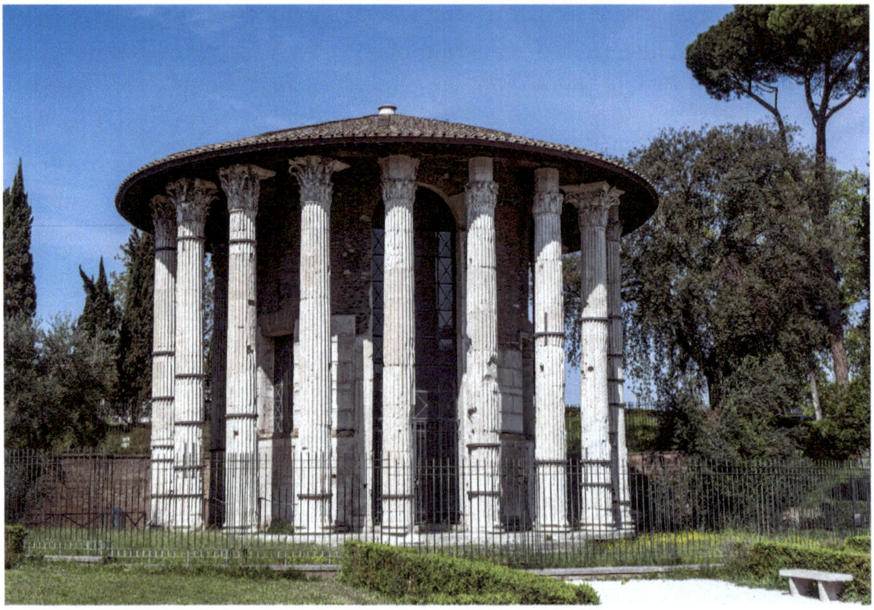

107. Round temple by the Tiber. Image: Wikimedia creative commons, https://en.wikipedia.org/wiki/Temple_of_Hercules_Victor#/media/File:Temple_of_Hercules_Victor_Rome_April_2019.jpg.

course enhance its perceived appropriateness for triumphal architecture. As Popkin shows, the use of Pentelic marble as well as the choice of Corinthian capitals worked together to visually trumpet Mummius' victory at Corinth.[40] Not all uses of marble could be linked so explicitly to Roman military triumphs, however. Alongside the ever-increasing architectural use of marble in Rome went the voracious importation of Greek marble sculpture into Italy, with hordes of statues adorning elite domestic spaces in addition to temples and public areas. As marble became more and more a part of the Italic landscape, the connotations of terracotta would have changed as a result. Indeed, beginning in the late Republic, our literary sources explicitly contrast the two, casting terracotta as the material of wholesome Italic tradition and marble as representative of foreign *luxuria*. Livy, for instance, puts these words in the mouth of Cato:

> infesta, mihi credite, signa ab Syracusis inlata sunt huic urbi. iam nimis multos audio Corinthi et Athenarum ornamenta laudantes mirantesque, et antefixa fictilia deorum Romanorum ridentes.

> Those statues from Syracuse were enemy standards brought against the city, believe me. Already I hear all too many people praising and admiring the artifacts of Corinth and Athens, and ridiculing the earthenware antefixes[41] of the Roman gods.[42]

The "ridiculing" of terracotta decoration and statuary is thus an indicator of moral decline – a decline propelled by exposure to foreign statues executed in luxurious materials. Of course, the comparison is unfair. The Greeks themselves had ancient and impressive traditions in architectural terracotta, and statuary in stone or bronze was far from being unknown in Italy. Still, the parallel Cato sets up is noteworthy rhetorically: foreigners use (unspecified) extravagant materials; good Romans respect the fictile images of Roman religious tradition.

A similar equation of non-terracotta materials with foreign *luxuria* appears in a musing of Pliny the Elder:

> mirumque mihi videtur, cum statuarum origo tam vetus Italiae sit, lignea potius aut fictilia deorum simulacra in delubris dicata usque ad devictam Asiam, unde luxuria.
>
> And it seems to me surprising that although the initiation of statuary in Italy dates so far back, the images of the gods dedicated in the shrines should have been more usually of wood or terracotta right down to the conquest of Asia, which introduced luxury here.[43]

The use of expensive materials for religious images is once again attributed to military conquest, with an implication of moral decline due to exposure to foreign luxury. *Potius* even suggests an element of preference for wood or terracotta, rather than simply of custom. At several points elsewhere in his treatise, Pliny notes that clay modeling is the most ancient form of sculpture and cites Varro's statement that the art of modeling clay was perfected in Italy and especially in Etruria.[44] He marvels at the durability (*firmitas*) of the terracotta pediments still visible in his own day, calling them "more deserving of respect than gold, and certainly more innocent."[45]

Propertius specifically lists terracotta as the material for images of deities in his visualization of early Rome, again linking the medium to notions of modesty, religion, and deep antiquity.[46] The Temple of Jupiter Optimus Maximus Capitolinus, arguably Rome's most iconic building, is frequently discussed in terms of its original terracotta decoration, which it retained long after marble had entered Roman architecture.[47] As Penelope Davies has noted, building restorations in the late Republic "tended toward conservatism."[48] This is certainly the case for Pompey's Temple of Hercules, which Vitruvius tells us followed an araeostyle design featuring a terracotta roof.[49] As his sumptuous theatre attests, Pompey was not a man who balked at spending vast sums of money on a building, nor at embellishing it with luxurious imported materials. His conservative approach to the Temple of Hercules reflects a deliberate choice, likely related to terracotta's perceived appropriateness for a restored ancient temple.[50] The antique connotations of clay as a building material seem to have become commonplace by the late Republic and are also highlighted in Vitruvius' account of mankind's earliest architectural exertions.[51]

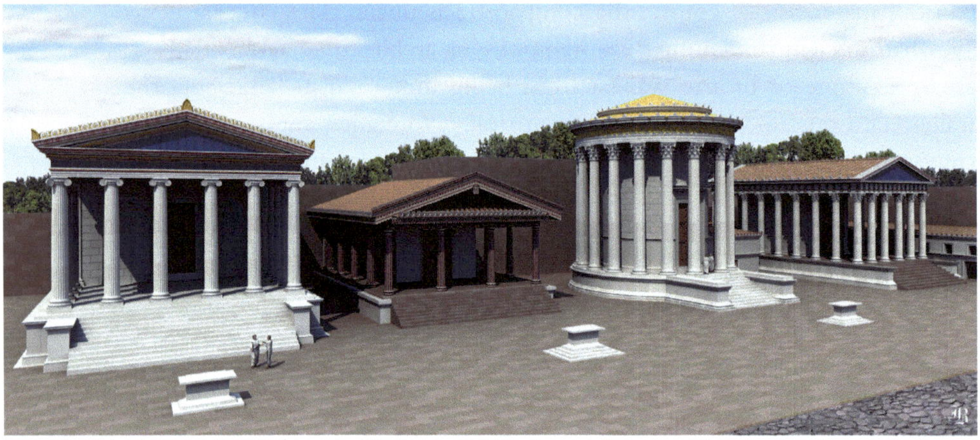

108. Hypothetical reconstruction of the area sacra di Largo Argentina c. 100 BCE, showing the contrast between temples built of different materials. Note in particular the comparatively squat dimensions of Temple C, second from left. Reconstruction John Burge.
Courtesy of Penelope Davies and John Burge.

This stereotype of terracotta as the material of the ancient – and specifically of Italic religious tradition – persisted beyond the opening of the quarries at Luni and the sudden availability of an actually native type of marble. The visual landscape of Rome and other Italic towns must have played an important role here. As temples built of Luna marble sprang up under Augustus, they would have contrasted sharply with the older, terracotta-laden structures that surrounded them. Not only would the textures of the materials have differed but their architectural forms as well – the old temples appearing top-heavy with their bulky terracotta roofs compared to the more vertical dimensions of the new stone constructions (Figure 108).[52] It is easy to imagine how orators and authors might have seized on the visual contrast that permeated Rome's architecture to decry a perceived moral decline and to promote an idealized version of a humble and pious Italic heritage.

Though a staunch promoter of Luna marble, Augustus (or, at least, the artisans in his service) was carefully attuned to the symbolic connotations of terracotta, which he turned to his advantage. Campana reliefs proved particularly expedient in this regard. As Hallett has shown, it is certainly not by accident that the otherwise luxuriously constructed Palatine complex was teeming with terracotta decoration.[53] What's more, several of the reliefs even go out of their way to emphasize their terracotta material. It had been common, beginning in the 2nd century BCE, to add a white primer coat before painting in order to help bring out the vivid colors on the surface.[54] Some of the most carefully worked Campana reliefs from the Palatine, however, not only eschew this white layer but even leave the figures' skin the natural color of the clay (most visible in Figure 97, though see also

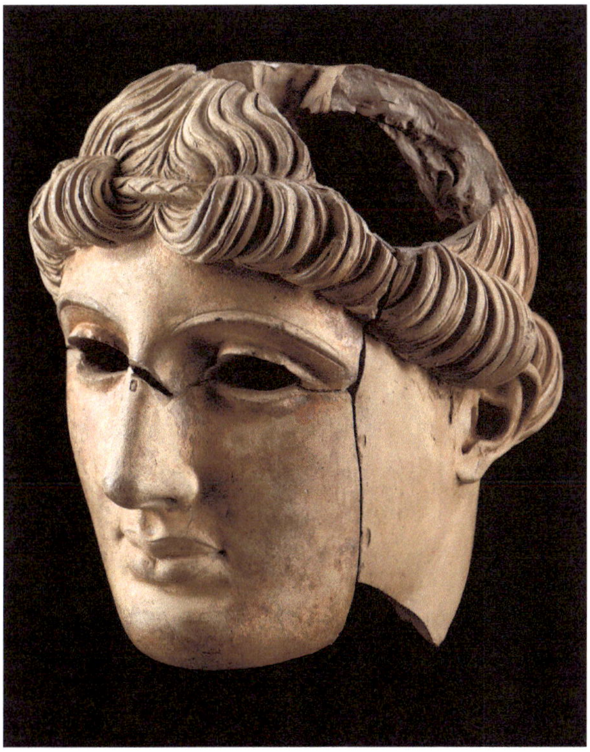

109. Head of a life-sized terracotta statue from the Palatine Hill. Rome: Museo Palatino. By permission of the Ministero della Cultura – Parco Archeologico del Colosseo.

Figure 98).[55] These reliefs, which would already have stood out in relation to the stone buildings of the Augustan complex, thus explicitly broadcast their terracotta material.

While a number of Campana reliefs were uncovered during Carettoni's excavations in the 1960s, it is Pensabene's monumental publication that has only recently made clear the vast scale of terracotta ornament on the Augustan Palatine. Over 1,600 fragments of architectural terracottas are known from this area. Most are Campana reliefs, but "traditional" terracotta simas, antefixes, and waterspouts were uncovered as well.[56] Archaizing terracotta statues of remarkable workmanship also come from the Palatine complex and would similarly have contrasted with the stone and bronze statues that likely stood alongside them (Figure 109).[57]

The Campana reliefs from the Augustan Palatine belong to both of the broad categories outlined above – some showing mythological scenes (e.g., Figures 97–98) while others feature figures amid swirling vegetation (Figures 100–101, 103, 105–106).[58] In the context of Octavian/Augustus' new complex, the use of vegetal motifs derived from traditional temple terracottas is highly charged symbolically. The vines and flowers are presented as explicitly numinous. Repeated across walls or the edges of porticoes, they would have created an ambience of bucolic sacredness, inhabited by divine figures whose vague appearance opened them to diverse (but always religious) interpretations. The terracotta material of these plaques would have stood out on the gleaming, marble-filled Palatine, further emphasizing the antique connotations of the plaques' imagery. As Hallett has argued, the use of terracotta (and specifically of Campana reliefs) on the Augustan Palatine "was intended to make reference to the traditional architectural ornament of the temples of central Italy, and ... to sound an unmistakably *Italian* patriotic note."[59]

Terracotta decoration was in reality one of many retrospective features of the Palatine complex. The Apollo temple itself was distyle in form – as close to the araeostyle design of traditional Etrusco-Italic temples as was structurally possible in marble.[60] Just southwest of the temple, large openings were apparently cut into the ground to reveal an Archaic structure below, "almost like archaeological artifacts."[61] In this same area, the "Hut of Romulus" stood rebuilt of humble materials to emphasize its antiquity, forming another medial contrast with the new complex.[62] Nearby too was the Lupercal, the Scalae Caci, the black meteorite in the Temple of Magna Mater – in short, a veritable museum to Rome's deep mythic history.[63] In this context, the religious and ancient connotations of the Campana reliefs would only have been heightened.

6.4 TERRACOTTA REMEDIATED

The translation of vegetal motifs from traditional temple decoration is clearest in the case of the Campana reliefs, which mimic their terracotta forbears in material, manufacture, and often in architectural placement as well. Campana reliefs, which represent the last gasp of terracotta as a dominant decorative medium in Roman/Italic architecture, endured into the early 2nd century CE but seem to have gradually declined in popularity after the early Empire. They represent a fundamentally transitional moment in the shift from terracotta to marble. Just as Campana reliefs were salvaging and reframing traditional vegetal motifs, these same designs were adopted for Rome's "new" architectural medium of marble.[64]

As I have argued elsewhere, this phenomenon is especially visible on the prominent vegetal panels of the Ara Pacis Augustae (Figure 110).[65] Many of the panels' features (the scrolling vines, profuse s-spirals, and repeated patterns, as well as the placement of acanthus and rows of palmettes) derive directly from temple terracottas. On a marble monument that proclaims the new Augustan peace, the emphasis on these traditional motifs is hardly accidental. They sit precisely at eye level and occupy more than half of the exterior of the enclosure walls. As on temple terracottas, paint would have rendered them even more noticeable and would have linked them chromatically to the

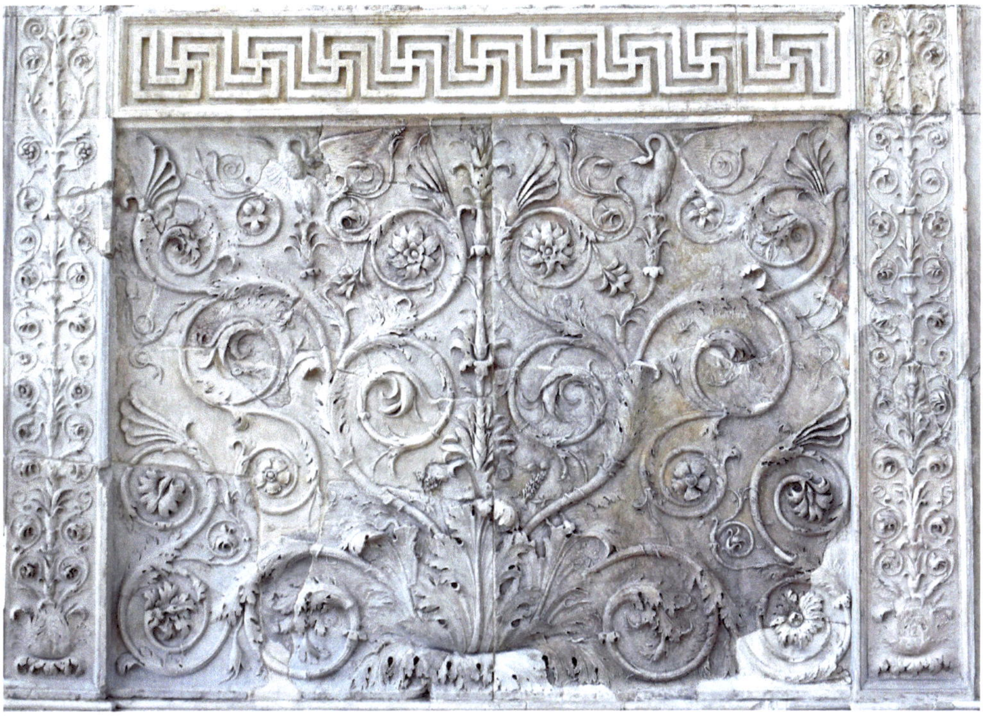

110. Ara Pacis vegetal frieze, short side (lower left of the east wall of the outer enclosure). Rome: Museo dell'Ara Pacis Augustae.
Author's photo. © Roma, Sovrintendenza Capitolina ai Beni Culturali.

bucolic greenery of the surrounding Campus Martius (Figure 111).[66] It is significant that the placement of this vegetal universe on the Ara Pacis has been reversed compared to temple architecture. Rather than crowning the monument, the vines and flowers of Italic religious tradition form the literal foundation of the Augustan project, which is illustrated above in figural form through a mix of mythological and processional scenes.[67]

Although the most famous example, the Ara Pacis is not the only monument on which traditional vegetal motifs are remediated in stone. Fragments belonging to at least two marble monuments date close to the Ara Pacis' construction and reveal a similar botanic emphasis.[68] Robert Cohon has attributed them to an atelier originating on the coast of Asia Minor. Regardless of the artists' origins, however, the appearance of these vegetal motifs must have stood in dialogue with the numerous architectural terracottas that still dominated Rome's temples. On the marble slabs, which likely decorated walls and pilasters, vines branch off into curls ending in flowers, they form s-spirals, they yield bursting offshoots (Figures 112–113). They occupy the composition entirely. Although carved in stone, they would have evoked for many viewers the ubiquitous vegetal motifs of Italic temple architecture (e.g., Figure 114).

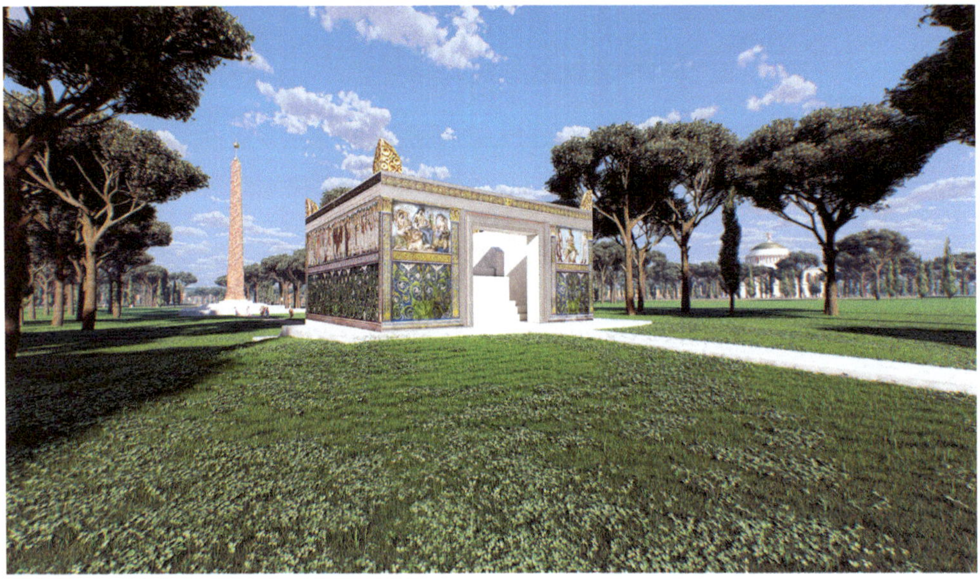

111. View of the Ara Pacis, with reconstructed color, in the Campus Martius.

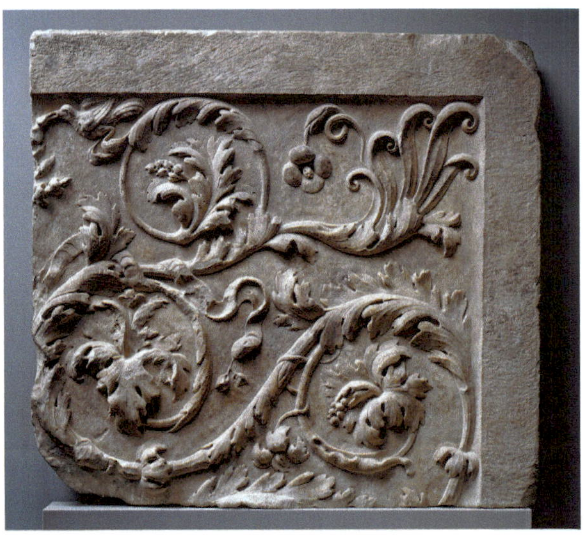

112. Marble relief with scrollwork. Atlanta: Carlos Collection of Ancient Art, Michael C. Carlos Museum, 2004.9.1.
Photo: Bruce M. White, 2004. Courtesy of the Michael C. Carlos Museum, Emory University.

A similar situation occurs on a marble frieze attributed to the Temple of Divus Julius (Figure 115).[69] Here, a winged female deity is represented with branching acanthus leaves in place of legs, much like the earlier *donnafiore* (Figure 104) and the subsequent figures from the Campana reliefs (Figure 103).

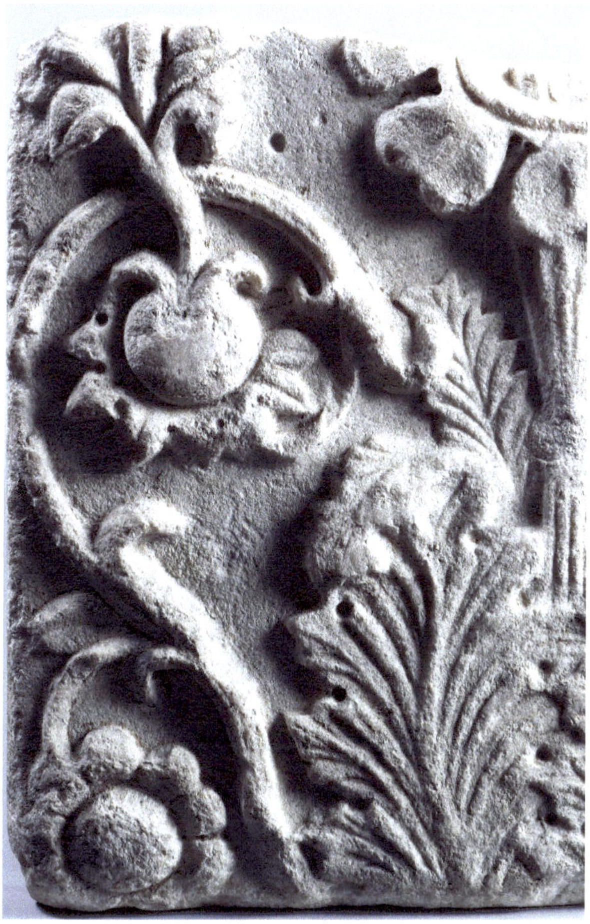

113. Relief with scrollwork. Paris: Musée du Louvre, MA4455;MNE579. © RMN-Grand Palais / Art Resource, NY (detail).

She is surrounded by swirling vines and flowers, one of which she reaches out her hand to grasp.

Of course, vegetal motifs such as these were not limited to architectural terracottas, and similar designs are well known from vase-painting, wall-painting, and monuments of the Hellenistic world. Temple terracottas, however, are particularly important since their use spans so large a chronological and geographical swath of Italic architectural history. Architectural terracottas constituted the primary decorative medium for Italic temples before the introduction of Luna marble, and many of these temples were still standing in the Augustan period. Artisans and elite viewers may have been familiar with the visual motifs of luxury items and Hellenistic monuments and may therefore have read more complex references into the vegetal imagery of Augustan stonework. But *all* viewers would have seen countless examples of architectural terracottas. When faced with something like the Ara Pacis' vegetal panels, their

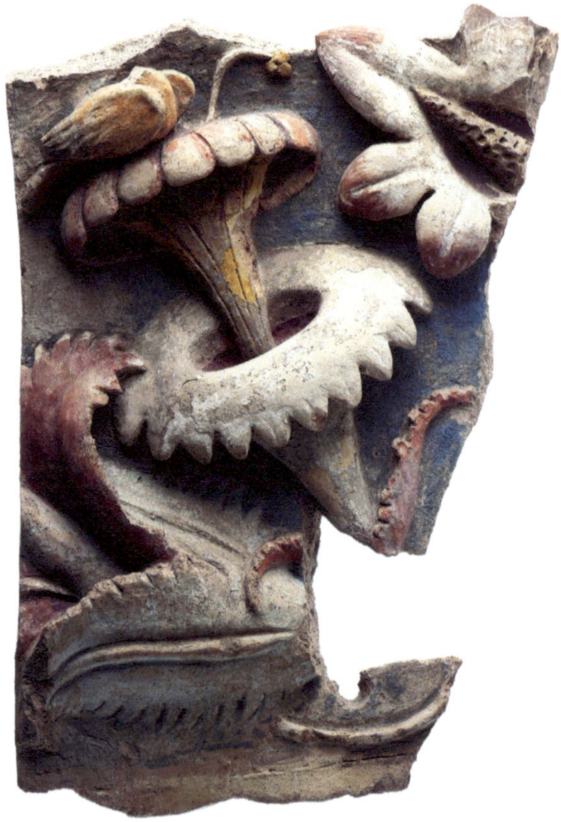

114. Terracotta plaque with floral motifs, 3rd century BCE. Geneva: Museum of Art and History, HR 0002.
© Museum of Art and History, City of Geneva, loan Association Hellas et Roma. Photograph by Bettina Jacot-Descombes.

first point of reference would have been the swirling vegetation of traditional temple decoration. The iconography of the Divus Julius frieze must similarly have recalled for viewers terracotta revetments and Campana reliefs, many of which adorned the Palatine just above the forum with closely matching imagery. The likely placement of this frieze on a prestigious temple would have reinforced the association with terracotta decoration.

Remediated vegetal imagery constitutes one of the lasting legacies of architectural terracottas in Roman visual culture.[70] Part of a marble *pluteus* or balustrade from the Sanctuary of Hercules at Tivoli dating to the Julio-Claudian period is decorated on its front with a swirling vine that branches off symmetrically from a central acanthus (Figure 116a).[71] Each vine spirals in turn, ending with a central flower precisely as they had on addorsed palmette plaques for centuries. At the top, a stylized formation of leaves recalls the two palmettes that terminated the vines on Campana reliefs with flanking female worshipers (Figures 105–106). Indeed, the same general principle is here

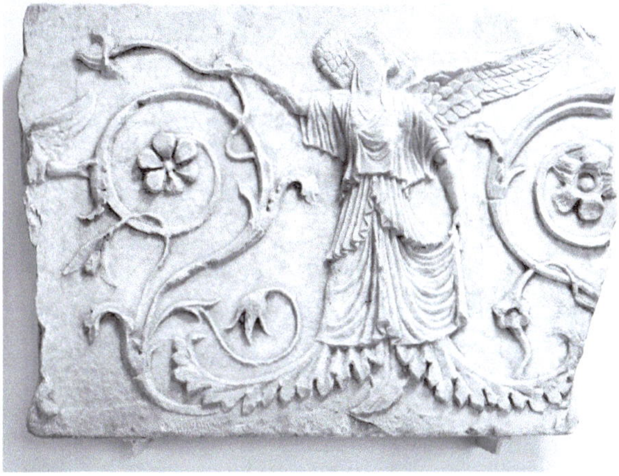

115. Marble frieze attributed to the Temple of Divus Julius, showing a winged female deity amid vegetation, with acanthus in place of legs.
Photo by H. Koppermann, 63.1233, courtesy of the Deutsches Archäologisches Institut – Rom.

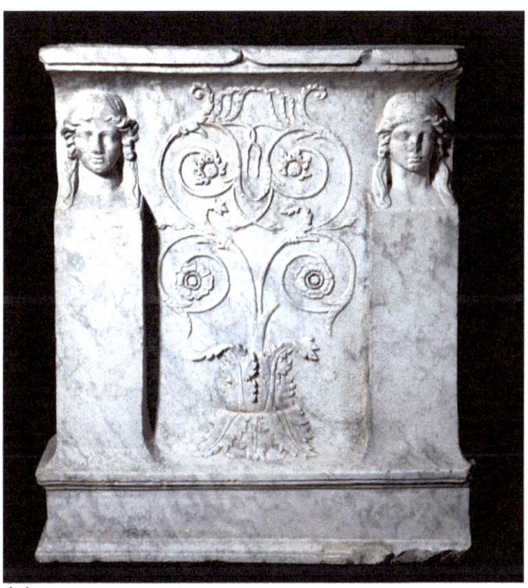

(a)

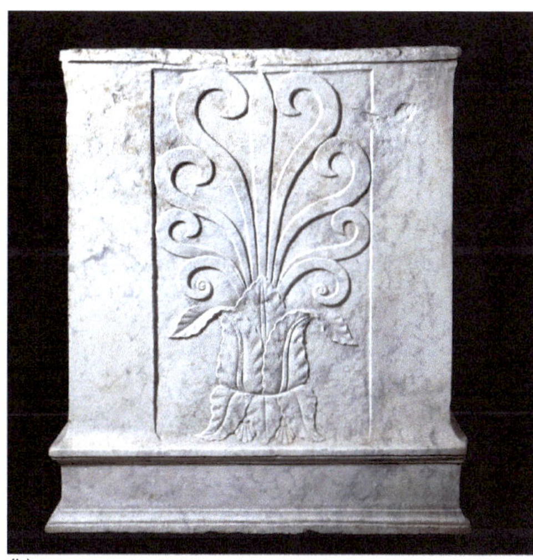

(b)

116. (A AND B) Marble *pluteus* with vegetal motifs, from the Sanctuary of Hercules at Tivoli.
By permission of the Istituto autonomo Villa Adriana e Villa d'Este-VILLAE, Tivoli (Ministero della Cultura).

evoked by the placement of symmetrical female herms on either side of a central floral design. The opposite side of the block is dominated almost entirely by a large palmette which closely mirrors the palmettes of terracotta antefixes and perforated acroteria (Figure 116b). Here, at a sacred site in which the temple and surrounding structures were executed on a monumental scale, traditional "humble" religious architecture is recalled on the stone-carved vines of the balustrade. Starting with the Campana reliefs, this vegetal imagery has been first reframed and then finally remediated. It is an Augustan interpretation of a bucolic religious past that has been carefully and beautifully absorbed into the visual language of a new Rome.

6.5 SYMBOLS OF *ITALIA*

The story of architectural terracottas in the Early Empire is thus one more instance of invented traditions. It is an Augustan creation of the past, a careful collage of images, styles, and materials tailored for a new political reality. It is a malleable and open imagery – one that, like the famous seated female figure on the Ara Pacis's east enclosure wall, allows its viewers to debate details but is resoundingly clear in its overarching message of piety, prosperity, and deeply rooted tradition.[72]

Before the imperial period, terracottas had visually referenced a temple's physical surroundings and mythic history. As terracottas fell from use, these more subtle differentiations and meanings slowly dissipated and were subsumed by the overarching symbolic value that was now assigned to them. Their material, which had once been unremarkable, was now explicitly highlighted as representative of humble (and thus morally admirable) Italic traditions. The vines and flowers that had long covered them were placed in new compositional arrangements, which drew attention to the vegetal motifs and set them within an explicitly religious imagery. The material and iconography of temple terracottas thus came to be associated with an idealized (re)vision of Italic history. Rather than representing local cults and their competing assertions of primacy, these terracottas expressed a unified religious past that was fully consistent with the Augustan present.[73] They expressed, in fact, Augustus' *tota Italia,* retrospectively stamped across Italy's cult landscape.

NOTES

1 *Antiche opera in plastica.* Campana's collection is now dispersed throughout several museums, including the Louvre and the Hermitage.

2 For the various building contexts of Campana reliefs, see Rizzo 1977; Tortorella 1981a, 2019; and the useful bibliography provided in Christensen and Johannsen 2015: 116 nn. 468–471.

3 See, for instance, Reinhardt's observations in the Introduction to Reinhardt 2024.

4 Tortorella 1981a, 1981b; Strazzulla 1984, 1987, 1995; Laubenheimer, Odiot, and Leclere 1989; Laubenheimer 1997; Braito 2016, Tortorella 2024.

5 Cosa: *Cosa II*: 296–300; Gabii: Dupré 1982: 154–162; Falerii Veteres (Sassi Caduti): Andrén 1940: 119–121; Strazzulla 1993: 306 and n. 40; Carlucci 2020: 91–94. For Campana relief production in Gaul, see Laubenheimer 1997. For Greece, see Partida 2024.

6 On the development of Campana reliefs in relation to earlier forms of architectural terracottas, see Känel 2024.

7 There is some inconsistency in the terminology for these types, as the German scholarly tradition distinguishes crestings ("Krönungen") from attachment plaques ("Aufsatzplatten"), whereas Italian literature often groups both within the category of "lastre di coronamento." Attachment plaques are also sometimes referred to as "cresting plaques" in English.

8 Von Rohden and Winnefeld 1911: 43–45; Borbein 1968, 16; Calderone 1975: 65–66, Painter 2002; Tortorella 2018. See also the frieze from the Casa di Medea at Vetulonia, Bruder 2022: 407–410.

9 Borbein 1968: 14–17.

10 Some plaques from the Palatine, for instance, are unusually large: 70–74 cm in height and 61–62 cm in width.

11 Of particular importance are a group of Campana reliefs from a house in Tusculum, where brick stamps confirm a Hadrianic date for the construction of the house: Rizzo 1977: 61–62.

12 There are, of course, many ways in which Campana reliefs could be (and have been) grouped. I have chosen to discuss them in terms of these two groupings since most of the earlier examples fit into these categories, and the broadness of the categories makes it easier to trace overarching similarities. Given the wide iconographic range of Campana reliefs, however, not all examples even from the early period fit neatly into these groupings.

13 *Cosa II*: 296–300.

14 *Cosa II*: 296, 300; Strazzulla 1985: 100. Tortorella notes that they could well have decorated the middle of the temple's external walls, as panels or as a running horizontal band: Tortorella 2018: 203.

15 For Campana reliefs of roughly similar date found in sanctuaries, see Tortorella 2019.

16 *Cosa II*: 296–300.

17 From the Palatine hill: Carettoni 1972: 125–128; Strazzulla 1985: 100; and from the foot of the Campidoglio: Rossini 2007. Fragments of the relief showing Apollo and Hercules, possibly even from the same mold as the Palatine and Campidoglio examples, were found at the Sanctuary of Hercules at Tivoli: Ten 1998–1999: 344–345; Tortorella 2019: 208. See also Partida 2024 for similar plaques from Dyme.

18 Most of these are described in von Rohden and Winnefeld 1911, esp. 3–130, with accompanying catalogue.

19 On modern biases against Neo-Attic works, with references to earlier discussions of the category, see Reinhardt 2018: 301–303.

20 For recent discussions of the frame in Roman wall painting, see Platt 2017; Platt and Squire 2017b; Squire 2017; and Jones 2019. Specially prized terracotta panels may also have been cut out and literally framed during Augustan renovations: Plin. *HN* xxxv.154–155, Hallett 2018: 188–191. On the physical and aesthetic relationship between Campana reliefs, wall painting, and stucco, see Tortorella 2018. On the upper and lower moldings of Campana reliefs, see Albers 2024.

21 Andrén 1940: 451 IV:8; cf. von Rohden and Winnefeld 1911 taf. IV.1.

22 Andrén 1940: 120; von Rohden and Winnefeld 1911: 198–200.

23 Von Rohden and Winnefeld 1911, 170–171, Abb. 333–335. For the Palatine fragments, see Pensabene 2017: 163–165, 313, cat. 1172–1173, pl. 138. Castriota 1995: 76–77 identifies the figure as Eros, while Pensabene (rightly, I believe) suggests a vaguer divine evocation (Pensabene 2017: 163).

24 Von Rohden and Winnefeld 1911: 244, taf. VII. Other examples of female heads emerging from buds or leaves include von Rohden and Winnefeld 1911 taf. LX 3–5.

25 Von Rohden and Winnefeld 1911, 73, taf. XXIV, 2. Several fragments of the same type were also found on the Palatine: Pensabene 2017: 155, 238–239, 316, cat. 448–449, 1192–1193, pl. 55, 141.

26 Von Rohden and Winnefeld 1911: 290–291, taf. CIII, 2. A single fragment of this type was found at the Velabrum at the foot of the Palatine, Pensabene 2017: 171, 360–361, cat. 1547.

27 Such iconography is known from Temple B at Pietrabbondante already in the late 2nd century BCE (Strazzulla 2006: fig. 3.8), as well as Civitella di Chieti (Iaculli 2006: 164–167, figs. 16.7–16.8), Tarquinia (Romanelli 1948: 262–263, fig. 45a), Nemi, (Diosono and Plebani 2013: 175–177, figs. 8–9), and Monte Rinaldo (Belfiori 2020a: 206–208), among others. A matrix for an antefix from Rimini preserves similar imagery (Pensa 1983: 387 tav. XXXI, 2).

28 Borbein 1968: 193–195 ("Frauen seitlich einer Pflanze") and pl. 4–8. The Louvre relief shown in Figure 105 has been restored, but other surviving fragments make the composition clear. The first iterations of the type are dated to the Augustan period, with subsequent versions produced for several more decades. For the version found on the Palatine, see Pensabene 2017: 141, 236, cat. 431, pl. 51.

29 Zanker 1988: 182.

30 Von Rohden and Winnefeld 1911 taf. VIII. For the Palatine fragments, see Pensabene 2017: 141–142, 288–289 cat. 1003 and 351 cat. 1458.

31 Von Rohden and Winnefeld 1911 taf. CXVIII, 2; Perry 1997: 35–36, fig. 17; Pensabene 2017: 166–167, 299 cat. 1058.

32 De Angelis 2008; Touchette 2015; Hallett 2018: 199; Thomas 2007: 189. For the symbolic value of terracotta in the early Empire, see Section 6.3.

33 Suet. *Aug.* 28.3.

34 Vell. Pat. 1.11.5, Vitr. *De arch.* 3.2.5; "Iuppiter Stator, aedes ad Circum," *LTUR* III, 157–159 (Viscogliosi); "Iuppiter Stator, aedes (2)" in Richardson 1992: 225–226; Stamper 2005: 54–55; Davies 2017: 95–97.

35 Popkin 2015: 291–295.

36 "Hercules, aedes Aemiliana," *LTUR* III, 11–12 (Coarelli); Rakob and Heilmeyer 1973; Ziolkowski 1988; "Hercules Victor, aedes" in Richardson 1992: 188–189; Stamper 2005: 68–79; Popkin 2015: 295–296; Davies 2017: 96–99.

37 For instance, the Pentelic marble remains beneath San Salvatore in Campo, probably to be identified with The Temple of Mars *in circo* ("Mars in Circo" *LTUR* III, 226–29 (Zevi); "Mars, aedes in Circo Flaminio" in Richardson 1992: 245) and the Temple of Neptune *in circo* ("Neptunus, aedes in Campo, aedes in Circo," *LTUR* V, 279–280 (Tucci); "Neptunus, aedes" in Richardson 1992: 267; Tucci 1997). Sulla is also said to have carried off columns from the Olympieion in Athens for use on the Temple of Jupiter Optimus Maximus on the Capitoline (Pliny, *HN* 36.45; Plut. *Publ.* 15). On the importation and logistical elements of Pentelic marble use in Roman architecture during the Republic, see Bernard 2010.

38 Popkin 2015. On the connotations of marble: Fant 1999; Pensabene 1998, 2002, M. Bradley 2006; Davies 2012; Hallett 2018. Barry 2011 and Popkin 2015: 299 highlight the connections between white marble, notions of divinity, and victory temples.

39 Gros 1976; Bernard 2010: 46. This remained true for imported colored marbles, Ward-Perkins 1951: 96–99, Pensabene 2002: 9–15, Bradley 2006; Beck 2022.

40 Popkin 2015: 296.

41 The precise meaning of *antefixa* here is unclear. Yardley defines *antefixa* as "statues of gods placed on the pediments of Etruscan and Roman temples" (Yardley 2017, Loeb edition of Livy Book 34 n. 14). Briscoe 1981: 52 also implies that the term refers to pedimental statuary, disagreeing with Puchstein's interpretation (*RE*, i. 2348) that it relates to all the decoration of a temple. The OLD defines *antefixa* as "ornamental figures or tiles placed at the edge of a roof, antefixes," but antefixes in the modern sense is probably too narrow a definition. I would favor the more literal interpretation of the first part of the OLD definition, or that of Lewis & Short: "The little ornaments, images, statues, etc., affixed to the roofs and gutters of houses or temples." It is unlikely that Livy's usage refers only to antefixes or to pedimental statuary when the entire roof would have been decked with

terracotta ornamentation, each element attached to another and forming a coherent overall impression of a roof to which terracottas have been affixed.

42 Livy 34.4.4. Text and translation after Yardley's 2017 Loeb edition. These comments may well be Livy's invention (Gruen 1992: 70; and 52–83 on Cato's relation to Hellenism). Either way, the speech still reveals an attitude that was circulating by the Augustan period.

43 Pliny *HN* 34.34. Text and translation after Rackham's 1952 Loeb edition.

44 Pliny *HN* 35.153, 157.

45 Pliny *HN* 35.158: *fastigia quidem templorum etiam in urbe crebra et municipiis, mira caelatura et arte suique firmitate, sanctiora auro, certe innocentiora.* Text: Rackham 1952, translation modified from the same. On the notion of *firmitas* as one of clay's important features, see Reinhardt 2022: 144.

46 Prop. 4.1.5.

47 For instance, Cic., *Div.* 1.10; Ov., *Fast.* 1.201–202; Vitr. 3.3.5; Plut., *Publ.* 13; Pliny, *HN* 28.16. For the extant architectural terracottas from the Temple of Jupiter Optimus Maximus Capitolinus, see especially Galluccio 2016 and Hopkins 2016.

48 Davies 2017: 194; Davies 2018.

49 Vitr. *De arch.* 3.3.5.

50 On Pompey's restoration of the temple in relation to political rivalry, see Davies 2017: 187–188.

51 Vitr. *De arch.* 2.1.3–6. Vitruvius (*De arch.* 2.1.5) also notes an ancient structure on the Areopagus in Athens that even in his own day was still covered with clay, suggesting like Pliny the unique durability of the material: "Athenis Areopagi antiquitatis exemplar ad hoc tempus luto tectum."

52 Vitruvius (*De arch.* 3.3.5) describes buildings with terracotta roofs as top-heavy, low, and broad (*barycephalae, humiles, latae*).

53 Hallett (2018) sees the use of archaizing styles and materials in early Augustan architecture as part of an "Archaic revival." On the symbolic value of the material of terracotta on the Augustan Palatine, see Touchette 2015 and Hallett 2018, as well as Känel 2001: 205 for the late Republic/early Empire more generally. Hallett (2018: 199) considers that "by the late 30s BC, terracotta had come to be regarded as the authentic material of the old gods in Italy; and in this way it arguably obtained a kind of cachet it had never had before."

54 For a discussion of Roman fired clay building materials in terms of natural color and added paint, see Reinhardt 2022. Notes on color and added underlayers on architectural terracottas were first laid out in von Rohden and Winnefeld 1911 and Koch 1912. For a more recent overview, Rescigno and Sampaolo 2006.

55 Reinhardt 2022: 136–137.

56 Numerous additional architectural terracottas have been found in other areas of the Palatine as well and were used without interruption on the Palatine's various temples and other buildings from the 6th century BCE through the 1st century CE. These are discussed in Pensabene 2017 Tomo 1 and Tomo 2.

57 The statues have been attributed to the 1st century BCE school of Pasiteles and show a strong interest in Archaic and Classical prototypes: La Rocca 1987: 41, 46; Tomei 1992; Fuchs 1999; Touchette 2015: 301–302.

58 Zink 2011 has suggested that some of these types may belong to a building that pre-dates the Augustan complex, but the vast number of Campana reliefs from various sectors/layers of the Palatine (Pensabene 2017) now indicate that many must have adorned the Augustan complex as well.

59 Hallett 2018: 194. On the broader theme, see also Dench's thoughtful diachronic discussion of "the idea of Italy" as it developed over the Republic and Empire (Dench 2005: 152–221).

60 Vitr. *De arch.* 3.3.4; Kellum 1985: 169; Touchette 2015: 304. On the excavations and extant remains, see Carettoni 1966–1967, "Apollo Palatinus" *LTUR* I, 54–57 (Gros), "Apollo Palatinus" *LTUR* V, 225 (Claridge), Richardson 1992: 14, Stamper 2005: 115–118, Zink

2011. As Stephan Zink has pointed out, the archaizing tendencies of the Palatine Apollo temple are particularly evident when considered alongside the roughly contemporary Temple of Apollo Sosianus: "The Palatine temple was not just a last remnant of Republican architecture but, in the guise of a prestigious marble temple, marks a deliberate recourse to Republican traditions" (Zink 2008: 63).

61 Zink 2015: 369.

62 Dion Hal., *Ant. Rom.* 1.79.11; "Casa Romuli (Cermalus)," *LTUR* I, 241–242 (Coarelli), Richardson 1992: 74.

63 "Lupercal," *LTUR* III, 198–199 (Coarelli); Richardson 1992: 238–239. "Scalae Caci," *LTUR* IV, 239–240 (Pensabene); Richardson 1992: 344. "Magna Mater Aedes," *LTUR* III, 206–208 (Pensabene); Richardson 1992: 242–243; Stamper 2005: 118–119. For a general survey of this area, see Stamper 2005: 115–119, Coarelli 2014.

64 On remediation, Bolter and Grusin 1999. Cook 2018 offers a recent analysis of remediation in Roman sculpture.

65 Crawford-Brown 2022.

66 On the Ara Pacis's polychromy, Rossini 2010; Caneva 2010: 131–140; Foresta 2011, 2012a, 2012b.

67 The scenes of Rome's founding that occupy the west enclosure wall would further have reinforced this message, as would the marble evocation of a simple wooden fence on the interior precinct wall.

68 These are discussed in detail in Cohon 2004.

69 "Iulius, Divus, aedes," *LTUR* III, 116–119 (Gros); Kraus 1953, 39–40; Montagna Pasquinucci 1973, esp. 265–272 and pl. VIIb–IXb for the friezes with winged female deities amid vines; Pollini 2012: 294–295.

70 For more on the "afterlives" of architectural terracottas during the Roman Empire, see Chapter 7.

71 Reggiani 1998: 28–29.

72 On this much-debated figure as being deliberately polysemic, Galinsky 1966 and especially 1992; Torelli 1982.

73 Similarly, Eric Orlin has argued that Augustan temple restorations, festival revivals, and Italic cults were re-read in order to build "a single imagined community" (Orlin 2022: 119; see also Orlin 2007).

SEVEN

CONCLUSION

7.1 AFTERLIVES

Once removed from the roof, temple terracottas returned to the earth. Damage from fire, storms, or simple wear and tear necessitated that either individual elements or the roof's entire decorative program be replaced from time to time. In such cases, the previous terracottas were not simply disposed of but were carefully deposited within the area of the temenos.[1] Now obsolete, these terracottas might be used as part of a new foundation or terrace fill, allowing them to literally support a new sacred structure. In other cases, representative elements were selected and ritually buried in sacred pits beside a temple wall, often together with an inscription.[2] Such practices attest to the strong symbolic charge that these terracottas retained even after they had lost any functional architectural application. With the advent of the Empire, terracotta was mostly abandoned for temple decoration. Nevertheless, occasional glimpses in the archaeological record suggest that the long-held reverence for these objects did not disappear entirely.

A good example comes from Cosa, where the wealthy owners of the House of Diana installed a small shrine against the northwest wall of their garden in the mid-1st century CE.[3] Three steps led up to a temple-like structure that was framed by columns and featured a statue of the goddess Diana in its cella. The rest of the garden was outfitted in reference to this shrine, with a bench facing it, a small altar, and herms. The garden's old niche was renovated with white marble for its floor and cowry shells on its walls, "giving it the air of a miniature grotto."[4] It may have functioned as a lararium in its own right and certainly constituted part of the garden's sacred space.

Around this niche, three fragments of Campana reliefs (Figures 117–119) and two fragments of architectural terracottas with vegetal decoration were

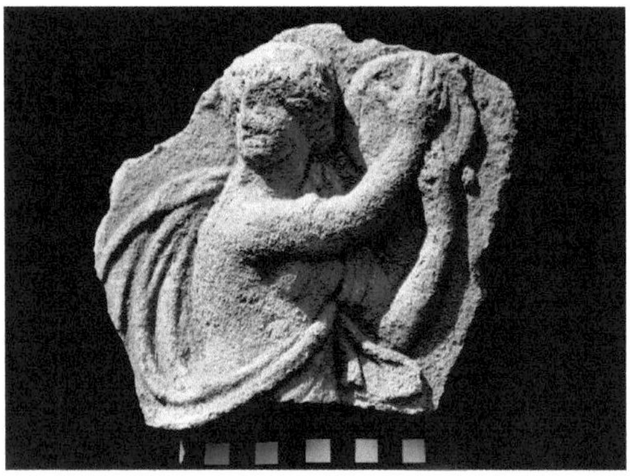

117. Fragment of a Campana relief from Cosa's summit, cut for reuse in the garden shrine of the House of Diana.
Courtesy of the American Academy in Rome, Cosa Archaeological Collection.

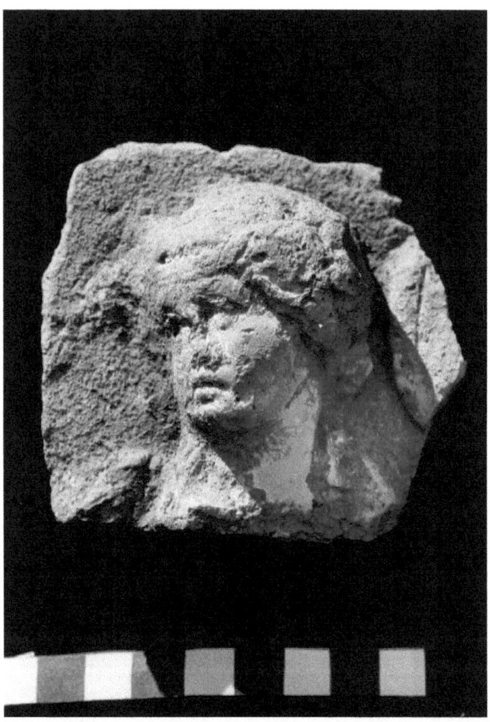

118. Fragment of a Campana relief from Cosa's summit, cut for reuse in the garden shrine of the House of Diana.
Courtesy of the American Academy in Rome, Cosa Archaeological Collection.

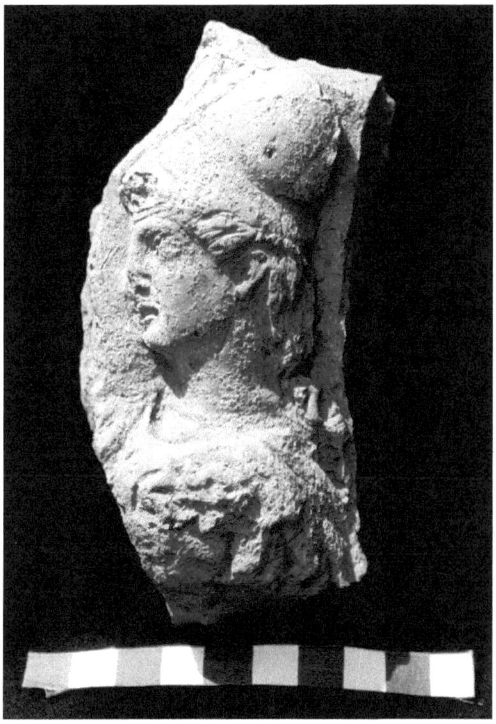

119. Fragment of a Campana relief from Cosa's summit, cut for reuse in the garden shrine of the House of Diana.
Courtesy of the American Academy in Rome, Cosa Archaeological Collection.

found.[5] The Campana reliefs belong to types known from the summit and were presumably taken from there. Interestingly, however, each relief appears to have been deliberately cut in order to isolate the head of a figure. The excavators suggested that these pieces were specifically selected and reworked for use as part of the niche's decoration.[6]

The reuse of terracotta decoration from the summit cannot be attributed to economic necessity in the lavish House of Diana. Rather, it suggests that these objects still held a certain status even after they had fallen into disuse. Their archaizing material and style, together with their visibly worn surfaces, would have given them an antique appearance, lending an air of solemnity to the sacred garden. A similar reuse of temple terracottas in elite construction is attested at other sites, as well. At Pompeii, a terracotta relief with Apollo and Olympos was found in the garden of the House of the Golden Bracelet, and plaques with Nereids were uncovered at the House of the Faun.[7] Pliny reports that during Augustan renovations of the Temple of Ceres in Rome, the old terracotta decoration by the famous coroplasts Damophilus and Gorgasus were cut out and framed.[8] These terracottas were evidently seen as precious legacies of the ancient temple.

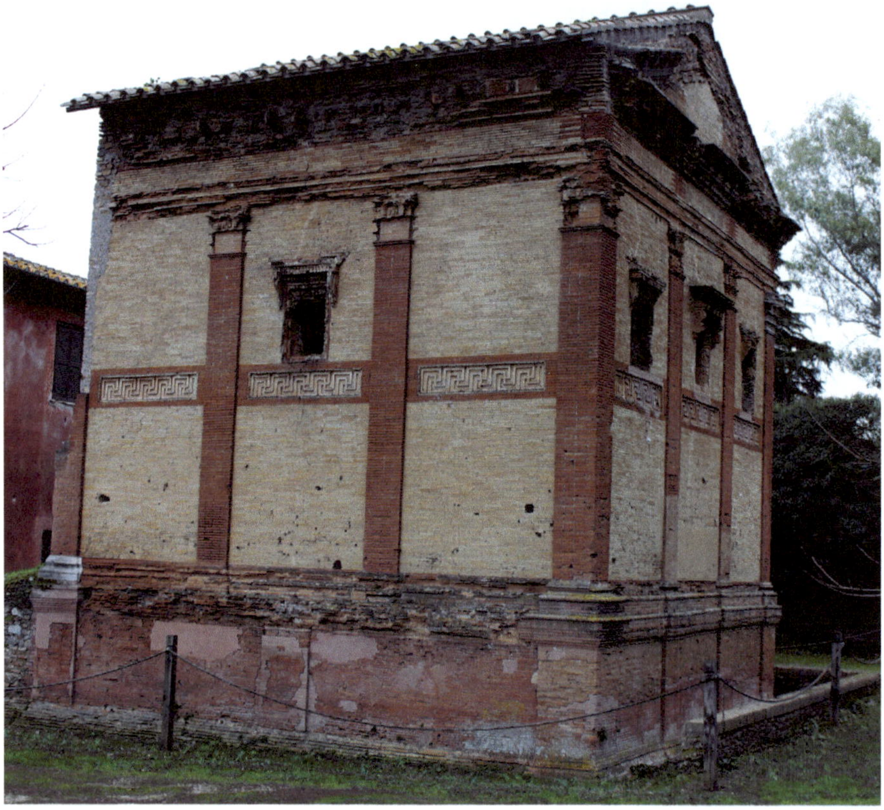

120. So-called Temple of Deus Rediculus, Rome, c. 160 CE.
Photo: Arne Reinhardt.

Even when Rome had largely marbleized and temple terracottas were no longer readily accessible, the association of terracotta decoration with notions of antiquity and permanence seems to have endured. A striking case is the group of Antonine temple-tombs constructed on the outskirts of imperial Rome.[9] Built at a time when marble revetment was the norm in elite architecture, these tombs not only left their brick material conspicuously exposed but emphasized it through the use of contrasting colors (Figure 120).[10] Their walls and pediments were adorned with terracotta decoration, much of which mimics the motifs of earlier temple terracottas (Figure 121).[11] Edmund Thomas has suggested that these tombs reflect "a desire on [the Roman elite's] part to emulate the Italic temples of the past and to re-create Rome's indigenous culture" and that the form and material of these structures constituted "a monument to their occupants' ethnic identity and the historical culture of their families."[12] The medium of clay here takes on an even more expansive symbolic value. It is associated not only with local identity and religious tradition but, in this sepulchral context, also with *firmitas* – an idea of permanence and stability.[13] Just as they had in the centuries

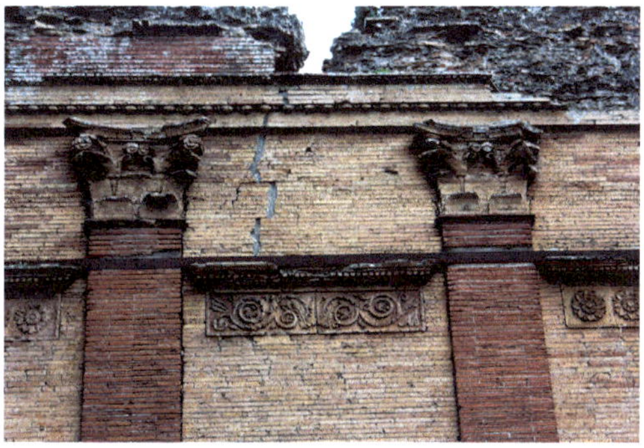

121. Terracotta ornamentation on the so-called Temple of Fortuna Muliebre, Rome. Photo: Arne Reinhardt.

prior, the connotations of terracotta ornament continued to shift, evolving to reflect the concerns of a specific place and moment.

7.2 THE ROOF, THE EARTH, THE ANCIENT

A terracotta roof transforms and transports the very substance of the land on which people live, work, and worship, and lifts it toward the sky – toward the realm of the gods. It is thus particularly evocative as a medium for temple decoration. Terracotta is, by its very nature, bound to place and rooted in the local landscape. It readily carries connotations of stability, antiquity, and permanence.

Perhaps we should not be surprised, then, that coroplasts and commissioners showed little interest in innovating new terracotta types for their temples during the last centuries BCE. That they were capable of such innovations is clear from the countless unusual and inventive terracottas designed for porticoes and private houses in this period (Figure 122). For temples, however, the rule was tradition and conservatism, with a specifically local frame of reference.

In considering 3rd–1st century temple decoration, we might recall Dionysius of Halicarnassus' description of Roman attitudes towards the hut of Romulus on the Palatine hill:

> βίος δ' αὐτοῖς ἦν βουκολικὸς καὶ δίαιτα αὐτουργὸς ἐν ὄρεσι τὰ πολλὰ πηξαμένοις διὰ ξύλων καὶ καλάμων σκηνὰς αὐτορόφους: ὧν ἔτι καὶ εἰς ἐμὲ ἦν τις τοῦ Παλλαντίου ἐπὶ τῆς πρὸς τὸν ἱππόδρομον στρεφούσης λαγόνος Ῥωμύλου λεγομένη, ἣν φυλάττουσιν ἱερὰν οἷς τούτων ἐπιμελὲς οὐδὲν ἐπὶ τὸ σεμνότερον ἐξάγοντες, εἰ δέ τι πονήσειεν ὑπὸ χειμῶνος ἢ χρόνου τὸ λεῖπον ἐξακούμενοι καὶ τῷ πρόσθεν ἐξομοιοῦντες εἰς δύναμιν.

> But [Romulus and Remus'] life was that of herdsmen, and they lived by their own labor, generally upon the mountains in huts which they built, roofs and all, out of sticks and reeds. One of these, called the hut of Romulus, remained even to my day on the flank of the Palatine hill which faces towards the Circus, and it is preserved holy by those who

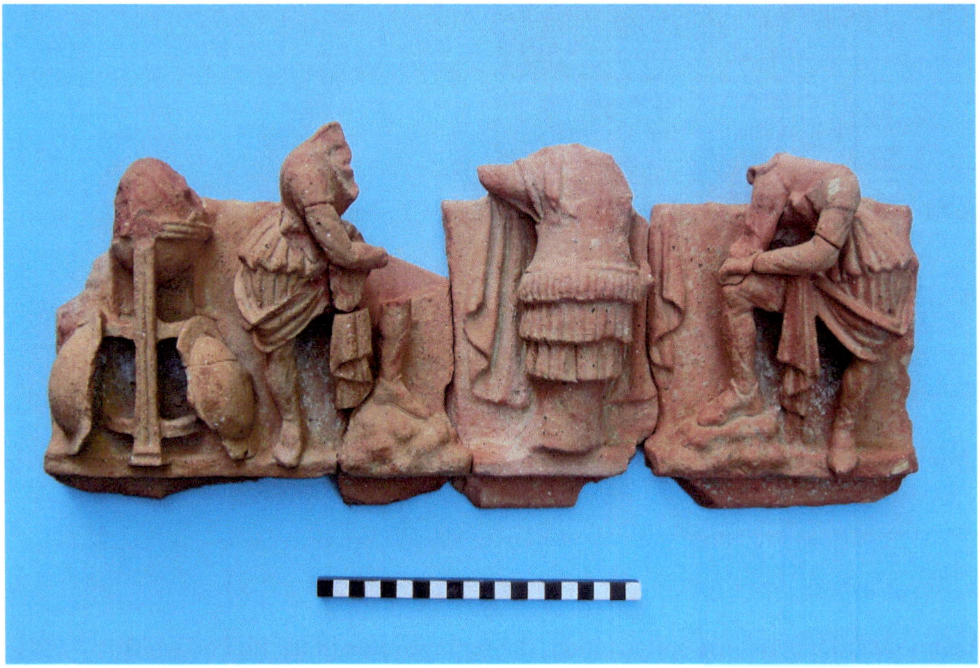

122 Terracotta figural frieze plaque from domus I.2, Fregellae. Courtesy of the Ministero della Cultura – Soprintendenza Archeologia, Belle Arti e Paesaggio per le province di Frosinone e Latina.
Photograph courtesy of Rudolf Känel.

> have charge of these matters; they add nothing to it to render it more stately, but if any part of it is injured, either by storms or by the lapse of time, they repair the damage and restore the hut as nearly as possible to its former condition.[14]

Although notionally a private dwelling, the hut of Romulus functioned as a sacred structure – a monument to Rome's mythic founding.[15] Its power lay in its location and in the antiquity of its *appearance*. Every stick and reed of its structure might have been added two days prior, but the reality of recent materials meant nothing if these materials emulated their predecessors and if the hut as a whole looked old. Romulus' hut thus offers a useful framework for considering attitudes toward earlier temple decoration. They too were designed to appear old and were deeply rooted in their physical settings – even when a lack of communal history meant that such roots had to be invented. As the architectural terracottas of 3rd–1st century central Italy vividly attest, cultural memory is no less powerful for being fictitious.

The long scholarly neglect of temple terracottas from this period is probably largely due to the fact that they repeat so insistently and change so little. To a casual observer, this can give the impression that they are merely monotonous and unimaginative. But it is precisely this feature, as I hope to have shown, that makes them such precious windows into the shifting and convoluted world of central Italy during Roman expansion and colonization. In the face of change, they proclaimed stability.

The terracotta types of the "standard temple kit" drew meticulously on earlier designs, making their use on temples built several centuries later a deliberate act of archaizing. What is especially striking in the 3rd–1st centuries BCE is that these old-fashioned motifs were employed on *new* temples in *new* towns. The past was privileged and promoted, and temples that lacked a past were superficially furnished with one by means of terracotta decoration.

As I have argued, much of this can be explained by the shifting political landscape of Italy during this period. The foundation of colonies across the peninsula created a disorienting environment for colonists and conquered alike. Contrary to traditional interpretations, which have tended to view terracottas from this period as simple markers of loyalty to Rome, these objects reveal a persistent desire to integrate new towns into the local (i.e., non-Roman) landscape. This did not always work in the same way since the connotations of particular terracotta types could change over time and from place to place. Still, two principal tendencies are widely detectable across 3rd–1st century central Italy: (1) the use of old-fashioned terracottas to give temples an antique and venerable appearance and (2) the inclusion of specifically local visual referents. Both presumably functioned to integrate new temples into the landscape and to assert their religious authority. In the case of colonies, architectural terracottas served the further end of providing the community with something it fundamentally lacked – a coherent visual identity. This was critical not just on an aesthetic level but as part of a broader effort to define the community and to provide it with some sense of its place in the mythic and religious history of the region.

With the large-scale exploitation of the Luna marble quarries and the dawn of the Augustan Principate, the connotations of temple terracottas underwent a fundamental shift. Architectural terracottas were structurally superfluous on stone buildings but were nevertheless retained and even highlighted in specific situations. The stone "Temple B" at Minturnae employed terracotta *potnia theron* antefixes. Their old-fashioned material would have been particularly noticeable in this otherwise lithic context and would have made explicit their visual quotation of Minturnae's earlier tripartite temple that stood just down the road. On the Palatine complex, praised for its glimmering surfaces and elaborate ornamentation, terracotta Campana reliefs offered a bridge between the old and new Rome. With their archaizing material and iconography, and with their reinterpretation of traditional vegetal motifs, these reliefs proclaimed continuity with an idealized past, rooting the changing city in the visual language of tradition and *pietas*. In this way, architectural terracottas simultaneously gained and lost meaning. They no longer referenced precise groups or cults. Rather, they stood in for a pious and homogenous Italic collective, perfectly integrated with the broader Augustan paradigm of *tota Italia*. They gave a face to an ancient unified past that had never existed, thus fulfilling their final role in the ongoing march of invented traditions.

NOTES

1 On terracottas as "sacred rubbish," see Glinister 2000.
2 For instance, at Satricum (Bouma 1993), Pyrgi (Colonna 1964: 53–56), beneath the Lapis Niger in the Roman forum (Lowe 1978: 143–144; Carafa 1998: 49–57 and fig. 53 a, b), at Minturnae (Johnson 1935: 29–36), and Luni (Frova 1973: coll. 32, 823–824), among others.
3 Cosa V: 38–55
4 Cosa V: 43.
5 Cosa V: 214–215.
6 Cosa V: 43, 215.
7 House of the Golden Bracelet: De Caro 2007: 76 and fig. 6.3. House of the Faun: De Caro 2003: 58; Naples Archaeological Museum Inv. 21515–21518.
8 Pliny *HN* xxxv.154–155, and see the discussion in Hallett 2018: 188–191.
9 Thomas 2007, esp. 188–189, Reinhardt 2022: 140–144.
10 Reinhardt 2022: 140–142.
11 Thomas 2007: 189.
12 Thomas 2007: 189.
13 On fired clay's connotations of *firmitas*, see Reinhardt 2022: 144.
14 Dion. Hal. *Ant. Rom.* 1.79.11. Trans. Cary.
15 Indeed, Christopher Siwicki (2020: 141–167) has recently argued that the reason the Hut of Romulus apparently contradicts more typical Roman approaches to innovative restoration relates precisely to its religious nature.

WORKS CITED

Aberson, M., M. C. Biella, M. Di Fazio, P. Sánchez, M. Wullschleger, eds. 2016. *L'Italia centrale e la creazione di una "koiné" culturale? I percorsi della "Romanizzazione."* Bern: Peter Lang.

Adriani, A. 1938. "Scavi di Minturno. 1931–1933. Catalogo di sculture." *NSc* 14.6, 159–226.

Åkerström, Å. 1966. *Die architektonische Terrakotten Kleinasiens.* Lund: Gleerup.

Albers, J. 2024. "Reliefs aus Ton und Stein. Überlegungen zur Ornamentik der sog. Campanareliefs und der Dekoration in Stein im spätrepublikanischen und frühkaiserzeitlichen Mittelitalien." In *Campana-Reliefs: Neue Forschungen zu römischem Architekturdekor aus Terrakotta, Akten der Internationalen Tagung Heidelberg, 8.–10. April 2021*, ed. A. Reinhardt. Heidelberg: Propylaeum, 109–123.

Alcock, S. E. 2002. *Archaeologies of the Greek Past. Landscape, Monuments, and Memories.* Cambridge: Cambridge University Press.

Almagro-Gorbea, M. 1981. "L'area del tempio di Giunone Gabina nel VI-V secolo a.C." *Archeologia Laziale* IV, 297–304.

ed. 1982. *El santuario de Juno en Gabii. Excavaciones 1956–1969.* Rome: Escuela Española de Historia y Arqueología en Roma.

Ambrosini, L. 2019. "Produzione di lastre di rivestimento con fregi dorici a Palestrina in età ellenistica." In *Deliciae Fictiles V: Networks and Workshops. Architectural Terracottas and Decorative Roof Systems in Italy and Beyond*, ed. P. Lulof, I. Manzini, and C. Rescigno. Oxford: Oxbow Books, 407–416.

Ammerman, A. J., I. Iliopoulos, F. Bondioli et al. 2008. "The Clay Beds in the Velabrum and the Earliest Tiles in Rome." *JRA* 21, 7–30.

Andersen, J. 2014. "Architect and Patron." In *A Companion to Roman Architecture*, ed. R. B. Ulrich and C. K. Quenemoen. Malden: Wiley Blackwell, 127–139.

Andrén, A. 1934–1935. "Terrecotte decorative e figurate di Ardea." *BollStudiMediterranei* 5, 22–31.

1940. *Architectural Terracottas from Etrusco-Italic Temples.* Lund: C. W. K. Gleerup.

1971 [1974]. "Osservazioni sulle terrecotte architettoniche etrusco-italiche." *OpRom* 8, 1–16.

Andrén, A., and E. Berggren. 1969. "Blera (Località Selvasecca) – Villa rustica etrusco-romana con manifattura di terrecotte architettoniche." *NSc* 8.23, 51–71.

Anselmino, L. 1977. *Terrecotte architettoniche dell'Antiquarium comunale di Roma, 1. Antefisse.* Rome: Antiquarium comunale di Roma.

1981. "Le antefisse fittili dal I a.C. al II d.C." In *Società romana e produzione schiavistica, vol. 2: merci, mercati e scambi nel Mediterraneo*, ed. A. Giardina and A. Schiavone. Rome: Ed. Laterza, 209–218.

Assmann, A. 1999. *Erinnerungsräume: Formen und Wandlungen des kulturellen Gedächtnisses.* Munich: Verlag C. H. Beck.

Assmann, J. 1992. *Das kulturelle Gedächtnis: Schrift, Erinnerung und politische Identität in frühen Hochkulturen.* Munich: Verlag C. H. Beck.

1995. "Collective Memory and Cultural Identity," trans. J. Czaplicka. *New German Critique* 65, 125–133.

1997. *Moses the Egyptian: The Memory of Egypt in Western Monotheism.* Cambridge, MA: Harvard University Press.

2000. *Religion und kulturelles Gedächtnis. Zehn Studien.* Munich: Verlag C. H. Beck.

2010. "Communicative and Cultural Memory." In *A Companion to Cultural Memory Studies*, ed. A. Erll and A. Nünning. Berlin: de Gruyter, 109–118.

2011. *Cultural Memory and Early Civilization: Writing, Remembrance, and Political Imagination.* Cambridge: Cambridge University Press.

Assmann, J., and T. Hölscher, eds. 1988. *Kultur und Gedächtnis.* Frankfurt: Suhrkamp.

Bacci, F. 2019. "Antefisse e lastre populoniesi: idee e maestranze itineranti alla luce delle nuove acquisizioni." In *Deliciae Fictiles V. Networks and Workshops*, ed. P. Lulof, I. Manzini, and C. Rescigno. Oxford: Oxbow Books, 521–526.

Barletta, B. A. 1996. "The Campanian Tradition in Archaic Architecture." *MAAR* 41, 1–67.

Barnett, R. D. 1957. *A Catalogue of the Nimrud Ivories with Other Examples of Ancient Near Eastern Ivories in the British Museum.* London: British Museum.

Barone, G., P. Mazzoleni, S. Raneri, G. Spagnolo, and A. Santostefano. 2017. "Coroplastic Art in Sicily: An Investigation on Provenance and Manufacturing Technology of Greek Architectural Terracottas from Gela (Italy)." *Mediterranean Archaeology and Archaeometry* 17.1, 89–101.

Barry, F. 2011. "A Whiter Shade of Pale: Relative and Absolute White in Roman Sculpture and Architecture." In *Revival and Invention: Sculpture through Its Material Histories*, ed. S. Clerbois and M. Droth. New York: Peter Lang, 31–62.

Barry, W. D. 1996. "Roof Tiles and Urban Violence in the Ancient World." *Roman and Byzantine Studies* 37.1, 55–74.

Barton, I. M. 1982. "Capitoline Temples in Italy and the Provinces (especially Africa)." *ANRW* II.12.1, 259–342.

Becatti, G. 1971. *Ninfe e divinità marine. Ricerche mitologiche, iconografiche, e stilistiche.* StMisc 17. Rome: De Luca Editore.

Beck, D. 2022. "Use, Aesthetics and Semantics of Coloured Marble Columns in the Western Mediterranean during the Late Republic and Early Roman Empire." In *Materiality in Roman Art and Architecture. Aesthetics, Semantics and Function*, ed. A. Huag, A. Hielscher, and M. Taylor Lauritsen. Berlin: de Gruyter, 95–112.

Beiner, G. 2018. *Forgetful Remembrance. Social Forgetting and Vernacular Historiography of a Rebellion in Ulster.* Oxford: Oxford University Press.

Belfiori, F. 2019. "Disiecta membra dal Piceno: Nuove considerazioni sulle terrecotte architettoniche di Offida (AP)." *Picus* XXXIX, 117–140.

2020a. "La decorazione architettonica." In E. Giorgi, F. Demma, and F. Belfiori, *Il santuario di Monte Rinaldo. La ripresa delle ricerche (2016–2019).* Bologna: Bononia University Press, 173–238.

2020b. "Roman Colonization, Sanctuaries and Cult in the Middle-Adriatic area between the 3rd and 2nd centuries BC." In *Boundaries Archaeology: Economy, Sacred Places, Cultural Influences in the Ionian and Adriatic Areas.* Panel 7.3, Archaeology and Economy in the Ancient World 39, ed. E. Giorgi, G. Lepore, and A. Gamberini. Heidelberg: Propylaeum, 5–23.

2022. *Mare Superum. Romani, Latini e l'Italia adriatica di mezzo (sviluppi culturali e fenomenologia religiosa, secoli III-I a.C.).* Rome: "L'Erma" di Bretschneider.

Bellini, G. R. 2006. "Il castrum di Minturnae." *Lazio & Sabina* 3, 269–272.

ed. 2021. *Antica Minturnae. L'Appia ritrovata.* Rome: Officina Edizioni.

Bellini, G. R., and H. von Hesberg, eds. 2015. *Minturnae. Nuovi contributi alla conoscenza della Forma Urbis.* Rome: Edizioni Quasar.

Bernard, S. 2010. "Pentelic Marble in Architecture at Rome and the Republican Marble Trade." *JRA* 23, 35–54.

2018. *Building Mid-Republican Rome: Labor, Architecture, and the Urban Economy.* New York: Oxford University Press.

2019a. "The Status and Mobility of Coroplasts and Building Workers in the Epigraphy of Central Italy, 300–50 BC." In *Deliciae*

Fictiles V. Networks and Workshops, ed. P. Lulof, I. Manzini, and C. Rescigno. Oxford: Oxbow Books, 499–507.

2019b. "The Brundisium elogium (*AE* 1954.216) and the History of Republican Colonization." In *Cosa and the Colonial Landscape of Republican Italy (Third and Second Centuries BCE)*, ed. A. U. De Giorgi. Ann Arbor: University of Michigan Press, 44–66.

Bianchi, U. 1950. "Disegno storico del culto capitolino nell'Italia romana e nelle province dell'Impero." *MemAccLinc* 2, 349–415.

Biella, M. C. 2004. "Falerii Veteres: Alcune novità tra archeologia e archivistica." *Archeologia Classica* 55, 325–362.

2020. "Falerii Veteres – Falerii Novi: Il record archeologico." In *Displacements: Continuità e discontinuità urbana nell'Italia centrale tirrenica*, ed. M. C. Biella. Rome: Edizioni Quasar, 67–82.

Bispham, E. 2006. "Coloniam Deducere. How Roman was Roman Colonization during the Middle Republic?" In *Greek and Roman Colonisation. Origins, Ideologies and Interactions*, ed. G. J. Bradley and J.-P. Wilson. Swansea: Classical Press of Wales, 73–160.

Bispham, E., and C. Smith, eds. 2000. *Religion in Archaic and Republican Rome and Italy: Evidence and Experience*. Edinburg: University of Edinburgh.

Blagg, T. F. C. 1983. *Mysteries of Diana: The Antiquities from Nemi in Nottingham Museums*. Nottingham: Castle Museum.

2000. "The Votive Model. Etrusco-Italic Temples from Nemi." In *Nemi – Status Quo: Recent Research at Nemi and the Sanctuary of Diana*, ed. J. Rasmus Brandt, A. M. Leander Touati, and J. Zahle. Rome: "L'Erma" di Bretschneider, 83–90.

Bleckmann, B. 2002. *Die römische Nobilität im Ersten Punischen Krieg. Untersuchungen zur aristokratischen Konkurrenz in der Republik*. Berlin: Akademie Verlag.

Bolder-Boos, M. 2011. *Heiligtümer römischer Bürgerkolonien: archäologische Untersuchungen zur sakralen Ausstattung republikanischer coloniae civium Romanorum*. Rahden/Westf.: Verlag Marie Leidorf.

2014. "Tutelary Deities in Roman Citizen Colonies." In *Roman Republican Colonization. New Perspectives from Archaeology and Ancient History*, ed. T. D. Stek and J. Pelgrom. Rome: Palombi, 279–293.

Bolter, J. D., and R. A. Grusin. 1999. *Remediation: Understanding New Media*. Cambridge, MA: MIT Press.

Bonamici, M. 1992. "L'edicola di Ponte Rotto a Vulci." In *La coroplastica templare etrusca fra il IV e il II secolo a.C.: Atti del XVI convegno di studi etruschi e italici, Orbetello 25–29 aprile 1988*, ed. G. Maetzke. Florence: Leo S. Olschki Editore, 127–141.

Bonghi Jovino, M. 1990. "Artigiani e botteghe nell'Italia preromana. Appunti e riflessioni per una sistema di analisi." In *Artigiani e botteghe nell'Italia preromana*, ed. M. Bonghi Jovino. Rome: "L'Erma" di Bretschneider, 19–59.

2010. "The Tarquinia Project: A Summary of 25 Years of Excavation." *AJA* 114.1, 161–180.

Borbein, A. H. 1968. *Campanareliefs. Typologische und stilkritische Untersuchungen*. Heidelberg: F. H. Kerle.

Bouma, J. W. 1993. "Architectural Terracottas Unearthed in a Votive Deposit in Borgo Le Ferriere ('Satricum'), 6th–3rd centuries BC." In *Deliciae Fictiles I*, ed. E. Rystedt, C. Wikander, O. Wikander. Stockholm: Svenska Institutet, 291–297.

Bourdin, S. 2012. *Les peuples de l'Italie préromaine: Identités, territoires et relations inter-ethniques en Italie centrale et septentrionale (VIIe–Ier s. av. J.-C.)*. Rome: École française de Rome.

Bradley, G. J. 2000. *Ancient Umbria. State, Culture, and Identity in Central Italy from the Iron Age to the Augustan Era*. Oxford: Oxford University Press.

2006. "Colonization and Identity in Republican Italy." In *Greek and Roman Colonisation. Origins, Ideologies and Interactions*, ed. G. J. Bradley and J.-P. Wilson. Swansea: Classical Press of Wales, 161–187.

Bradley, G. J., and J.-P. Wilson. 2006. *Greek and Roman Colonization: Origins, Ideologies and*

Interactions. Swansea: Classical Press of Wales.

Bradley, M. 2006. "Colour and Marble in Early Imperial Rome." *Cambridge Classical Journal* 52, 1–22.

Braito, S. 2016. "Iscrizioni di produzione sulle 'Lastre Campana': Il caso di Annia Arescusa." In *Le iscrizioni con funzione didascalico-esplicativa. Committente, destinatario, contenuto e descrizione dell'oggetto nell'instrumentum inscriptum. Atti del VI Incontro Instrumenta Inscripta*, ed. M. Buora and S. Magnani. Trieste: Editreg, 465–477.

Brandt, J. R., and J. W. Iddeng. 2012. "Some Concepts of Ancient Festivals." In *Greek and Roman Festivals. Content, Meaning, and Practice*, ed. J. R. Brandt and J. W. Iddeng. Oxford: Oxford University Press, 1–10.

Brendel, O. 1969. "Ganymede Group from Cosa." *AJA* 73, 232.

Briquel, D. 1991. *L'origine lydienne des Etrusques: Histoire de la doctrine dans l'Antiquité*. Rome: Ecole française de Rome.

Briscoe, J. 1981. *A Commentary on Livy Books XXXIV–XXXVII*. Oxford: Clarendon Press.

Brown, F. E. 1967. "Scavi a Cosa-Ansedonia, 1965–66." *BdA* 52, 37–41.

1969. "Excavations at Cosa, 1965–1968." *AJA* 73, 232.

1980. *Cosa, The Making of a Roman Town*. Ann Arbor: University of Michigan Press.

Bruder, S. K. 2022. *Man lebt, wie man wohnt: Untersuchungen zur Wohnhausarchitektur Mittel- und Norditaliens vom ausgehenden 6. bis zum beginnenden 2. Jh. v. Chr.* Heidelberg: Propylaeum.

Bruni, S. 1985. "Antefisse inedite da Populonia." *Rassegna di archeologia classica e postclassica* 5, 119–130.

Bruno, V. 2001. "Cosa's Maritime Neighbors." In *New Light from Ancient Cosa: Classical Mediterranean Studies in Honor of Cleo Rickman Fitch*, ed. N. W. Goldman. New York: Lang, 51–82.

Bruschetti, P. 1992. "Terrecotte architettoniche dal Lago Trasimeno." In *La coroplastica templare etrusca fra il IV e il II secolo a.C.: Atti del XVI convegno di studi etruschi e italici, Orbetello 25–29 aprile 1988*, ed. G. Maetzke. Florence: Leo S. Olschki Editore, 319–323.

Bulle, H. 1918. *Archaisierende griechische Rundplastik*. München: Verlag.

Buranelli, F. 1992. "Divagazioni vulcenti." In *La coroplastica templare etrusca fra il IV e il II secolo a.C.: atti del XVI convegno di studi etruschi e italici, Orbetello 25–29 aprile 1988*, ed. G. Maetzke. Florence: Leo S. Olschki Editore, 143–153.

Büsing, H. 1977. "Ranke und Figur an der Ara Pacis Augustae." *AA* 92.2, 247–257.

Calderone, A. 1975. "Sulle terracotte 'Campana.'" *Bollettino d'arte* 60, 65–74.

Campanile, I., and I. Cangiano. 2019. "Le terrecotte architettoniche del Tempio della Pace: il prodotto di una fabbrica templare pestana." In *Deliciae Fictiles V: Networks and Workshops, Fifth International Conference on Architectural Terracottas and Decorative Roof Systems in Italy*, ed. P. Lulof, I. Manzini, and C. Rescigno. Oxford: Oxbow Books, 273–277.

Caneva, G. 2009. "The Augustus Botanical Code; the Message of the Ara Pacis." *Bocconea* 23, 63–77.

2010. *Il codice botanico di Augusto; Roma – Ara Pacis; parlare al popolo attraverso le immagini della natura*. Rome: Gangemi Editore.

Cappelli, A. 1930. "Talamone. Rinvenimenti archeologici nell'impianto di una macchina idrovora a Bengodi." *NS* 6.6, 300–302.

Carandini, A., ed. 1985. *La Romanizzazione dell'Etruria: il territorio di Vulci*. Milan: Electa.

Carafa, P. 1998. *Il Comizio di Roma dalle origini all'età di Augusto*. Rome: "L'Erma" di Bretschneider.

Carettoni, G. 1966/67. "I problemi della zona augustea del Palatino alla luce dei recenti scavi." *RendPontAcc* 39, 55–75.

1972. "Terracotte 'Campana' dallo scavo del Tempio di Apollo Palatino." *RendPontAcc* XLIV, 123–139.

Carlucci, C. 2004. "Il II Tempio dello Scasato a Falerii: Restituzione del sistema decorativo." In *Scavo nello scavo. Gli Etruschi non visti*, ed. A. M. M. Sgubini. Rome: Union Printing Edizioni, 29–44.

2011. "Roma. Novità dal Colle Palatino." In *Tetti di terracotta. La decorazione architettonica fittile tra Etruria e Lazio in età arcaica.* Atti delle giornate di studio, Sapienza, Università di Roma. Rome: Officina edizioni, 202–215.

2020. "Segnali di frequentazione e discontinuità. Le fasi più recenti dei santuari di Falerii." In *Displacements. Continuità e discontinuità urbana nell'Italia centrale tirrenica,* ed. M. C. Biella. Rome: Edizioni Quasar, 83–98.

2021. *Terrecotte architettoniche etrusco-laziali. I sistemi decorativi della II fase iniziale.* Rome: "L'Erma" di Bretschneider.

Carlucci, C., and M. A. De Lucia Brolli. 2017. "La città e gli edifici pubblici. Matrici di terrecotte architettoniche da Falerii." *Sc. Ant.* 23.2, 171–179.

Carroll, M. 2010. "Exploring the Sanctuary of Venus and Its Sacred Grove: Politics, Cult and Identity in Roman Pompeii." *PBSR* 78, 63–106, 347–351.

2017. "Temple Gardens and Sacred Groves." In *Gardens of the Roman Empire,* ed. W. F. Jashemski, K. L, Gleason, K. J. Hartswick, and A.-A. Malek. Cambridge: Cambridge University Press, 152–164.

Caskey, J. L. 1954. "Excavatons at Lerna, 1952–1953." *Hesperia* 23.1, 3–30.

Castriota, D. 1995. *The Ara Pacis Augustae and the Imagery of Abundance in Later Greek and Early Roman Imperial Art.* Princeton: Princeton University Press.

Cataldi, M. 1985. "Il tempio detto Ara della Regina a Tarquinia: terrecotte architettoniche." In *Santuari d'Etruria,* ed. G. Colonna. Milan: Electa, 73–77.

Cébeillac-Gervasoni, M. ed. 1983. *Les "Bourgeoisies" municipales italiennes aux IIe et Ier siècles av. J.-C: Actes du Colloque International du CNRS n. 609 (Naples 1981).* Naples: Publications du Centre Jean Bérard,

1990. "L'évergétisme des magistrats du Latium et de la Campanie des Gracques à Auguste à travers les témoignages épigraphiques." *MEFRA* 102:2, 699–722.

ed. 1996. *Les élites municipales de l'Italie péninsulaire des Gracques à Néron : actes de la table ronde de Clermont-Ferrand, 28–30 novembre 1991.* Rome: École Française de Rome.

Celuzza, M. 1985. "Tecnica e tipologia dei rivestimenti fittili." In *Settefinestre. Una villa schiavistica nell'Etruria romana,* ed. A. Carandini. Modena: Edizioni Panini, 91–99.

2002. "Zona D. Talamone." In *Paesaggi d'Etruria. Valle dell'Albegna, Valle d'Oro, Valle del Chiarone, Valle del Tafone,* ed. A. Carandini, F. Cambi, M. Celuzza, and E. Fentress. Rome: Edizioni di Storia e Letteratura, 168–171.

Christensen, J., and K. B. Johannsen. 2015. *Thorvaldsen's Ancient Terracottas. A Catalogue of the Ancient Greek, Etruscan and Roman Terracottas in Thorvaldsens Museum.* Copenhagen: Thorvaldsens Museum.

Ciampoltrini, G. 1985. "Talamone e l'area costiera. La città e l'aristocrazia fra IV e I secolo a.C." In *La Romanizzazione dell'Etruria: il territorio di Vulci,* ed. A. Carandini. Milan: Electa, 115–118.

1995a. "Il vecchio, il mare, la nave. Una proposta per il fregio con thiasos marino di Telamone." *Parola del Passato* 50, 67–77.

1995b. "Un pocolom e le mura di Orbetello." *ArchClass* 47, 289–302.

2011. "Talamone." In *Bibliografia topografica della colonizzazione greca in Italia e nelle isole tirreniche. XX Sutera-Toppo Daguzzo,* ed. M. I. Gulletta and C. Cassanelli. Pisa, Rome, Naples: Scuola normale superiore, École française de Rome, Centre Jean Bérard Naples, 16–37.

Ciampoltrini, G., and P. Rendini. 1992. "Porti e traffici nel Tirreno settentrionale fra IV e III secolo a.C. Contributi da Telamone e dall'Isola del Giglio." *Annali della Scuola Normale Superiore di Pisa. Classe di Lettere e Filosofia* 22.4, 985–1004.

Ciasca, A. 1959. "Regione VII. Santa Severa. Le restanti terrecotte architettoniche." *Santa Severa (Roma). Scavi e ricerche nel sito dell'antica Pyrgi (1957-1958),* ed. G. Foti, G. Colonna, and A. Ciasca. Atti dell'accademia Nazionale dei Lincei. *NSc* s 8 v. 13, 191–224.

Cifani, G. 2018. "Visibility Matters. Notes on Archaic Monuments and Collective Memory in Mid-Republican Rome."

In *Omnium annalium monumenta: Historical Writing and Historical Evidence in Republican Rome*, ed. K. Sandberg and C. J. Smith. Leiden: Brill, 390–403.

Ciuffi, G. 1854. *Memorie storiche ed archeologiche della città di Traetto*. Naples: F. Serafini.

Clackson, J. 2014. "Local Languages in Italy and the West." In *The Oxford Handbook of Roman Epigraphy*, ed. C. Bruun and J. Edmondson. New York: Oxford University Press, 699–720.

Coarelli, F. 1976. "Architettura e arti figurative in Roma: 150–50 a.C." In *Hellenismus in Mittelitalien. Kolloquium in Göttingen vom 5. bis 9. Juni 1974*, ed. P. Zanker. Göttingen: Vandenhoeck & Ruprecht, 21–51.

1982a. *Lazio*. Rome: Laterza.

1982b. "L'altare del tempio e la sua iscrizione." In *El santuario de Juno en Gabii. Excavaciones 1956–1969*, ed. M. Almagro-Gorbea. Rome: Escuela Española de Historia y Arqueología en Roma, 125–130.

ed. 1986. *Fregellae, 2. Il santuario di Esculapio*. Rome: Edizioni Quasar.

1987. *I santuari del Lazio in età repubblicana*. Rome: La Nuova Italia Scientifica.

ed. 1989. *Minturnae*. Rome: Nuova Editrice Romana.

1993. "I luci del Lazio: la documentazione archeologica." In *Les bois sacrés. Actes du colloque international organisé par le Centre Jean Bérard et L'Ecole Pratique des Hautes Etudes (Ve section), Naples 23–25 novembre 1989*. Naples: Centre Jean Bérard, 45–52.

2008. "Scorta Minturnensia." In *Dalle sorgenti alla foce. Il bacino del Liri-Garigliano nell'antichità: culture, contatti, scambi*, ed. C. Corsi and E. Polito. Rome: Quasar, 105–111.

2012. *Palatium: Il Palatino dalle origini all'impero*. Rome: Quasar.

2014. "Palatine." In *Rome and Environs*. Berkeley: University of California Press, 131–157.

Coarelli, F., and A. La Regina 1984. *Abruzzo, Molise*. Rome: Laterza.

Coarelli, F., and P. Arthur. 1989. *Minturnae*. Roma: NER.

Cofer, C. 2015. "The Ara Pacis Augustae and the Ancient Understanding of Grafting." PhD diss., Bryn Mawr College.

Cohon, R. 2004. "Forerunners of the Scrollwork on the Ara Pacis Augustae Made by a Western Asiatic Workshop." *JRA* 17, 83–106.

Coles, A. J. 2009. "Not Effigies Parvae Populi Romani: Gods, Agency, and Landscape in Mid-Republican Colonization." PhD diss., University of Pennsylvania.

Colivicchi, F. 2008. "Hellenism and Romanization at Ancona: A Case of 'Invented Tradition.'" *JRA* 21, 31–46.

Colonna, G. 1964. "I dati dello scavo." In M. Pallottino, L. Vlad Borelli and G. Gabini, "Scavi nel santuario etrusco di Pyrgi." *ArchClass* 16, 50–57.

ed. 1985. *Santuari d'Etruria*. Milan: Electa.

2000. "Il santuario di Pyrgi dalle origini mitistoriche agli altorilievi frontonali dei Sette e di Leucotea." *ScAnt* 10, 251–336.

Comella, A. 1985. "Nota sulla coroplastica falisca." *Studi in onore di Giovanni Lilliu per il suo settantesimo compleanno*. Cagliari: Istituto di antichità e arte. Facoltà di lettere, 83–98.

1993. *Le terrecotte architettoniche del santuario dello Scasato a Falerii: Scavi 1886–1887*. Naples: Edizioni Scientifiche Italiane.

Connerton, P. 1989. *How Societies Remember*. Cambridge: Cambridge University Press.

Cook, E. M. 2018. "Legacies of Matter: The Reception and Remediation of Material Traditions in Roman Sculpture." PhD diss., Columbia University.

Cozza, A. 1888. "Civita Castellana (antica Faleria). Avanzi di un antico tempio in contrada Lo Scasato." *NSc*, 414–433.

Crawford, M. H. et al. 2011. *Imagines Italicae. A Corpus of Italic Inscriptions*. London: Institute of Classical Studies.

Crawford-Brown, S. 2019a. "Regionalism or *Romanitas*? Network Approaches to Architectural Terracottas at Minturnae and Cosa." In *Cosa and the Colonial Landscape of Republican Italy (Third and Second Centuries BCE)*, ed. A. U. De Giorgi. Ann Arbor: University of Michigan Press, 182–203.

2019b. "*Daedala Tecta*: Architectural Terracottas and Cultural Memory in Republican Italy." PhD diss, University of Pennsylvania.

2019c. "Mixing Traditions: The Architectural Terracottas from Minturnae." In *Deliciae Fictiles V: Networks and Workshops, Fifth International Conference on Architectural Terracottas and Decorative Roof Systems in Italy*, ed. P. Lulof, I. Manzini, and C. Rescigno. Oxford: Oxbow Books, 366–370.

2022. "Down from the Roof: Reframing Plants in Augustan Art." *JRA* 35, 33–63.

Cristofani, M. 1973. *Volterra. Scavi 1969–1971.* NSc Suppl. Rome: Accademia Nazionale dei Lincei.

ed. 1981a. *Gli Etruschi in Maremma. Popolamento e attività produttive.* Milan. Silvana Editoriale.

1981b. "Riflessioni sulla decorazione architettonica di prima fase in Etruria e a Roma." In *Gli Etruschi e Roma. Atti dell'incontro di studio in onore di Massimo Pallottino: Roma, 11–13 dicembre 1979.* Rome: G. Bretschneider, 189–198.

ed. 1990. *La Grande Roma dei Tarquini.* Rome: "L'Erma" di Bretschneider.

Damgaard Andersen, H. 1996. "The Origin of Potnia Theron in Central Italy." *Hamburger Beiträge zur Archäologie* 19/20, 73–113.

Davies, P. 2012. "On the Introduction of Stone Entablatures in Republican Rome." In *Monumentality in Etruscan and Early Roman Architecture. Ideology and Innovation*, ed. M. L. Thomas and G. E. Meyers. Austin: University of Texas Press, 139–165.

2017. *Architecture and Politics in Republican Rome.* Cambridge: Cambridge University Press.

2018. "Constructing, Deconstructing and Reconstructing Civic Memory in Late Republican Rome." In *Omnium Annalium Monumenta: Historical Writing and Historical Evidence in Republican Rome*, ed. K. Sandberg and C. Smith. Leiden: Brill, 477–511.

2020. "Striving against Oblivion. Tombs and Cemeteries in the Mid-Republic." In *Roma medio repubblicana. Dalla conquista di Veio alla battaglia di Zama*, ed. A. D'Alessio, M. Serlorenzi, C. Smith, and R. Volpe. Rome: Quasar, 451–466.

De Angelis, F. 2008. "Pliny the Elder and the Identity of Roman Art." *RES: Anthropology and Aesthetics* 53/54: 79–92.

De Caro, S. 2003. *I mosaici. La casa del fauno.* Naples: Electa Napoli.

2007. "The First Sanctuaries." In *The World of Pompeii*, ed. J. J. Dobbins and P. W. Foss. New York: Routledge, 73–81.

De Giorgi, A. U., R. T. Scott, A. Glennie, A. Smith. 2019. "Cosa (Orbetello, GR): 70 Years of Excavations and New Directions." *Bollettino di archeologia online* X.3–4, 57–70.

De Grummond, E. 2000–2001. "Maenads and Meaning: Antefixes from Tarquinia in American Collections." *The University of Michigan Museum of Art and Archaeology Bulletin* XIII, 7–30.

De Grummond, N. T. 2006. *Etruscan Myth, Sacred History, and Legend.* Philadelphia: University of Pennsylvania Museum of Archaeology and Anthropology.

Dench, E. 2005. *Romulus' Asylum.* New York: Oxford University Press.

De Tommaso, G., E. Paribeni, and E. Sorge. 2011. "Il grande tempio di Luni. Nuovi dati dal restauro del Frontone B." In *Deliciae Fictiles IV: Architectural Terracottas in Ancient Italy: Images of Gods, Monsters and Heroes*, ed. P. Lulof and C. Rescigno. Oxford: Oxbow Books, 250–257.

Della Seta, A. 1918. *Museo di Villa Giulia.* Rome: Danesi.

Diefenbach, S. 2007. *Römische Erinnerungsräume: Heiligenmemoria und kollektive Identitäten im Rom des 3. bis 5. Jahrhunderts n. Chr.* Berlin: De Gruyter.

Dietrich, N., and M. Squire, eds. 2018. *Ornament and Figure in Graeco-Roman Art: Rethinking Visual Ontologies in Classical Antiquity.* Berlin: Walter de Gruyter.

Diffendale, D. P. 2018. "Disiecta Fictilia: Some Republican-era Moldmade Architectural

Terracottas from the Magazzino at Sant'Omobono." In *Ricerche nell'area dei templi di Fortuna e Mater Matuta.* Vol. II, ed. P. Brocato, M. Ceci, and N. Terrenato. Ricerche 14, Collana del Dipartimento di Studi Umanistici, Università della Calabria, 159–175.

Diosono, F., and F. R. Plebani. 2013. "La terrazza inferiore e la terrazza mediana. Le terrecotte architettoniche e la coroplastica." In *Il Santuario di Diana a Nemi: Le terrazze e il ninfeo. Scavi 1989–2009,* ed. F. Coarelli, G. Ghini, F. Diosono, P. Braconi. Rome: "L'Erma" di Bretschneider, 167–186.

Diosono, F., and G. D'Angelo. 2019. "Nemi in contesto. La decorazione fittile delle diverse fasi del tempio di Diana tra vecchie collezioni e nuovi dati stratigrafici." In *Deliciae Fictiles V. Networks and Workshops,* ed. P. Lulof, I. Manzini, and C. Rescigno. Oxford: Oxbow Books, 397–406.

Diosono, F., A. Fraddosio, A. La Notte, N. Pecere, and M. D. Piccioni. 2022. "'Seismic Shield' Properties of Foundations and Podiums of Roman-Italic Temples in Central Italy: the Case Study of Temple B in Pietrabbondante." In *Living with Seismic Phenomena in the Mediterranean and Beyond between Antiquity and the Middle Ages,* ed. R. Compatangelo-Soussignan, F. Diosono, F. Le Blay. Oxford: Archaeopress, 379–398.

Dupré, X. 1982. "Terracotas Arquitectonicas." In *El santuario de Juno en Gabii. Excavaciones 1956–1969,* ed. M. Almagro-Gorbea. Rome: Escuela Española de Historia y Arqueología en Roma, 131–194.

Edlund-Berry, I. 1987. *The Gods and the Place: Location and Function of Sanctuaries in the Countryside of Etruria and Magna Graecia (700–400 B.C.).* Stockholm: Svenska Institutet i Rom.

2008. "The Language of Etrusco-Italic Architecture: New Perspectives on Tuscan Temples." *AJA* 112.3, 441–447.

2022. "With a Sense of Place and Time. The Use of Mouldings in Etrusco-Italic and Republican Roman Architecture." In *Approaches to Ancient Etruria,* ed. M. Moltesen and A. Rathje. Acta Hyperborea 16. Copenhagen: Museum Tusculanum Press, 33–80.

Edlund-Berry, I., G. Greco, and J. Kenfield, eds. 2006. *Deliciae Fictilies III. Architectural Terracottas in Ancient Italy.* Oxford: Oxbow Books.

Ekserdjian, A. 2023. "The Gods of Hellenistic Central Italy: Theology, Representation, and Response." PhD diss., Columbia University.

Enea nel Lazio: Archeologia e mito. Bimillenario virgiliano: Roma 22 Settembre–31 Dicembre 1981, Campidoglio, Palazzo dei conservatori. 1981. Rome: Fratelli Palombi.

Erdkamp, P. 2008. "Mobility and Migration in Italy in the Second Century BC." In *People, Land, and Politics: Demographic Developments and the Transformation of Roman Italy, 300 BC–AD 14,* ed. L. de Ligt and S. Northwood. Leiden: Brill, 417–449.

2011. "Soldiers, Roman Citizens, and Latin Colonists in Mid-Republican Italy." *Ancient Society* 41, 109–146.

Erll, A. 2010. "Cultural Memory Studies: An Introduction." In *A Companion to Cultural Memory Studies,* ed. A. Erll and A. Nünning. Berlin: de Gruyter, 1–15.

2011. *Memory in Culture,* trans. S. B. Young. Houndmills and New York: Palgrave Macmillan.

Erll, A., and A. Nünning. 2010. *A Companion to Cultural Memory Studies.* Berlin: de Gruyter.

Fant, J. C. 1999. "Augustus and the City of Marble." In *Archéomatériaux: Marbres et autres roches. ASMOSIA IV,* ed. M. Schvoerer. Bordeaux: CRPAA, 277–280.

Farney, G. 2007. *Ethnic Identity and Aristocratic Competition in Republican Rome.* Cambridge: Cambridge University Press.

Farrell, J. 1997. "The Phenomenology of Memory in Roman Culture." *The Classical Journal* 92.4, 373–383.

Fentress, E. 2000. "Frank Brown, Cosa, and the Idea of a Roman City." In *Romanization and the City: Creations, Transformations and*

Failures, ed. E. Fentress. JRA Suppl. 38. Portsmouth, RI: Journal of Roman Archaeology, 11–24.

Fentress, E., and P. Perkins. 2016. "Cosa and the *Ager Cosanus*." In *A Companion to Roman Italy*, ed. A. E. Cooley. West Sussex: Wiley Blackwell, 378–400.

Fernández-Götz, M., D. Maschek, and N. Roymans. 2020. "The Dark Side of the Empire: Roman Expansionism between Object Agency and Predatory Regime." *Antiquity* 94.378, 1630–1639.

Ferrante, C., J.-C. Lacam, and D. Quadrino, eds. 2015. *Regio I. Fondia, Formia, Minturno, Ponza*. Rome: Quasar.

Ferrea, L. 2002. *Gli dei di terracotta. La ricomposizione del frontone da Via di San Gregorio*. Milan: Electa.

Flower, H. I. 1996. *Ancestor Masks and Aristocratic Power in Roman Culture*. New York: Clarendon Press of Oxford University Press.

2006. *The Art of Forgetting: Disgrace and Oblivion in Roman Political Culture*. Chapel Hill: The University of North Carolina Press.

Foresta, S. 2011. "La policromia dell'Ara Pacis e i colori del Campo Marzio settentrionale." In *Colore e Colorimetria: Contributi Multidisciplinari. Vol. VII A*, ed. M. Rossi and A. Siniscalco. Santarcangelo di Romagna: Maggioli S.p.A., 333–340.

2012a. "La policromia dell'Ara Pacis Augustae: Osservazioni sulla storia dell'arte romana." In *Colore e Colorimetria: Contributi Multidisciplinari. Vol. VIII A*, ed. M. Rossi. Santarcangelo di Romagna: Maggioli S.p. A., 689–696.

2012b. "La funzione della policromia nell'interpretazione storico-artistica dell'Ara Pacis Augustae dal 1894 alla metà del '900." *EIDOLA International Journal of Classical Art History* 9, 87–106.

Forte, M. 1991. *Le terrecotte ornamentali dei templi lunensi. Catalogo delle terrecotte architettoniche a stampo conservate al Museo Archeologico Nazionale di Firenze*. Florence: Leo S. Olschki Editore.

Forte, M., P. Desantis, and S. Sani 1992. "Le terrecotte architettoniche di Luni: La ricomposizione del rivestimento fittile del Grande Tempio e del Capitolium." In *La coroplastica templare etrusca fra il IV e il II secolo a.C.: atti del XVI convegno di studi etruschi e italici, Orbetello 25–29 aprile 1988*, ed. G. Maetzke. Florence: Leo S. Olschki Editore, 185–223.

Fischer-Hansen, T. 2008. "Votive and Architectural Terracottas: The Archaic and Post-archaic Period." In *The Temple of Castor and Pollux II.2. The Finds and Trenches*, ed. K. Slej and M. Cullhed. Rome: "L'Erma" di Bretschneider, 283–302.

Frapiccini, N., and M. Silvestrini. 2016. "Interventi di archeologia urbana: nuovi indizi della romanizzazione a Camerino." In *Dalla Valdelsa al Conero. Ricerche di archeologia e topografia storica in ricordo di Giuliano de Marinis*, ed. G. Baldini and P. Giroldini. Florence: All'Insegna del Giglio, 305–314.

Frova, A., ed. 1973. *Scavi di Luni: Relazione preliminare delle campagne di scavo 1970–1971*. Rome: "L'Erma" di Bretschneider.

Fuchs, M. 1999. *"In hoc etiam genere Graeciae nihil cedamus": Studien zur Romanisierung der späthellenistischen Kunst im 1. Jh. v. Chr.* Mainz: Philipp von Zabern.

Fugazzotto, M., A. Stroscio, P. Mazzoleni, C. Panella, A. Russo, S. Raneri, and G. Barone. 2021. "Ceramic Technology and Paintings of Archaic Architectural Slabs, louteria and Antefixes from the Palatine Hill in Rome (Italy)." *Archaeometry* 64, 118–133.

Fullerton, M. D. 1990. *The Archaistic Style in Roman Statuary*. Mnemosyne Supplement 110. Leiden: Brill.

Gabba, E. 1982. "Riflessioni sulla 'storiografia locale' antica (fino al II secolo d.C.)." In *La Storia locale: temi, fonti e metodi della ricerca*, ed. C. Violante. Bologna: Società editrice il mulino, 33–39.

Gabrielli, C. 2003. "Lucius Postumius Megellus at Gabii: A New Fragment of Livy." *CQ* 53.1, 247–259.

Galinsky, K. 1966. "Venus in a Relief on the Ara Pacis Augustae." *AJA* 70.2, 223–243.
1969. *Aeneas, Sicily, and Rome*. Princeton: Princeton University Press.
1992. "Venus, Polysemy, and the Ara Pacis Augustae." *AJA* 96.3, 457–475.
ed. 2014. *Memoria Romana: Memory in Rome and Rome in Memory*. Ann Arbor: The University of Michigan Press.
ed. 2016. *Memory in Ancient Rome and Early Christianity*. Oxford: Oxford University Press.
Galinsky, K., and K. Lapatin, eds. 2015. *Cultural Memories in the Roman Empire*. Los Angeles: J. Paul Getty Museum.
Galli, M., and O. Cordovana, ed. 2007. *Arte e memoria culturale nell'età della Seconda Sofistica*. Catania: Edizioni del Prisma.
Galluccio, F. 2016. "Il mito torna realtà. Le decorazioni fittili del tempio di Giove Capitolino della fondazione all'età medio repubblicana." In *Campidoglio: Mito, Memoria, Archeologia*, ed. C. Parisi Presicce and A. Danti. Rome: Campisano Editore.
García Giménez, R., R. Vigil de la Villa, P. Recio de la Rosa, M. D. Petit Domínguez, and M. I. Rucandio. 2005. "Analytical and Multivariate Study of Roman Age Architectural Terracotta from Northeast of Spain." *Talanta* 65, 861–868.
Gatti, S. 1995. "I Latini di Praeneste: nuove acquisizioni." *Eutopia* IV.2, 95–122.
Gazzetti, G. 1985. "La città e il territorio dopo la conquista. La città." In *La Romanizzazione dell'Etruria: il territorio di Vulci*, ed. A. Carandini. Milan: Electa, 61–64.
Glendinning, M. 2002. "Recovering the Lost Art of Phrygian Roof Tiling." *Expedition* 44.2, 28–35.
2005. "A Decorated Roof at Gordion: What Tiles Are Revealing about the Phrygian Past." In *The Archaeology of Midas and the Phrygians. Recent Work at Gordion*, ed. L. Kealhofer. Philadelphia: University of Pennsylvania Press, 82–100.
Ghini, G., and F. Diosono. 2012. "Il Santuario di Diana a Nemi: recenti acquisizioni dai nuovi scavi." In *Sacra Nominis Latini. I santuari del Lazio arcaico e repubblicano*, ed. E. Marroni. Ostraka – Volume speciale 2012. Naples: Loffredo Editore, 121–139.
Glennie, A. 2022. "Waterlessness and Rainwater Harvesting on a Monumental Scale: Largescale Non-domestic Water Collection, Storage, and Control at Cosa in the Roman Republican and Imperial Periods." PhD diss., Florida State University.
Glinister, F. 2000. "Sacred Rubbish." In *Religion in Archaic and Republican Rome and Italy: Evidence and Experience*, ed. E. Bispham and C. Smith. London: Routledge, 54–70.
Gombrich, E. H. 2002. *The Preference for the Primitive: Episodes in the History of Western Taste and Art*. London: Phaidon.
Goodman, P. J. 2016. "Urban Peripheries." In *A Companion to Roman Italy*, ed. A. E. Cooley. West Sussex: Wiley-Blackwell.
Gosden, C. 2005. "What Do Objects Want?" *Journal of Archaeological Method and Theory* 12.2, 193–211.
Gowing, A. M. 2005. *Empire and Memory: The Representation of the Roman Republic in Imperial Culture*. Cambridge: Cambridge University Press.
Grabar, O. 1992. *The Mediation of Ornament*. Princeton: Princeton University Press.
ed. 2010. *Special Issue: Ornement/Ornamental. Perspective: Actualité en Histoire de l'Art* 1.
Graham, E.-J. 2021. *Reassembling Religion in Roman Italy*. Abingdon and New York: Routledge.
Greco, E. 1988. "Archeologia della colonia latina di Paestum." *DArch* 6.2, 79–86.
Grønne, C. 1992. "The Architectural Terracottas." In *The Temple of Castor and Pollux. The Pre-Augustan Temple Phases with Related Decorative Elements*, ed. I. Nielsen and B. Poulsen. Rome: Edizioni de luca, 157–176.
Gros, P. 1976. *Aurea Templa. Recherches sur l'architecture religieuse de Rome à l'époque d'Auguste*. Rome: École française de Rome.
Gruen, E. S. 1990. *Studies in Greek Culture and Roman Policy*. Leiden: Brill.
1992. *Culture and National Identity in Republican Rome*. Ithaca: Cornell University Press.

Gualtieri, M., G. Rossini, and B. Moroni. 2002. "Campana plaques from Ossaia – La Tufa (Cortona, Arezzo): From Archaeological Hypothesis to Archaeometric Results." *Periodico di Mineralogia* 71, 145–166.
Guarino, A. 2010. *Le terrecotte architettoniche a stampo da Vigna Parrocchiale. Scavi 1983–1989.* Pisa, Rome: Fabrizio Serra Editore.
Guest, C. L. 2016. *The Understanding of Ornament in the Italian Renaissance.* Leiden: Brill.
Gullini, G. 1973. "La datazione e l'inquadramento stilistico del santuario della Fortuna Primigenia a Palestrina." *ANRW* 1.4, 746–799.
Hackländer, N. 1996. *Der archaistische Dionysos: Eine archäologische Untersuchung zur Bedeutung archaistischer Kunst in hellenistischer und römischer Zeit.* Frankfurt: Peter Lang.
Halbwachs, M. 1925. *Les cadres sociaux de la mémoire.* Paris: Alcan.
1941. *La topographie légendaire des Évangiles en Terre sainte: Étude de mémoire collective.* Paris: Alcan.
1950. *La mémoire collective.* Paris: Presses Universitaires de France.
Hallett, C. 2005. "Emulation versus Replication: Redefining Roman Copying." *JRA* 18, 419–435.
2012. "The Archaic Style in Sculpture in the Eyes of Ancient and Modern Viewers." In *Making Sense of Greek Art,* ed. V. Coltman. Exeter: University of Exeter Press, 70–100.
2018. "Terracotta, Antiquarianism, and the 'Archaic Revival' of Early Augustan Rome." In *Visual Histories of the Classical World. Essays in Honour of R. R. R. Smith,* ed. C. M. Draycott, R. Rajan, K. Welch, and W. T. Wootton. Turnhout: Brepols, 181–203.
Hampe, R., and A. Winter. 1965. *Bei Töpfern und Zieglern in Süditalien, Sizilien und Griechenland.* Mainz: Verlag des Römisch-Germanischen Zentralmuseums Mainz.
Harari, M. 1997. "Tarquinia e il territorio suburbano nel rilevamento da alta quota: Una lettura topografica." In *Tarquinia: Testimonianze archeologiche e ricostruzione storica. Scavi sistematici nell'abitato (Campagne 1982–1988),* ed. M. Bonghi Jovino and C. Chiaramonte Treré. Rome: "L'Erma" di Bretschneider, 5–17.
Harnett, E. 1986. "The Sculpture of Roman Minturnae." PhD diss., Bryn Mawr College.
1998. "Some Lost Sculptures from Minturnae." In *Stephanos: Studies in Honor of Brunilde Sismondo Ridgway,* ed. K. J. Hartswick and M. C. Sturgeon. Philadelphia: University of Pennsylvania, 101–104.
Hingley, R. 2005. *Globalizing Roman Culture: Unity, Diversity and Empire.* London and New York: Routledge.
Hitchner, R. B. 2012. "Roads, Integration, Connectivity, and Economic Performance in the Roman Empire." In *Highways, Byways, and Road Systems in the Pre-Modern World,* ed. S. E. Alcock, J. Bodel, and R. J. A. Talbert. Malden, MA and Oxford: Wiley-Blackwell, 222–234.
Hobsbawm, E., and T. Ranger. 1983. *The Invention of Tradition.* Cambridge: Cambridge University Press.
Hölkeskamp, K.-J. 1993. "Conquest, Competition and Consensus: Roman Expanion in Italy and the Rise of the 'Nobilitas.'" *Historia* 42.1, 12–39.
Holland, L. L. 2002. "Worshiping Diana: The Cult of a Roman Goddess in Republican Italy.PhD diss., University of North Carolina at Chapel Hill.
Hölscher, T. 2004. *The Language of Images in Roman Art.* Trans. A Snodgrass and A. Künzl-Snodgrass. Cambridge: Cambridge University Press.
2009. "Architectural Sculpture: Messages? Programs? Towards Rehabilitating the Notion of 'Decoration.'" In *Structure, Image, Ornament: Architectural Sculpture in the Greek World,* ed. Schultz, P. and R. von den Hoff. Oxford: Oxbow, 54–67.
Hopkins, J. N. 2010. "The Colossal Temple of Jupiter Optimus Maximus in Archaic Rome." In *Arqueología de la construcción, 2. Los procesos constructivos en el mundo romano: Italia y provincias orientales,* ed. S. Camporeale, H. Dessales, and A Pizzo.

Archivio Español de Arqueología Suppl. 57. Merida: Archivio Español de Arqueología, 15–33.

2014. "The Capitoline Temple and the Effects of Monumentality on Roman Temple Design." In *Monumentality in Etruscan and Early Roman Architecture: Ideology and Innovation*, ed. M. Thomas and G. E. Meyers. Austin: University of Texas Press, 111–138.

2016. *The Genesis of Roman Architecture*. New Haven and London: Yale University Press.

2022. "The Connective Evidence for Early Roman Urbanism. Terracottas and Architectural Accretion." In *Architecture in Ancient Central Italy*, ed. C. R. Potts. Cambridge: Cambridge University Press, 95–124.

2023. "Engagements in and beyond Rome in the 5th c. BCE: Architectural Remains as Evidence for Action across Geo-temporal Boundaries." *JRA* 35.2, 654–682.

2024. *Unbound from Rome. Art and Craft in a Fluid Landscape, ca. 650–250 BCE*. New York and London: Yale University Press.

Hunt, A. 2016. *Reviving Roman Religion: Sacred Trees in the Roman World*. Cambridge: Cambridge University Press.

Iaculli, G. 1993. *Il tempio italico di Colle S. Giorgio (Castiglione Messer Raimondo)*. Penne: Cassa rurale ed artigiana di Castiglione Messer Raimondo.

2006. "Note sulla tecnica di esecuzione di alcune terrecotte della Civitella di Chieti." In *Deliciae Fictiles III*, ed. I. Edlund-Berry, G. Greco, and J. Kenfield. Oxford: Oxbow Books, 164–175.

Isayev, E. 2017. *Migration, Mobility and Place in Ancient Italy*. Cambridge: Cambridge University Press.

Jazwa, K. A. 2018. "The Construction of Early Helladic II Ceramic Roofing Tiles from Mitrou, Greece: Influence and Interaction." *Mediterranean Archaeology and Archaeometry* 18.2, 153–173.

Jerram, L. 2013. "Space: A Useless Category for Historical Analysis?" *History and Theory* 52, 400–419.

Johnson, J. 1933a. *Excavations at Minturnae. Volume II: Inscriptions*. Philadelphia: University of Pennsylvania Press.

1933b. " Minturnae: A Resumé of the Initial Campaign." *Bollettino dell'Associazione internazionale degli studi mediterranei* 1–2, 13–26.

1934. "An Egyptian Landscape at Minturnae." *University Museum Bulletin* 5, 13–20.

1935. *Excavations at Minturnae. Volume I: Monuments of the Republican Forum*. Philadelphia: University of Pennsylvania Press.

1940. "Minturnae." *RE Suppl.* 7, 458–494.

Johnston, A. C., and M. Mogetta. 2020. "Debating Early Republican Urbanism in Latium Vetus: The Town Planning of Gabii, between Archaeology and History." *JRS* 110, 91–121.

Jolivet, V., and E. Lovergne. 2011. "Matrici di età ellenistica dal sito di Civita Musarna (Viterbo)." In *Deliciae Fictiles IV: Architectural Terracottas in Ancient Italy: Images of Gods, Monsters and Heroes*, ed. P. Lulof and C. Rescigno. Oxford: Oxbow Books, 514–516.

Jones, N. B. 2019. *Painting, Ethics, and Aesthetics in Rome: Greek Culture in the Roman World*. Cambridge: Cambridge University Press.

Kaderka, K. 2018. *Les décors tympanaux des temples de Rome*. Bordeaux: Ausonius.

Känel, R. 1991. "Zwei etruskisch-italische Terrakottaplatten mit vegetabilem Dekor in Genf." *Antike Kunst* 34.2, 170–177.

2000. "Das Dianaheiligtum in Nemi: Die Baudekoration aus Terrakotta." In *Nemi – Status Quo: Recent Research at Nemi and the Sanctuary of Diana*, ed. J. Rasmus Brandt, A. M. Leander Touati, and J. Zahle, eds. Rome: "L'Erma" di Bretschneider, 131–139.

2001. "Bilderzyklen aus Terrakotta: Untersuchungen zur etruskisch-italischen Baudekoration des 3. und 2. Jahrhunderts v. Chr." PhD diss., University of Munich (published in Microfiche in 2004).

2010. "Bemerkungen zum Terrakotta-Bauschmuck hellenistischer Wohnhäuser in Mittelitalien." In *Etruskisch-italische und römisch-republikanische Häuser*, ed. M. Bentz and C. Reusser. Wiesbaden: Dr. Ludwig Reichert Verlag, 263–271.

2015. "Das Aesculapius-Heiligtum in Fregellae und sein Bauschmuck aus Terrakotta." In *The Impact of Rome on Cult Places and Religious Practice in Ancient Italy*, ed. T. D. Stek and G.-J. Burgers. London: University of London, 67–95.

2019. "Der sog. THVMA-Meister. Beobachtungen zur Aktivität eines griechischen Koroplasten in Fregellae." In *Deliciae Fictiles V. Networks and Workshops*, ed. P. Lulof, I. Manzini, and C. Rescigno. Oxford: Oxbow Books, 377–386.

Känel, R., and S. Stangoni. 2019. "Le terrecotte architettoniche e la decorazione frontonale del tempio suburbano sulla via Latina." In *Fregellae. Il tempio del Foro e il tempio suburbano sulla via Latina*, ed. G. Battaglini, F. Coarelli, and F. Diosono. Rome: Giorgio Bretschneider, 111–144.

2024. "Alles neu? Die Campana-Reliefs und ihre etruskisch-italischen Vorläufer." In *Campana-Reliefs: Neue Forschungen zu römischem Architekturdekor aus Terrakotta, Akten der Internationalen Tagung Heidelberg, 8.–10. April 2021*, ed. A. Reinhardt. Heidelberg: Propylaeum, 87–108.

Keay, S., and N. Terrenato, eds. 2001. *Italy and the West. Comparative Issues in Romanization.* Oxford: Oxbow.

Keller, J. 2004. "Römische Interessengeschichte. Eine Studie zu Interessenvertretung, Interessenkonflikten und Konfliktlösung in der römischen Republik des 2. Jahrhunderts v. Chr." PhD diss., LMU München.

2007. "Rome and Her Italian Allies: Conflicting Interests and Disintegration." In *Roman by Integration: Dimensions of Group Identity in Material Culture and Text*, ed. R. E. Roth, J. Keller, and E. Flaig. JRA Suppl. 66. Portsmouth, RI: Journal of Roman Archaeology, 43–57.

Kellum, B. A. 1985. "Sculptural Programs and Propaganda in Augustan Rome: The Temple of Apollo on the Palatine." In *The Age of Augustus: Interdisciplinary Conference Held at Brown University, April 30th–May 2nd, 1982*, ed. R. Winkes. Providence: Center for Old World Archaeology and Art, Brown University, 169–176.

1994. "What We See and What We Don't See: Narrative Structure and the Ara Pacis Augustae." *Art History* 17.1, 26–45.

Knoop, R. R. 1987. *Antefixa Satricana: Sixth-Century Architectural Terracottas from the Sanctuary of Mater Matuta at Satricum (Le Ferriere).* Assen: Van Gorcum.

1993. "Towards a Reappraisal of Della Seta's Three-Phase System." In *Deliciae Fictiles I*, ed. E. Rystedt, C. Wikander, and O. Wikander. Stockholm: Svenska Institutet, 61–66.

Koch, H. 1912. *Dachterrakotten aus Campanien mit Ausschluss von Pompei.* Berlin: Georg Reimer.

Kohlberger-Schaub, T. 2015. "L'area B a Minturnae – L'evoluzione di un santuario urbano." In *Minturnae. Nuovi contributi alla conoscenza della forma urbis*, ed. G. R. Bellini and H. von Hesberg. Rome: Edizioni Quasar, 147–156.

Kolb, A., ed. 2019. *Roman Roads. New Evidence – New Perspectives.* Berlin: De Gruyter.

Kosmopoulos, D. 2021. *Architettura templare italica in epoca ellenistica.* Rome: "L'Erma" di Bretschneider.

Kraus, T. 1953. *Die Ranken der Ara Pacis: Ein Beitrag zur Entwicklungsgeschichte der Augusteischen Ornamentik.* Berlin: Gerb. Mann.

Krauskopf, I. 2000. "I sette contro Tebe nell'arte etrusca arcaica e classica." *ScAnt* 10, 497–510.

Lackner, E.-M. 2008. *Republikanische Fora.* Munich: Biering & Brinkmann.

Laffi, U. 1983. "I senati locali nell'Italia repubblicana." In *Les "bourgeoisies" municipales italiennes aux IIe et Ier siècles av. J.-C : Actes du Colloque International du CNRS n. 609 (Naples 1981)*, ed. M. Cébeillac-Gervasoni. Naples: Publications du Centre Jean Bérard, 59–74.

2017. "Italici in colonie latine e Latini in colonie romane." In *Itinerari di storia:*

In ricordo di Mario Pani, ed. M. Chelotti, M. Silvestrini, and E. Todisco. Bari: Edipuglia, 51–61.

Laird, M. L. 2016. "Diversity in Architecture and Urbanism." In *A Companion to Roman Italy*, ed. A. E. Cooley. Malden and Oxford: Wiley Blackwell, 181–216.

La Rocca, E. 1987. *L'Auriga dell'Esquilino*. Rome: "L'Erma" di Bretschneider.

L'Orange, H. P. 1985. "The Floral Zone of the Ara Pacis Augustae," trans. Donald Mills. In *The Roman Empire: Art Forms and Civic Life*. New York: Rizzoli, 209–228.

La Regina, A. 1966. "Le iscrizioni osche di Pietrabbondante e la questione di Bovianum Vetus." *Rheinisches Museum* 109, 260–286.

1976. "Osco." In La Regina, A., M. Lejeune, A. Prosdocimi "Sannio: Pietrabbondante." *StEtr* 44, 283–288.

Laubenheimer, F. 1997. "Les plaques Campana gauloises." In *Le moulage en terre cuite dans l'antiquité. Création et production dérivée, fabrication et diffusion*, ed. A. Muller. Villeneuve d'Ascq: Presses Universitaires du Septentrion, 397–415.

Laubenheimer, F., T. Odiot, and H. Leclere. 1989. "Sous Auguste, un atelier de potiers italianisant à Saint-Just (Ardèche)." *Melanges Pierre Lévêque* 2, 295–329.

Laurence, R. 1999. *The Roads of Roman Italy: Mobility and Cultural Change*. London: Routledge.

Ledderose, L. 2000. *Ten Thousand Things. Module and Mass Production in Chinese Art*. Princeton: Princeton University Press.

Lefebvre, H. 1974. *La production de l'espace*. Paris: Éditions Anthropos.

Liberatore, D. 2006. "Le terrecotte architettoniche della Civitella di Chieti: il frontone delle Muse." In *Deliciae Fictiles III*, ed. I. Edlund-Berry, G. Greco, and J. Kenfield. Oxford: Oxbow Books, 181–193.

Lipps, J., and D. Maschek, eds. 2014. *Antike Bauornamentik: Grenzen und Möglichkeiten ihrer Erforschung*. Wiesbaden: Dr. Ludwig Reichert Verlag.

Livi, V. 2002. "A Story Told in Pieces: Architectural Terracottas from Minturnae." *Expedition* 44, 24–35.

2006. "Religious Locales in the Territory of Minturnae: Aspects of Romanization." In *Religion in Republican Italy*, ed. C. E. Schultz and P. B. Harvey. Cambridge: Cambridge University Press, 90–116.

2019. "Il santuario della dea Marica in età romana. Un contributo dallo studio delle terrecotte architettoniche." In *Deliciae Fictiles V. Networks and Workshops*, ed. P. Lulof, I. Manzini, and C. Rescigno. Oxford: Oxbow Books, 371–376.

2022. "Minturnae (Latina) – Altorilievi frontonali dal deposito del Tempio B di Minturnae. Osservazioni preliminari." *NSc*, ns 1 2, 153–179.

Lomas, K. 1997. "The Idea of a City: Élite Ideology and the Evolution of Urban Form in Italy, 200 BC–AD 100." In *Roman Urbanism: Beyond the Consumer City*, ed. H. M. Markins. London and New York: Routledge, 21–41.

2003. "Public Building, Urban Renewal and Euergetism in Early Imperial Italy." In *"Bread and Circuses." Euergetism and Municipal Patronage in Roman Italy*, ed. K. Lomas and T. Cornell. New York: Routledge, 28–45.

2017. *The Rise of Rome. From the Iron Age to the Punic Wars (1000–264 BC)*. London: Profile Books.

Lowe, C. 1978. "The Historical Significance of Early Latin Votive Deposits (up to 4th Century BC)." In *Papers in Italian Archaeology I*, ed. H. McK. Blake, T. W. Potter, and D. B. Whitehouse. Oxford: BAR, 141–152.

Lulof, P. 2000. "Archaic Terracotta Acroteria Representing Athena and Heracles: Manifestations of Power in Central Italy." *JRA* 13, 207–219.

2006. "'Roofs from the South': Campanian Architectural Terracottas in Satricum." In *Deliciae Fictiles III*, ed. I. Edlund-Berry, G. Greco, and J. Kenfield. Oxford: Oxbow Books, 235–242.

Lulof, P. S., and E. M. Moorman. 1997. *Deliciae Fictiles II: Proceedings of the 2nd International Conference on Archaic Architectural Terracottas from Italy Held at the Netherlands Institute in Rome 12–13 June 1996*, ed. P. S. Lulof and E. M. Moormann. Amsterdam: Thesis.

Lulof, P. S., and C. Rescigno, eds. 2011. *Deliciae Fictiles IV: Architectural Terracottas in Ancient Italy: Images of Gods, Monsters and Heroes*. Oxford: Oxbow Books.

Lulof, P. S., and C. Smith. 2017. "The Age of Tarquinius Superbus. History and Archaeology." In *The Age of Tarquinius Superbus: Central Italy in the Late 6th Century*, ed. P. Lulof and C. Smith. Leuven: Peeters, 3–13.

Lulof, P. S., I. Manzini, and C. Rescigno, eds. 2019. *Deliciae Fictiles V: Networks and Workshops, Fifth International Conference on Architectural Terracottas and Decorative Roof Systems in Italy*. Oxford: Oxbow Books.

Manderscheid, H. 2015. "Dalla scarsità all'abbondanza: gestione idrica e architettura dell'acqua a Minturnae." In *Minturnae. Nuovi contributi alla conoscenza della forma urbis*, ed. G. R. Bellini and H. von Hesberg. Rome: Edizioni Quasar, 111–118.

2021. *"Nil Magis Mirandum in Toto Orbe Terrarum": Wasserbewirtschaftung, Hydrotechnik und Wasserarchitektur von Minturnae*. Wiesbaden: Harrassowitz.

Markowitsch, H. J. 2010. "Cultural Memory and the Neurosciences." In *A Companion to Cultural Memory Studies*, ed. A. Erll and A. Nünning. Berlin: de Gruyter, 275–283.

Marzolff, P., 2017. "Beobachtungen am ältesten keramischen Dachdecksystem." In *Werkspuren. Materialverarbeitung und handwerkliches Wissen im antiken Bauwesen*, ed. D. Kurapkat and U. Wulf-Rheidt. Regensburg: Verlag Schnell und Steiner, 179–190.

Maschek, D. 2008a. "Figur und Ornament. Das Tänzerinnenmonument von der Via Prenestina und die Produktion von Architekturdekor im römischen Suburbium des 1. Jhs. v. Chr." *Jahreshefte des Österreichischen Archäologischen Institutes* 77, 185–217.

2008b. "Neue Überlegungen zur Produktionsdynamik und kulturhistorischen Bedeutung mittelitalischer Rankenornamentik des ersten Jahrhunderts vor Christus." *RM* 114, 99–176.

2010. "Augustus und die Pracht der Blüten. Überlegungen zu den Rankenplatten aus den Horti Sallustiani in Rom." *Römische Historische Mitteilungen* 52: 79–119.

2012. *Rationes decoris. Aufkommen und Verbreitung dorischer Friese in der mittelitalischen Architektur des 2. und 1. Jahrhunderts v. Chr.* Vienna: Phoibos Verlag.

2014. "Der Tempel neue Kleider? Rezeptionsästhetische und semantische Aspekte von Bauornamentik im spätrepublikanischen Mittelitalien." In *Antike Bauornamentik: Grenzen und Möglichkeiten ihrer Erforschung*, ed. J. Lipps and D. Maschek. Wiesbaden: Dr. Ludwig Reichert Verlag, 181–202.

2022. "The Meaning of Building Materials in Late Republican Architecture: Moving from Semantics to Pragmatics." In *Materiality in Roman Art and Architecture. Aesthetics, Semantics and Function*, ed. A. Huag, A. Hielscher, and M. Taylor Lauritsen. Berlin: de Gruyter, 151–162.

Massa-Pairault, F.-H. 1973. "Un nouvel atelier de Volterra autour du 'Maître de Myrtilos.'" *MEFRA* 85.1, 91–135

1985a. *Recherches sur l'art et l'artisanat étrusco-italiques à l'époque hellénistique*. Rome: École française de Rome.

1985b. "Talamone e l'area costiera. Il tempio e il frontone." In *La Romanizzazione dell'Etruria: il territorio di Vulci*, ed. A. Carandini. Milan: Electa, 119–121.

1992. *Iconologia e politica nell'Italia antica: Roma, Lazio, Etruria dal VII al I secolo a.C.* Milan: Longanesi.

ed. 1999a. *Le mythe grec dans l'Italie antique: fonction et image. Actes du colloque international organisé par l'École française de Rome, l'Istituto italiano per gli studi filosofici (Naples) et l'UMR 126 du CNRS (Archéologies d'Orient et d'Occident): Rome, 14–16 novembre 1996.* Rome: École française de Rome.

1999b. "Mythe et identité politique. L'Étrurie du IVe siècle à l'époque hellénistique." In *Le mythe grec dans l'Italie antique: fonction et image. Actes du colloque international organisé par l'École française de Rome, l'Istituto italiano per gli studi filosofici (Naples) et l'UMR 126 du CNRS (Archéologies d'Orient et d'Occident): Rome, 14–16 novembre 1996*, ed. F.-H. Massa-Pairault. Rome: École française de Rome, 521–554.

2000. "Programmi decorativi dei templi etruschi e latini tardoarcaici." *ScAnt* 10, 427–456.

Massa-Pairault, F.-H., and J.-M. Pailler. 1979. *La maison aux salles souterraines. I: les terres cuites sous le péristyle.* Rome: École française de Rome.

Mastrocinque. A. 1993. "Eracle 'iperboreo' in Etruria." In *Ercole in Occidente*, ed. A. Mastrocinque. Trento: Università degli Studi di Trento, 49–61.

Mattingly, D. J., ed. 1997. *Dialogues in Roman Imperialism. Power, Discourse, and Discrepant Experience in the Roman Empire.* JRA Suppl. 23. Portsmouth, RI: Journal of Roman Archaeology.

2011. *Imperialism, Power, and Identity: Experiencing the Roman Empire.* Princeton: Princeton University Press.

McCann, A. M. 1987. "The Lagoon Temple." In *The Roman Port and Fishery of Cosa: A Center of Ancient Trade*, ed. A. M. McCann. Princeton: Princeton University Press, 129–136.

Megale, C. 2007. "Una lastra architettonica con ratto di Ganimede da Populonia." In *Materiali per Populonia 6*, ed. L. Botarelli, M. Coccoluto, and C. Mileti. Pisa: Edizioni ETS, 213–220.

Meiggs, R. 1960. *Roman Ostia.* Oxford: Clarendon Press.

Mengarelli, R. 1936. "Il luogo e i materiali del tempio di Hera a Caere." *StEtr* 10, 67–86.

Meritt, L. S., and I. Edlund-Berry. 2000. *Etruscan and Republican Roman Mouldings.* Philadelphia: University of Pennsylvania Press.

Mertens-Horn. M. 1990. "Archaische Tondächer westgriechischer Typologie in Delphi und Olympia." *Hesperia* 59, 235–248.

Mesolella, G. 2012. *La decorazione architettonica di Minturnae, Formiae, Tarracina: l'età augustea e giulio-claudia.* Rome: "L'Erma" di Bretschneider.

Meyers, G., A. Steiner, Z. Ni, and S. Mertzman. 2019. "Roof Tile Production in a Diverse Craft Industry: New Geochemical Evidence from Poggio Colla." In *Deliciae Fictiles V. Networks and Workshops*, ed. P. Lulof, I. Manzini, and C. Rescigno. Oxford: Oxbow Books, 537–540.

Miles, N. C. 2016. "Die Himmel über Berlin: Constructing and Resisting Citizenship through Occupations of the Divided City's Aerial Space." *Opticon1826*, 1–17.

Millett, M. 1990. *The Romanization of Britain: An Essay in Archaeological Interpretation.* Cambridge: Cambridge University Press.

2007. "Urban Topography and Social Identity in the Tiber Valley." In *Roman by Integration: Dimensions of Group Identity in Material Culture and Text*, ed. R. Roth and J. Keller. JRA Suppl. 66. Portsmouth, RI: Journal of Roman Archaeology, 71–82.

Mingazzini, P. 1938. "Il santuario della dea Marica alle foci del Garigliano." In *MonAnt* 37, 693–984.

Mogetta, M. 2019. "Monumentality, Building Techniques, and Identity Construction in Roman Italy: The Remaking of Cosa, post-197 BCE." In *Size Matters: Understanding Monumentality Across Ancient Civilizations*, ed. F. Buccellati, S. Hageneuer, S. van der Heyden, and F. Levenson. Bielefeld: Transcript Verlag, 241–268.

2021. *The Origins of Concrete Construction in Roman Architecture: Technology and Society in Republican Italy.* Cambridge: Cambridge University Press.

Moltesen, M. 2009. "Diana and Her Followers in a Late Republican Temple Pediment from Nemi: A Preliminary Note." In *From Artemis to Diana: The Goddess of Man and Beast*, ed. T. Fischer-Hansen and B. Poulsen. Copenhagen: Museum Tusculanum Press, 345–367.

Montagna Pasquinucci, M. 1973. "La decorazione architettonica del tempio del divo

Giulio nel Foro Romano." *MonAnt Serie miscellanea I*, 4: 257–280.

Moore, D. 2021. "The Etruscan Roots of the Reinheim Armring." *Germania* 99, 37–55.

Moser, C. 2019. *The Altars of Republican Rome and Latium: Sacrifice and the Materiality of Roman Religion*. New York: Cambridge University Press.

Mouritsen, H. 1998. *Italian Unification: A Study in Ancient and Modern Historiography*. London: Institute of Classical Studies.

Muccigrosso, J. 1998. "Factional Competition and Monumental Construction in Mid-Republican Rome." PhD diss., University of Michigan.

Mullen, A. 2011. "Latin and Other Languages: Societal and Individual Bilingualism." In *A Companion to the Latin Language*, ed. J. Clackson. Chichester: Wiley-Blackwell, 527–548.

Nair, S. 2015. *At Home with the Sapa Inca. Architecture, Space, and Legacy at Chinchero*. Austin: University of Texas Press.

Necipoğlu, G., and A. Payne, eds. 2016. *Histories of Ornament: From Global to Local*. Princeton: Princeton University Press.

Nielsen, E. 1987. "Some Preliminary Thoughts on New and Old Terracottas." *OpRom* 16, 91–119.

1994. "Interpreting the Lateral Sima at Poggio Civitate." In *Murlo and the Etruscans. Art and Society in Ancient Etruria*, ed. R. D. De Puma and B. P. Small. Madison: University of Wisconsin Press, 64–71.

Nielsen, M. 1993. "Cultural Orientations in Etruria in the Hellenistic Period. Greek Myths and Local Motifs on Volterran Urn Reliefs." *Acta Hyperborea* 5, 319–357.

2004. "The Three Ages of Man. Myth and Symbol Between Chiusi and Athens." In *Myth and Symbol II: Symbolic Phenomena in Ancient Greek Culture*, ed. S. des Bouvrie. Bergen: The Norwegian Institute at Athens, 25–41.

Nielsen, M., and A. Rathje. 2009. "Artumes in Etruria – the Borrowed Goddess." In *From Artemis to Diana. The Goddess of Man and Beast*, ed. T. Fischer-Hansen and B. Poulsen. Copenhagen: Museum Tusculanum Press, 261–301.

Nilson, K. A., C. B. Persson, S. Sande, and J. Zahle. 2009. *The Temple of Castor and Pollux III: The Augustan Temple*. Rome: "L'Erma" di Bretschneider.

Nijboer, A. J. 1991. "Funerary Symbols on the Temple Decorations from the Talamonaccio." *PIA* 2, 17–28.

Nonnis. D. 2019. "I frammenti dell'iscrizione monumentale in terracotta del tempio sub-urbano sulla via Latina." In *Fregellae. Il tempio del Foro e il tempio suburbano sulla via Latina*, ed. G. Battaglini, F. Coarelli, and F. Diosono. Rome: Giorgio Bretschneider, 145–149.

Nora, P. 1984. *Les Lieux de mémoire*. Paris: Gallimard.

1989. "Between Memory and History: Les Lieux de Mémoire." *Representations* 26, 7–24.

Olick, J. K., and J. Robbins. 1998. "Social Memory Studies: From 'Collective Memory' to the Historical Sociology of Mnemonic Practices." *Annual Review of Sociology* 24, 105–140.

Olick, J. K., V. Vinitzky-Seroussi, and D. Levy. 2011. *The Collective Memory Reader*. New York: Oxford University Press.

Orlin, E. 2007. "Augustan Religion and the Reshaping of Roman Memory." *Arethusa* 40.1. *Reshaping Rome: Space, Time, and Memory in the Augustan Transformation*, 73–92.

2022. "Mos et Ritus Sacrorum: Religion in the Construction of Augustan Italy." In *Nos sumus Romani qui fuimus ante ... Memory of Ancient Italy*, ed. M. Aberson, M. C. Biella, M. di Fazio, M. Wullschleger. Lausanne: Peter Lang Verlag, 119–128

Padilla Peralta, D., and S. Bernard. 2022. "Middle Republican Connectivities." *JRS* 112, 1–37.

Painter, K. 2002. "Campana Reliefs." In *The Via Gabina Villas. Sites 10, 11 and 13*, http://viagabina.rice.edu/campana/index.html.

Panella, C., C. Rescigno, and A. F. Ferrandes. 2021. *Architetture perdute. Decorazioni architettoniche fittili dagli scavi tra Palatino, Velia e valle del Colosseo (VII–IV secolo a. C.)*. Naples: Naus Editoria.

Parisi Presicce, C., and A. Danti. 2016. "Le indagini archeologiche nell'area dell'ex Ospedale Teutonico." In *Campidoglio: Mito, memoria, archeologia*, ed. C. Parisi Presicce and A. Danti. Rome: Campisano Editore, 229–235.

Parker, A. J. 1992. *Ancient Shipwrecks of the Mediterranean and the Roman Provinces*. Oxford: Tempus Reparatum.

Partida, E. C. 2024. "Campana Reliefs Produced in Achaea (Greece)." In *Campana-Reliefs: Neue Forschungen zu römischem Architekturdekor aus Terrakotta, Akten der Internationalen Tagung Heidelberg, 8.–10. April 2021*, ed. A. Reinhardt. Heidelberg: Propylaeum, 61–85.

Patterson, J. R. 2000. *Political Life in the City of Rome*. London: Bristol Classical Press.

Pedacchioni, A. 2019. "Le terrecotte architettoniche del tempio del Foro." In *Fregellae. Il tempio del Foro e il tempio suburbano sulla via Latina*, ed. G. Battaglini, F. Coarelli, and F. Diosono. Rome: Giorgio Bretschneider, 29–42.

Pelgrom, J. 2008. "Settlement Organization and Land Distribution in Latin Colonies before the Second Punic War." In *People, Land, and Politics, Demographic Developments and the Transformation of Roman Italy, 300 BC–AD 14*, ed. L. de Ligt and S. Northwood. Leiden: Brill, 333–372.

Pelgrom, J., and T. D. Stek. 2014. "Roman Colonization under the Republic: Historiographical Contextualization of a Paradigm." In *Roman Republican Colonization. New Perspectives from Archaeology and Ancient History*, ed. T. D. Stek, and J. Pelgrom. Rome: Palombi, 11–41.

Pellegrino, A. 1986. "Il culto di Vulcano ad Ostia: nuove testimonianze." In *Decima miscellanea greca e romana*. Rome: Istituto italiano per la storia antica, 289–301.

Pensa, M. 1983. "La decorazione architettonica fittile in Emilia-Romagna: Aspetti e problemi." *Studi sulla città antica. L'Emilia-Romagna*. Rome: "L'Erma" di Bretschneider, 383–397.

Pensabene, P. 1998. "Il fenomeno del marmo nella Roma tardo-repubblicana e imperiale." In *Marmi antichi II: Cave e tecnica di lavorazione, provenienze e distribuzione*, ed. P. Pensabene. Rome: "L'Erma" di Bretschneider, 333–390.

1999. *Terrecotte del Museo Nazionale Romano I. Gocciolatoi e protomi da sime*. Rome: "L'Erma" di Bretschneider.

2001. "Contributo delle terrecotte architettoniche alla definizione dei luoghi di culto dell'area sud occidentale del Palatino." *Ostraka* 10, 81–103.

2002. "Il fenomeno del marmo nel mondo romano." In *I marmi colorati della Roma imperiale*, ed. M. De Nuccio and L. Ungaro. Venice: Marsilio, 3–67.

2017. *Scavi del Palatino 2. Culti, architettura e decorazioni. Tomo 2, La "Casa dei Grifi," la Casa di Ottaviano-Augusto e il Tempio di Apollo*. Rome: 'L'Erma' di Bretshneider.

Pensabene, P., and M. R. Sanzi Di Mino. 1983. *Museo Nazionale Romano: Le terrecotte III, 1, Antefisse*. Rome: De Luca Editore.

Percossi Serenelli, E. 2009. "Su alcuni tipi di terrecotte architettoniche da Potentia." In *Omaggio a Nereo Alfieri. Contributi all'archeologia marchigiana*, ed. G. De Marinis and G. Paci. Tivoli: Edizioni TORED, 439–490.

Perret, J. 1942. *Les origines de la légende troyenne de Rome*. Paris: Société d'édition "Les Belles lettres."

Perry, E. 2005. *The Aesthetics of Emulation in the Visual Arts of Ancient Rome*. Cambridge: Cambridge University Press.

Perry, R. 1997. *Die Campanareliefs*. Mainz: Philipp von Zabern.

Pignocchi, G. 1996. "Le terrecotte architettoniche del Colle della Guardia (Offida-AP)." *Picus* XVI–XVII, 203–229.

Platt, V. 2017. "Framing Pictorial Space: Introduction." In *The Frame in Classical Art: A Cultural History*, ed. V. Platt and M. J. Squire. Cambridge: Cambridge University Press, 102–116.

Platt, V., and M. J. Squire. 2017a. *The Frame in Classical Art: A Cultural History*. Cambridge: Cambridge University Press.

2017b. "Framing the Visual in Greek and Roman Antiquity: An Introduction." In *The Frame in Classical Art: A Cultural History*, ed. V. Platt and M. J. Squire. Cambridge: Cambridge University Press, 3–99.

Poccetti, P. 1979. *Nuovi documenti italici: A complemento del manuale di E. Vetter*. Pisa: Giardini Editori e Stampatori.

Pollini, J. 2012. "The Acanthus of the Ara Pacis as an Apolline and Dionysiac Symbol of Anamorphosis, Anakyklosis, and Numen Mixtum." In *From Republic to Empire: Rhetoric, Religion, and Power in the Visual Culture of Ancient Rome*. Norman: University of Oklahoma Press, 271–308.

Pommer, R. 1983. "The Flat Roof: A Modernist Controversy in Germany." *Art Journal* 43.2, 158–169.

Popkin, M. L. 2015. "Decorum and the Meanings of Materials in Triumphal Architecture of Republican Rome." *JSAH* 74.3, 289–311.

2016. *The Architecture of the Roman Triumph. Monuments, Memory, and Identity*. New York: Cambridge University Press.

2022. *Souvenirs and the Experience of Empire in Ancient Rome*. New York: Cambridge University Press.

Popkin, M. L., and D. Y. Ng. 2022. *Future Thinking in Roman Culture. New Approaches to History, Memory, and Cognition*. London and New York: Routledge.

Porter, J. I. 2010. *The Origins of Aesthetic Thought in Ancient Greece: Matter, Sensation, and Experience*. Cambridge: Cambridge University Press.

Poucet, J. 1985. *Les origines de Rome*. Brussels: Facultés universitaires Saint-Louis.

Poulsen, B., and C. Grønne. 1988. "Ricerche nel Vicus Tuscus lungo il lato ovest del Tempio dei Castori." *Archeologia Laziale* IX, 27–31.

1992. "Cult, Myth and Politics." In *The Temple of Castor and Pollux. The Pre-Augustan Temple Phases with Related Decorative Elements*, ed. I. Nielsen and B. Poulsen. Rome: Edizioni De Luca, 46–53.

Pullen, D. J. 1986. "A 'House of the Tiles' at Zygouries? The Function of Monumental Early Helladic Architecture." In *Early Helladic Architecture and Urbanization. Proceedings of a Seminar Held at the Swedish Institute in Athens, June 8, 1985*, ed. R. Hägg and D. Konsola. Göteborg: Paul Åströms Förlag, 79–84.

Pupilli, L., and C. Costanzi. 1990. *Fermo*. Bologna: Calderini.

Quinn, J. C., and A. Wilson. 2013. "Capitolia." *JRS* 103, 117–173.

Radet, G. 1909. *Cybélé: Étude sur les transformations plastiques d'un type divin*. Bordeaux: Féret.

Rakob, F., and W.-D. Heilmeyer. 1973. *Der Rundtempel am Tiber in Rom*. Mainz: von Zabern.

Ramage, A. 1978. *Lydian Houses and Architectural Terracottas*. Cambridge, MA: Harvard University Press.

Reggiani, A. M., ed. 1998. *Tivoli: il santuario di Ercole vincitore*. Milan: Electa.

Reinhardt, A. 2018. "Delectari varietate: Zur Erklärung der repetitiven Darstellung auf dem, Puteal Tegel.'" In *Ornament and Figure in Graeco-Roman Art: Rethinking Visual Ontologies in Classical Antiquity*, ed. N. Dietrich and M. Squire. Berlin: de Gruyter, 299–325.

2022. "Diverging Trends in the Visual Appearance of Fired Clay in Roman Architecture: 'Campana Plaques' and Terracotta Facades." In *Materiality in Roman Art and Architecture. Aesthetics, Semantics and Function*, ed. A. Haug, A. Hielscher, and M. Taylor Lauritsen. Berlin: de Gruyter, 131–148.

ed. 2024. *Campana-Reliefs: Neue Forschungen zu römischem Architekturdekor aus Terrakotta, Akten der Internationalen Tagung Heidelberg, 8.–10. April 2021*. Heidelberg: Propylaeum.

Rescigno, C. 1998. *Tetti campani. Età arcaica. Cuma, Pitecusa e gli altri contesti*. Rome: G. Bretschneider.

Rescigno, C., and V. Sampaolo. 2006. "Appunti sull'impiego del colore sulle terrecotte architettoniche capuane." *Mediterranea* II 2005, 133–163.

Ricci, L. 2019. "Hellenistic Monumental Sanctuaries in Late Republican Latium: The Advantages of a Semantic Approach." *Graeco-Latina Brunensia* 24: 1, 181–194.

Richardson, L. 1992. *A New Topographical Dictionary of Ancient Rome*. Baltimore: The Johns Hopkins University Press.

Ridgway, B. S. 1977. *The Archaic Style in Greek Sculpture*. Princeton: Princeton University Press.

Riis, P. J. 1941. *Tyrrhenika: An Archaeological Study of the Etruscan Sculpture in the Archaic and Classical Periods*. Copenhagen: Einar Munksgaard.

1981. *Etruscan Types of Heads: A Revised Chronology of the Archaic and Classical Terracottas of Etruscan Campania and Central Italy*. København: Royal Danish Academy of Sciences and Letters.

Rizzo, M. A. 1977. "Su alcuni nuclei di lastre 'Campana' di provenienza nota." *Rivista dell'Istituto Nazionale d'Archeologia e Storia dell'Arte*, 23–24, 5–93.

Robinson, E. C. 2021. *Urban Transformation in Ancient Molise: The Integration of Larinum into the Roman State*. New York: Oxford University Press.

Roller, L. E. 1999. *In Search of God the Mother: The Cult of Anatolian Cybele*. Berkeley and Los Angeles: University of California Press.

Romanelli, P. 1939. "Gruppo fittile rinvenuto a Tarquinia." *Le Arti* I, 436–441.

1948. "Tarquinia. Scavi e ricerche nell'area della città." *NSc*, 193–270.

Ronzitti Orsolini, G. 1971. *Il mito dei Sette a Tebe nelle urne volterrane*. Florence: La Nuova Italia.

Rose, C. B. 2002. "Bilingual Trojan Iconography." In *Mauerschau: Festschrift für Manfred Korfmann*, ed. R. Aslan, S. Blum, G. Kastl, F. Schweizer, and D. Thumm. Remshalden-Grunbach: B.A. Greiner, 329–350.

2008. "Forging Identity in the Roman Republic: Trojan Ancestry and Veristic Portraiture." In *Role Models in the Roman World: Identity and Assimilation*, ed. S. Bell and I. L. Hansen. Ann Arbor: University of Michigan Press, 97–123.

2015. "The Homeric Memory Culture of Roman Ilion." In *Cultural Memories in the Roman Empire*, ed. K. Galinksy and K. Lapatin. Los Angeles: J. Paul Getty Museum, 134–152.

Roselaar, S. T. 2010. *Public Land in the Roman Republic. A Social and Economic History of Ager Publicus in Italy, 396–89 BCE*. New York: Oxford University Press.

2011. "Colonies and Processes of Integration in the Roman Republic." *MERFA* 123.2, 527–555.

Rosenstein, N. S. 1990. *Imperatores Victi: Military Defeat and Aristocratic Competition in the Middle and Late Republic*. Berkeley: University of California Press.

Rossi, C. 2011. "Santuario in loc. Le Salzare, Fosso dell'Incastro, Ardea (Roma). Il frontone del tempio tardo repubblicano." In *Deliciae Fictiles IV: Architectural Terracottas in Ancient Italy: Images of Gods, Monsters and Heroes*, ed. P. Lulof and C. Rescigno. Oxford: Oxbow Books, 287–294.

2018. "La decorazione architettonica fittile del Tempio A." In *Castrum Inui. Il Santuario di Inuus alla foce del Fosso dell'Incastro*, ed. M. Torelli and E. Marroni. Rome: Giorgio Bretschneider, 343–362.

Rossini, G. 2007. "Lastre Campana dalle pendici del Campidoglio." In *Museo e territorio V*, ed. M. Angle and A. Germno. Rome: Bonsignori, 81–90.

Rossini, O. 2010. "I colori dell'Ara Pacis: Storia di un esperimento." *Archeomatica* 3: 20–25.

Roth, R. 2007. "Introduction: Roman Culture between Homogeneity and Integration." In *Roman by Integration: Dimensions of Group Identity in Material Culture and Text*, ed. R. Roth and J. Keller. JRA Suppl. 66. Portsmouth, RI: Journal of Roman Archaeology, 7–10.

2013. "Trading Identities." In *Creating Ethnicities and Identities in the Roman World*, ed. A. Gardner, E. Herring, and K. Lomas. London: University of London, 93–111.

2017. "Beyond Romanisation: Settlement, Networks and Material Culture in Italy,

c. 300–90 BC." In *The Peoples of Ancient Italy*, ed. G. D. Farney and G. Bradley. Berlin: De Gruyter, 295–317.

Roth, R., and J. Keller, eds. 2007. *Roman by Integration: Dimensions of Group Identity in Material Culture and Text*. JRA Suppl. 66. Portsmouth, RI: Journal of Roman Archaeology.

Rous, B. D. 2009. "No Place for Cult. The Sacred Landscape of Latium in the Late Republic." *BABESCH* 84, 53–84.

2010. "Triumphs of Compromise: An Analysis of the Monumentalisation of Sanctuaries in Latium in the Late Republican Period (Second and First Centuries BC)." PhD diss., University of Amsterdam.

2011. "An Age without Images: Architectural Decoration in the Late Republican Period." In *Deliciae Fictiles IV: Architectural Terracottas in Ancient Italy: Images of Gods, Monsters and Heroes*, ed. P. Lulof and C. Rescigno. Oxford: Oxbow Books, 84–94.

Roymans, N., and M. Fernández-Götz. 2019. "Reconsidering the Roman Conquest: New Archeological Perspectives." *JRA* 32, 415–420.

Ruegg, D. S. 1988. "Minturnae: A Roman River Seaport on the Garigliano River, Italy." In *Archaeology of Coastal Changes: Proceedings of the First International Symposium "Cities on the Sea – Past and present," Haifa, Israel, September 22–29*, ed. A. Raban. Oxford: B.A.R., 209–228.

1995. *Underwater Investigations at Roman Minturnae: Liris-Garigliano River*. Jonsered: Paul Åströms Förlag.

Russo, G., E. Ceccaroni, A. M. Conte, L. Medeghini, C. De Vito, and S. Mignardi. 2022. "Archaeometric Study of Roman Painted Terracottas from the Sanctuary of Hercules in Alba Fucens (Abruzzo, Italy). *Minerals* 12, 346. https://doi.org/10.3390/min12030346.

Rystedt, E. 1983. *Acquarossa IV: Early Etruscan acroteria from Acquarossa and Poggio Civitate (Murlo)*. Stockholm: P. Aström.

Rystedt, E., C. Wikander, and Ö. Wikander. 1993. *Deliciae Fictiles: Proceedings of the First International Conference on Central Italic Architectural Terracottas at the Swedish Institute in Rome, 10–12 December 1990*. Stockholm: Svenska Institutet.

Salmon, E. T. 1969. *Roman Colonization under the Republic*. Ithaca: Cornell University Press.

Santostefano, A. 2019. "Tra sapere tecnico e sperimentazione: la fabbrica di Gela attraverso l'analisi di terrecotte architettoniche da due aree santuariali." In *Deliciae Fictiles V. Networks and Workshops*, ed. P. Lulof, I. Manzini, and C. Rescigno. Oxford: Oxbow Books, 165–177.

Sauron, G. 1982. "Le Message symbolique des rinceaux de l'Ara Pacis Augustae." *Comptes-rendus des séances de l'Académie des Inscriptions et Belles-Lettres* 126.1, 81–101.

Scatozza Höricht, L. A. 2019. "Un sistema di rivestimento fittile condiviso a Pitecusa, Cuma e Pompei nel primo Ellenismo." In *Deliciae Fictiles V. Networks and Workshops*, ed. P. Lulof, I. Manzini, and C. Rescigno. Oxford: Oxbow Books, 284–292.

Scheid, J. 1993. "Lucus, nemus. Qu'est-ce qu'un bois sacré?" In *Les bois sacrés. Actes du colloque international organisé par le Centre Jean Bérard et l'École Pratique des Hautes Études*, ed. O. Le Cazanove and J. Scheid. Naples: Centre Jean Bérard, 13–20.

2012. "The Festivals of the Forum Boarium Area. Reflections on the Construction of Complex Representations of Roman Identity." In *Greek and Roman Festivals. Content, Meaning, and Practice*, ed. J. R. Brandt and J. W. Iddeng. Oxford: Oxford University Press, 289–304.

Schmidt, E. 1922. *Archaistische Kunst in Griechenland und Rom*. München: B. Heller.

Schultz, P., and R. von den Hoff, ed. 2009. *Structure, Image, Ornament: Architectural Sculpture in the Greek World*. Oxford: Oxbow.

Scott, R. T. 1992. "The Decorations in Terracotta from the Temples at Cosa." In *La coroplastica templare etrusca fra il IV e il II secolo a.C. Atti del XVI convegno di studi etruschi ed italici, Orbetello, 25–29 aprile 1988.* Firenze: L.S. Olschki, 91–100.

2019. "Cosa: How Perfect! How Come?" In *Cosa and the Colonial Landscape of Republican Italy (Third and Second Centuries BCE)*, ed. A. U. De Giorgi. Ann Arbor: University of Michigan Press, 21–29.

Scott, R. T., A. U. De Giorgi, S. Crawford-Brown, A. Glennie, and A. Smith. 2015. "Cosa Excavations: The 2013 Report." *Orizzonti* XVI, 11–22.

Scullard, H. H. 1981. *Festivals and Ceremonies of the Roman Republic.* London: Thames and Hudson.

Sewell, J. 2005. "Trading Places? A Reappraisal of the Fora at Cosa." *Ostraka* 14.1, 91–114.

2010. *The Formation of Roman Urbanism, 338–200 B.C.: Between contemporary foreign influence and Roman tradition.* JRA Suppl. 79. Portsmouth, RI: Journal of Roman Archaeology.

2014. "Gellius, Philip II and a Proposed End to the 'Model-Replica' Debate." In *Roman Republican Colonization. New Perspectives from Archaeology and Ancient History*, ed. T. D. Stek and J. Pelgrom. Rome: Palombi, 125–139.

Shepherd, E. J. 2006. "Laterizi da copertura e da costruzione." *Rassegna di Archeologia classica e postclassica* 22B, 165–200.

2007. "Considerazioni sulla tipologia e diffusione dei laterizi da copertura nell'Italia tardo-repubblicana." *BullCom* CVIII, 55–88.

2015. "Tegole piane di età romana: Una tipologia influenzata dalle culture 'locali,' una diffusione stimolata dall'espansione militare." *Archeologia dell'Architettura* XX, 120–132.

2016. "Tegole di copertura in età romana: Questioni di forma, posa in opera e impiego." *Costruire in Laterizio* 168, 54–59.

Siwicki, C. 2020. *Architectural Restoration and Heritage in Imperial Rome.* Oxford: Oxford University Press.

Small, J. P. 1981. *Studies Related to the Theban Cycle on Late Etruscan Urns.* Rome: Giorgio Bretschneider.

Smith, C. 2012. "The Feriae Latinae." In *Greek and Roman Festivals. Content, Meaning, and Practice*, ed. J. R. Brandt and J. W. Iddeng. Oxford: Oxford University Press, 267–288.

Söderlind, M. 2006. "The Function of the Terracottas from Selvasecca." In *Deliciae Fictiles III*, ed. I. Edlund-Berry, G. Greco, and J. Kenfield. Oxford: Oxbow Books, 116–121.

Solin, H. 1999. "Epigrafia repubblicana. Bilancio, novità, prospettive." In *XI Congresso Internazionale di Epigrafia Greca e Latina, Roma 1997. Atti, I.* Rome: Quasar, 379–404.

Sironen, T. 1997. "Un graffito in latino arcaico su un frammento di terracotta da Fregellae." *Zeitschrift für Papyrologie und Epigraphik* 115, 242–244.

Spartz, E. 1962. "Das Wappenbild des Herrn und der Herrin der Tiere in der minoisch-mykenischen und frühgriechischen Kunst." PhD diss., University of Munich.

Squire, M. 2017. "Framing the Roman 'Still Life': Campanian Wall-painting and the Frames of Mural Make-believe." In *The Frame in Classical Art: A Cultural History*, ed. V. Platt and M. J. Squire. Cambridge: Cambridge University Press, 188–253.

Stamper, J. 2005. *The Architecture of Roman Temples: The Republic to the Middle Empire.* Cambridge and New York: Cambridge University Press.

Steinhardt, N. 2019. *Chinese Architecture: A History.* Princeton: Princeton University Press.

Stek, T. D. 2009. *Cult Places and Cultural Change in Republican Italy: A Contextual Approach to Religious Aspects of Rural Society after the Roman Conquest.* Amsterdam: Amsterdam University Press.

Stek, T. D., and G.-J. Burgers. 2015. *The Impact of Rome on Cult Places and Religious Practices in Ancient Italy.* London: Institute of Classical Studies.

Stek, T. D., and J. Pelgrom, eds. 2014. *Roman Republican Colonization. New Perspectives from Archaeology and Ancient History.* Rome: Palombi.

Stoddart, S. 2020. *Power and Place in Etruria. The Spatial Dynamics of a Mediterranean Civilization, 1200–500 BC*. Cambridge: Cambridge University Press.

Stolle, R. 1999. *Ambitus et Invidia. Römische Politiker im Spannungsfeld zwischen persönlichem Ehrgeiz und Forderungen der Standesloyalität 200–133 v.Chr.* Frankfurt am Main/New York: Lang.

Stopponi, S. 1979. "Terrecotte architettoniche dal santuario di Punta della Vipera." In *Studi in onore di Filippo Magi*, ed. M. Bergamini Simoni. Perugia: E.U.COOP, 249–283.

2006. "Volsiniensia disiecta membra." In *Deliciae Fictiles III*, ed. I. Edlund-Berry, G. Greco, and J. Kenfield. Oxford: Oxbow Books, 210–221.

Stortoni, E. 2013. "La raccolta archeologica del Museo Comunale di Fermo: note su alcune terrecotte architettoniche romane." *Il Capitale Culturale. Studies on the Value of Cultural Heritage* 7, 285–303.

Strauss, E. J. 2007. "Roman Cargoes: Underwater Evidence from the Eastern Mediterranean." PhD diss., University College London.

Strazzulla, M. J. 1977. "Le terrecotte architettoniche nell'Italia centrale." In *Caratteri dell'ellenismo nelle urne etrusche*, ed. M. Martelli and M. Cristofani. Florence: Centro Di, 41–49.

1981. "Le terrecotte architettoniche. Le produzioni dal IV al I sec. a.C." In *Società romana e produzione schiavistica*, ed. A. Giardina and A. Schiavone. Bari: Laterza, 187–198.

1984. "Terrecotte architettoniche del Museo Civico di Bassano del Grappa." *Archeologia Veneta* 7, 167–190.

1985. "Cosa e il suo territorio. Le terrecotte architettoniche." In *La Romanizzazione dell'Etruria: il territorio di Vulci*, ed. A. Carandini. Milan: Electa, 97–100.

1987. *Le terrecotte architettoniche della Venetia romana: Contributo allo studio della produzione fittile nella Cisalpina (II a.C.–II d.C.).* Roma: "L'Erma" di Bretschneider.

1992. "Le terrecotte architettoniche frontonali di Luni nel problema della coroplastica templare nelle colonie in territorio etrusco." In *La coroplastica templare etrusca fra il IV e il II secolo a.C.: atti del XVI convegno di studi etruschi e italici, Orbetello 25–29 aprile 1988*, ed. G. Maetzke. Florence: Leo S. Olschki Editore, 161–183.

1993. "Fortuna etrusca e Fortuna romana: Due cicli decorativi a confronto (Roma, via S. Gregorio e Bolsena)." *Ostraka* 2.2, 317–349.

1995. "Alcune considerazioni sulle lastre Campana con bollo: le sime con pantere e tirso." In *Splendida civitas nostra: Miscellanea di studi archeologici in onore di Antonio Frova*, ed. G. Cavalieri Manasse and E. Roffia. Rome: Quasar, 409–415.

2006a. "Ancora sul frontone di via di San Gregorio: alcune considerazioni." *ScAnt* 13, 249–264.

2006b. "Le terrecotte architettoniche nei territori italici." In *Deliciae Fictiles III*, ed. I. Edlund-Berry, G. Greco, and J. Kenfield. Oxford: Oxbow Books, 25–42.

2007. "L'uso delle immagini nell'edilizia pubblica dell'ellenismo a Roma e nel mondo etrusco-italico." In *Images et modernité hellénistiques: appropriation et représentation du monde d'Alexandre à César*, ed. F.-H. Massa-Pairault and G. Sauron. Rome: École française de Rome, 139–161.

2010. "L'architettura religiosa di Roma tra tradizione e innovazione." In *I giorni di Roma: L'età della conquista*, ed. E. La Rocca and C. Parisi Presicce. Rome: Skira, 83–94.

Strazzulla, M. J., L. Ferrea, L. Anselmino. 1990–1991. "Il frontone di via di San Gregorio ed il tempio della Fortuna Respiciens sul Palatino: una nuova ipotesi." *RendPontAc* 63, 193–262.

Tarpin, M. 2014. "Strangers in Paradise. Latins (and Other Non-Romans) in Colonial Context: A Short Story of Territorial Complexity." In *Roman Republican Colonization. New Perspectives from Archaeology and Ancient History*, ed. T. D.

Stek and J. Pelgrom. Rome: Palombi, 161–191.

Taylor, D. M. 1957. *Cosa: Black-Glaze Pottery*. MAAR 25. Ann Arbor: University of Michigan Press.

Taylor, M., and H. C. Bradshaw. 1916. "Architectural Terra-cottas from Two Temples at Falerii Veteres." *PBSR* 18.1, 1–34.

Taylor, R. 2002. "Temples and Terracottas at Cosa." *AJA* 106:1, 59–83.

Ten, A. 1998. "Santuario di Ercole Vincitore a Tivoli: Nuove acquisizioni." *RendPontAcc* 71, 327–345.

Terrenato, N. 1998a. "The Romanization of Italy: Global Acculturation or Cultural Bricolage?" In *TRAC 97: Proceedings of the 7th Theoretical Roman Archaeology Conference*. Oxford: Oxbow, 20–27.

1998b. "Tam firmum municipium: The Romanization of Volaterrae and Its Cultural Implications." *JRS* 88, 94–114.

2019. *The Early Roman Expansion into Italy: Elite Negotiation and Family Agendas*. Cambridge: Cambridge University Press.

Thomas, E. 2007. *Monumentality and the Roman Empire: Architecture in the Antonine Age*. Oxford: Oxford University Press.

Tomei, M. A. 1992. "Statue di terracotta dal Palatino." *RM* 99, 171–228.

Torelli, M. 1965. "Tempio etrusco in località 'Punta della Vipera.'" *BdA* 50, 125–126.

1967. "Terza campagna di scavi a Punta della Vipera (S. Marinella)." *SE* XXXV, 331–352.

1982. *Typology and Structure of Roman Historical Reliefs*. Ann Arbor: University of Michigan Press.

1993. "Fictiles fabulae. Rappresentazione e romanizzazione nei cicli figurati fittili repubblicani." *Ostraka* 2, 269–299.

1995. *Studies in the Romanization of Italy*. Edmonton: University of Alberta Press.

1997. *Il rango, il rito e l'immagine. Alle origini della rappresentazione storica romana*. Milan: Electa.

1999. *Tota Italia: Essays in the Cultural Formation of Roman Italy*. Oxford: Oxford University Press.

2004. "Gli dei di terracotta: Il frontone di Via di S. Gregorio in una mostra romana." *Ostraka* 13.1, 133–161.

2018. "Storia del santuario di Castrum Inui e dei suoi culti: Inuus, Indiges, Aeneas." In *Castrum Inui. Il Santuario di Inuus alla foce del Fosso dell'Incastro*, ed. M. Torelli and E. Marroni. Rome: Giorgio Bretschneider, 481–539.

Tortorella, S. 1981a. "Le lastre campana." In *Società romana e produzione schiavistica. Vol. 2: Merci, mercati e scambi nel Mediterraneo*, ed. A. Giardina and A. Schiavone. Bari: Laterza, 219–235.

1981b. "Le lastre Campana: problemi di produzione e di iconografia." In *L'art décoratif à Rome à la fin de la République et au début du Principat: table ronde organisé par l'École française de Rome (Rome, 10–11 mai 1979)*, ed. X. Lafon. Rome: École française de Rome, 61–80.

2018. "Terrecotte architettoniche, stucchi, pitture. Affinità reciproche tra generi diversi di arte decorativa." *Archeologia Classica* 69, 197–222.

2019. "Lastre fittili architettoniche del tipo Campana in edifici sacri: un aggiornamento." In *Una lezione di archeologia globale. Studi in onore di Daniele Manacorda*, ed. M. Modolo, S. Pallecchi, G. Volpe, E. Zanini. Bari: Edipuglia, 205–213.

2024. "Lastre Campana. Aspetti della produzione e ruolo delle *figlinae* polivalenti." In *Campana-Reliefs: Neue Forschungen zu römischem Architekturdekor aus Terrakotta, Akten der Internationalen Tagung Heidelberg, 8.–10. April 2021*, ed. A. Reinhardt. Heidelberg: Propylaeum, 37–59.

Touchette, L.-A. 2015. "Archaism and Eclecticism." In *The Oxford Handbook of Roman Sculpture*, ed. E. A. Friedland, M. G. Sobocinski, and E. K. Gazda. New York: Oxford University Press, 292–306.

Tucci, P. L. 1997. "Dov'erano il tempio di Nettuno e la nave di Enea?" *BullCom* 98: 15–42.

Tuck, A. 2006. "The Social and Political Context of the 7th Century Architectural

Terracottas at Poggio Civitate (Murlo)." In *Deliciae Fictiles III*, ed. I. Edlund-Berry, G. Greco, and J. Kenfield. Oxford: Oxbow Books, 130–135.

2010. "Mistress and Master: The Politics of Iconography in Pre-Roman Central Italy." In *The Master of the Animals in Old World Iconography*, ed. D. B. Counts and B. Arnold. Budapest: Archaeolingua, 211–221.

2021. *Poggio Civitate (Murlo)*. Austin: University of Texas Press.

Tulving, E., and F. I. M. Craik, eds. 2000. *The Oxford Handbook of Memory*. New York: Oxford University Press.

Turfa, J. M. 2022. "The Silent Roofing Revolution: The Etruscan Tie-Beam Truss." In *Architecture in Ancient Central Italy*, ed. C. R. Potts. Cambridge: Cambridge University Press, 31–61.

Vagnetti, L. 1966. "Nota sull'attività dei coroplasti etruschi." *Archeologia Classica* 18, 110–114.

Valentini, G. 1969. "Il motivo della Potnia Theron sui vasi di bucchero." *StEtr* 37, 413–442.

1970. "Un nuovo tipo di Potnia Theron sui vasi di bucchero." *StEtr* 38, 361–362.

van Dommelen, P.A.R. and N. Terrenato, eds. 2007. *Articulating Local Cultures. Power and Identity under the Expanding Roman Republic.* JRA Suppl. 63. Portsmouth, RI: Journal of Roman Archaeology.

van Eck, C. 2020. "Ornament in Europe. From Antiquity to the Twentieth Century." In *Oxford Bibliographies: Architecture, Planning, and Preservation*. Oxford: Oxford University Press. www.oxfordbibliographies.com/display/document/obo-9780190922467/obo-9780190922467-0042.xml.

Vermeulen, F. 2021. "The Introduction of 'Classical' Urban Concepts in Central Adriatic Italy: A Sign of Romanization and Hellenization?" In *Imperium Romanum. Romanization between Colonization and Globalization*, ed. O. Belvedere and J. Bergemann. Palermo: Palermo University Press, 109–123.

Versluys, M. J. 2013. "Material Culture and Identity in the Late Roman Republic." In *A Companion to the Archaeology of the Roman Republic*, ed. J. DeRose Evans. Oxford: Wiley Blackwell, 429–440.

2015. "Roman Visual Material Culture as Globalising Koine." In *Globalisation and the Roman World. World History, Connectivity and Material Culture*, ed. M. Pitts and M. J. Versluys. New York: Cambridge University Press, 141–174.

von Freytag Löringhoff, B. 1986. *Das Giebelrelief von Telamon und seine Stellung innerhalb der Ikonographie der "Sieben gegen Theben."* Mainz: Philipp von Zabern.

von Vacano, O. W. 1985. *Gli Etruschi a Talamone. La baia di Talamone dalla preistoria ai giorni nostri*. Bologna: Cappelli editore.

von Vacano, O. W., and B. von Freytag Löringhoff. 1982. *Talamone. Il mito dei Sette a Tebe: catalogo della mostra. Firenze, Museo archeologico 14 febbraio–3 ottobre 1982.* Rome: Vision, Viella, David.

von Rohden, H., and H. Winnefeld. 1911. *Architektonische römische Tonreliefs der Kaiserzeit.* Berlin and Stuttgart: W. Spemann.

Wallace-Hadrill, A. 2008. *Rome's Cultural Revolution*. Cambridge: Cambridge University Press.

Walter, U. 2004. *Memoria und res publica. Zur Geschichtskultur im republikanischen Rom.* Frankfurt: Verlag Antike.

Ward-Perkins, J. 1951. "Tripolitania and the marble trade." *JRS* 41: 89–104.

Webster, J. 2001. "Creolizing the Roman Provinces." *AJA* 105:2, 209–225.

Welch, K. E. 2006. "Art and Architecture in the Roman Republic." In *A Companion to the Roman Republic*, ed. N. Rosenstein and R. Morstein-Marx. Malden, MA: Blackwell, 496–542.

Wertsch, J. V. 2009. "Collective Memory." In *Memory in Mind and Culture*, ed. P. Boyer and J. V. Wertsch. Cambridge: Cambridge University Press, 117–137.

Wescoat, B. D. 2015. "The Patronage of Greek and Roman Architecture." In *The Oxford Handbook of Greek and Roman Art and Architecture*, ed. C. Marconi. Oxford: Oxford University Press, 176–202.

Wikander, C. 1988. *Acquarossa I. The Painted Architectural Terracottas. Part 2. Typological and Decorative Analysis.* Stockholm: Svenska Institutet i Rom.

1993. "The Decorative Systems of the Archaic Sima." In *Deliciae Fictiles I*, ed. E. Rystedt, C. Wikander, and O. Wikander. Stockholm: Svenska Institutet, 87–91.

Wikander, Ö. 1993. *Acquarossa VI. The Roof-Tiles. Part 2. Typology and Technical Features.* Stockholm: Svenska Institutet i Rom.

1994. "The Archaic Etruscan Sima." In *Murlo and the Etruscans. Art and Society in Ancient Etruria*, ed. R. D. De Puma and B. P. Small. Madison: University of Wisconsin Press, 47–63.

2017. *Roof-tiles and Tile-roofs at Poggio Civitate (Murlo). The Emergence of Central Italic Industry.* Stockholm: Svenska Institutet i Rom.

Wikander, C., and Ö. Wikander. 2006. "Architectural Terracottas in Theory and Practice. Reflections on Thirty Years of Experience." In *Deliciae Fictiles III*, ed. I. Edlund-Berry, G. Greco, and J. Kenfield. Oxford: Oxbow Books, 42–44.

Winter, N. A. 1993a. *Greek Architectural Terracottas: From the Prehistoric to the End of the Archaic Period.* Oxford: Clarendon Press.

1993b. "Kroisos' Role in the Diffusion of Greek Mainland Architectural Terracottas to Ionia." In *Les Grands Ateliers d'architecture dans le monde égéen du VIe siècle av. J.-C. Actes du colloque d'Istanbul, 23–25 mai 1991*, ed. J. des Courtils and J.-Ch. Moretti. Istanbul: Institut Français d'Études Anatoliennes-Georges Dumézil, 29–33.

1997. "Work-in-progress on a New Synthesis of Etruscan Architectural Terracottas. In *Deliciae Fictiles II: proceedings of the 2nd International Conference on Archaic Architectural Terracottas from Italy held at the Netherlands Institute in Rome 12–13 June 1996*, ed. P. S. Lulof and E. M. Moormann. Amsterdam: Thesis, 237–239.

2002. "Commerce in Exile: Terracotta Roofing in Etruria, Corfu and Sicily, a Bacchiad Family Enterprise." *EtrStud* 9, 227–236.

2009. *Symbols of Wealth and Power: Architectural Terracotta Decoration in Etruria and Central Italy, 640–510 B.C.* Ann Arbor: University of Michigan Press.

2022. "Architectural Terracottas of Central Italy within Their Wider Mediterranean Context." In *Architecture in Ancient Central Italy*, ed. C. R. Potts. Cambridge: Cambridge University Press, 62–94.

Winter, N. A., I. Iliopoulos, and A. J. Ammerman. 2009. "New Light on the Production of Decorated Roofs of the 6th c. B.C. at Sites in and around Rome." *JRA* 22, 6–28.

Wiseman, T. P. 1985. *Roman political life: 90 B.C.–A.D. 69.* Exeter: University of Exter Press.

Witcher, R. E. 2000. "Globalisation and Roman Imperialism: Perspectives on Identities in Roman Italy." In *The Emergence of State Identities in Italy in the First Millennium B.C.*, ed. E. Herring and K. Lomas. London: Accordia Research Institute, 213–225.

Woolf, G. 1998. *Becoming Roman. The Origins of Provincial Civilization in Gaul.* Cambridge: Cambridge University Press.

Zagdoun, M.-A. 1989. *La sculpture archaïsante dans l'art hellénistique et dans l'art romain du Haut-Empire.* BÉFAR 269. Paris: Boccard.

Zanker, P. 1988. *The Power of Images in the Age of Augustus*, trans. A. Shapiro. Ann Arbor: University of Michigan Press.

Zink, S. 2008. "Reconstructing the Palatine Temple of Apollo: A Case Study in Early Augustan Temple Design." *JRA* 21: 47–63.

2011. "Octavian's Sanctuary of Apollo on the Palatine: Architecture, Site, and the Development of a Sacred Topography." PhD diss., Univ. of Pennsylvania.

2015. "The Palatine Sanctuary of Apollo: The Site and Its Development, 6th to 1st c. B.C." *JRA* 28: 358–370.

Ziolkowski, A. 1988. "Mummius' Temple of Hercules Victor and the Round Temple on the Tiber." *Phoenix* 42:4: 309–333.

INDEX